PRESIDENT LINCOLN
ASSASSINATED!!

PRESIDENT
LINCOLN
ASSASSINATED!!

THE FIRSTHAND STORY OF THE MURDER, MANHUNT, TRIAL, AND MOURNING

··· COMPILED AND INTRODUCED BY ···

HAROLD HOLZER

A SPECIAL PUBLICATION OF THE LIBRARY OF AMERICA

Introduction, headnotes, chronology and volume compilation copyright © 2014 by
Literary Classics of the United States, Inc., New York, N.Y.

For sources and acknowledgments see page 431.

Distributed to the trade in the United States
by Penguin Random House Inc.
and in Canada by Penguin Random House Canada Ltd.

Library of Congress Control Number: 2014946644
ISBN 978–1–59853–373–6

10 9 8 7 6 5 4 3 2 1

Printed in the United States of America

Contents

MOURNING AND REMEMBERING LINCOLN

Illustrations
(following page 302)

1. Ford's Theatre playbill for April 14, 1865.

2. The last photograph of Lincoln, March 6, 1865, by Henry F. Warren.

3. Mary Lincoln in mourning attire.

4. The presidential box at Ford's Theatre.

5. Ford's Theatre c. 1860–65.

6. *Lincoln Borne by Loving Hands* by Carl Bersch, c. 1895.

7. Drawing of Lincoln's deathbed scene by Hermann Faber.

8. Fanny Seward in 1866.

9. Broadside reward poster issued by the War Department.

10–13. Co-conspirators David Herold, Lewis Powell (alias Payne), and George Atzerodt, photographs by Alexander Gardner. The last known portrait of Mary Surratt.

14. John Wilkes Booth, c. 1860–65.

15. Sergeant Boston Corbett, the man who shot Booth.

16. Lincoln's catafalque in New York City, photograph by George Stacy.

17. The funeral train on a Lake Michigan pier in Chicago.

18. Mourners in front of the Lincoln home in Springfield, Illinois.

19. Lincoln's funeral procession in New York City, photograph by Robert N. Dennis.

20. "The Founder and the Preserver of the Union. (*Apotheosis*)" by Thurston, Herline & Co.

21. "Britannia Sympathises With Columbia" by John Tenniel.

22. "The Reward of the Just" by D. T. Wiest.

23. Hanging of the conspirators, July 7, 1865, photograph by Alexander Gardner.

Introduction

Shortly before he fell victim to an assassin's bullet, a spectrally haggard, sleep-deprived Abraham Lincoln had a portentous dream—or so his longtime friend and aide, Ward Hill Lamon, later remembered. Not until ten days after was the President ready to unburden himself by sharing the details of his haunting nightmare. And then he told not only Lamon, but also his chronically anxious wife, Mary—even though he insisted that he did not believe in dreams and urged his listeners to take no heed, either.[1]

Awakened from a deep slumber by the sound of "subdued sobs," as Lincoln began his recollection, he dreamt that he left his bed to prowl the empty White House in search of the source of the commotion. Slowly he headed downstairs alone, greeted only by the ever louder "mournful sounds" of "pitiful sobbing." Finally reaching the East Room, he came face-to-face with what he called a "sickening surprise."

"Before me was a catafalque," Lincoln told his enthralled listeners, "on which rested a corpse wrapped in funeral vestments" and encircled by military guards and "a throng" of tearful mourners. "Who is dead in the White House?" Lincoln recalled demanding of one of the soldiers. "The President," came the sad reply; "he was killed by an assassin!" A "loud burst of grief from the crowd" then woke the dreamer from his slumber. Quoting *Hamlet*, Lincoln admitted, "I slept no more that night," for "to sleep" was "perchance to dream."

"That is horrid," Mary Lincoln declared when her husband finished his chilling story. "I wish you had not told it."

"Well," drawled her husband, as if liberated from the disturbing vision, "it is only a dream, Mary. Let us say no more about it."[2] In fact he

[1] Yet on June 9, 1863, Lincoln had telegraphed Mary (who was in Philadelphia with their young son Tad), "Think you better put 'Tad's' pistol away. I had an ugly dream about him." See Don E. Fehrenbacher, ed., *Abraham Lincoln: Speeches and Writings*, 2 vols. (New York: Library of America, 1989), 2:453.
[2] Dorothy Lamon, ed., *Recollections of Abraham Lincoln 1847–1865 by Ward Hill Lamon* (Chicago: A. C. McClurg & Co., 1895), 115–16. Some scholars have cast doubt on Lamon's written recollections, most of which were gathered by his daughter thirty years after Lincoln's death—and two years after her father's. Modern historians especially question Lamon's

repeated it for Lamon twice more in the days before the Civil War—and Lincoln's life as well—came to an end during a week of seismically contrasting peace and violence, a week like none other in American history.

No dream but a horrific reality gripped the nation that mid-April of 1865: a shocking presidential murder, fear that the entire federal government was under attack, and a massive dragnet to capture the assassination conspirators, followed by their widely reported trial and punishment. Uniquely, the insatiable appetite for news of the crime manifested itself even as the first public funeral took place to honor the once-partisan, frequently mocked, now almost universally beloved martyr. As this collection of firsthand recollections, eyewitness reportage, and retrospective lamentations will demonstrate, Americans managed simultaneously in the spring and summer of 1865 to mourn passionately their fallen leader and to hungrily consume the latest updates about the hunt for his killer.

Americans had never before been whipsawed by such emotional upheaval, or produced such an avalanche of breathlessly read journalism and literature about a single violent event. While other volumes have variously analyzed the biggest crime of the nineteenth century, probed the grief it inspired, or detailed the dramatic hunt for the conspirators and their subsequent trial, conviction, and execution, what this collection makes vividly clear is how all these stories unfolded simultaneously before stunned contemporaries. The accounts are presented here in their original form—just as they first transfixed American readers a century and a half ago—laying bare the nation's concurrent obsessions with justice, vengeance, and deification. Here are the very words that contemporary citizens digested as these horrifying and mournful events first unfolded, with dirge competing with drama.

Certainly no manhunt in American history ever assumed the high drama—or attracted the vast audience—as did the pursuit of Abraham Lincoln's killer and his gang. Unknown to all but a handful of plotters—and perhaps the Confederate government as well, it was later charged—these conspirators had hatched their plan to murder Lincoln in the

---

assertion that Lincoln confided to him that his Gettysburg Address had fallen on the audience "like a wet blanket." Still, it is difficult to believe that Lamon wholly invented the elaborate story he revealed here, especially since the President was known to have experienced similarly morbid dreams or visions in the past.

jubilant days following Confederate General Robert E. Lee's surrender to Ulysses S. Grant at Appomattox Court House, Virginia, on April 9.

A lightning bolt of vengeance was the last thing on the public's mind that week, though the constant threat of assassination had long concerned those closest to Lincoln. Dreams aside, the risk had been very much on Ward Hill Lamon's mind—as well as Lincoln's—for years. One summer evening in 1862, a would-be murderer, or perhaps a confused Union sentry, had put a bullet through the President's trademark stovepipe hat as the tall target rode alone on horseback from the White House toward his summer residence at the Soldiers' Home three miles north of downtown Washington. No one ever identified the shooter, though Lincoln himself dismissed him as "a disloyal bushwhacker." Lamon insisted he never ride alone again, and Lincoln reluctantly agreed, though he was heard to scoff: "Oh, assassination of public officers is not an American crime."[3]

Nonetheless, more than one White House visitor noticed a bulging folder stored in the pigeonhole desk in Lincoln's private office. The President kept it filed under "A"—for "Assassination"—and filled it with the scrawled threats that arrived routinely at the mansion ("the brutalities, enmities, and infamies of the President's letter-bag," according to his correspondence clerk, William O. Stoddard).[4] In fact, Lincoln had been receiving such mail ever since his nomination for president five years earlier. "[T]hey have ceased to give me any apprehension," he assured artist-in-residence Francis B. Carpenter in 1864, jocularly adding: "Oh, there is nothing like getting *used* to things!"[5] In a more fatalistic vein, Lincoln confided to journalist Noah Brooks: "I long ago made up my mind that if anybody wants to kill me, he will do it. If I wore a shirt of mail and kept myself surrounded by a bodyguard, it would be all the same. There are a thousand ways of getting at a man if it is desirable that he should be killed."[6] Just recently, the President had walked safely

[3] Lamon, *Recollections of Abraham Lincoln, 1847–1865*, 262; Benjamin F. Butler in Allen Thorndike Rice, ed., *Reminiscences of Abraham Lincoln by Distinguished Men of His Time* (New York: North American Publishing Company, 1886), 144.

[4] Stoddard quoted—and the assassination file discussed—in Harold Holzer, *Dear Mr. Lincoln: Letters to the President* (New York: Addison-Wesley, 1993), 335–36.

[5] F[rancis]. B. Carpenter, *Six Months at the White House with Abraham Lincoln: The Story of a Picture* (New York: Hurd & Houghton, 1866), 62–63.

[6] Noah Brooks, "Personal Reminiscences of Lincoln," *Scribner's Monthly* 15 (February–March 1878): 674.

through the streets of the conquered Confederate capital of Richmond, accompanied only by his twelve-year-old son, Tad, and a small contingent of armed sailors. The April 4 visit had buoyed Lincoln's spirits, for the city's black population had welcomed him ecstatically as a Messiah, even if most white residents remained sullenly in their homes. "Why, Doctor, I walked alone on the street," Lincoln exulted to the Rev. Phineas Gurley when he returned home to Washington, "and any one could have shot me from a second story window."[7]

Such threats seemed far from the President's mind on the warm afternoon of Good Friday, April 14, 1865, when, duly accompanied by a military escort, Lincoln took his wife for a leisurely carriage ride through Washington. His recent nightmare forgotten, the President had brightened noticeably. "I never saw him so supremely cheerful," Mary remembered; "—his manner was even playful . . . he was almost boyish, in his mirth." The long, bloody, hideously destructive Civil War was all but over, and a suddenly unburdened Lincoln savored the relaxing ride through the open air, telling his wife that he was "bent on the theater" later that night, religious holiday notwithstanding. "We must *both*, be more cheerful in the future," Lincoln urged Mary. "[B]etween the war & the loss of our darling Willie [the beloved son who had died in 1862] we have both, been very miserable."[8]

Along their ride the couple combined business with pleasure, inspecting three battle-scarred Union ironclads at the Washington Navy Yard. On they drove, chatting about retiring to Illinois after his newly commenced term ended, even pondering a future pilgrimage to the Holy Land. Finally they returned to the White House to dress for their evening out at Ford's Theatre. Lincoln usually favored Shakespearean tragedy, but tonight he planned to take his wife to a rollicking English farce called *Our American Cousin*. It was time for laughter, not lamentation.

The last words he heard, at around 10:15 that night, were: "Don't

---

[7] Gurley quoted in Ervin Chapman, *Latest Light on Abraham Lincoln and War-Time Memories*, 2 vols. (New York: Fleming H. Revell, 1917), 2:500.

[8] Mary Lincoln to Francis B. Carpenter, November 15, 1865, and to James Smith, December 17, 1866, in Justin G. Turner and Linda Levitt Turner, eds., *Mary Todd Lincoln: Her Life and Letters* (New York: Alfred A. Knopf, 1972), 284, 400, also editors' note, 216. See also p. 356 in this volume for the letter to Carpenter.

know the manners of good society, eh? Well, I guess I know enough to turn you inside out, old gal—you sockdologizing old mantrap."

At that precise moment, as the audience howled with laughter, a gunshot rang out in the theater, and an ominous puff of smoke billowed from the balcony-level presidential box above the stage. Was it part of the play? For a few seconds, no one in the playhouse seemed to know. Then, as if in a nightmare worthy of Lincoln himself, a menacing, dark-clad figure vaulted over the rail of the box, caught his spur in the patriotic bunting that draped it, and awkwardly landed on the stage. Quickly recovering, the acrobatic intruder, recognized by many in the house as the actor John Wilkes Booth, turned toward the audience and hissed the Latin motto of Virginia, based on Brutus's alleged declaration at the assassination of Caesar: "*sic semper tyrannis*" ("thus always to tyrants"). Then he hurried unimpeded toward the wings and vanished backstage as the paralyzed throng watched in shock. By then, reacting to Mary Lincoln's piercing screams, most ticket-holders in the sold-out theater realized that this was no nightmare: Booth had shot the President.

In the ensuing pandemonium, a doctor in the crowd somehow made his way up to the comatose Lincoln's side and eased him from his rocking chair onto the floor. Sticking a nonsterile finger into the bullet hole he discovered in the back of the President's head, he relieved the pressure on Lincoln's brain caused by bleeding within the skull. Although the President's labored breathing improved, the doctor realized at once that he had been mortally wounded and could not possibly survive. Surely, however, he must not be allowed to die in a theater—a setting most religious Americans held in disrepute—especially on the anniversary of Christ's crucifixion.

Gingerly, a small knot of unnamed and unknown theatergoers— hundreds would later claim the honor—cradled the stricken leader and carried him out of the box, down the balcony stairs, into the street, and, with nowhere else to go, up the winding steps that led into William A. Petersen's modest brick boardinghouse directly across the road. There, in the tiny back bedroom of the Petersen house, furnished with a bed too small to accommodate his giant frame except diagonally, America's sixteenth president would linger for nine more hours before breathing his last at 7:22 the following morning, April 15, 1865—just six days after the Civil War had ended with the Union intact and the principle of majority rule upheld.

One of the last of the war's 750,000 dead, the Union commander-in-chief had not even been given time to enjoy the laurels many believed he deserved. Phineas Gurley, the same minister who just days before had heard Lincoln boast that he had walked unharmed in Richmond, now found himself at the stricken President's bedside at the Petersen house, offering a prayer after he succumbed to an assassin after all.

Perhaps nothing symbolized the violently sudden transformation of mood about to roil the North—from wildest celebration to deepest confusion, rage, and ultimately sadness—more vividly than the confusing scene that unfolded on Tenth Street minutes after Booth shot Lincoln. In a revealing corollary drama unreported to the public and all but unknown since, an artist named Carl Bersch happened to be perched on the porch of a nearby residence looking down at the street, drawing pad in hand. Bersch was engaged in sketching a group of Union soldiers and musicians sharing an exuberant victory procession up the thoroughfare, when he noticed a sudden, unexpected commotion from the direction of the theater door across Tenth Street. As a "hushed committee" emerged bearing the President's long, inert frame through the crowd, the parade scattered, the music stopped, and the military march melted into a blur of disarray. Bersch presciently incorporated the "solemn and reverent cortege" into his sketch, which showed Lincoln's body practically driving a wedge into the cluster of stunned celebrants now parting in disbelief to create an aisle for the precious cargo. Later, the artist expanded his daub into a large painting he entitled *Lincoln Borne by Loving Hands*— the only known visual record of an end-of-war celebration interrupted and subdued by the murder of Abraham Lincoln.[9]

Bersch's canvas perfectly evoked the seismic changes in private and public emotions that overtook the country once shock and grief supplanted jubilation in April 1865. The surprise attack thrust the martyred Lincoln into the sacred role of symbolic final casualty of the Civil War. But it also made his assailants the most hated fugitives in America, even among many Southerners who reviled the northern President but now feared they would be blamed for his murder. In response, Americans

---

[9] Carl Bersch to Angelica Bode, April 16, 1866; Gerda Vey (Bersch's granddaughter) to Bruce Catton, April 9, 1960; *"Carl Bersch—Artist and Portrait Painter,"* unidentified, undated clipping, all in Ford's Theatre collection.

became voyeurs and mourners at the same time, whipsawed by emotional upheaval that conflated vengeance with sorrow. No one seemed able to decide what was hardest to bear: the anxiety, the fury, or the grief.

At once, one man tried to bring order to the mayhem. Even as Lincoln lay dying, Secretary of War Edwin M. Stanton took charge of investigating his assassination and capturing his killer, using a parlor in the Petersen house as his headquarters. All through that sorrowful night, Stanton resolutely ordered troops to pursue Booth, while calmly dispatching a series of updates on the President's condition to New York for publication in the newspapers. Even before Lincoln breathed his last, a dragnet had begun that would ensnare dozens of Washington suspects (most of them innocent), and unleash an armed search-and-capture mission for the infamous gunman in both southern Maryland and northern Virginia.

Who were the alleged conspirators—and more importantly, *where* were they? All of Washington, and soon all of the country, became transfixed by these urgent questions as Stanton's War Department (whose provost marshals began functioning as a kind of national police force) launched a massive manhunt to identify and capture them, even creating, by some accounts, the first wanted poster illustrated by real photographs. For eleven days—even as hundreds of thousands of heartbroken admirers gathered in Northern cities at elaborate funerals for the slain president—Booth remained at large while Americans pursued every detail of the search as avidly as the pursuers themselves chased their prey.

The breathless wait continued until, one by one, almost all of Booth's co-conspirators were captured and their leader shot to death on April 26, in a Virginia tobacco barn, by an overzealous army sergeant who quickly became a Northern hero. But was Sergeant Boston Corbett's victim really John Wilkes Booth? With the assassin's body spirited off to a Union ironclad for a secret autopsy, conspiracy theorists then and now cast doubts on the official identification, and closure remained difficult to achieve.

In the meantime, the national mood—principally in the North—shifted overnight from celebratory to sorrowful. Victory observances were aborted. In Washington, church bells resumed their recent pealing—but the rhythmic clanging that had sounded so triumphant the previous week now seemed to toll mournfully. Bonfires were extinguished, fireworks and illuminations doused, and rallies cancelled. City after city adorned public buildings with so much thick black crape that recognizable architecture all but vanished behind the abundance of bunting. Private citizens took to wearing black-ribboned badges adorned with small photographs of the martyred President, and placing Lincoln statuettes and portraits in their shop windows. In Springfield, Illinois, the martyr's hometown, even his horse, Old Robin, was swathed in a black blanket fringed with gold tassels and photographed outside of Lincoln's house for posterity and public sale. Distributors of black cloth and Lincoln portraits immediately raised prices to meet the sudden demand and profited handsomely.

People wept, privately and publicly alike, in their homes, in the streets, both alone and in congregations attending Easter and Passover services that took on profound new meaning, for Lincoln's death almost providentially coincided with Christian and Jewish holy days marking, respectively, martyrdom and freedom. Both Christian ministers and Jewish rabbis took to their pulpits to liken the slain President to a second Jesus or a born-again Moses.

Yet Lincoln's most outraged grievers—among them his suddenly converted political foes and newspaper critics—did more than lament as the once-partisan politician morphed into a deity. Mourners also focused with unprecedented intensity on the pursuit of Booth. For weeks, as soldiers rounded up and interrogated conspiracy suspects in Washington and pursued others into the South, the nation's newspaper readers followed the quest with the same passionate interest they had, until days before, devoted to news of Civil War battles. The public had good reason to fear that, after being subdued on the battlefield, the rebellion had assumed a more insidious and treacherous reincarnation. When the full extent of Booth's conspiracy became known, it was clear that his plan had indeed reached beyond killing the President. It had marked for decapitation, on April 14, 1865, the executive branch of the federal government.

At around the same time that Booth shot Lincoln, as Americans quickly learned, a onetime Confederate soldier named Lewis Powell, alias Payne, first lied, then forced his way into Secretary of State William H. Seward's Washington home. As Seward's daughter remembered the scene of horror in a gripping account featured in this collection, Powell stabbed him repeatedly with a large knife as the helpless victim lay prone in his bed. Lincoln's chief advisor survived, though permanently disfigured, only because a metal brace fitted around his neck after a recent carriage accident prevented his would-be assassin from inflicting a fatal blow.

The plot proved even wider. Ford's Theatre had proudly advertised Ulysses S. Grant as the Lincolns' special guest at *Our American Cousin* that night, and Booth planned to target him as well. He certainly would have tried had not the general cancelled earlier in the day, ostensibly to reunite with his children in New Jersey, almost surely to prevent an awkward reunion between Julia Grant and Mary Lincoln, who despised each other. Vice President Andrew Johnson, too, would have been attacked that evening, had not the conspirator assigned to murder him, a hard-drinking German-born carriage repairman named George Atzerodt, panicked in a haze of whiskey at the last moment and abandoned his assignment to complete the multifaceted strike against Union leaders. The delusional and racist Booth was certain that these dramatic strikes against the federal leadership would embolden defeated Southerners once again to take up arms and prevent the government from promoting black equality. But as his diary entries in these pages show, Booth aspired not only to embolden the defeated South, but to exact revenge on the "tyrant" he held responsible for its subjugation. Only days earlier, hearing Lincoln speak publicly at the White House about granting voting rights to "very intelligent" African Americans and "those who serve our cause as soldiers," an infuriated Booth had vowed to a confidant—in a chilling incident recounted in this collection—"That is the last speech he will ever make."[10]

Three days later, Booth made good on his promise, and despite the resulting maelstrom of conflicting emotion, professional reporters somehow managed to provide vivid summaries, often overnight, of both eulogies and interrogations. Words in turn immediately inspired pictures—examples of which also appear on these pages. Bersch was not the only artist to commemorate the Lincoln assassination. Painters, engravers, and lithographers all responded to the highly lucrative

---

[10] Speech on Reconstruction, April 11, 1865, in Fehrenbacher, ed., *Abraham Lincoln: Speeches and Writings*, 2:699; Booth's vow reported in testimony of Thomas T. Eckert before the House Judiciary Committee, May 30, 1867; see p. 9 of this volume.

public demand for such images — often inventing wildly inaccurate depictions to attract buyers (one even showed Satan tempting Booth to Lincoln's murder). Artists accompanied these with reverential, often exaggerated scenes of the martyr's deathbed, in which the tiny back bedroom of the Petersen house successively expanded to accommodate nearly all of official Washington, in the most absurd examples assuming the proportions of a palace chamber. Finally, the image-makers concocted visions of Lincoln's rise into heaven — where he was often portrayed embracing his longtime hero, George Washington: the founder and the preserver of the Union united in an imagined afterlife. Through this flood of words and images, some designed as ephemera for immediate consumption in the pictorial weeklies, others as permanent decoration for private homes, Americans visualized the story of the century from every possible angle — even the martyr's imagined ascent into the afterlife.

Back on earth, Lincoln's actual remains were embalmed to the point of petrifaction so they could be displayed at public funerals not only in Washington, but in Baltimore, Harrisburg, Philadelphia, New York, Albany, Buffalo, Cleveland, Columbus, Indianapolis, Michigan City, Chicago, and finally, beneath signs reading "HOME IS THE MARTYR," his own Springfield, Illinois. For those who lived outside these centers of mass mourning, well-placed journalists provided timely and detailed descriptions.

First, it seemed that all of Washington massed for the initial funeral of the first president to be assassinated — the leader who had died at the height of his powers, at the crest of his fame. An inconsolable Mary Lincoln, however, refused to attend the White House ceremony, keeping to her darkened room and perhaps remembering that Lincoln's ominous dream had come true. It was left to the public — along with the eulogists, artists, and writers — to pay their respects.

Over time, more people gazed on Lincoln's mummified countenance than had ever glimpsed any president in life or death. Baltimore, the first stop after the capital in the long funeral schedule, happened to be the very "Mob City" where in 1861, enemies of the Union had posed such a credible threat to Lincoln's safety that the President-elect had passed through it at night, in secret, and some foes falsely claimed, in absurd disguise. "[N]ot one hand reached forth to greet me, not one voice broke the stillness to cheer me," an uncharacteristically bitter Lincoln later remembered of that pre-dawn visit, in a passage he wisely omitted from an 1864 speech.[11]

Now, in a scene suggesting a mass conversion, or at least a demonstration of atonement on an unprecedented scale, tens of thousands of Baltimore mourners lined up despite a pounding rain to pay their respects at Lincoln's bier. It proved to be such an outpouring of grief that most of the disappointed admirers at the back of the line never got the chance to glimpse the open coffin, which was closed and carted away according to the tight, pre-arranged schedule, so the President's remains could arrive at their next stop on time. Where had all these emotional supporters been when Lincoln had arrived, in life, just four years earlier? (Only an anemic 2.5 percent of Maryland voters had cast ballots for Lincoln back in 1860.) No one seemed to know, Lincoln had won the state by a handsome margin in 1864, and few of Baltimore's citizens now admitted their earlier opposition.

Similar scenes of mass grief played out repeatedly as Lincoln's body headed north, then west, to its final resting place. Mourners crowded alongside railroad tracks to catch a glimpse of the funeral train and the perpetually illuminated car transporting Lincoln and the exhumed remains of his late son Willie home. In city after city chosen to host official ceremonies, streets overflowed with onlookers competing for vantage points from which best to view the hearse when it rolled by. Dirges played, church bells tolled, and determined admirers routinely lined up for the chance to view the remains. In one venue, the City of Brotherly Love, where Lincoln had once declared at Independence Hall that he would "rather be assassinated on this spot than to surrender" the principles the Founders had crafted there, tens of thousands of people, frustrated by seven-hour-long waits and a failure by the authorities to organize the queues, erupted into a panicked mob. When overmatched police finally dispersed the angry crowd, Philadelphians left in their wake a sea of lost hats, abandoned skirt hoops, and the scattered booty of pickpockets—the weird detritus of mass mourning.[12]

---

[11] Draft of Address for Sanitary Fair at Baltimore, Maryland, before April 18, 1864, in Fehrenbacher, ed., *Abraham Lincoln: Speeches and Writings*, 2:588.
[12] Speech at Independence Hall, February 22, 1861, in *Abraham Lincoln, Speeches and Writings*, 2:213; scene at Philadelphia described in Dorothy Meserve Kunhardt and Philip B. Kunhardt Jr., *Twenty Days* (New York: Harper and Row, 1965), 146–50.

Then came New York, which hosted the largest funeral of all. There, unjustly, African Americans had to battle for the mere right to march in the long procession honoring "Our Emancipator," as one of their banners declared. But the city's largely Democratic arrangements committee denied them their rightful place, as readers of this volume will discover—clearly having failed to absorb the right lessons from Manhattan's shameful Draft Riots two years earlier, when resentment over conscription spilled over into deadly persecution of innocent blacks. Secretary of War Stanton promptly overruled local officials and insisted that the city find a place for these grief-stricken mourners. So the city did—but at the very back of a four-and-a-half-hour-long line of marchers stretching so far that by the time their two hundred–member contingent reached the railroad depot along the Hudson River to bid farewell to Lincoln's coffin, the remains had long before left the city. Still, more than a hundred thousand mourners had gazed briefly at Lincoln's remains lying in state at City Hall, and half a million New Yorkers, black as well as white, had witnessed the funeral procession.

Among these mourners were military and civilian contingents, labor groups, religious organizations, aged veterans of the War of 1812, young children, and "Negroes . . . all of whom," one reporter marveled, were "bathed in tears." Even the once anti-Lincoln *New York Herald* called the "triumphant procession" for Lincoln "greater, grander, more genuine than any living conqueror or hero ever enjoyed." This book presents original reports of these historic events: accounts that must have made the millions of mourners who could not join the hundreds of thousands of attendees feel that they, too, were present to honor their fallen chief.

Featured on these pages, too, is Frederick Douglass's long-ignored declaration in a eulogy at Cooper Union—site of the 1860 speech that had helped make Lincoln president—that the late leader deserved history's acknowledgment as "the black man's President." Here is one landmark assessment that surprisingly—for Douglass was a genuine celebrity in his own right at the time—went unreported or merely paraphrased by the white press in 1865, and remains largely unknown even now. This is believed to be its first appearance in print outside the Douglass archives.

All through the torrid late spring and early summer of 1865, after writers fanned Lincoln's growing reputation with accounts of these heartfelt panegyrics and giant public demonstrations of grief, newspaper readers experienced the military trial in Washington of eight of the alleged conspirators and, ultimately, the hanging of four of them (including Mary Surratt, the first woman to be executed by the federal government). And thus ended the irresistibly gripping drama that writers had helped make nearly as monumental as the recently ended Civil War itself.

The poets were not far behind the journalists and orators in responding to, and trying to make sense of, the mayhem. The greatest literary talents of the age—among them Herman Melville and Walt Whitman—quickly crafted tributes to Lincoln in verse. The author of *Moby-Dick*, for one, likened Ford's Theatre to Golgotha, and Lincoln to Jesus Christ. And though Whitman spent weeks composing his elaborate elegy "When Lilacs Last in the Dooryard Bloom'd," it was one of Whitman's most uncharacteristic efforts, the singsong "O Captain! My Captain," that proved so popular that its author would be compelled to recite it for the rest of his life. Although Whitman often left the somewhat disingenuous impression that he regretted he had ever written it, so repetitious were the requests for its performance, "Captain" became his most famous creation—destined to be memorized by schoolchildren alongside Lincoln's own Gettysburg Address well into the twentieth century. Dramatists and essayists from Ibsen to Emerson had their say as well, while less elegant but equally heartfelt tributes poured in from unlikelier writers, including a widow-to-widow condolence letter to Mary Lincoln from Queen Victoria.

Amidst this frenzy of journalism and tribute, some voices prudently remained muted or unpublished, among them Northerners who regarded Lincoln as a tyrant who had deserved to die, and Southerners who regretted his passing only because they feared it would trigger retribution. Their silence was understandable. In an explosive atmosphere teetering between reverence and revenge, even antiwar Northern Copperheads or homesick soldiers who blurted out their joy that Lincoln had been killed often suffered near-fatal beatings or harsh official punishment. When, for example, Seaman James Tozier of the USS *Powhatan* called for three cheers when he learned of Lincoln's murder, he was court-martialed and sentenced to a year in prison. After drinking to excess, a Union soldier, James Walker of the 8th California Infantry, publicly declared Lincoln a "Yankee son of a bitch" who "ought to have been killed long ago." His recommended punishment was death by firing squad, though a court commuted the sentence. In all, dozens of imprudent enlisted men were dishonorably discharged for suggesting, in the words of one Michigan soldier who dared to blurt out, and in Lincoln's own hometown, "The man who killed Lincoln did a good thing."[13]

In marked contrast, many Upper South newspapers quickly and prudently expressed shock and sympathy, with the *Richmond Whig* characterizing Lincoln's death as the "heaviest blow which has fallen on the people of the south," and the *Raleigh Standard* expressing its "profound grief" over the tragedy. Not all Southerners who spoke on the record offered condolences. So many Northerners suspected that Confederate President Jefferson Davis had personally ordered Lincoln's murder that prosecutors named him as an unindicted co-conspirator at the trial of Booth's gang. (The testimony directly linking Davis and his agents in Canada to the assassination was later shown to be perjured, and the former Confederate president was never charged in connection with the crime.) Days after he fled south in a futile effort to keep the Confederacy's "Lost Cause" alive, word reached Davis that Lincoln had been murdered. Demonstrating that, like his late Northern counterpart, he, too, knew his Shakespeare, Davis allegedly reacted with chilling sangfroid by quoting *Macbeth*: "If it were done, it were better it were well done." On the other hand, he was also said to have confided to his secretary of the navy about the murder that while he had "no special regard for Mr. Lincoln . . . I fear it will be disastrous to our people." Davis's true feelings remained difficult to parse, and years of reflection did little to break through his impenetrable shell: his voluminous 1881 history of the Confederate government merely referred in passing to "the death of Mr. Lincoln."[14]

To be sure, multiple expressions of regret from the war-ravaged South were also hard to find. The *Chattanooga Daily Rebel* defiantly wrote: "Abe has gone to answer before the bar of God for the innocent blood

---

[13] See Thomas P. Lowry, "Not Everybody Mourned Lincoln's Death," in Harold Holzer, Craig L. Symonds, and Frank J. Williams, eds., *The Lincoln Assassination: Crime and Punishment, Myth and Meaning* (New York: Fordham University Press, 2010), 95–114.

[14] Lewis F. Bates, testimony for the prosecution, May 30, 1865, in Benjamin Perley Poore, ed., *The Conspiracy Trial for the Murder of the President*, 3 vols. (Boston: J. E. Tilton & Co., 1866), 2:242; Davis declaration cited in Stephen Mallory Papers, Southern Historical Collection, University of North Carolina, Chapel Hill; Jefferson Davis, *The Rise and Fall of the Confederate Government* (New York: D. Appleton, 1881), 2:719.

which he has permitted to be shed, and his efforts to enslave a free people."[15] Private citizens in these states could be equally contemptuous, as the candid diarists represented in this volume—like Sarah Morgan and Emma LeConte—reveal. But they wisely kept their views hidden, their personal journals locked, fearful of reprisals. In one brazen show of defiance, a photography studio in Charleston, South Carolina, the birthplace of the rebellion, placed photographs of Booth on sale soon after the assassination. Yet it must also be said that curious collectors snatched up just such souvenirs in New York and other Northern cities as well. Even in a period of mass mourning, curiosity trumped propriety. Astonishingly, even the Lincoln family's own photograph album boasted a *carte de visite* of the man who had murdered its patriarch.[16]

A watershed moment occurred in 1876, shortly before Reconstruction would abruptly be abandoned as a concession to the South to settle a disputed presidential election. In April of that year, Frederick Douglass rose in Washington to deliver the dedicatory address at the unveiling of a new statue of Lincoln. Thomas Ball's heroic bronze depicted the late President as an emancipator, lifting a half-naked African American from his knees—a racially insensitive embarrassment today, yet funded entirely by African-American donors. On the eleventh anniversary of the assassination, Douglass revised his 1865 assessment, and called the late President "preeminently the *white man's President* [emphasis added], entirely devoted to the welfare of white men." Only later in the oration did Douglass acknowledge that Lincoln had "delivered us from . . . bondage." Perhaps Douglass, like so many other black leaders, had grown impatient for the permanent guarantee of equal rights for his people.

There was reason to believe that Douglass was right—once again. For two years later, with Reconstruction (Union occupation of the South, in the view of many Lost Cause Southerners) now ended, it somehow seemed fitting and proper that one of the era's most prestigious honors

[15] Reprinted in the *Philadelphia Evening Bulletin*, May 10, 1865. In April 1865 the *Daily Rebel* was being published in Selma, Alabama. I am grateful to Laurie Verge, William C. Davis, and Edward Steers Jr. for their help in locating this quotation.
[16] See Thomas Reed Turner, *Beware the People Weeping: Public Opinion and the Assassination of Abraham Lincoln* (Baton Rouge: Louisiana State University Press, 1982), 90–91, 97; Mark E. Neely Jr. and Harold Holzer, *The Lincoln Family Album: Photographs from the Personal Collection of a Historic American Family* (New York: Doubleday, 1990), 108–9.

—an invitation to speak at the unveiling at the U.S. Capitol of a newly acquired painting celebrating the Emancipation Proclamation—should go to the former vice president of the Confederacy, Alexander Hamilton Stephens.[17] To some unreconstructed abolitionists and Union veterans, the Georgian was still a traitor, the same man who had once proudly declared slavery to be the "corner-stone" of the Confederacy.[18]

Many senators and representatives probably knew that the diminutive yet passionate old orator had once served alongside fellow Whig Abraham Lincoln in the House of Representatives. As a freshman congressman, Lincoln had once been moved to tears by one of that "little slim, pale-faced, consumptive" orator's floor speeches.[19] During the secession crisis of 1860–61, Lincoln had tried mightily to convince the Georgian to resist disunion—and even briefly considered offering him a cabinet post in return. Near the end of the war that neither had been able to prevent, the two men had reunited briefly and, as it turned out, acrimoniously at the ill-fated Hampton Roads Peace Conference of 1865 (as dramatized in Steven Spielberg's 2012 film *Lincoln*). There, the President had bluntly told his onetime colleague that there was now no room for compromise, whatever further blood might be shed: the South could never become a separate country and there would be no retreat from emancipation, no hope of preventing ratification of the Thirteenth Amendment to the Constitution. Now, thirteen more years later, Stephens proved as generous in his praise before Congress as Lincoln had been immovable in his resistance at Hampton Roads. The onetime Confederate leader proved the perfect oracle of what had come to be accepted as sectional reconciliation, even if his address never acknowledged the thwarted hopes of many Republicans for civil and voting rights for African Americans.

Taken together, this decades-long onslaught of emotion, attention, and praise—pictorial and narrative, journalistic and poetic, public and

---

[17] The work was Francis B. Carpenter's *First Reading of the Emancipation Proclamation Before the Cabinet*, which dated to 1864. After a protracted campaign to see it displayed in the Capitol, the painting was purchased years later by a patron and donated to Congress.

[18] Alexander H. Stephens: "Corner-Stone" Speech, March 21, 1861, in Brooks D. Simpson, Stephen W. Sears, and Aaron Sheehan-Dean, ed., *The Civil War: The First Year Told by Those Who Lived It* (New York: Library of America, 2011), 221–36.

[19] Lincoln to William H. Herndon, February 2, 1848, in Fehrenbacher, ed., *Abraham Lincoln: Speeches and Writings*, 1:174.

private—failed to secure full citizenship rights for the people Frederick Douglass called Abraham Lincoln's "stepchildren." But it effectively transformed Lincoln into nothing less than the nation's first secular saint, elevating a vigorously opposed political leader into a sanctified hero. The image the writers created was so powerfully resonant that it survived virtually intact and unchallenged for nearly a hundred years, until historians and civil rights leaders of the 1960s began reexamining and reassessing the past in search of the brilliant but flawed man behind the gilded myth. Yet not even the barrage of subsequent revisionism has succeeded in ousting Lincoln from his customary perch atop all historians' surveys of greatest presidents. Nor has it stemmed the unbroken outpouring of books devoted to reexamining his presidency, most of which invariably conclude that his leadership saved the nation.

In this sesquicentennial year of the crime that propelled Lincoln into the pantheon of myth, this collection of prose and poetry, reportage and recollection, is offered as contemporary evidence of a transfiguration that played out against the backdrop of the effort to avenge the crime of the century—or was it that the prolonged manhunt for Booth only made the sanctification of his victim more complete? Though unsolved mysteries about Booth's conspiracy remain—principally whether the Confederate government authorized and financed it—and while debates about the culpability of alleged individual conspirators continue to rage, here are the very words that originally triggered these doubts: reports that now take modern readers from the earliest news reports of Lincoln's murder to the lamentations that novelists and poets added to the written record of what a character in Lincoln's favorite play, *Macbeth*, called "the deep damnation of his taking off."

As a coda, this volume concludes with a few selected words by Lincoln himself—who, during the bloody war, became in effect the nation's mourner-in-chief, repeatedly and eloquently trying to forge meaning from almost unimaginable death and loss. In some of these letters, he offers personal recognition to individual heroes who died that the nation might live. And in two of his most widely acclaimed speeches, he first dedicates hallowed ground to "the brave men, living and dead," who fought for a "new birth of freedom," and then later invokes the idea that slaves had suffered so violently, for so long, that God now willed that

Americans North *and* South pay for the bloodshed "drawn with the lash" with yet more bloodshed "drawn with the sword." Although he had once insisted that "assassination of public officials is not an American crime," perhaps the exhausted president had come by 1865 to foresee—or at least dream of—himself as the tragedy's final sacrifice. After all, he had once reportedly told his old Springfield law partner, "I feel as if I should meet with some terrible end"—a premonition he repeated more than a dozen times.[20]

With all the words in this collection—from Lincoln and his contemporaries alike—the crime of the nineteenth century is again evoked, and the resulting sanctification of its victim recalled and assessed. Readers who reimagine the tragedy and absorb its literature will here have an unprecedented opportunity to consider, for example, Frederick Douglass's shifting views, and decide this and other questions of reputation and fact for themselves.

One early observer who did precisely that—reassess Lincoln's suddenly transfigured reputation—was the English writer Tom Taylor, a frequent and acerbic critic of Lincoln while the American President lived, and ironically the author of the 1858 play *Our American Cousin*, which Lincoln had been enjoying at Ford's Theatre when his life was taken.

Just three weeks after the assassination—in an example of poetic atonement to be found in full on these pages—the guilt-ridden Taylor apologized in verse both for his relentless earlier assaults and for his inability to appreciate the late President while he lived. In remarkable words written to accompany a woodcut cartoon showing Britannia sympathizing with Columbia at Lincoln's bier, Taylor belatedly but generously acknowledged Lincoln as a hero of both "the Old World and the New." In so doing, Taylor spoke as meaningfully about the almost universal post-assassination approbation for Lincoln as he did about the lacerating criticism and ridicule that had preceded it, and from which the martyred President had been liberated, as this volume shows, only by virtue of his heroic death. As Taylor wrote:

---

[20] Benjamin F. Butler in Rice, ed., *Reminiscences of Abraham Lincoln by Distinguished Men of His Time*, 144; Herndon quoted in Don E. Fehrenbacher and Virginia Fehrenbacher, *Recollected Words of Abraham Lincoln* (Stanford, CA: Stanford University Press, 1996), 252.

Yes, he had lived to shame me from my sneer,
   To lame my pencil, and confute my pen—
To make me own this hind of princes peer,
   This rail-splitter a true-born king of men.

HAROLD HOLZER

THE ASSASSINATION OF THE
PRESIDENT AND THE PUNISHMENT
OF THE CONSPIRATORS

Charles Carleton Coffin

Scenes in Richmond

Worn down by the pressures of Washington and eager to be at the front when the war ended, President Lincoln arrived at Ulysses S. Grant's headquarters at City Point, Virginia, on March 24, 1865, for an extended visit. On April 2 Union troops ended a nine-month-long siege by breaking through the Confederate lines at Petersburg, forcing Robert E. Lee to retreat westward and Jefferson Davis to flee Richmond. As the Confederate government abandoned its capital, the city's military commander ordered the destruction of its tobacco and cotton stockpiles. The fires rapidly spread and devastated much of Richmond before Union forces arrived the next morning. When Lincoln telegraphed Edwin M. Stanton of his intention to visit Petersburg on April 3, he received a stern admonition from his secretary of war: "Allow me respectfully to ask you to consider whether you ought to expose the Nation to the consequence of any disaster to yourself in the pursuit of a treacherous and dangerous Enemy like the rebel army." Hours later the President told Stanton that he planned to go to Richmond the next day, and added: "I will take care of myself." The arrival in Richmond on April 4 of Lincoln and his twelve-year-old son, Thomas (Tad), was witnessed by Charles Carleton Coffin (1823–1896), who had been reporting on the war for the *Boston Journal* since 1861.

RICHMOND, April 4, 1865.

To the Editor of The Boston Journal:

President Lincoln is in Richmond. The hated, despised, ridiculed, the brute, the beast, the baboon of the Yankee nation, as the Richmond editors have named him, is here, in the house from which Jeff. Davis fled in haste and terror on Sunday last! The thought sets one's brain in a whirl, and yet it is my business to write coolly of the great events now transpiring in this city. To write connectedly I will make simply a record of personal observations, taking up the narrative broken abruptly in my letter of yesterday by the departure of the mail messenger.

APPEARANCE OF THE CITY.

Language fails me in any attempt to describe correctly the appearance of the city as I passed through the streets this morning at an early hour. The ruins were still smoking. The fire was still flaming furiously in several places. The pavements were hot to my feet, so intense had been

the flames. Granite columns, iron pillars, marble facings broken into
thousands of pieces, with cart loads of bricks, blocked the streets. The
firemen were still at work. One of the engineers stated that nearly a
thousand buildings of all kinds had been burned. The Bank of Richmond, Bank of the Commonwealth, Traders' Bank, Bank of Virginia,
Farmers' Bank, a score of private banking houses, the American
Hotel, the Columbian Hotel, the *Enquirer* and the *Dispatch* printing
offices, the Confederate Post Office Department, the State Court
House, the Mechanics' Institute, all the insurance offices, the Confederate War Department, the Confederate Arsenal, the Laboratory, Dr.
Read's Presbyterian Church, several foundries and machine shops, the
Henrico county Court House, the Danville and the Petersburg depots,
the three bridges across the James, Haxall's great flouring mills (the
largest in the world), all the best stores of the city, were destroyed. The
Libby Prison was not burned. It still stands a monument of rebel cruelty and inhumanity. In vain were the protests of the citizens to General Ewell; he detailed men to set the fires. When the rebel authorities
fired Charleston, negro troops from Massachusetts saved the city from
utter destruction; and here Massachusetts, in common with other soldiers of the North, white and negro alike, threw down their guns and did
what they could to save the city. General Devens' division was the first
to enter the city after Major Stevens with the cavalry detachment. He
detailed soldiers to battle with the flames. Some mounted the roof of
the Capitol, and others the Governor's Mansion, and extinguished the
flames, which were kindled again and again.

"If it had not been for the soldiers the whole city would have been
destroyed," was the remark of a Richmond citizen to-day. So the despised Yankees, the greasy mechanics and mudsills, became the saviors
of their fond old city, which the leaders of the rebellion, who claim to
be cavaliers, set on fire in their impotent rage. What cared they even
if they made their best friends houseless and homeless and penniless?
Jeff. Davis, Secretary Breckinridge, Gen. Lee and Gen. Ewell have been
feasted by many families who to-day are poverty stricken, who have lost
property, houses, lands, and all those who are in mourning for loved ones
who have fallen on the battle field, through the insane ambition and malignant hate of those in whom they blindly trusted.

When the rebel rear guard left the city they broke open the stores;

panes of window glass, which cost hundreds of dollars, were smashed without compunction; dry goods, boots, shoes, jewelry, everything was taken which pleased their fancy. Why should they not plunder after the example set them by their leaders?

The rebel soldiers are to be judged leniently. They have suffered privation and hardship, but their leaders have reveled in luxury, have had places of power, have plundered and robbed the nation, and with provident forethought have hundreds of thousands of dollars in London and Paris.

The poor people and negroes who have had hard work to keep soul and body together, improved the opportunity to help themselves to what was left. There was a grand rush to the stores. Some very ludicrous scenes. One negro had three Dutch ovens on his head, piled one above another, a stew pan in one hand and a skillet in another. Women had bags of flour in their arms, baskets of salt and pails of molasses, or sides of bacon. No miser ever gloated over his gold so eagerly as they over their supply of provisions. They had all but starved, but now they could eat till satisfied.

VISIT TO THE CAPITOL.

The Capitol square was full of furniture, beds, bedding, barrels, baskets, pots, kettles, pianos, sofas, looking glasses, crockery, and hundreds of women and children who had passed the night in the open air, among the soldiers of Gen. Devens' division, who cheerfully shared with them their rations.

The capitol outside and in, like the Confederacy, is exceedingly dilapidated. The windows are broken, the carpets faded, the paint dingy, the desks rickety. The members of the Legislature had left their letters and papers behind. Gen. Weitzel was in the Senate Chamber issuing his orders. Gen. Shepley, Military Governor, was also there; also Gen. Devens.

ADMIRAL FARRAGUT.

The door opened and a smooth faced man with a keen eye, firm, quick, resolute step entered. He wore a plain blue blouse with three stars on the collar. It was the old hero who opened the way to New Orleans, and who fought the battle of the Mobile forts from the mast head of his vessel—Admiral Farragut. He was accompanied by Gen. Gordon of Massachusetts, now commanding the Department of Norfolk. They heard the news yesterday noon and made all haste up the James, landing at Varina and taking horses to the city. It was a pleasure to take the brave Admiral's hand, and answer his eager questions as to what Grant had done. Being latest of all present from Petersburg I could give him the desired information. "Thank God, it is about over," said he, meaning the rebellion.

ARRIVAL OF PRESIDENT LINCOLN.

I was standing upon the bank of the river, viewing the scene of desolation, when a boat, pulled by twelve sailors, came up stream. It contained President Lincoln and his son, Admiral Porter, Capt. Penrose of the army, Capt. A. H. Adams of the navy, Lieut. W. W. Clemens of the signal corps. Somehow the negroes on the bank of the river ascertained that the tall man wearing a black hat was President Lincoln. There was a sudden shout. An officer who had just picked up fifty negroes to do work on the dock, found himself alone. They left work and crowded round the President. As he approached I said to a colored woman:

"There is the man who made you free."

"What, massa?"

"That is President Lincoln."

"Dat President Linkum?"

"Yes."

She gazed at him a moment, clapped her hands and jumped straight up and down, shouting "Glory, glory, glory!" till her voice was lost in the universal cheer.

There was no carriage near, so the President, leading his son, walked three-quarters of a mile up to Gen. Weitzel's headquarters—Jeff. Davis's mansion. What a spectacle it was! Such a hurly-burly—such wild indescribable ecstatic joy I never witnessed. A colored man acted as guide. Six sailors, wearing their round blue caps and short jackets and bagging pants, with navy carbines, was the advance guard. Then came the President and Admiral Porter, flanked by the officers accompanying him and the correspondent of *The Journal*, then six more sailors with carbines—twenty of us all told—amid a surging mass of men, women and children, black, white and yellow, running, shouting, dancing, swinging their caps, bonnets and handkerchiefs. The soldiers saw him and swelled the crowd, cheering in wild enthusiasm. All could see him, he was so tall—so conspicuous.

One colored woman, standing in a doorway, as the President passed along the sidewalk, shouted: "Thank you, dear Jesus, for this! thank you, Jesus!" Another standing by her side was clapping her hands and shouting: "Bless de Lord!"

A colored woman snatched her bonnet from her head, whirled it in the air, screaming with all her might, "God bless you, massa Linkum."

A few white women looking out from the houses waved their handkerchiefs. One lady in a large and elegant building looked awhile, and then turned away her head as if it was a disgusting sight.

President Lincoln walked in silence, acknowledging the salutes of officers and soldiers and of the citizens, *black and white!* It was the man of the people among the people. It was the great deliverer, meeting the delivered. Yesterday morning the majority of the thousands who crowded the streets and hindered our advance were slaves. Now they were free, and behold him who had given them their liberty. Gen. Shepley met the President in the street, and escorted him to Gen. Weitzel's quarters. Major Stevens hearing that the President was on his way suddenly summoned a detachment of the Massachusetts 4th Cavalry, and cleared the way.

After a tedious walk the mansion of Jeff. Davis was reached. The immense crowd swept round the corner of the street and packed the space in front. Gen. Weitzel received the President at the door. Cheer upon cheer went up from the excited multitude—two-thirds of whom were colored.

The officers who had assembled were presented to the President in the reception room of the mansion.

Judge Campbell, once on the Supreme bench of the United States, who became a traitor, came in and had a brief private interview with the President in the drawing-room. Other citizens called—those who have been for the Union through all the war.

The President then took a ride through the city, accompanied by Admiral Porter, Gens. Shepley, Weitzel and other officers. Such is the simple narrative of this momentous event, but no written page of illuminated canvas can give the reality of the event—the enthusiastic bearing of the people—the blacks and poor whites who have suffered untold horrors during the war, their demonstrations of pleasure, the shouting, dancing, the thanksgivings to God, the mention of the name of Jesus—as if President Lincoln were next to the son of God in their affections—the jubilant cries, the countenances beaming with unspeakable joy, the tossing up of caps, the swinging of arms of a motley crowd—some in rags, some bare-foot, some wearing pants of Union blue, and coats of Confederate gray, ragamuffins in dress through the hardships of war, but yet of stately bearing—men in heart and soul—free men henceforth and forever, their bonds cut asunder in an hour—men from whose limbs the chains fell yesterday morning, men who through many weary years have prayed for deliverance—who have asked sometimes if God were dead—who, when their children were taken from them and sent to the swamps of South Carolina and the cane brakes of Louisiana, cried to God for help and cried in vain, who told their sorrows to Jesus and asked for help, but who had no helper—men who have been whipped, scourged, robbed, imprisoned, for no crime. All of these things must be kept in remembrance if we would have the picture complete.

No wonder that President Lincoln who has a child's heart, felt his soul stirred; that the tears almost come to his eyes as he heard the thanksgivings to God and Jesus, and the blessings uttered for him from thankful hearts. They were true, earnest and heartfelt expressions of gratitude to God. There are thousands of men in Richmond to-night who would lay down their lives for President Lincoln—their great deliverer—their best friend on earth. He came among them unheralded, without pomp or parade. He walked through the streets as if he were only a private citizen and not the head of a mighty nation. He came not as a conqueror—not with bitterness in his heart, but with kindness. He came as a friend, to alleviate sorrow and suffering—to rebuild what has been destroyed.

CARLETON.

Thomas T. Eckert

Testimony Before the House Judiciary Committee

The President returned to Washington on the evening of April 9, Palm Sunday, just a few hours before Grant telegraphed the War Department with news of Lee's surrender earlier that day at Appomattox Court House. When Lincoln spoke to a large crowd gathered at the White House on the evening of April 11, he devoted only a single paragraph of his speech to the recent Union victories before turning to the difficulties of reconstruction. Publicly addressing for the first time the question of black suffrage in Louisiana, he said: "It is also unsatisfactory to some that the elective franchise is not given to the colored man. I would myself prefer that it were now conferred on the very intelligent, and on those who serve our cause as soldiers." Listening in the crowd was the actor John Wilkes Booth, who had been plotting for months to abduct the President and then exchange him for Confederate prisoners of war. Two of his co-conspirators later provided accounts of Booth's reaction to Lincoln's words. In *Katy of Catoctin*, his 1886 novel about the Lincoln assassination, George Alfred Townsend, a former correspondent for the *New York World*, depicted Booth telling his co-conspirator David Herold: "That means nigger citizenship. Now, by God! I'll put him through." In a footnote, Townsend wrote that Booth's remarks had been related to him by Herold's defense counsel, Frederick Stone. Another version of Booth's response was given by Major Thomas T. Eckert (1825–1910), superintendent of the War Department telegraph office and acting assistant secretary of war in April 1865. In testimony before the House Judiciary Committee on May 30, 1867, Eckert described his questioning of the conspirator Lewis Powell, alias Payne, after Powell's arrest.

Q. Did he make any statement with regard to what other persons were to be assassinated?

A. No, sir, nothing, except as to the President and Mr. Seward. He knew in reference to the intention to assassinate the President, because Booth tried to get him to shoot the President the night of the celebration after the fall of Richmond. The President made a speech that night from one of the windows of the White House, and he and Booth were in the grounds in front. Booth tried to persuade him to shoot the President while in the window, but he told Booth he would take no such risk; that he left then and walked around the square, and that Booth remarked: "That is the last speech he will ever make."

9

Lawrence A. Gobright

Associated Press Dispatch

Two nights after the President's speech, Washington celebrated the Union triumph at Appomattox with fireworks and a grand illumination of the city. The following night, April 14, Good Friday, Lawrence A. Gobright (1816–1891), the Washington correspondent for the Associated Press since 1846, was reading a newspaper in his office when a "hurried and excited" visitor told him that the President had been assassinated at Ford's Theatre. Gobright rushed to the scene and examined the box where Lincoln had been shot, then learned that Secretary of State William H. Seward, who was recovering from a carriage accident, had been attacked in his home. After visiting the Seward house, Gobright talked to several witnesses from Ford's Theatre and spoke with House Speaker Schuyler Colfax about Lincoln's condition before sending a remarkably accurate dispatch across the telegraph wires for publication nationwide.

WASHINGTON, April 14.

President Lincoln and wife, with other friends, this evening visited Ford's Theatre, for the purpose of witnessing the performance of the "American Cousin."

It was announced in the papers that General Grant would be present. But that gentleman took the late train of cars for New Jersey.

The theatre was densely crowded, and everybody seemed delighted with the scene before them. During the third act, and while there was a temporary pause for one of the actors to enter, a sharp report of a pistol was heard, which merely attracted attention, but suggesting nothing serious, until a man rushed to the front of the President's box, waving a long dagger in his right hand, and exclaiming, "*Sic semper tyrannis*," and immediately leaped from the box, which was in the second tier, to the stage beneath, and ran across to the opposite side, making his escape, amid the bewilderment of the audience, from the rear of the theatre, and mounting a horse, fled.

The screams of Mrs. Lincoln first disclosed the fact to the audience that the President had been shot; when all present rose to their feet, rushed toward the stage, many exclaiming, "Hang him! hang him!"

The excitement was of the wildest possible description, and of course there was an abrupt termination of the theatrical performance.

There was a rush toward the President's box, when cries were heard, "Stand back and give him air!" "Has any one stimulants?" On a hasty examination, it was found that the President had been shot through the head, above and back of the temporal bone, and that some of the brain was oozing out. He was removed to a private house opposite to the theatre, and the Surgeon-General of the Army, and other surgeons, were sent for to attend to his condition.

On an examination of the private box, blood was discovered on the back of the cushioned chair in which the President had been sitting; also on the partition, and on the floor. A common single-barrelled pocket-pistol was found on the carpet.

A military guard was placed in front of the private residence to which the President had been conveyed. An immense crowd was in front of it, all deeply anxious to learn the condition of the President. It had been previously announced that the wound was mortal, but all hoped otherwise. The shock to the community was terrible.

At midnight the Cabinet went thither. Messrs. Sumner, Colfax, and Farnsworth; Judge Curtis, Governor Oglesby, General Meigs, Colonel Hay, and a few personal friends, with Surgeon-General Barnes and his immediate assistants were around his bedside. The President was in a state of syncope, totally insensible, and breathing slowly. The blood oozed from the wound at the back of his head.

The surgeons exhausted every possible effort of medical skill, but all hope was gone!

The parting of his family with the dying President is too sad for description. The President and Mrs. Lincoln did not start for the theatre until fifteen minutes after eight o'clock. Speaker Colfax was at the White House at the time, and the President stated to him that he was going, although Mrs. Lincoln had not been well, because the papers had announced that General Grant and they were to be present, and, as General Grant had gone North, he did not wish the audience to be disappointed.

He went to the theatre with apparent reluctance, and urged Mr. Colfax to accompany him; but that gentleman had made other engagements, and with Mr. Ashmun, of Massachusetts, bade him good-bye.

When the excitement at the theatre was at its wildest height, reports were circulated that Secretary Seward had also been assassinated.

REPORTED ASSASSINATION OF MR. SEWARD.—On reaching this gentleman's residence, a crowd and military guard were found at the door, and on entering, it was ascertained that the reports were true.

Everybody there was so excited, that scarcely an intelligible word could be gathered; but the facts are substantially as follows:—

About ten o'clock, a man rang the bell, and the call having been answered by a colored servant, he said he had come from Doctor Verdi, Secretary Seward's family physician, with a prescription, at the same time holding in his hand a small piece of folded paper, and saying in answer to a refusal, that he must see the Secretary, as he was intrusted with particular directions concerning the medicine. He still insisted on going up, although repeatedly informed that no one could enter the chamber. The man pushed the servant aside, and walked heavily toward the Secretary's room, and was then met by Mr. Frederick W. Seward, of whom he demanded to see the Secretary, making the same representation which he did to the servant. What further passed in the way of colloquy is not known, but the man struck him on the head with a billy, severely injuring the skull, and felling him to the floor almost senseless. The assassin then rushed into the chamber and attacked Major Seward, Paymaster United States Army, and Mr. Hansell, a messenger of the State Department, and two male nurses, disabling them all. He then rushed upon the Secretary, who was lying in bed in the same room, and inflicted three stabs in the neck, but severing, it is thought and hoped, no arteries, though he bled profusely. The assassin then rushed down-stairs, mounted his horse at the door, and rode off before an alarm could be sounded, and in the same manner as the assassin of the President.

It is believed that the injuries of the Secretary are not fatal, nor those of either of the others, although both the Secretary and the Assistant Secretary are very seriously injured.

Secretaries Stanton and Welles, and other prominent officers of the Government, called at Secretary Seward's house, to inquire into his condition, and there, for the first time, heard of the assassination of the President. They then proceeded to the house where he was lying, exhibiting, of course, intense anxiety and solicitude. An immense crowd was gathered in front of the President's house, and a strong guard was also stationed there, many persons supposing that he would be brought to his home.

The entire city to-night presents a scene of wild excitement accompanied by violent expressions of indignation and the profoundest sorrow. Many shed tears. The military authorities have dispatched mounted patrols in every direction, in order, if possible, to arrest the assassins. The whole metropolitan police are likewise vigilant for the same purpose.

The attacks, both at the theatre and at Secretary Seward's house, took place at about the same hour, ten o'clock, thus showing a preconcerted plan to assassinate those gentlemen. Some evidences of the guilt of the party who attacked the President are in possession of the police. Vice-President Johnson is in this city, and his headquarters are guarded by troops.

Edwin M. Stanton

Telegrams to John A. Dix

Secretary of War Edwin M. Stanton (1814–1869) was one of Lincoln's best appointments, and a powerful testament to his ability to overcome personal grievances. When the two men first met before the war as co-counsels in a patent case, the nationally prominent Stanton had excluded Lincoln from the trial and treated the "low-down country lawyer" with open contempt. Despite this humiliation, Lincoln chose Stanton, a Democrat, to replace Simon Cameron as secretary of war in January 1862. Often brusque to the point of rudeness, Stanton proved to be an honest, energetic, and efficient administrator, and grew to respect the President. In the last year of the war Stanton began writing telegrams to John A. Dix, the Union commander in New York City, that were released to the press as de facto government communiqués. The four telegrams Stanton sent to Dix in the hours immediately following the shooting testify to his ability to manage chaotic events and to the speed with which his investigation identified Lincoln's assassin.

———————

WAR DEPARTMENT,
April 15, 1865 — 1.30 A.M. (Sent 2.15 A.M.)

Major-General DIX,
New York:

Last evening, about 10.30 P.M., at Ford's Theater, the President, while sitting in his private box with Mrs. Lincoln, Miss Harris, and Major Rathbone, was shot by an assassin, who suddenly entered the box and approached behind the President. The assassin then leaped upon the stage, brandishing a large dagger or knife, and made his escape in the rear of the theater. The pistol-ball entered the back of the President's head, and penetrated nearly through the head. The wound is mortal. The President has been insensible ever since it was inflicted, and is now dying. About the same hour an assassin (whether the same or another) entered Mr. Seward's home, and, under pretense of having a prescription, was shown to the Secretary's sick chamber. The Secretary was in bed, a nurse and Miss Seward with him. The assassin immediately rushed to the bed, inflicted two or three stabs on the throat and two on the face. It is hoped the wounds may not be mortal; my apprehension is that they will prove fatal. The noise alarmed Mr. Frederick Seward, who was in an adjoining room, and hastened to the door of his father's room, where he met the assassin, who inflicted upon him one or more dangerous wounds. The recovery of Frederick Seward is doubtful. It is not probable that the President will live through the night. General Grant and wife were advertised to be at the theater this evening, but he started to Burlington at 6 o'clock this evening. At a Cabinet meeting yesterday, at which General Grant was present, the subject of the state of the country and the prospects of speedy peace was discussed. The President was very cheerful and hopeful; spoke very kindly of General Lee and others of the Confederacy, and the establishment of government in Virginia. All the members of the Cabinet except Mr. Seward are now in attendance upon the President. I have seen Mr. Seward, but he and Frederick were both unconscious.

EDWIN M. STANTON,
Secretary of War.

WASHINGTON CITY,
No. 458 Tenth Street, April 15, 1865—3 A.M.
(Sent 3.20 A.M.)

Major-General DIX:
(Care Horner, New York.)

The President still breathes, but is quite insensible, as he has been ever since he was shot. He evidently did not see the person who shot him, but was looking on the stage as he was approached behind.

Mr. Seward has rallied, and it is hoped he may live. Frederick Seward's condition is very critical. The attendant who was present was stabbed through the lungs, and is not expected to live. The wounds of Major Seward are not serious. Investigation strongly indicates J. Wilkes Booth as the assassin of the President. Whether it was the same or a different person that attempted to murder Mr. Seward remains in doubt. Chief Justice Cartter is engaged in taking the evidence. Every exertion has been made to prevent the escape of the murderer. His horse has been found on the road, near Washington.

EDWIN M. STANTON,
Secretary of War.

————————

WASHINGTON CITY,
No. 458 Tenth Street, April 15, 1865—4.10 A.M.
(Sent 4.44 A.M.)

Major-General DIX:

   The President continues insensible and is sinking. Secretary Seward remains without change. Frederick Seward's skull is fractured in two places, besides a severe cut upon the head. The attendant is still alive, but hopeless. Major Seward's wounds are not dangerous. It is now ascertained with reasonable certainty that two assassins were engaged in the horrible crime, Wilkes Booth being the one that shot the President, the other a companion of his whose name is not known, but whose description is so clear that he can hardly escape. It appears from a letter found in Booth's trunk that the murder was planned before the 4th of March, but fell through then because the accomplice backed out until "Richmond could be heard from." Booth and his accomplice were at the livery stable at 6 this evening, and left there with their horses about 10 o'clock, or shortly before that hour. It would seem that they had for several days been seeking their chance, but for some unknown reason it was not carried into effect until last night. One of them has evidently made his way to Baltimore, the other has not yet been traced.

EDWIN M. STANTON,
Secretary of War.

————————

WASHINGTON CITY, *April 15, 1865.*

Major-General DIX,
   New York:
   Abraham Lincoln died this morning at 22 minutes after 7 o'clock.

EDWIN M. STANTON,
Secretary of War.

Edwin M. Stanton

Letter to Charles Francis Adams

With both Secretary of State Seward and his son Frederick, the assistant secretary of state, seriously wounded, Stanton took it upon himself to officially notify Adams, the U.S. minister in Great Britain, of Lincoln's murder. Stanton's letter reached London on April 26. It was forwarded to American legations throughout Europe and printed in the foreign press.

WAR DEPARTMENT,
Washington City, April 15, 1865—11.40 A.M.

Hon. CHARLES FRANCIS ADAMS,
    Minister of the United States to Her Britannic Majesty:

SIR: It has become my distressing duty to announce to you that last night His Excellency Abraham Lincoln, President of the United States, was assassinated about the hour of 10.30 o'clock in his private box at Ford's Theater in this city. The President about 8 o'clock accompanied Mrs. Lincoln to the theater. Another lady and gentleman were with them in the box. About 10.30, during a pause in the performance, the assassin entered the box, the door of which was unguarded, hastily approached the President from behind, and discharged a pistol at his head. The bullet entered the back of his head and penetrated nearly through. The assassin then leaped from the box upon the stage, brandishing a large knife or dagger and exclaiming "*Sic semper tyrannis,*" and escaped in the rear of the theater. Immediately upon the discharge the President fell to the floor insensible, and continued in that state until 7.20 o'clock this morning, when he breathed his last.

About the same time this murder was being committed at the theater another assassin presented himself at the door of Mr. Seward's residence, gained admission by pretending he had a prescription from Mr. Seward's physician, which he was directed to see administered, hurried up to the third-story chamber, where Mr. Seward was lying. He here encountered Mr. Frederick Seward, struck him over the head, inflicting several wounds, and fracturing the skull in two places, inflicting, it is feared, mortal wounds. He then rushed into the room where Mr. Seward was in bed, attended by a young daughter and a male nurse. The male attendant was stabbed through the lungs, and it is believed will die. The assassin then struck Mr. Seward with a knife or dagger twice in the throat and twice in the face, inflicting terrible wounds. By this time Major Seward, the eldest son of the Secretary, and another attendant reached the room, and rushed to the rescue of the Secretary. They were also wounded in the conflict, and the assassin escaped. No artery or important blood vessel was severed by any of the wounds inflicted upon him, but he was for a long time insensible from the loss of blood. Some hopes of his possible recovery are entertained.

Immediately upon the death of the President notice was given to Vice-President Johnson, who happened to be in the city, and upon whom the office of President now devolves. He will take the office and assume the functions of President to-day. The murderer of the President has been discovered, and evidence obtained that these horrible crimes were committed in execution of a conspiracy deliberately planned and set on foot by rebels, under pretense of avenging the South and aiding the rebel cause. It is hoped that the immediate perpetrators will be caught. The feeling occasioned by these atrocious crimes is so great, sudden, and overwhelming that I cannot at present do more than communicate them to you at the earliest moment.

Yesterday the President called a Cabinet meeting, at which General Grant was present. He was more cheerful and happy than I had ever seen, rejoiced at the near prospect of firm and durable peace at home and abroad, manifested in marked degree the kindness and humanity of his disposition, and the tender and forgiving spirit that so eminently distinguished him. Public notice had been given that he and General Grant would be present at the theater, and the opportunity of adding the lieutenant-general to the number of victims to be murdered was no doubt seized for the fitting occasion of executing the plans that appear to have been in preparation for some weeks. But General Grant was compelled to be absent, and thus escaped the designs upon him.

It is needless for me to say anything in regard to the influence which this atrocious murder of the President may exercise upon the affairs of this country, but I will only add that horrible as are the atrocities that have been resorted to by the enemies of this country, they are not likely in any degree to impair the public spirit or postpone the complete and final overthrow of the rebellion.

In profound grief for the events which it has become my duty to communicate to you, I have the honor to be, very respectfully, your obedient servant,

EDWIN M. STANTON.

P. S.—You will please communicate these deplorable events to all the ministers and diplomatic agents of the United States with whom you are in communication.

EDWIN M. STANTON,
Secretary of War.

Henry R. Rathbone

Affidavit

Although it had been announced in the *Washington Evening Star* that General Grant and his wife would accompany the Lincolns to the theater on April 14, personal friction between Mary Lincoln and Julia Grant caused the general to decline the invitation that afternoon, using as a pretext his urgent desire to reunite with his children in New Jersey. Major Thomas T. Eckert, the assistant secretary of war, also declined, saying that Stanton needed him to work late at the War Department. Only then was an invitation extended to Clara Harris, the daughter of Senator Ira Harris of New York, and to her stepbrother and fiancé, Major Henry R. Rathbone (1837–1911), an infantry officer who had fought at Antietam and Fredericksburg and been wounded at Petersburg in the battle of the Crater.

Henry R. Rathbone, Brevet Major in the Army of the United States, being duly sworn, says, that on the 14th day of April, instant, at about twenty-minutes past eight o'clock in the evening, he, with Miss Clara H. Harris, left his residence at the corner of Fifteenth and H streets, and joined the President and Mrs. Lincoln and went with them in their carriage to Ford's Theatre in Tenth street. The box assigned to the President is in the second tier on the right-hand side of the audience, and was occupied by the President and Mrs. Lincoln, Miss Harris, and this deponent, and by no other person. The box is entered by passing from the front of the building in the rear of the dress circle to a small entry or passageway, about eight feet in length and four feet in width. This passageway is entered by a door which opens on the inner side. The door is so placed as to make an acute angle between it and the wall behind it on the inner side. At the inner end of this passageway is another door, standing squarely across, and opening into the box. On the left-hand side of the passageway, and being near the inner end, is a third door, which also opens into the box. This latter door was closed. The party entered the box through the door at the end of the passageway. The box is so constructed that it may be divided into two by a movable partition, one of the doors described opening into each. The front of the box is about ten or twelve feet in length, and in the centre of the railing is a small pillar overhung with a curtain. The depth of the box from front to rear is about nine feet. The elevation of the box above the stage, including the railing, is about ten or twelve feet.

When the party entered the box, a cushioned arm chair was standing at the end of the box furthest from the stage and nearest the audience. This was also the nearest point to the door by which the box is entered. The President seated himself in this chair, and, except that he once left the chair for the purpose of putting on his overcoat, remained so seated until he was shot. Mrs. Lincoln was seated in a chair between the President and the pillar in the centre above described. At the opposite end of the box, that nearest the stage, were two chairs, in one of these, standing in the corner, Miss Harris was seated. At her left hand, and along the wall running from that end of the box to the rear, stood a small sofa. At the end of this sofa, next to Miss Harris, this deponent was seated. The distance between this deponent and the President, as they were sitting, was about seven or eight feet, and the distance between this deponent and the door was about the same. The distance between the President, as he sat, and the door was about four or five feet. The door, according to the recollection of this deponent, was not closed during the evening.

When the second scene of the third act was being performed, and this deponent was intently observing the proceedings upon the stage, with his back towards the door, he heard the discharge of a pistol behind him, and looking around, saw through the smoke a man between the door and the President. At the same time deponent heard him shout some word which deponent thinks was 'Freedom.' This deponent instantly sprang towards him and seized him. He wrested himself from the grasp and made a violent thrust at the breast of deponent with a large knife. Deponent parried the blow by striking it up, and received a wound several inches deep in his left arm between the elbow and the shoulder. The orifice of the wound is about an inch and a half in length, and extends upwards towards the shoulder several inches. The man rushed to the front of the box and deponent endeavored to seize him again, but only caught his clothes as he was leaping over the railing of the box. The clothes, as deponent believes, were torn in this attempt to seize him. As he went over upon the stage, deponent cried out with a loud voice, "Stop that man." Deponent then turned to the President. His position was not changed. His head was slightly bent forward and his eyes were closed. Deponent saw that he was unconscious, and, supposing him mortally wounded, rushed to the door for the purpose of calling medical aid. On reaching the outer door of the passageway as above described, deponent found it barred by a heavy piece of plank, one end of which was secured in the wall and the other rested against the door. It had been so securely fastened that it required considerable force to remove it. This wedge or bar was about four feet from the floor. Persons upon the outside were beating against the door for the purpose of entering. Deponent removed the bar and the door was opened. Several persons who represented themselves to be surgeons were allowed to enter. Deponent saw there Colonel Crawford, and requested him to prevent other persons from entering the box. Deponent then returned to the box and found the surgeons examining the President's person. They had not yet discovered the wound. As soon as it was discovered it was determined to remove him from the theatre. He was carried out, and this deponent then proceeded to assist Mrs. Lincoln, who was intensely excited, to leave the theatre. On reaching the head of the stairs deponent requested Major Potter to aid him in assisting Mrs. Lincoln across the street to the house to which the President was being conveyed. The wound which deponent had received had been bleeding very profusely, and, on reaching the house, feeling very faint from the loss of blood, he seated himself in the hall, and soon after fainted away and was laid upon the floor. Upon the return of consciousness deponent was taken in a carriage to his residence.

In the review of the transaction, it is the confident belief of the deponent that the time which elapsed between the discharge of the pistol and the time when the assassin leaped from the box, did not exceed thirty seconds. Neither Mrs. Lincoln nor Miss Harris had left their seats.

H. R. Rathbone.

Subscribed and sworn before me
this 17th day of April, 1865,

A. B. Olin,
Justice of the Supreme Court of the
District of Columbia.

Harry Hawk

Letter to William Hawk

Actor Harry Hawk (1837–1916) played "Asa Trenchard," the Vermont rustic whose comic encounters with his English relatives provide much of the humor in the 1858 comedy *Our American Cousin*. Questioned by Stanton and other investigators on the night of the assassination, he was one of the first witnesses to identify Booth as the President's assailant. Hawk's letter to his father was published in the *Chicago Journal* and reprinted in the *Washington Evening Star* on April 24, 1865.

───────────

Mr. William J. Hawke, of this city, who resides at No. 254 State street, has received a letter from his son Harry, who is a member of Laura Keene's theatrical company, who were playing "Our American Cousin" at Ford's Theatre, in Washington on the night of the horrid tragedy. He gives some new facts in reference to the assassination and the assassin. We are permitted to publish the letter, which is as follows:—

Washington, Sunday, April 16.—This is the first opportunity I have had to write to you since the assassination of our dear President on Friday night, as I have been in custody, nearly ever since. I was one of the principal witnesses of that sad affair, being the only one on the stage at the time of the fatal shot.

I was playing "Asa Trenchard," in the "American Cousin." The "old lady" of the theatre had just gone off the stage, and I was answering her exit speech when I heard the shot fired. I turned, looked up at the President's box, heard the man exclaim, "*Sic Semper Tyrannis*," saw him jump from the box, seize the flag on the staff and drop to the stage; he slipped when he gained the stage; but he got upon his feet in a moment, brandished a large knife, saying, "The South shall be free!" turned his face in the direction I stood, and I recognized him as John Wilkes Booth. He ran towards me, and I seeing the knife, thought I was the one he was after, ran off the stage and up a flight of stairs. He made his escape out of a door, directly, in the rear of the theatre, mounted a horse and rode off.

The above all occurred in the space of a quarter of a minute, and at the time I did not know that the President was shot, although, if I had tried to stop him he would have stabbed me.

I am now under one thousand dollars bail to appear as a witness when Booth is tried, if caught.

All the above I have sworn to. You may imagine the excitement in the theatre, which was crowded, with cries of "Hang him!" "Who was he!" etc., from every one present.

In about fifteen minutes after the occurrence the President was carried out and across the street. I was requested to walk down to the police head-quarters and give my evidence. They then put me under one thousand dollars' bond, to appear at ten o'clock next morning. I then walked about the city for some time, as the city was wild with excitement, and then went to bed. At half-past three I was called by an aid of the President, to go to the house where he was lying, to give another statement before Judge Carter, Secretary Stanton and other high officials assembled there. I did so, and went to bed again. On Saturday, I gave bail.

It was the saddest thing I ever knew. The city only the night before was illuminated, and everybody was so happy. Now it is all sadness. Everybody looks gloomy and sad.

On that night the play was going off so well, Mr. and Mrs. Lincoln enjoyed it so much. She was laughing at my speech when the shot was fired. In fact, it was one laugh from the time the curtain went up until it fell, and to think of such a sorrowful ending! It is an era in my life that I shall never forget. Inclosed is a piece of the fringe of the flag the President was holding when shot.

Helen Du Barry

Letter to Ann Amelia Bratt

Helen Du Barry (b. 1839) attended Ford's Theatre with her husband, Major Beekman Du Barry, an assistant to the army commissary general. The men she describes seeing with Lincoln were probably Charles Forbes, the guileless White House messenger who admitted Booth to the presidential box, and John F. Parker, an officer of the Washington Metropolitan Police who served on the detail guarding the White House. Parker was accused of negligence after the assassination, but was cleared by a police review board and returned to duty. It is possible that while Parker was told to escort Lincoln to the theater, he was never ordered to guard the President while he was there.

———————

WASHINGTON. D.C.
April 16th/65.

MY DEAR MOTHER

Beck has not come from the Office yet and I have not received your letter but as I have a good deal to write I will begin now. I suppose by to-morrow the mail will go out from Washin No trains left yesterday. What I have to write is with reference to the great Tragedy which has caused a Nation to mourn. I had the misfortune to be at Ford's Theatre on Friday evening & to hear the shot which deprived us of a President.

It was given out during the day that Mrs Lincoln had engaged a "*Box*" for the *President & Genl. Grant* and having a desire not only to see them but to see the "American cousin" performed, we determined to go. Before we went Beck knew that the Genl. would not be there as he was to leave for his home in the evening. We went a few moments before the time & waited some time for the President to arrive & as he did not come until late the performances commenced & we thought we were to be disappointed in not seeing him. In the mid'st of the 2nd scene there was a great applause & cheering and our attention was directed from the stage to the Dress circle—close to the wall—walked Miss Harris—Mrs Lincoln—Major Rathbun—a gentleman the President & another gentleman behind him. These two gentleman were *watchman* in citizens dress who have *always* accompanied the President since the War commenced We followed him with our eyes until he entered the Box

little thinking we were looking for the last time at him. He sat looking
on the stage his back to us and out of our sight behind the flags except
occasionnally when he would lean foward. Mrs Lincoln was in front of
him and we only saw her occasionally. We saw her smile & turn towards
him several times. It was while every one's attention was fastened upon
the stage that a pistol shot was heard causing every one to jump (as an
unexpected shot will) & look up at the President's Box merely because
that was the direction of the sound and supposing it to be part of the
performance we all looked again on the stage—when a man suddenly
vaulted over the railing of the box—turned back & then leaped to the
stage—striking on his heels & *falling* backward but recovered himself in
an instant and started across the stage to behind the scenes florishing a
knife—the blade of which appeared in the reflection of the bright lights
to be half as long as a man's arm—and making use of the expressions
you have seen in the Papers. He had nearly disappeared before we could
understand what it was or what had happened. We first thought it was
a crazy man—when he jumped on to the stage we all jumped to our feet
& stood spell bound—as he crossed the stage some few started towards
the stage crying—our President! our President is shot! catch him—hang
him! Miss Harris was seen to lean over the railing for water & that was
all that broke the stillness in that box. If those watch had called out as
soon as the man jumped to give us *an idea* of what had happened he could
have been caught as he stopped to recover himself after the fall. There
was not a soul to be seen in the Box and perfect stillness there—which
all added to our bewilderment—one man got up on a chair on hearing
that the man was caught—& said "take out the ladies & hang him here
on the spot." Beck fearing a mob hurried me out—leaving the audience
still standing awed & speechless. We waited outside until a young man
came out & said "He is dead—no doubt about it!"

Before we got out of the door some one said "It was J. Wilkes Booth"
and before I got out, the idea that our Chief was gone—almost our sole
dependence—overcome me & I could not control myself & sobbed
aloud We met several outside the door just coming in asking "For God's
sake tell me is it true? as if they had heard already rumors of the great
tragedy. The reason that we could not suddenly realize what had occurred was because we could not anticipate that an assassin could be in

the Box with the President. His only danger seemed to be from a shot fired by one of the audience

Booth entered the front door and asked some one there if Genl. Grant was there that night—then went along to the door of the Box— just where we had seen the President enter—knocked at the door & to the *watch* who opened it, said he wished to speak to the President, that he had a communication for him showing an Official envelope & giving him a card with the name of a Senator written on it. The watch stepped aside & the assassin entered & fired immediately while Mr Lincoln was looking on the stage

The excitement that night was intense & a mob of about 2000 went to the Old Capitol Prison to burn it & they called upon the people to come out & see the rebels burn. The Police & troops were out & put a stop to it or it would have been done. The assassin at Sewards first stabbed the nurse through the lungs & *killed* him I believe—knocked in the skull of Fred Seward with a butt of a pistol & stabbed another son—all had opposed his entrance and the old man hearing the scuffle at the door & thinking it was some one after him, rolled out of bed on to the floor and the assassin had to lean over the bed to stab him so he only had two cuts—on his neck & face—which will not prove serious if he has strength after his former sickness. There is no doubt that it was Booth who killed the President. Laura Keene says she can testify that it was him

The secessionists here have *all* draped their houses in crape—and ac- knowledge that it was the worst thing for the South that ever happened —their best friend is gone & Andy J.—will be more severe than ever Lin- coln was—Andy Johnson joined the Temperance Society after the Inau- garation and every one who saw him at his own Inauguration were much pleased with his manner as he seemed impressed with the responsibility before him.

There are rumored changes to be made in the Cabinet already There was a strange coincidence at the Theatre Friday evening. In the play the American Cousin won the prize at Archery and on receiving the medal was congratulated. He said he "had'nt done nothing—all it required was a steady hand a clear eye—to pull the trigger & the mark was hit" as he said it he looked right up at the President

That was in the play & he looked there merely because he was the
principal person present but afterwards it struck every one as a strange
coincidence

On Friday Beck received a letter from *Duane* who is a prisoner at
Point Lookout begging him to forget the Past & to find out for him if he
would be allowed to take the oath of allegiance to the U.S. that he was
sick enough of the Confederacy and very sorry he had ever had any thing
to do with it. That afternoon Beck went to the Comg Genl. of prisoners
but he was out—and of course after the awful tragedy Beck did not feel
like interceding for a rebel I do not know what he will do now—he may
go to Genl. Grant—if Hoffman won't do anything. Don't say anything
about it.

I suppose you have read all I have told you, in the Papers but being
there myself I supposed you would like to hear it over just as I saw it. The
Authorities think that there is no chance for the assassins to escape but
I think it is like hunting for a needle in a haystack. Your letter did not
come today and when ever it does not come by Sunday it is because you
have left it to tell the latest news of Adèle and when you wrote last she
was a little troubled with her throat. I had a letter from Maggie today

I will send this letter today before getting your's. If you send me word
how much cloth it takes for Adèle's sacque I can buy it here & make it if
I had the pattern. I have forgotten how wide the material was that Mrs
Foster bought—but if I know the length of her sacque & the width of
the half at the bottom I can tell how much it would take when I see Mrs
Foster about the width of the material. We are well & send love—with
kisses to adèle.

> Your aff dau
> HELEN DuB.

Charles A. Leale

Report on the Death of President Lincoln

A surgeon at the Armory Square military hospital in Washington, Charles A. Leale (1842–1932) had graduated from Bellevue Hospital Medical College in New York City only six weeks before the assassination. The first physician to come to the President's aid at Ford's Theatre, Leale wrote his report soon after the event, possibly within a day or two.

———————————

Having been the first of our profession who arrived to the assistance of our late President, and having been requested by Mrs. Lincoln to do what I could for him I assumed the charge until the Surgeon General and Dr Stone his family physician arrived, which was about 20 minutes after we had placed him in bed in the house of Mr. Peterson opposite the theatre, and as I remained with him until his death, I humbly submit the following brief account.

I arrived at Fords Theatre about 8¼ P.M. April 14/65 and procured a seat in the dress circle about 40 feet from the Presidents Box. The play was then progressing and in a few minutes I saw the President, Mrs Lincoln, Major Rathbone and Miss Harris enter; while proceeding to the Box they were seen by the audience who cheered which was reciprocated by the President and Mrs Lincoln by a smile and bow.

The party was preceded by an attendant who after opening the door of the box and closing it after they had all entered, took a seat nearby for himself.

The theatre was well filled and the play of "Our American Cousin" progressed very pleasantly until about half past ten, when the report of a pistol was distinctly heard and about a minute after a man of low stature with black hair and eyes was seen leaping to the stage beneath, holding in his hand a drawn dagger.

While descending his heel got entangled in the American flag, which was hung in front of the box, causing him to stumble when he struck the stage, but with a single bound he regained the use of his limbs and ran to the opposite side of the stage, flourishing in his hand a drawn dagger and disappearing behind the scene.

I then heard cries that the "President had been murdered," which were followed by those of "Kill the murderer" "Shoot him" etc, which came from different parts of the audience.

I immediately ran to the Presidents box and as soon as the door was opened was admitted and introduced to Mrs. Lincoln when she exclaimed several times, "O Doctor, do what you can for him, do what you can"! I told her we would do all that we possibly could.

When I entered the box the ladies were very much excited. Mr. Lincoln was seated in a high backed armchair with his head leaning towards his right side supported by Mrs. Lincoln who was weeping bitterly. Miss Harris was near her left and behind the President.

While approaching the President I sent a gentleman for brandy and another for water.

When I reached the President he was in a state of general paralysis, his eyes were closed and he was in a profoundly comatose condition, while his breathing was intermittent and exceedingly stertorous. I placed my finger on his right radial pulse but could perceive no movement of the artery. As two gentlemen now arrived, I requested them to assist me to place him in a recumbent position, and as I held his head and shoulders, while doing this my hand came in contact with a clot of blood near his left shoulder.

Supposing that he had been stabbed there I asked a gentleman to cut his coat and shirt off from that part, to enable me if possible to check the hemorrhage which I supposed took place from the subclavian artery or some of its branches.

Before they had proceeded as far as the elbow I commenced to examine his head (as no wound near the shoulder was found) and soon passed my fingers over a large firm clot of blood situated about one inch below the superior curved line of the occipital bone.

The coagula I easily removed and passed the little finger of my left hand through the perfectly smooth opening made by the ball, and found that it had entered the encephalon.

As soon as I removed my finger a slight oozing of blood followed and his breathing became more regular and less stertorous. The brandy and water now arrived and a small quantity was placed in his mouth, which passed into his stomach where it was retained.

Dr. C. F. Taft and Dr. A. F. A. King now arrived and after a moments consultation we agreed to have him removed to the nearest house, which we immediately did, the above named with others assisting.

When we arrived at the door of the box, the passage was found to be densely crowded by those who were rushing towards that part of the theatre. I called out twice "Guards clear the passage," which was so soon done that we proceeded without a moments delay with the President and were not in the slightest interrupted until he was placed in bed in the house of Mr. Peterson, opposite the theatre, in less than 20 minutes from the time he was assassinated.

The street in front of the theatre before we had left it was filled with the excited populace, a large number of whom followed us into the house.

As soon as we arrived in the room offered to us, we placed the President in bed in a diagonal position; as the bed was too short, a part of the foot was removed to enable us to place him in a comfortable position.

The windows were opened and at my request a Captain present made all leave the room except the medical gentlemen and friends.

As soon as we placed him in bed we removed his clothes and covered him with blankets. While covering him I found his lower extremities very cold from his feet to a distance several inches above his knees.

I then sent for bottles of hot water, and hot blankets, which were applied to his lower extremities and abdomen.

Several other Physicians and Surgeons about this time arrived among whom was Dr. R. K. Stone who had been the President's Physician since the arrival of his family in the city.

After having been introduced to Dr. Stone I asked him if he would assume charge (telling him at the time all that had been done and describing the wound,) he said that he would and approved of the treatment.

The Surgeon General and Surgeon Crane in a few minutes arrived and made an examination of the wound.

When the President was first laid in bed a slight ecchymosis was noticed on his left eyelid and the pupil of that eye was slightly dilated, while the pupil of the right eye was contracted.

About 11. P.M. the right eye began to protrude which was rapidly followed by an increase of the ecchymosis until it encircled the orbit extending above the supra orbital ridge and below the infra orbital foramen.

The wound was kept open by the Surgeon General by means of a silver probe, and as the President was placed diagonally on the bed his head was supported in its position by Surgeon Crane and Dr Taft relieving each other.

About 2 A.M. the Hospital Steward who had been sent for a Nelatons probe, arrived and examination was made by the Surgeon General, who introduced it to a distance of about 2½ inches, when it came in contact with a foreign substance, which laid across the track of the ball.

This being easily passed the probe was introduced several inches further, when it again touched a hard substance, which was at first supposed to be the ball, but as the bulb of the probe on its withdrawal did not indicate the mark of lead, it was generally thought to be another piece of loose bone.

The probe was introduced a second time and the ball was supposed to be distinctly felt by the Surgeon General, Surgeon Crane and Dr Stone.

After this second exploration nothing further was done with the wound except to keep the opening free from coagula, which if allowed to form and remain for a very short time, would produce signs of increased compression: the breathing becoming profoundly stertorous and intermittent and the pulse to be more feeble and irregular.

His pulse which was several times counted by Dr. Ford and noted by Dr King, ranged until 12 P.M. from between 40 to 64 beats per minute, and his respiration about 24 per minute, were loud and stertorous.

At 1 A.M. his pulse suddenly increasing in frequency to 100 per minute, but soon diminished gradually becoming less feeble until 2.54 A.M. when it was 48 and hardly perceptible.

At 6.40 A.M. his pulse could not be counted, it being very intermittent, two or three pulsations being felt and followed by an intermission, when not the slightest movement of the artery could be felt.

The inspirations now became very short, and the expirations very prolonged and labored accompanied by a gutteral sound.

6.50 A.M. The respirations cease for some time and all eagerly look at their watches until the profound silence is disturbed by a prolonged inspiration, which was soon followed by a sonorous expiration

The Surgeon General now held his finger to the carotid artery, Col. Crane held his head, Dr Stone who was sitting on the bed, held his left pulse, and his right pulse was held by myself.

At 7.20 A.M. he breathed his last and "the spirit fled to God who gave it."

During the night the room was visited by many of his friends. Mrs Lincoln with Mrs. Senator Dixon came into the room three or four times during the night.

The Presidents son Captn R. Lincoln, remained with his father during the greater part of the night.

Immediately after death had taken place, we all bowed and the Rev. Dr. Gurley supplicated to God in behalf of the bereaved family and our afflicted country.

True copy.

(signed) Charles A. Leale M. D.

Charles Sabin Taft

Abraham Lincoln's Last Hours

One of the first physicians to assist Leale in treating the stricken president was Dr. Charles Sabin Taft (1835–1900), a surgeon at the signal corps training camp in Georgetown. Taft recounted Lincoln's final hours in an article published in *Century Magazine* in February 1893.

FROM THE NOTE-BOOK OF AN ARMY SURGEON PRESENT AT THE ASSASSINATION, DEATH, AND AUTOPSY.

The notes from which this article is written were made the day succeeding Mr. Lincoln's death, and immediately after the official examination of the body. They were made, by direction of Secretary Stanton, for the purpose of preserving an official account of the circumstances attending the assassination, in connection with the medical aspects of the case.

On the fourth anniversary of the fall of Fort Sumter, the beloved President, his great heart filled with peaceful thoughts and charity for all, entered Ford's Theater amid the acclamations of the loyal multitude assembled to greet him. Mr. Lincoln sat in a high-backed upholstered chair in the corner of his box nearest the audience, and only his left profile was visible to most of the audience; but from where I sat, almost under the box, in the front row of orchestra chairs, I could see him plainly. Mrs. Lincoln rested her hand on his knee much of the time, and often called his attention to some humorous situation on the stage. She seemed to take great pleasure in witnessing his enjoyment.

All went on pleasantly until half-past ten o'clock, when, during the second scene of the third act, the sharp report of a pistol rang through the house. The report seemed to proceed from behind the scenes on the right of the stage, and behind the President's box. While it startled every one in the audience, it was evidently accepted by all as an introductory effect preceding some new situation in the play, several of which had been introduced in the earlier part of the performance. A moment afterward a hatless and white-faced man leaped from the front of the President's box down, twelve feet, to the stage. As he jumped, one of the spurs on his riding-boots caught in the folds of the flag draped over the front, and caused him to fall partly on his hands and knees as he struck the stage. Springing quickly to his feet with the suppleness of an athlete, he faced the audience for a moment as he brandished in his right hand a long knife, and shouted, "*Sic semper tyrannis!*" Then, with a rapid stage stride, he crossed the stage, and disappeared from view. A piercing shriek from the President's box, a repeated call for "Water! water!" and "A surgeon!" in quick succession, conveyed the truth to the almost paralyzed audience. A most terrible scene of excitement followed. With loud shouts of "Kill him!" "Lynch him!" part of the audience stampeded toward the entrance and some to the stage.

I leaped from the top of the orchestra railing in front of me upon the stage, and, announcing myself as an army surgeon, was immediately lifted up to the President's box by several gentlemen who had collected beneath. I happened to be in uniform, having passed the entire day in attending to my duties at the Signal Camp of Instruction in Georgetown, and not having had an opportunity to change my dress. The cape of a military overcoat fastened around my neck became detached in clambering into the box, and fell upon the stage. It was taken to police headquarters, together with the assassin's cap, spur, and derringer, which had also been picked up, under the supposition that it belonged to him. It was recovered, weeks afterward, with much difficulty.

When I entered the box, the President was lying upon the floor surrounded by his wailing wife and several gentlemen who had entered from the private stairway and dress-circle. Assistant Surgeon Charles A. Leale, U. S. V., was in the box, and had caused the coat and waistcoat to be cut off in searching for the wound. Dr. A. F. A. King of Washington was also present, and assisted in the examination. The carriage had been ordered to remove the President to the White House, but the surgeons countermanded the order, and he was removed to a bed in a house opposite the theater. The wound in the head had been found before leaving the box, but at that time there was no blood oozing from it. When the dying President was laid upon the bed in a small but neatly furnished room opposite the theater, it was found necessary to arrange his great length diagonally upon it. The room having become speedily filled to suffocation, the officer in command of the provost guard at the theater was directed to clear it of all except the surgeons. This officer guarded the door until relieved later in the evening by General M. C. Meigs, who took charge of it the rest of the night, by direction of Mr. Stanton.

A hospital steward from Lincoln Hospital did efficient service in speedily procuring the stimulants and sinapisms ordered. The wound was then examined. A tablespoonful of diluted brandy was placed between the President's lips, but it was swallowed with much difficulty. The respiration now became labored; pulse 44, feeble; the left pupil much contracted, the right widely dilated; total insensibility to light in both. Mr. Lincoln was divested of all clothing, and mustard-plasters were placed on every inch of the anterior surface of the body from the neck to the toes. At this time the President's eyes were closed, and the lids and surrounding parts so injected with blood as to present the appearance of having been bruised. He was totally unconscious, and was breathing regularly but heavily, an occasional sigh escaping with the breath. There was scarcely a dry eye in the room, and it was the saddest and most pathetic death-bed scene I ever witnessed. Captain Robert Lincoln, of General Grant's staff, entered the room and stood at the headboard, leaning over his dying father. At first his terrible grief overpowered him, but, soon recovering himself, he leaned his head on the shoulder of Senator Charles Sumner, and remained in silent grief during the long, terrible night.

About twenty-five minutes after the President was laid upon the bed, Surgeon-General Barnes and Dr. Robert King Stone, the family physician, arrived and took charge of the case. It was owing to Dr. Leale's quick judgment in instantly placing the almost moribund President in a recumbent position the moment he saw him in the box, that Mr. Lincoln did not expire in the theater within ten minutes from fatal syncope. At Dr. Stone's suggestion, I placed another teaspoonful of diluted brandy between the President's lips, to determine whether it could be swallowed; but as it was not, no further attempt was made.

Some difference of opinion existed as to the exact position of the ball, but the autopsy confirmed the correctness of the diagnosis upon first exploration. No further attempt was made to explore the wound. The injury was pronounced mortal. After the cessation of the bleeding, the respiration was stertorous up to the last breath, which was drawn at twenty-one minutes and fifty-five seconds past seven; the heart did not cease to beat until twenty-two minutes and ten seconds after seven. My hand was upon the President's heart, and my eye on the watch of the surgeon-general, who was standing by my side, with his finger upon the carotid. The respiration during the last thirty minutes was characterized by occasional intermissions; no respiration being made for nearly a minute, but by a convulsive effort air would gain admission to the lungs, when regular, though stertorous, respiration would go on for some seconds, followed by another period of perfect repose. The cabinet ministers and others were surrounding the death-bed, watching with suspended breath the last feeble inspiration; and as the unbroken quiet would seem to prove that life had fled, they would turn their eyes to their watches; then, as the struggling life within would force another fluttering respiration, they would heave deep sighs of relief, and fix their eyes once more upon the face of their chief.

The vitality exhibited by Mr. Lincoln was remarkable. It was the opinion of the surgeons in attendance that most patients would have died within two hours from the reception of such an injury; yet Mr. Lincoln lingered from 10:30 P.M. until 7:22 A.M.

Mrs. Lincoln (with Miss Harris, who was one of the theater party, a few other ladies, and the Rev. Dr. Gurley, Mrs. Lincoln's pastor) remained during the night in the front parlor of the house, occasionally visiting her dying husband. Whenever she sat down at the bedside, clean napkins were laid over the crimson stains on the pillow. Her last visit was most painful. As she entered the chamber and saw how the beloved features were distorted, she fell fainting to the floor. Restoratives were applied, and she was supported to the bedside, where she frantically addressed the dying man. "Love," she exclaimed, "live but for one moment to speak to me once—to speak to our children!"

When it was announced that the great heart had ceased to beat, Mr. Stanton said in solemn tones, "He now belongs to the Ages." Shortly after death, finding that the eyes were not entirely closed, one of the young surgeons reverently placed silver half-dollars upon them. The lower jaw fell slightly, and one of the medical men bound it up with his handkerchief. Secretary Stanton pulled down the window-shades, a guard was stationed outside the door, and the martyred President was left alone.

Immediately after death, the Rev. Dr. Gurley made a fervent prayer, inaudible, at times, from the sobs of those present. As the surgeons left the house, the clergyman was again praying in the front parlor. Poor Mrs. Lincoln's moans, which came through the half-open door, were distressing to hear. She was supported by her son Robert, and was soon after taken to her carriage. As she reached the front door she glanced at the theater opposite, and exclaimed several times, "Oh, that dreadful house! that dreadful house!"

Shortly after her departure, the body of the late President, surrounded by a guard of soldiers, was removed to the White House. A dismal rain was falling on a dense mass of horror-stricken people stretching from F street to Pennsylvania Avenue. As they made a passage for the hearse bearing the beloved dead, terrible execrations and mutterings were heard. A disparaging reference to the dead President was punished by instant death. One man who ventured a shout for Jeff. Davis was set upon and nearly torn to pieces by the infuriated crowd.

During the post-mortem examination Mrs. Lincoln sent in a messenger with a request for a lock of hair. Dr. Stone clipped one from the region of the wound, and sent it to her. I extended my hand to him in mute appeal, and received a lock stained with blood, and other surgeons present also received one.

It was my good fortune during the early part of the war to become acquainted with Mr. Lincoln. Busy as he was,—weary as he was,—with a burden of care and anxiety resting upon him such as no other President, before or since, has ever borne, he yet found time to visit the army hospitals. He came several times to the Church Hospital on H street, of which I had charge. He was always accompanied by Mrs. Lincoln. While she was distributing the flowers she had brought, Mr. Lincoln would accompany me on a tour of the ward. The convalescents stood "at attention" by their cots. He asked the name of every soldier, his State and regiment, and had a kindly and encouraging word for each one. If he came to a soldier who was above the average height, he would laughingly ask him to measure heights, back to back. He never found one there who overtopped him. Mrs. Lincoln always brought, in addition to a quantity of flowers from the White House conservatory, bottles of wine and jellies. She was a kind-hearted and sympathetic woman, and a devoted wife and mother. A gold-and-onyx initial sleeve-button that I took out of Mr. Lincoln's cuff when his shirt was hastily removed in searching for the wound, was subsequently presented to me by Mrs. Lincoln, and is still in my possession.

Charles Sabin Taft, M. D.

James Tanner

Letter to Henry F. Walch

After fighting in the Peninsula campaign with the 87th New York Infantry, James Tanner (1844–1927) was hit by a shell fragment at Second Bull Run and lost both of his legs below the knee. Fitted with artificial limbs, Tanner studied shorthand in Syracuse before becoming a clerk at the War Department in 1864. On the night of the assassination he served as a stenographer for Stanton and recorded the testimony of six witnesses, incuding the actor Harry Hawk and James Ferguson, a saloonkeeper who identified Booth without qualification as the assassin. Tanner described his experiences in a letter (written in Pitman shorthand) to a friend from business college.

ORDNANCE OFFICE

WAR DEPARTMENT

Washington. Apr. 17th, 1865.

Friend Walch:

Your very welcome letter was duly recd. by me and now I will steal a few minutes from my duties in the office to answer it.

Of course you must know most as well as I do about the terrible events which have happened in this city during the past few days. I have nothing else to write about so I will give you a few ideas about that, perhaps which you have not yet got from the papers.

Last Friday night, a friend invited me to attend the Theatre with him, which I did. I would have preferred the play at Ford's Theatre where the President was shot, but my friend chose the play at Grover's, which was "Alladdin, or the wonderful lamp." While sitting there, witnessing the play, about ten o'clock, or rather a little after, the entrance door was thrown open, and a man exclaimed, "President Lincoln is assassinated in his private box at Ford's. Turn out!" Instantly all was excitement, and a terrible rush commenced, and some one cried out, "Sit down, it is a ruse of the pickpockets." The audience generally agreed to this, for most of them sat down, and the play went on; soon however a gentleman came out from behind the scenes, and informed us that the sad news was too true. We instantly dispersed.

On going out in the street we were horrified to learn that Mr. Seward had been attacked and severely wounded in bed at his house. Myself and friend went up to Willard's which is a short distance above Grover's to learn what we could, but we could learn nothing there. The people were terribly excited. Ford's Theatre is on Tenth Street between "E" and "F". Grover's is on the Avenue near 14th, and just below Willard's; it is about four blocks up from Ford's. My boarding house is right opposite Ford's Theatre. We then got on the cars and went down to Tenth Street and up Tenth to Ford's, and to my boarding house. There was an immense throng there, very quiet and yet very much excited. The street was crowded. I only got across on account of my boarding there. The President had been carried into the adjoining house to where I board. I went up to my room on the second floor and out on the balcony which nearly over-hung the door of Mr. Petersen's house. Members of the Cabinet, the Chief Justice, Generals Halleck, Meiggs, Augur and others were going in and out, all looking anxious and sorrow stricken. By leaning over the railing I could learn from time to time of his Excellency's condition and soon learned that there were no hopes of him. Soon they commenced taking testimony in the room adjoining where he lay, before Chief Justice Carter, and General Halleck called for a Reporter. No one was at hand, but one of the Head Clerks in our office who boarded there, knew I could write short hand and told the General. He bade him call me, so he came to the door and asked me to come down and write the testimony. I went down, and the General passed me in, as the house was strictly guarded of course. I went into a room between the rear room and the front room. Mrs. Lincoln was in the front room, weeping as though her heart would break. In the back room lay His Excellency breathing hard, and with every breath a groan. In the room where I was were Generals Halleck, Meiggs, Augur and others,—all of the Cabinet excepting Mr. Seward—Chief Justice Chase, and Chief Justice Carter of the District of Columbia, Andrew Johnson and many other distinguished men. A solemn silence pervaded the whole throng. It was a terrible moment. Never in my life was I surrounded by half so impressive circumstances. Opposite me, at the table where I sat writing, sat Secretary Stanton writing despatches to General Dix and others, and giving orders for the guarding of Ford's and the surrounding country. At the left of me was Judge Carter propounding the questions to the witnesses, whose answers I was jotting

down in Standard Phonography. I was so excited when I commenced,
that I am afraid it did not much resemble Standard Phonography or any
other kind, but I could read it readily afterwards, so what was the difference? In fifteen minutes I had testimony enough down to hang Wilkes
Booth, the assassin, higher than ever Haman hung. I was writing short
hand for about an hour and a half when I commenced writing it out. I
thought I had been writing about two hours, when I looked at the clock
and it marked half past four, A.M. I commenced writing about twelve,
A.M. I could not believe that it was so late, but I looked at my watch,
which corroborated it. The surrounding circumstances had so engrossed
my attention that I had not noticed the flight of time. In the front room
Mrs. Lincoln was uttering the most heart broken exclamations all the
night long. As she passed through the hall back to the parlor after she had
taken leave of the President for the last time—as she went by my door,
I heard her moan, "Oh, My God, and have I given my husband to die?"
and I tell you, I never heard so much agony in so few words. The President was still alive, but sinking fast. He had been utterly unconscious
from the time the shot struck him and remained so until he breathed
his last. At 6:45 Saturday morning I finished my notes and passed into
the back room where the President lay. It was very evident that he could
not last long. There was quite a crowd in the room, which was small, but
I approached quite near the bed on which so much greatness lay, fast
loosing its hold on this world. The head of the bed was towards the door.
At the head stood Captain Robert Lincoln, weeping on the shoulder of
Senator Sumner. General Halleck stood just behind Robert Lincoln and
I stood just to the left of General Halleck and between him and General
Meiggs. Stanton was there, trying every way to be calm and yet he was very
much moved. The utmost silence pervaded, broken only by the sounds
of strong men's tears. It was a solemn time, I assure you. The President
breathed heavily until a few minutes before he breathed his last, then his
breath came easily, and he passed off very quietly.

As soon as he was dead, Rev. Dr. Gurley, who has been the President's
Pastor since his sojourn in this city, offered up a very impressive prayer. I
grasped for my pencil which was in my pocket, as I wished to secure his
words, but I was very much disappointed to find that my pencil had been
broken in my pocket. I could have taken it very easily, as he spoke very

favorably for reporting. The friends dispersed, Mrs. Lincoln and some going to the White House, which she had left the night before to attend the Theatre with him who never returned to it except in his coffin.

Secretary Stanton told me to take charge of the testimony I had taken, so I went to my room and took a copy of it to be delivered to him, as I wished to keep both my notes and the original copy which I made while there in the house. They will ever be cherished mementoes to me of the awful night and the circumstances with which I found myself so unexpectedly surrounded, and which will not soon be forgotten.

Saturday night I took the copy I had made to the Secretary's house, but as he was asleep I did not see him, so I left them with my card. I tell you, Walch, I would not regret the time and money I have spent on Phonography if it never brought me more than it did on that night, for then it brought me the privilege of standing by the death bed of the most remarkable man of modern times and one who will live in the annals of his Country as long as she continues to have a history.

Frank Leslie's Illustrated will have a good picture of the building made celebrated by this sad event (on that evening). I saw the sketch made by its Artist—of the Theatre—and it was very correct indeed. He also sketched the inside of the room where the President died, also the outside of the building as well as the adjoining buildings on both sides. You will see the house I board in has a balcony along the front of the two rooms on the second floor. I occupy both of these rooms.

You can imagine the feelings here by judging by the feelings in your own place, only I think it is more horrifying from the fact that the President lived in our midst and was universally beloved by the loyal portion of the people.

This morning there was published in the Chronicle the statements of one of the witnesses which I reported, Mr. James B. Ferguson by name. You will doubtless see it in your papers there, as it is most important. I have an idea, which is gaining ground here, and that is that the assassin had assistance in the Theatre and that the President was invited to be there for the express purpose of assassinating him. When that is once fully understood, I would not give three cents for the Theatre. The Theatre is very strictly guarded now, night and day.

I shall pack up my things tonight, the most of them, expecting to be called on 'most any time to make a hasty exit from my room, as the

Theatre is just opposite. Tell Professor Holmes I received the college journals he sent to me and have distributed them around in the office and sent some off by mail to my friends. Walch, if you write such confounded short letters in Phonography, what length do you write when you write in long hand? My regards with [   ] and write soon and long.

Very truly your friend,

James Tanner

Frances (Fanny) Seward

Diary, April 14, 1865

While Booth made his way into Lincoln's box at Ford's Theatre on the night of April 14, his co-conspirator Lewis Powell, alias Payne, approached the Seward house on Lafayette Square six blocks away. A strikingly handsome twenty-year-old former Confederate soldier who stood six feet, two inches, and weighed 175 pounds, Powell claimed to be delivering medicine for the secretary of state, who had been seriously injured in a carriage accident on April 5. Powell pushed his way past the servant who answered the door and went up to the third floor, where he was confronted by Frederick Seward, who served under his father as assistant secretary of state. When Powell discovered that his intended victim was resting in a nearby bedroom, he drew a revolver and tried to shoot Frederick; when it misfired, Powell struck him repeatedly, fracturing Frederick's skull and breaking the weapon. Wielding a large bowie knife, Powell then burst into Seward's bedroom and began struggling with George Robinson, a convalescing Union soldier who had been assigned to nurse the cabinet officer. Knocking Robinson to the floor, the powerfully built Powell reached Seward's bedside and slashed him repeatedly around the face and neck until Robinson was again able to intervene. The melee drew in Frederick's wife, Anna; his brother, Augustus, an army paymaster; and his sister, Fanny. Eventually Powell broke away and ran down the stairs. After wounding Emerick Hansell, a State Department messenger, he fled the house while shouting "I'm mad! I'm mad," and escaped on horseback, having failed in his mission. The secretary of state had been saved by his heavy neck brace, which shielded his major blood vessels from Powell's knife. Robinson, Hansell, and Augustus and Frederick Seward also survived their wounds. In the weeks that followed, Frances (Fanny) Adeline Seward (1844–1866) wrote about the attack on her father and brothers in her diary. She completed her narrative sometime before the sudden death of her semi-invalid mother, Frances, from heart failure on June 21, 1865.

Good Friday. April 14th 1865.

Father had a better night than any of late, and seemed the better after his refreshing sleep— He took solid food for the first time since his accident—breakfasted on soft egg, milk-toast, shad and coffee. Today a distinguished party perform the ceremony of raising the flag on Fort Sumter, taken from us 4 years ago.

So far I had written in pencil, in my pocket diary on the day of the date— I think I remember beginning the page, & wondering if I should have anything unusual to enter there later in the day. The rest of the page

is filled with out-lines of what occurred later—from which, & from a longer account written three weeks later at my earliest leisure—(to relieve
my mind of its weight of recollection) I write the following account. I
can only give my remembrances, which are very vivid in my own mind—
but I cannot describe all that took place, because in many instances I
cannot remember to have seen some who were in the room— Anna, for
instance—& Robinson part of the time.

First we had a quiet afternoon. Father so much better that he told
Donaldson he need not stay— I sat alone with him some time and read
"Enoch Arden" to him. He spoke very highly of it. In the evening a
torch-light procession of employees from the Navy Yard or Arsenal, visited the White House. I think it was earlier than that, that I was some
time with Mother, in our room—part of the time she was lying down. I
was telling her how any recital of suffering affected & haunted me—and
she told me it had always been so with her. I think we talked much together. Anna & I watched the procession, & listened to the music—they
played "Rally Round the Flag," & were singing too I believe, as they approached the White House. I came to my room to show Anna a book of
soldier's songs, in which was the "Year of Jubilee," of which I had been
telling her. Mother & she & I talked a little there. Then came the quiet
arrangements for the night, in father's room—Fred & Anna & Mother
had been up a great deal— That evening it was arranged that Gus should
rest till 11—then sit up till in the night when Donaldson would come—
Meantime I was to have the watch while Gus rested, & Robinson was to
be there till George, the german nurse, relieved him. I sat by the side of
the bed nearest the door, reading "Legends of Charlemagne," Robinson
was near. I saw that Father seemed inclined to sleep—so turned down
the gas, laid my book on a stand at the foot of the bed, & took a seat on
the other side. About 10 o'c—Dr Norris paid his visit—& left us all quiet.
Father fell into a light sleep. Fred came in at the door, & glancing at the
bed, saw his father slept, and said he would come in again. After he had
gone, Father opened his eyes with a little smile of recognition as he saw
me at the foot of the bed. He was lying close on the edge, farthest from
the door— I do not remember hearing voices outside, but something
led me to think that Fred was there with some one else. It occurred to
me that he might have some important reason for wishing to see Father
awake. Perhaps the President was there, or had sent over. I did not stop

to see if Father wakened thoroughly, but hastened to the door, opened it a very little, and found Fred standing close by it, facing me. On his right hand, also close by the door, stood a very tall young man, in a light hat & long overcoat. I said "Fred, Father is awake now." Something in Fred's manner led me at once to think that he did not wish me to say so, and that I had better not have opened the door. This confused me, & looking around I was glad to see Father going to sleep again. Holding the door as I did, I know the man could not see my father at all, nor could Fred, I think. I do not remember what Fred said to me. The man seemed impatient, & addressing me in a tone that struck me at once as much more harsh & full of determination than such a simple question justified, asked "Is the Secretary asleep." I paused to look at my father, & replied "Almost." Then Fred drew the door shut very quickly. I sat down again. I had no means of telling the errand of the man. I fancied some one had sent him—that he was, perhaps, a messenger from the telegraph office. Very soon I heard the sound of blows—it seemed to me as many as half a dozen—sharp and heavy, with lighter one's between. There had been an interval of quiet. I did not fully connect this with the person I had seen. I thought they were chasing a rat in the hall, remembering such a chase once. But when the blows continued, I could not tell what it meant, & said to Robinson, who was sitting at the head of the bed, on the side nearest the door, "What can be the matter? Do go and see." Then I was afraid something was wrong, and, being impatient to find out, started, myself. I thought Robinson & I reached the door at the same time. I did not see who opened it— It was he. I saw that two men came in, side by side. I was close by the door, & the one nearest me, was Fred. The side of his face was covered with blood, the rest very pale, his eyes full of intense expression. I spoke to ask him what was the matter,—he could not answer me. On his right hand was the assassin. I do not remember how his face looked, his arms were both stretched out, he seemed rushing toward the bed. In his the hand nearest me was a pistol, in the right hand a knife. I ran beside him to the bed imploring him to stop. I must have said "Don't kill him," for father wakened, he says, hearing me speak the word kill, & seeing first me, speaking to some one whom he did not see—then raised himself & had one glimpse of the assassin's face bending over, next felt the blows—and by their force (he being on the edge of the bed, where fear of hurting his broken arm, had caused him to lie for

some time) was thrown to the floor. I cannot remember seeing him—
nor seeing Payne—go around the bed—but Anna was in the room and
saw it. I have no remembrance of going around the foot of the bed, to
the other side, but I remember standing there, by the corner at the foot,
& thinking "This must be a fearful dream!" Then I looked about and
saw, first, what I had seen before I think, but more fully now, three men
struggling beside the bed. I knew who they all were then. I could not tell
the next day. But they were Fred & Robinson & the assassin—next I saw
all the familiar objects in the room, the bureau, the little stand, the book
I had been reading, all looked natural. Then I knew it was not a dream. I
remember pacing the room back & forth from end to end—screaming.
My screams wakened Gus. But I do not remember seeing him when he
came in—then Payne & the others were—

After a little time, it seemed to me—though all that had taken place must
have been almost in an instant, some vague idea of calling for assistance carried me into the hall. I think that at that time the assassin & those struggling
with him were by the door in Father's room, & that I passed them as I went
out. I have a very indistinct recollection of the next moment, when I seemed
to meet Mother on one side, and Anna on the other, both saying "What is
the matter," and I said something about the man, (Payne) who came out
struggling with some one, I afterwards learned it was Augustus. I think I
saw the assassin stab Hansell, as he, the assassin rushed headlong down the
stairs. I do not know just when—but I remember in the hall with Mother
and Anna asking me what happened, my saying "Is *that man* gone," and they
said "what man." The first recollection I have of seeing Augustus—except
when the assassin broke away from him, was with his forehead covered with
blood. It seemed to me that every man I met had blood on his face. It seems
to me that I saw Fred then. I did not open any window and cry "murder" as
the report of Robinson's statement said, neither did I leave the room as then
mentioned, but at the time I have stated.

I remember running back, crying out "Where's Father?," seeing the
empty bed. At the side I found what I thought was a pile of bed clothes—
then I knew that it was Father. As I stood my feet slipped in a great pool
of blood. Father looked so ghastly I was sure he was dead, he was white
& very thin with the blood that had drained from the gashes about his
face & throat. Fred was in the room till after Father was placed on the
bed. Margaret says she heard me scream "O my God! Father's dead." I

remember that Robinson came instantly, & lifting him, said his heart still beat—& he, with or without aid, laid him on the bed. Notwithstanding his own injuries Robinson stood faithfully at Father's side, on the right hand —I did not know what should be done. Robinson told me everything— about staunching the blood with cloths & water. He applied them on the right side, & I, kneeling on the bed, on the left, put them on a wound on that side of the neck. Father seemed to me almost dead, but he spoke to me, telling me to have the doors closed, & send for surgeons, & to ask to have a guard placed around the house. William had gone for Dr Verdi, & he came & had ice applied to the wounds. I ran down to the butlers pantry for ice & saw a great many persons gathered about the door. While Dr V. was on Father's right side, & I engaged as before, the doctor who was himself greatly excited kept saying to me—(I was talking & making some exclaimations I believe) "Don't get excited, don't get excited—" Then Father showed his conciousness by putting out his hand towards me in a soothing way, as if to bid me be calm, & reassure me. It seemed a great while to us before the doctors came, though they probably hastened on the earliest information of what had occurred. William, the colored boy, having been accustomed to go for Dr Verdi on former occasions, went for him the first thing, so he was here sooner. The Tayloes were passing—Mr & Mrs T. & came in—& stayed I think all night— Mrs Tayloe was in the hall or some other room, & Mr T. in Father's room. The Surgeon General came & stood by Father on the right, & Dr Norris came next & kneeling down to examine the wounds said something like "Assassination in the vilest form—" A clot of blood upon father's chest, which I had taken for a stab, was found to be only blood that had collected there outside. We were assured that no artery was severed, & the wounds were not fatal. The little entry outside fathers door, & the stairway beyond, were thronged with inquiring men of every description. M. C.s, policemen, members of the press—etc— Everyone was asking us to tell more than we knew ourselves. Anna, at Fred's door resisted their entrance with great firmness, & I was unwilling to have any one come into father's room—for I could not reason calmly, & suspected everyone. At first Mother had supposed that the whole occurrence consisted in Father's being more than usually delerious, & that in that condition he had injured Fred. She had an indistinct view of Gus and Payne struggling at the door, & supposed it to be father with a knife. She saw Fred's condition & went into his room, & was engaged with him. He was then unable to speak. So she was not in father's room at first. I cannot remember when she came in—but I remember her being there, ministering to him. She & Anna went to the attic to see if anyone was concealed there. Mother forbade me to go then— At one time I went, & searched in some of the rooms there, then went down to the parlor floor, & looked through three rooms & was going further when Fosburg told me he had searched. (Fosburg waited up stairs till Payne was out of the house—then appeared & stood at the foot of father's bed.) I remember going to the attic & tearing the clothing from the beds & bringing it down for father's bed when he had a severe chill. While the Surgeon General was here, I found between the door & the bed, just in front of the wash-stand, a hat which I supposed to be Payne's—as it afterwards proved to be— I showed it to Anna, & by her advice put it in the bureau drawer. The washbowl on the stand had the bottom broken out when I first looked at it. Near where I found the hat, the pistol was picked up— I found Robinson looking for the priming on the floor— he said it was missing, and if stepped on might do mischief—he soon found it. Dr Norris sewed up the great gash in father's cheek—which had lain open— I was standing by the door, against the wall while he did it. I imagined all the time that father suffered dreadfully. I thought I heard him moan. But Father has since told us that he remembers no feeling of pain, & that he thinks he both fell a sleep & woke during the operation—he remembered "being sewed up." The Surgeon General was sent for with the news of the assassination of the President. Mother saw the person who came for him, who told her of the fact. I remember hearing some one else tell her the President had been shot. The Surgeon General sent me out of the room part of the time while they were attending to Father, & told me he would send for me if I was wanted. Perhaps it was at this time, I went into Fred's room & saw him lying bloody & unconscious, on a lounge, where he was being attended to. I saw Mrs Tayloe in the hall. I went into Augustus' room—he was lying on the bed—& asked about Father—(he came in once or more to see him) he had five wounds on the head—& one on the hand. He told me they were not serious. I had seen Robinson before—putting on cold water upon his own wounds in the bath-room. For a long time he refused to do or have done anything done for them—& with head and shoulder wounded & bleeding, insisted on attending to Father. This last time I went in Gus's room, Robinson lay on the lounge at the side of the room. I went & spoke with him—he was very cheerful & called his wounds "only flesh wounds." I went across the hall into my own room. I was there twice. The first time they were dressing poor Hansell's back—(he was stabbed in the back) the second time he lay on the bed. Eliza the seamstress was there to attend to him. In the middle of the room sat Donaldson, his face buried in his hands—crying aloud, like a child. I touched his shoulder & said—"Donaldson, you were not hurt?" "No Miss Fanny" he said—"I wasn't here. If I had been here this wouldn't have happened. If I had been here I'd have been a dead man. Oh, why wasn't I here?" All the white wood work of the entry was covered with great dashes of blood. I did not want it washed off—but Margaret & Eliza told me some person had directed that it should be—so I did not interfere. It was a terrible sight—there was so much blood everywhere. The drugget on the stairs was sprinkled with it, all the way down to the floor below. On the inner side of the door of Father's room there was, in blood, the distinct impression of a hand, which seemed to have clenched it from without. While this was being wiped off I marked the door, to show where the place had been. When we found father there was such a pool of blood that our dresses were drabbled in it. Dr Norris's assistant, Dr Nottson came. Dr Norris bandaged Fred's wounds—which he supposed much less dangerous than they proved to be. The Surgeon General, having been summoned, went away. Father had been attended to & moved to the left side of the bed. As the Surgeon General left the room he shook hands with me telling me Father was safe. Dr Verdi at first for some time kept rushing around saying "Children, children, don't get excited—" While Father was being attended to, some of the time I stood over by the door, leaning against the wall. I think he came & said something of that sort once then. While I stood there Dr Norris came to me & said "You have been a pretty brave little girl tonight, can't you get me a shirt for your father?" & I went to get one of Augustus' who left his bed, & gave me two shirts. While I was sitting by Father's bed a gentlemanly officer in uniform came towards me, & said that he belonged to the medical department & asked if he could be of any assistance. I referred him to Dr Norris & he told me the doctor thought he should not need his help. I asked for his address, that we might send for him if he should be needed. He had probably already told me his name—Dr Wilson—and now informed me that his house was next to the Secretary of War. As he was going away I chanced to be going to the door and met Anna, & introduced him to her by telling her of his offer— She asked him to go and see Fred, & took him into the other room. A Dr White was here at that time—stayed in Fred's room—Dr Whelan

At one time all the doctors were in Fred's room, & Mother & I were with Father. Once I thought his wounds were bleeding afresh—but it proved to be only a clot of blood. At another time when the doctors were in the room, mother was sitting down—& I went to her. She was ill in some way I think—perhaps with palpitation. She showed feeling & anxiety that must have been anguish, but she bore up with the greatest fortitude— as we spoke together she told me she was afraid Fred could not live. By that time it had been ascertained that his injuries were very serious. I do not know whether it was before or after the Surgeon General left that Dr Wilson went to see Fred— He declined, on medical etiquette to examine the wounds till Dr Norris had removed the bandages put on by himself. It was found that Fred's injuries were of the most dangerous nature—the skull fractured. I met Mr Harrington in the entry—& he told me not to give up about Fred, described very serious injuries he had once sustained—had been trepanned. Fred was insensible. Father was conscious. Not very long after the attack, when Father's wounds had been dressed & himself moved to the right side of the bed, a number of distinguished gentlemen came in & stood about the bed. Mr Stanton, Gen. Halleck, & Mr Welles are all I remember. It was then that I first heard about the President, one of the gentlemen telling Mother that he was shot. As this group stood there Father related in a clear, distinct manner, his recollections of the whole scene—between each word he drew breath, as one dying might speak, & I feared the effort might cost his remaining strength. I think we gave him tea in the night—at his own request. I was in constant apprehension of some fatal turn in his symptoms— At length all was still in the room— We took our seats to watch through the night. Dr Norris remained much of the night—& when he went away left his assistant, Dr Nottson, saying that he was an accomplished physician. As we sat through those long dark hours the thoughts they brought were almost overwhelming. The thought that such cruel & inhuman beings, as the man who had attacked my father &

brothers, existed, made me wish myself dead, & out of such a world, anywhere seemed better. The anxiety of the condition of father & Fred was
fearful. Although a guard sat in the entry, I could not reason away a feeling that the assassin who had wounded so many might return & finish his
attempt. I had felt suspicious of every unknown face however friendly—
I was too shocked to reason. "I have supped full on horrors," rang over
& over in my mind—and I retraced the dreadful scene—& remembered
the moment when I felt almost beside myself, and Anna's hand laid on
my arm, & her voice "Fanny! Fanny!" recalled me, & I stopped screaming
to answer her inquiries & to remember that I must be quiet & calm.
Blood, blood, my thoughts seemed drenched in it—I seemed to breathe
its sickening odor. My dress was stained with it—Mother's was drabbled
with it—it was on everything. The bed had been covered with blood, the
blankets & sheet chopped with several blows of the knife. Night wore
away while we sat there—the gray light of morning came— "Risest thou
thus gray dawn again" repeated itself over & over in my mind—& that
light should come, & the sun rise, & the birds sing & the green leaves
rustle in the trees, seemed strange in such a world. Early in the morning,
by Father's side, Dr Nottson showed me a card on which some one told
one of the surgeons that the president was growing worse. Father asked
about it. In the morning came a note from Miss Dix to Mother, which
I answered, offering to be of assistance, & to send one or more women
nurses. Mr Stanton came. I think it must have been he—but perhaps
it was some one earlier, that answered Mother's inquiry as to whether
any thing later had been heard from the President— "Yes. He is dead."
He died at 7—& we heard of it within two hours. While Mr Stanton
was there by the bed Mother said very gently to Father— "Henry—the
President is gone." He received the news calmly, but seemed to know
the meaning of the words. He was not able to talk much of the time—
and communicated, as he had done before the last injury—by means of a
white slate & pencil—but—owing to his exhausted state, & to his broken
arm, it was almost impossible for him to write so that it could be read. I
remember that Mother said—in talking with the Secretary of War, "Are
you safe Mr Stanton," as if apprehensive of danger to him— "Not any
more than any one else" (or, the others,) he replied. He said Mrs Stanton
was down stairs— I went down and saw her in the library— Mr Stanton
came down, and I told him about the pistol—which was brought— I also

told him of the hat & showed it to him—he took charge of both. I told him my fear about the guard, there not being any at the back door. He was very kind—& relieved my solicitude at once. A little later in the morning I was called down to see Col. Pelouze, who said he had Mr Stanton's instructions to come to me, & to place the guard where I said. The guard was doubled—by Mr S.'s order, after my speaking to him. Many friends came to inquire— I saw none of them but Dept. people. The President died about half past seven in the morning. Miss Dix sent a note which I answered—(she offered assistance) quite early she came over—& saw Mother & Father. Father conversed with her by using his slate. It was very difficult to read the writing—he was so weak. The following sentence, addressed to Miss Dix—I copied from the slate for her. "Neither the friends nor the enemies of our America have left me anything to complain of. The friends of America ought to have watched Mr Lincoln better. His life however is the forfeit. The Nation will do him Justice."

I copied three other sentences which he wrote on the slate that day—these: "—the blows inflicted before or after the assault on you, Augustus, & Frederick?" "I was fast asleep and only saw Fanny — up, and the assassin. I next — — and would kill me. Then the blow, dashing blood in floods." (I have to leave blanks where the words were illegible.) "I saw all my strength was weakness last night. I thought that if I had still reserved forces I should make them take me safely through in two or three days. I am very moderate. I have drunk tea all day—making no point of it."

Gideon Welles

Diary, April 14–21, 1865

A former journalist from Connecticut whom President Lincoln sometimes called "Father Neptune," the extravagantly bearded and ludicrously bewigged Secretary of the Navy Gideon Welles (1802–1878) had successfully presided over the wartime expansion and modernization of the naval service. By April 1865 Welles and Seward were the only members of Lincoln's original cabinet remaining in the administration, serving along with Stanton and Hugh McCulloch (secretary of the treasury), James Speed (attorney general), William Dennison (postmaster general), and John P. Usher (secretary of the interior). Welles recorded in his diary his recollections of the assassination and its immediate aftermath, culminating in the departure from Washington of the funeral train that would carry Lincoln's body back to Illinois.

I had retired to bed about half-past ten on the evening of the 14th of April, and was just getting asleep when my wife said some one was at our door. Sitting up in bed I heard some one twice call to John, my son whose sleeping room was directly over the front door. I arose at once and raised a window, when my messenger James called to me that Mr. Lincoln the President had been shot, and that Secretary Seward and his son, Assistant Secretary Frederick Seward, were assassinated. James was much alarmed and excited. I told him his story was very incoherent and improbable, that he was associating men who were not together and liable to attack at the same time. Where, I inquired, was the President when shot? James said he was at Ford's Theatre on 10th Street. Well, said I Secretary Seward is an invalid in bed in his house on 15th Street. James said he had been there, stopped in at the house to make inquiry before alarming me.

I immediately dressed myself, and against the earnest remonstrance and appeals of my wife went directly to Mr. Seward's. James accompanied me. As we were crossing 15th Street, I saw four or five men in earnest consultation under the lamp on the corner by St. John's Church. Before I had got half across the street, the lamp was suddenly extinguished and the knot of persons rapidly dispersed. For a moment and but a moment I was disconcerted to find myself in darkness but recollecting that it was late and about time for the moon to rise, I proceeded on, not having lost

54

five steps, merely making a pause without stopping. Hurrying forward into 15th Street I found it pretty full of people especially near the residence of Secretary Seward, where there were very many soldiers as well as citizens already gathered.

Entering the house I found the lower hall and office full of persons, and among them most of the foreign legations, all anxiously inquiring what truth there was in the horrible rumors afloat. I replied that my object in calling was to ascertain the facts. Proceeding through the hall to the stairs, I found one, and I think two of the servants there checking the crowd. They were frightened and seemed relieved to see me. I hastily asked what truth there was in the story that an assassin or assassins had entered the house and assaulted the Secretary. I was assured that it was true, and that Mr. Frederick was also badly injured. They wished me to go up, but no others. At the head of the first stairs I met the elder Mrs. Seward or her sister I think who desired me to proceed up. On reaching the third story I met Mrs. Frederick Seward who, although evidently distressed, was, under the circumstances exceedingly composed. I inquired for the Secretary's room which she pointed out—the southwest room. As I entered, I met Miss Fanny Seward with whom I exchanged a single word, and proceeded to the foot of the bed. Dr. Verdi and I think two others were there. The bed was saturated with blood. The Secretary was lying on his back, the upper part of his head covered by a cloth, which extended down over his eyes. His mouth was open, the lower jaw dropping down. I exchanged a few words in a whisper with Dr. V. Secretary Stanton who came almost simultaneously with me spoke in a louder tone. We almost immediately withdrew and went into the adjoining front room, where lay Frederick Seward upon his right side. His eyes were open but he did not move them, nor a limb, nor did he speak. Doctor White told me he was unconscious and more dangerously injured than his father.

As we descended the stairs, I asked Stanton what he had heard in regard to the President that was reliable. He said the President was shot at Ford's Theatre, that he had seen a man who was present and witnessed the occurrence. I remarked that I would go immediately to the White House. Stanton told me the President was not there but was down at the theatre. Then, said I let us go immediately there. He said that was his intention, and asked me, if I had not a carriage, to go with him.

In the lower hall we met General Meigs, whom he requested to take charge of the house, and to clear out all who did not belong there. General Meigs requested Stanton not to go down to 10th Street, others remonstrated against his going. Stanton I thought hesitated. I remarked that I should go immediately, and I thought it his duty also. He said he should certainly go, but the remonstrants increased and gathered round him. I remarked that we were wasting time, and pressing through the crowd entered the carriage and urged Stanton, who was detained after he had placed his foot on the step. I was impatient. Stanton, as soon as he had seated himself, said the carriage was not his. I said that was no objection. He invited Meigs to go with us, and Judge Cartter of the Supreme Court mounted with the driver. At this moment Major Eckert rode up on horseback and protested vehemently against Stanton's going to 10th Street—said he had just come from there, that there were thousands of people of all sorts there and he considered it very unsafe for the Secretary of War to expose himself. I replied that I knew not where he would be safe, and the duty of both of us was to attend the President immediately. Stanton concurred. Meigs called to some soldiers to go with us, and there was one on each side of the carriage. The streets were full of people. Not only the sidewalk but the carriage-way was to some extent occupied, all or nearly all hurrying towards 10th Street. When we entered that street we found it pretty closely packed.

The President had been carried across the street from the theatre, to the house of a Mr. Peterson. We entered by ascending a flight of steps above the basement and passing through a long hall to the rear the President lay extended on a bed breathing heavily. Several surgeons were present, at least six, I should think more. Among them I was glad to observe Dr. Hall, who, however soon left. I inquired of one of the Surgeons Dr. H., I think, the true condition of the President and was told he was dead to all intents, although he might live three hours or perhaps even longer.

The giant sufferer lay extended diagonally across the bed which was not long enough for him. He had been stripped of his clothes. His large arms, which were occasionally exposed were of a size which one would scarce have expected from his spare appearance. His slow, full respiration lifted the clothes. His features were calm and striking. I had never seen them appear to better advantage than for the first hour, perhaps, that I was there. After that his right eye began to swell and became discolored.

Senator Sumner was there, I think, when I entered. If not he came in soon after, as did Speaker Colfax, Mr. Secretary McCulloch and the other members of the Cabinet, with the exception of Mr. Seward. A double guard was stationed at the door and on the sidewalk, to repress the crowd which was excited and anxious.

The room was small and overcrowded. The surgeons and members of the Cabinet were as many as should have been in the room, but there were many more, and the hall and other rooms in the front or main house were full. One of them was occupied by Mrs. Lincoln and her attendants. Mrs. Dixon and Mrs. Kinney came about twelve o'clock. About once an hour Mrs. Lincoln would repair to the bedside of her dying husband and remain until overcome by her emotion.

A door which opened upon a porch or gallery, and the windows were kept open for fresh air. The night was dark, cloudy and damp, and about six it began to rain. I remained until then without sitting or leaving, when, there being a vacant chair at the foot of the bed, I occupied for nearly two hours, listening to the heavy groans, and witnessing the wasting life of the good and great man who was expiring before me.

About 6 A.M. a fainting sickness came over me and for the first time after entering the room, a little past eleven, I left it and the house, and took a short walk in the open air. It was a dark and gloomy morning, and rain set in before I returned to the house, some fifteen minutes. Large groups of people were gathered every few rods, all anxious and solicitous. Some one stepped forward as I passed, to inquire into the condition of the President, and to ask if there was no hope. Intense grief exhibited itself on every countenance when I replied that the President could survive but a short time. The colored people especially—and there were at this time more of them perhaps than of whites—were painfully affected.

Returning to the house, I seated myself in the back parlor where the Attorney-General and others had been engaged in taking evidence concerning the assassination. Stanton, and Speed, and Usher were there, the latter asleep on the bed—there were three or four others also in the room. While I did not feel inclined to sleep as did many, I was somewhat indisposed and had been for several days—the excitement and atmosphere from the crowded rooms oppressed me physically.

A little before seven, I went into the room where the dying President was rapidly drawing near the closing moments. His wife soon after made her last visit to him. The death struggle had begun. Robert, his son stood at the head of the bed and bore himself well, but on two occasions gave way to overpowering grief and sobbed aloud, turning his head and leaning on the shoulder of Senator Sumner. The respiration became suspended at intervals, and at length entirely ceased at twenty-two minutes past seven.

A prayer followed from Dr. Gurley; and the Cabinet, with the exception of Mr. Seward and Mr. McCulloch immediately thereafter assembled in the back parlor, from which all other persons were excluded, and signed a letter which had been prepared by Attorney-General Speed to the Vice President, informing him of the event, and that the government devolved upon him.

Mr. Stanton proposed that Mr. Speed, as the law officer, should communicate the letter to Mr. Johnson with some other member of the Cabinet. Mr. Dennison named me. I saw that it disconcerted Stanton, who had expected and intended to be the man and to have Speed associated with him. As I was disinclined to any effort for myself personally I named Mr. McCulloch as the first in order after the Secretary of State.

I arranged with Speed with whom I rode home for a Cabinet meeting at twelve meridian at the room of the Secretary of the Treasury, in order that the government should experience no detriment, and that prompt and necessary action might be taken to assist the new Chief Magistrate in promoting the public tranquillity. We accordingly met at noon. Mr. Speed reported that the President had taken the oath which was administered by the Chief Justice, and had expressed a desire that affairs should proceed without interruption. Some discussion took place as to the propriety of an inaugural address, but the general impression was that it would be inexpedient. I was most decidedly of that opinion.

President Johnson, who was invited to be present, deported himself with gentlemanly and dignified courtesy, and on the subject of an inaugural was of the opinion that his acts would best disclose his policy. In all essentials it would be the same as that of the late President. He desired the members of the Cabinet to go forward with their duties without any interruption. Mr. Hunter, Chief Clerk of the State Department was designated to act *ad interim* as Secretary of State. I suggested Mr. Speed, but I saw it was not acceptable in certain quarters. Stanton especially expressed a hope that Hunter should be assigned to the duty.

A room for the President as an office was proposed, and Mr.

McCulloch offered the adjoining room. I named the State Department as appropriate and proper until there was a Secretary of State, or so long as the President wished, but objections arose at once. The papers of Mr. Seward would be disturbed—it would be better here, etc., etc. Stanton I saw had a purpose.

On returning to my house the morning of Saturday, I found Mrs. Welles who had been confined to the house from indisposition for a week had been twice sent for by Mrs. Lincoln and had yielded, and imprudently gone, although the weather was inclement. She remained at the Executive Mansion through the day.

For myself, wearied, shocked, exhausted but not inclined to sleep, the day passed off strangely.

On Sunday the 16th the President and Cabinet met by agreement at 10 A.M. at the Treasury. The President was half an hour behind time. Stanton was more than an hour later and brought with him papers, and had many suggestions relative to our measures before the Cabinet at our last meeting with President Lincoln. The general policy of treating the Rebels and the Rebel States was fully discussed. President Johnson is not disposed to treat treason lightly, and the chief Rebels he would punish with exemplary severity.

Stanton has divided his original plan and made the reestablishing of State government applicable to North Carolina, leaving Virginia which has a loyal government and governor, to arrange that matter of election to which I had excepted, but elaborating it for North Carolina and the other States.

Being at the War Department Sunday evening, I was detained conversing with Stanton and finally Senator Sumner came in. He was soon followed by Gooch and Dawes from Massachusetts and some two or three others—general officers also came in. Stanton took from his table in answer to an inquiry from some one, his document which had been submitted to the Cabinet and which was still a Cabinet measure.

It was evident the gentlemen were there by appointment and that I came as an intruder. Stanton did not know how to get rid of me and they supposed I was there by arrangement; I felt embarrassed and was very glad after he had read to them his first programme for Virginia, and had got about half through with the other, when a line was brought me at this time by the messenger, giving me an opportunity to leave.

On Monday the 17th I was actively engaged in bringing forward business issuing orders, and arranging for the funeral solemnities of President Lincoln. Secretary Seward and his son continue in a low condition, and Mr. Fred Seward's life is precarious.

Tuesday, 18. Details in regard to the funeral, which takes place on the 19th, occupied general attention and little else was done at the Cabinet meeting. From every part of the country comes lamentation. Every house, almost, has some drapery, especially the homes of the poor. Profuse exhibition is displayed on the public buildings and the houses of the wealthy, but the little black ribbon or strip of black cloth from the hovel of the poor negro or the impoverished white is more touching.

I have tried to write something consecutively since the horrid transactions of Friday night, but I have no heart for it, and the jottings down are mere mementos of a period, which I will try to fill up when more composed, and I have some leisure or time for the task.

Sad and painful, wearied and irksome, the few preceding incoherent pages have been written for future use, for they are fresh in my mind and may pass away with me but cannot ever be forgotten by me.

The funeral on Wednesday the 19th was imposing and sorrowful. All felt the solemnity, and sorrowed as if they had lost one of their own household. By voluntary action business was everywhere suspended, and the people crowded the streets.

The Cabinet met by arrangement in the room occupied by the President at the Treasury. We left a few minutes before meridian so as to be in the East Room at precisely twelve o'clock, being the last to enter. Others will give the details.

I rode with Stanton in the procession to the Capitol. The front of the procession reached the Capitol, it was said, before we started, and there were as many, or more who followed us. A brief prayer was made by Mr. Gurley in the rotunda, where we left the remains of the good and great man we loved so well. Returning, I left Stanton who was nervous and full of orders as usual, and I took in my carriage President Johnson and Preston King, their carriage having been crowded out of place. Coming down Pennsylvania Avenue after this long detention we met the marching procession in broad platoons all the way to the Kirkwood House on Twelfth Street.

There were no truer mourners when all were sad, than the poor colored people who crowded the streets, joined the procession and exhibited their feelings and anxiety for the man whom they regarded as a benefactor and father. Women, as well as men, with their little children thronged the streets covering it and trouble and distress depicted on their countenances and in their bearing. The vacant holiday expression had given way to real grief. Seward, I am told sat up in bed and viewed the procession and hearse of the President, and I know his emotion. Stanton who rode with me was uneasy & left the carriage four or five times.

On the morning of Friday the 21st I went by appointment or agreement to the Capitol at 6 A.M. Stanton had agreed to call for me before six and take me in his carriage, the object being to have but few present when the remains were taken from the rotunda where they had lain in state through Thursday, and were visited and seen by many thousands. As I knew Stanton to be uncertain and in some respects unreliable, I ordered my own carriage and I wished also to take my sons with me to the last opportunity they or I would have to manifest our respect and love for the man who had been the steady and abiding friend of their father. Stanton, as I expected, was late, and then informed me he had not, as he agreed, informed Governor Dennison of our purpose. He said he had to go for another friend, and wished me to take up Governor D. Not until I had got to his house was I aware of Stanton's neglect. It was then about six. Governor D. sent me word he would be ready in three minutes. I think he was not five. Stanton I perceived did not tell me the truth about another visitor. He moved in great state himself being escorted by the cavalry corps which usually attended the President.

We reached the Capitol and entered the rotunda just as Mr. Gurley was commencing an earnest and impressive prayer. When it was concluded, the remains were removed and taken to the depot where a car and train were prepared for the commencement of the long and circuitous journey to his last earthly resting place in Springfield, in the great prairies of the West. We were, as we had intended, an hour in advance of the time, and thus avoided the crowd which before the train departed thronged the roads and depot.

John Wilkes Booth

Diary, April 17, 1865

Although it is dated from April 13 to 14, 1865, the fugitive assassin probably wrote this entry in his pocket diary on April 17 as he hid from Union patrols in the pine woods of Zekiah Swamp near the Potomac in Charles County, Maryland. Born near Bel Air, Maryland, in 1838, John Wilkes Booth was the son of the well-known Anglo-American actor Junius Booth and the younger brother of the celebrated Shakespearean performer Edwin Booth. John Wilkes followed them onto the stage and successfully toured the country as a leading man until May 1864. A fervent Confederate sympathizer and supporter of slavery, in August 1864 Booth began recruiting potential co-conspirators in a plot to abduct Lincoln in Washington, take him to Richmond, and use him as a hostage to force the resumption of prisoner exchanges between the Union and Confederate armies. During the winter of 1864–65 he recruited additional accomplices and planned an escape route through southern Maryland across the Potomac into Virginia. An attempt by Booth and several collaborators to ambush the President on March 17, 1865, as he returned to the White House from a military hospital failed when Lincoln changed his schedule. When the fall of Richmond and Lee's surrender made the abduction plot impossible, Booth plotted three simultaneous murders. On the evening of April 14 he gave his final instructions to Lewis Powell; George Atzerodt, a twenty-nine-year-old carriage painter from Port Tobacco, Maryland; and David Herold, a twenty-two-year-old druggist's clerk from Washington. Booth would murder Lincoln; Powell, accompanied by Herold as a guide, would assassinate Seward; and Atzerodt would kill Andrew Johnson at the Kirkwood House hotel. In the event, Herold left Powell outside the Seward house, while Atzerodt lost his nerve, got drunk, and fled without ever approaching the vice president. Booth and Herold both escaped on horseback across the Navy Yard bridge, rendezvoused in Prince Georges County, Maryland, and made their way to the home of Dr. Samuel Mudd, who treated Booth for a fractured left fibula. While Booth claimed that he broke his leg when he jumped onto the stage of Ford's Theatre, it is possible that the fracture was the result of a subsequent horse fall.

April 13th   14 Friday the Ides
 Until to day nothing was ever *thought* of sacrificing to our country's wrongs. For six months we had worked to capture. But our cause being almost lost, something decisive & great must be done. But its failure is owing to others, who did not strike for their country with a heart. I struck boldly and not as the papers say. I walked with a firm step through

a thousand of his friends, was stopped, but pushed on. A Col- was at his side. I shouted Sic semper *before* I fired. In jumping broke my leg. I passed all his pickets, rode sixty miles that night, with the bones of my leg tearing the flesh at every jump. I can never repent it, though we hated to kill: Our country owed all her troubles to him, and God simply made me the instrument of his punishment. The country is not what it *was*. This forced union is not what I *have* loved. I care not what *becomes* of me. I have no desire to out-live my country. This night (before the deed), I wrote a long article and left it for one of the Editors of the National Inteligencer, in which I fully set forth our reasons for our proceedings. He or the Govmt

John Wilkes Booth

"To whom it may concern"

In November 1864 Booth had visited his sister, Asia, in Philadelphia while on his way to New York City, where he would appear with his actor brothers Edwin and Junius in a special performance of *Julius Caesar*. During his stay Booth gave his sister a packet for safekeeping that contained two letters. One was addressed to their mother, while the other was probably intended for Asia's husband, John Sleeper Clarke, a successful comic actor and theater manager. Clarke turned the second letter over to the U.S. marshal in Philadelphia on April 18, and it was published in the *Philadelphia Inquirer* the next day. Ironically, the phrase "To whom it may concern" had been used by Lincoln in July 1864 to address a message communicating his terms for peace—complete reunion and emancipation—to Confederate envoys in Canada. On the afternoon of April 14, 1865, Booth gave a letter to his friend and fellow actor John Matthews and asked that it be delivered to the Washington *National Intelligencer*. Matthews testified before Congress in July 1867 that he opened the letter immediately after the assassination, read it "a couple of times," and then burned it for fear of being implicated in Booth's plot. Soon afterward, Matthews wrote to the *National Intelligencer* that the letter covered three pages, the first two "written in the spirit and style" of the "To whom it may concern" letter of 1864, and with a concluding paragraph "in these words": "For a long time I have devoted my energies, my time and money, to the accomplishment of a certain end. I have been disappointed. The moment has arrived when I must change my plans. Many will blame me for what I am about to do, but posterity, I am sure, will justify me. Men who love their country better than gold and life.

John W. Booth, Payne, Herold, Atzerodt."

———————

————, ————, 1864

MY DEAR SIR,—You may use this as you think best. But as *some* may wish to know *when*, *who* and *why*, and as I know not *how* to direct, I give it (in the words of your master)

"TO WHOM IT MAY CONCERN":

Right or wrong, God judge me, not man. For be my motive good or bad, of one thing I am sure, the lasting condemnation of the North.

I love peace more than life. Have loved the Union beyond expression. For four years have I waited, hoped and prayed for the dark clouds to break, and for a restoration of our former sunshine. To wait longer would be a crime. All hope for peace is dead. My prayers have proved as idle as my hopes. God's will be done. I go to see and share the bitter end.

I have ever held the South were right. The very nomination of ABRA-HAM LINCOLN, four years ago, spoke plainly, war—war upon Southern rights and institutions. His election proved it. "Await an overt act." Yes, till you are bound and plundered. What folly! The South was wise. Who thinks of argument or patience when the finger of his enemy presses on the trigger? In a *foreign war* I, too, could say, "country, right or wrong." But in a struggle *such as ours*, (where the brother tries to pierce the brother's heart,) for God's sake, choose the right. When a country like this spurns justice from her side she forfeits the allegiance of every honest freeman, and should leave him, untrameled by any fealty soever, to act as his conscience may approve.

People of the North, to hate tyranny, to love liberty and justice, to strike at wrong and oppression, was the teaching of our fathers. The study of our early history will not let *me* forget it, and may it never.

This country was formed for the *white*, not for the black man. And looking upon *African Slavery* from the same stand-point held by the noble framers of our constitution. I for one, have ever considered *it* one of the greatest blessings (both for themselves and us,) that God has ever bestowed upon a favored nation. Witness heretofore our wealth and power; witness their elevation and enlightenment above their race elsewhere. I have lived among it most of my life, and have seen *less* harsh treatment from master to man than I have beheld in the North from father to son. Yet, Heaven knows, *no one* would be willing to do *more* for the negro race than I, could I but see a way to *still better their* condition.

But LINCOLN's policy is only preparing the way for their total annihilation. The South *are not, nor have they been fighting* for the continuance of slavery. The first battle of Bull Run did away with that idea. Their causes *since* for *war* have been as *noble* and *greater far than those that urged our fathers on. Even* should we allow they were wrong at the beginning of this contest, *cruelty and injustice* have made the wrong become the *right*, and they stand *now* (before the wonder and admiration of the world) as a noble band of patriotic heroes. Hereafter, reading of *their deeds*, Thermopylae will be forgotten.

When I aided in the capture and execution of JOHN BROWN (who was a murderer on our Western border, and who was fairly *tried* and *convicted*, before an impartial judge and jury, of treason, and who, by the way, has since been made a god), I was proud of my little share in the transaction, for I deemed it my duty, and that I was helping our common country to perform an act of justice. But what was a crime in poor JOHN BROWN is now considered (by themselves) as the greatest and only virtue of the whole Republican party. Strange transmigration! *Vice* to become a *virtue*, simply because *more* indulge in it.

I thought then, *as now*, that the Abolitionists *were the only traitors* in the land, and that the entire party deserved the same fate of poor old BROWN, not because they wish to abolish slavery but on account of the means they have ever endeavored to use to effect that abolition. If BROWN were living I doubt whether he *himself* would set slavery against the Union. Most or many in the North do, and openly curse the Union, if the South are to return and retain a *single right* guarantied to them by every tie which we once *revered as sacred*. The South can make no choice. It is either extermination or slavery for *themselves* (worse than death) to draw from. I know *my* choice.

I have also studied hard to discover upon what grounds the right of a State to secede has been denied, when our very name, United States, and the Declaration of Independence, *both* provide for secession. But there is no time for words. I write in haste. I know how foolish I shall be deemed for undertaking such a step as this, where, on the one side, I have many friends, and everything to make me happy, where my profession *alone* has gained me an income of *more than* twenty thousand dollars a year, and where my great personal ambition in my profession has such a great field for labor. On the other hand, the South have never bestowed upon me one kind word; a place now where I have no friends, except beneath the sod; a place where I must either become a private soldier or a beggar. To give up all of the *former* for the *latter*, besides my mother and sisters whom I love so dearly, (although they so widely differ with me in opinion,) seems insane; but God is my judge. I love *justice* more than I do a country that disowns it; more than fame and wealth; more (Heaven pardon me if wrong,) more than a happy home. I have never been upon a battle-field; but O, my countrymen, could you all but see the *reality* or effects of this horrid war, as I have seen them, (in *every State* save Virginia,)

I know you would think like me, and would pray the Almighty to create in the Northern mind a sense of *right* and *justice*, (even should it possess no seasoning of mercy,) and that he would dry up this sea of blood between us, which is daily growing wider. Alas! poor country, is she to meet her threatened doom? Four years ago I would have given a thousand lives to see her remain (as I had always known her) powerful and unbroken. And even now, I would hold my life as naught to see her what she was. O, my friends, if the fearful scenes of the past four years had never been enacted, or if what has been had been but a frightful dream, from which we could now awake, with what overflowing hearts could we bless our God and pray for his continued favor. How I have loved the *old flag*, can never now be known. A few years since and the entire world could boast of *none* so pure and spotless. But I have of late been seeing and hearing of the *bloody deeds* of which she has *been made the emblem*, and would shudder to think how changed she had grown. O, how I have longed to see her break from the mist of blood and death that circles round her folds, spoiling her beauty and tarnishing her honor. But no, day by day has she been dragged deeper and deeper into cruelty and oppression, till now (in my eyes) her once bright red stripes look like bloody gashes on the face of Heaven. I look now upon my early admiration of her glories as a dream. My love (as things stand to-day) is for the South alone. Nor do I deem it a dishonor in attempting to make for her a prisoner of this man, to whom she owes so much of misery. If success attends me, I go penniless to her side. They say she has found that "last ditch" which the North have so long derided, and been endeavoring to force her in, forgetting they are our brothers, and that it's impolitic to goad an enemy to madness. Should I reach her in safety and find it true, I will proudly beg permission to triumph or die in that same "ditch" by her side.

A Confederate doing duty upon his own responsibility,

J. WILKES BOOTH.

Edwin M. Stanton

Reward Announcement

After escaping from the Seward residence, Lewis Powell had hid for three days on the northeast outskirts of Washington before appearing at Mary Surratt's boardinghouse, where he was arrested on April 17 by Union officers. In the early hours of April 20 George Atzerodt was arrested at a cousin's house in Germantown, Maryland, after talking too freely about the assassination. Later that day Secretary of War Stanton announced rewards for the capture of Booth and Herold, who were still hiding in the woods of southern Maryland, and of John H. Surratt, Mary Surratt's son. A Confederate agent and courier involved in Booth's abduction plot, Surratt was in Elmira, New York, when Lincoln was shot. He quickly fled to Montreal and would elude federal authorities until the fall of 1866. Stanton's warning that accomplices to the assassination would be tried before a military commission reflected his firm conviction that the murder in wartime of the commander-in-chief by enemy sympathizers should be punished under the laws of war.

SURRATT.   BOOTH.   HEROLD.

WAR DEPARTMENT,
Washington, April 20, 1865.

$100,000 REWARD.

The murderer of our late beloved President Abraham Lincoln is still at large.

Fifty thousand dollars reward will be paid by this Department for his apprehension, in addition to any reward offered by municipal authorities or State executives.

Twenty-five thousand dollars reward will be paid for the apprehension of John H. Surratt, one of Booth's accomplices.

Twenty-five thousand dollars reward will be paid for the apprehension of David E. Herold, another of Booth's accomplices.

Liberal rewards will be paid for any information that shall conduce to the arrest of either of the above-named criminals or their accomplices.

All persons harboring or secreting the said persons, or either of them, or aiding or assisting their concealment or escape, will be treated as accomplices in the murder of the President and the attempted assassination of the Secretary of State, and shall be subject to trial before a military commission and the punishment of death.

Let the stain of innocent blood be removed from the land by the arrest and punishment of the murderers.

All good citizens are exhorted to aid public justice on this occasion. Every man should consider his own conscience charged with this solemn duty, and rest neither night nor day until it be accomplished.

EDWIN M. STANTON,
Secretary of War.

Descriptions.—Booth is five feet seven or eight inches high, slender build, high forehead, black hair, black eyes, and wore a heavy black mustache, which there is some reason to believe has been shaved off.

John H. Surratt is about five feet nine inches. Hair rather thin and dark; eyes rather light; no beard. Would weigh 145 or 150 pounds. Complexion rather pale and clear, with color in his cheeks. Wore light clothes of fine quality. Shoulders square; cheek bones rather prominent; chin narrow; ears projecting at the top; forehead rather low and square, but broad. Parts his hair on the right side. Neck rather long. His lips are firmly set. A slim man.

David E. Herold is five feet six inches high, hair dark, eyes dark, eyebrows rather heavy, full face, nose short, hand short and fleshy, feet small, instep high, round bodied, naturally quick and active; slightly closes his eyes when looking at a person.

Notice.—In addition to the above, State and other authorities have offered rewards amounting to almost $100,000, making an aggregate of about $200,000.

John Wilkes Booth

Diary, April 22, 1865

On the night of April 20 Booth and Herold tried to cross the Potomac in a boat provided by Thomas Jones, a local Confederate agent. Caught in strong currents and alarmed by the presence of Union patrol boats on the river, they were forced to return to Maryland and take shelter in a shack along Nanjemoy Creek. While in hiding, Booth read newspapers supplied by Jones and became increasingly dismayed at the public response to his crime. Unaware that John Matthews had burned his letter to the *National Intelligencer*, Booth attributed its failure to appear in print to government suppression. Although he dated this entry in his pocket diary April 21, it is likely that Booth wrote it on April 22.

Friday 21—

After being hunted like a dog through swamps, woods, and last night being chased by gun boats till I was forced to return wet cold and starving, with every mans hand against me, I am here in despair. And why; For doing what Brutus was honored for, what made Tell a Hero. And yet I for striking down a greater tyrant than they ever knew am looked upon as a common cutthroat. My action was purer than either of theirs. One, hoped to be great himself. The other had not only his countrys but his own wrongs to avenge. I hoped for no gain. I knew no private wrong. I struck for my country and that alone. A country groaned beneath this tyranny and prayed for this end. Yet now behold the cold hand they extend to me. God *cannot* pardon me if I have done wrong. Yet I cannot see any wrong except in serving a degenerate people. The little, the very little I left behind to clear my name, the Govmt will not allow to be printed. So ends all. For my country I have given up all that makes life sweet and Holy, brought misery on my family, and am sure there is no pardon in Heaven for me since man condemns me so. I have only *heard* what has been done (except what I did myself) and it fills me with horror. God try and forgive me and bless my mother. To night I will once more try the river with the intent to cross, though I have a greater desire to return to Washington and in a measure clear my name which I feel I can do. I do not repent the blow I struck. I may before God but not to man.

I think I have done well, though I am abandoned, with the curse of

Cain upon me. When if the world knew my heart, *that one* blow would have made me great, though I did desire no greatness.

To night I try to escape these blood hounds once more. Who who can read his fate. God's will be done.

I have too great a soul to die like a criminal. Oh may he, may he spare me that and let me die bravely.

I bless the entire world. Have never hated or wronged anyone. This last was not a wrong, unless God deems it so. And its with him, to damn or bless me. And for this brave boy with me who often prays (yes before and since) with a true and sincere heart, was it a crime in him, if so why can he pray the same I do not wish to shed a drop of blood, but "I must fight the course" Tis all thats left me.

Clara Harris

Letters to Mary and to M——

In the weeks following the assassination Clara Harris (1834–1883), the daughter of Republican senator Ira Harris of New York, wrote to two friends about the events of April 14 and the slow recovery of her stepbrother and fiancée, Major Henry R. Rathbone, from wounds inflicted by Booth's knife as the assassin struggled to flee the presidential box. Clara Harris's letters upend the long-standing myth that Lincoln bled profusely after being shot, a fact doctors contradicted to little avail once actress Laura Keene, who at one point had cradled the wounded President's head in her lap, exhibited her blood-saturated dress on subsequent theatrical tours. In fact, as Harris's letters suggest, it was Rathbone, stabbed in an artery, who bled profusely on the dress, and the blood displayed for years by Laura Keene was undoubtedly his. Harris and Rathbone would marry in 1867 and have three children together. Haunted by feelings of guilt over having failed to stop Booth, Henry Rathbone became increasingly erratic and delusional. On December 23, 1883, while they were living in Germany, he accused Clara of plotting to leave him, then shot and stabbed her to death before slashing himself several times. Judged insane by a German court, Rathbone lived in an asylum until his death in 1911.

Washington April 25th

My dear Mary:

I received your kind note last week, & should have answered it before, but that I have really felt, as though could not settle myself quietly, even to the performance of such a slight duty as that—Henry has been suffering a great deal with his arm, but it is now doing very well,—the knife went from the elbow nearly to the shoulder, inside,—cutting an artery, nerves & veins—He bled so profusely as to make him very weak—My whole clothing, as I sat in the box was saturated literally with blood, & my hands & face—you may imagine what a scene—poor Mrs Lincoln all through that dreadful night would look at me with horror & scream, oh! my husband's blood,—my dear husband's blood—which it was not, though I did not know it at the time—the President's wound, did not bleed externally at all—the brain was instantly suffused—

When I sat down to write I did not intend alluding to these fearful events, at all, but I really cannot fix my mind on anything else—though I try my best to think of them as little as possible—I cannot sleep & really feel wretchedly—only to think that fiend is still at large—There was a report here yesterday that every house in the District of Columbia was to be searched to-day—I hoped it was true, as the impression seems to be gaining ground that Booth is hidden in Washington—Is not that a horrible thought!

Mr Johnson is at present living in Mr Hooper's house, opposite us—a guard are walking the street in front constantly—

It will probably be two or three weeks before Mrs Lincoln will be able to make arrangements for leaving—she has not left her bed since she returned to the White House that morning—

We expect to be able to leave next week for New York—but on what day, it would be impossible yet to say—I will write you in time however, so that I shall be sure to see you, while there—

Please give my love to all the family, & believe me

Ever truly yours,
Clara H.

1865

WASHINGTON, April 29th.

MY DEAR M——: I was very glad to hear from you again, your letter proving that in all the events of your *matronly* life our old friendship is not forgotten.

You may well say that we have been passing through scenes sad indeed. That terrible Friday night is to me yet almost like some dreadful vision. I have been very intimate with Mrs. Lincoln and the family ever since our mutual residence in Washington, which began at the same time, and we have been constantly in the habit of driving and going to the opera and theater together. It was the only amusement, with the exception of receiving at their own house, in which the President and Mrs. Lincoln were permitted, according to custom, to indulge, and to escape from the crowds who constantly thronged to see them, more than from any decided taste for such things. They were in the habit of going very often to hear Forest, Booth, Hackett and such actors, when playing in Washington.

The night before the murder was that of the general illumination here, and they drove all through the streets to see it; a less calculating

villain might have taken that opportunity for his crime, or the night before, when the White House alone was brilliantly illuminated, and the
figure of the President stood out in full relief to the immense crowd
below, who stood in the darkness to listen to his speech. He spoke from
the center window of the Executive Mansion. I had been invited to pass
the evening there, and stood at the window of an adjoining room with
Mrs. Lincoln, watching the crowd below as they listened and cheered.
Of course Booth was there, watching his chance. I wonder he did not
choose that occasion; but probably he knew a better opportunity would
be offered. After the speech was over, we went into Mr. Lincoln's room;
he was lying on the sofa, quite exhausted, but he talked of the events
of the past fortnight, of his visit to Richmond, of the enthusiasm everywhere felt through the country; and Mrs. Lincoln declared the past
few days to have been the happiest of her life. Their prospects indeed
seemed fair—peace dawning upon our land, and four years of a happy
and honored rule before one of the gentlest, best and loveliest men I
ever knew. I never saw him out of temper—the kindest husband, the
tenderest father, the truest friend, as well as the wisest statesman. "Our
beloved President"—when I think that I shall never again stand in his
genial presence, that I have lost his friendship so tried and true, I feel
like putting on the robe of mourning which the country wears.

My own dear father was deeply attached to Mr. Lincoln; they thoroughly sympathized in many things, and Mr. Lincoln, perhaps being able
to discern in him an honest, unselfish nature, in that akin to his own, was
wont with him to throw off the restraints of the politician and talk over
things as with an old friend.

The shock has been a terrible one to him; he feels his death to be a
deep, personal affliction.

You were right in supposing the Major Rathbone who was with us to
be the "Henry" whom you knew in Albany.

We four composed the party that evening. They drove to our door in
the gayest spirits; chatting on our way—and the President was received
with the greatest enthusiasm.

They say we were watched by the assassins; ay, as we alighted from the
carriage. Oh, how could any one be so cruel as to strike that kind, dear,
honest face! And when I think of that fiend barring himself in alone with
us, my blood runs cold. My dress is saturated with blood; my hands and

face were covered. You may imagine what a scene! and so, all through that dreadful night, when we stood by that dying bed. Poor Mrs. Lincoln was and is almost crazy.

Henry narrowly escaped with his life. The knife was struck at his heart with all the force of a practiced and powerful arm; he fortunately parried the blow, and received a wound in his arm, extending along the bone, from the elbow nearly to the shoulder. He concealed it for some time, but was finally carried home in a swoon; the loss of blood had been so great from an artery and veins severed. He is now getting quite well, but cannot as yet use his arm.

I hope you will pardon me this dreadfully long letter. I did not realize how much I was writing. I have been quite ill, and have as yet answered scarcely any of the numerous letters I have received in the last two weeks.

We are preparing to close our house here for the summer, and return to Albany on the 8th of May. My sister Amanda is to be married on the 25th of next month, to Mr. I. Ewing Miller, of Columbus, Ohio and we must all hasten on to the wedding. It would give us all great pleasure if you and Mr. Johnson could be present. It will be a quiet morning wedding. Please give my kindest regards to your husband. My sisters are in Albany or they would unite with my mother in love to yourself. Again I must apologize for the length of this letter. I am not given to such errors, and will promise never to transgress in that way again.

Ever yours sincerely.

CLARA H. HARRIS.

P. S. Please give my love to *Mrs. Stevenson*, if you see her.   C. H. H. LANGSIDE, GLASGOW.

Elizabeth Keckly

FROM *Behind the Scenes*

"Mrs. Lincolns condition is very pitiable—she has hysteria & has sometimes been very delerious," wrote Elizabeth Blair Lee, a friend of Mary Lincoln, on April 17. Five days later Lee told her husband: "Mrs. Lincoln is better physically & her nervous system begins to rally from the terrible shock—I thought her mind have recovered in part its tone—but her grief is terrible & altogether for her husband as her all in life—this makes her sorrow doubly touching." A member of the politically influential Blair family, Lee alternated her visits to the White House with those of Mary Jane Welles, the wife of navy secretary Gideon Welles. But no one spent more time with the grieving First Lady than Elizabeth Keckly (1818–1907), a former slave who had become a successful Washington dressmaker. Keckly began making dresses for Mary Lincoln in 1861 and became her confidante and close friend. She wrote about the assassination in her memoir *Behind the Scenes, or, Thirty Years a Slave, and Four Years in the White House* (1868). Its publication caused Mary Lincoln to break off their friendship.

The days passed without any incident of particular note disturbing the current of life. On Friday morning, April 14th—alas! what American does not remember the day—I saw Mrs. Lincoln but for a moment. She told me that she was to attend the theatre that night with the President, but I was not summoned to assist her in making her toilette. Sherman had swept from the northern border of Georgia through the heart of the Confederacy down to the sea, striking the death-blow to the rebellion. Grant had pursued General Lee beyond Richmond, and the army of Virginia, that had made such stubborn resistance, was crumbling to pieces. Fort Sumter had fallen;—the stronghold first wrenched from the Union, and which had braved the fury of Federal guns for so many years, was restored to the Union; the end of the war was near at hand, and the great pulse of the loyal North thrilled with joy. The dark war-cloud was fading, and a white-robed angel seemed to hover in the sky, whispering "Peace—peace on earth, good-will toward men!" Sons, brothers, fathers, friends, sweethearts were coming home. Soon the white tents would be folded, the volunteer army be disbanded, and tranquillity again reign. Happy, happy day!—happy at least to those who fought under the banner of the Union. There was great rejoicing throughout the North. From the Atlantic to the Pacific, flags were gayly thrown to the breeze, and at night every city blazed with its tens of thousand lights. But scarcely had the fireworks ceased to play, and the lights been taken down from the windows, when the lightning flashed the most appalling news over the magnetic wires. "The President has been murdered!" spoke the swift-winged messenger, and the loud huzza died upon the lips. A nation suddenly paused in the midst of festivity, and stood paralyzed with horror—transfixed with awe.

Oh, memorable day! Oh, memorable night! Never before was joy so violently contrasted with sorrow.

At 11 o'clock at night I was awakened by an old friend and neighbor, Miss M. Brown, with the startling intelligence that the entire Cabinet had been assassinated, and Mr. Lincoln shot, but not mortally wounded. When I heard the words I felt as if the blood had been frozen in my veins, and that my lungs must collapse for the want of air. Mr. Lincoln shot! the Cabinet assassinated! What could it mean? The streets were alive with wondering, awe-stricken people. Rumors flew thick and fast, and the wildest reports came with every new arrival. The words were repeated with blanched cheeks and quivering lips. I waked Mr. and Mrs. Lewis, and told them that the President was shot, and that I must go to the White House. I could not remain in a state of uncertainty. I felt that the house would not hold me. They tried to quiet me, but gentle words could not calm the wild tempest. They quickly dressed themselves, and we sallied out into the street to drift with the excited throng. We walked rapidly towards the White House, and on our way passed the residence of Secretary Seward, which was surrounded by armed soldiers, keeping back all intruders with the point of the bayonet. We hurried on, and as we approached the White House, saw that it too was surrounded with soldiers. Every entrance was strongly guarded, and no one was permitted to pass. The guard at the gate told us that Mr. Lincoln had not been brought home, but refused to give any other information. More excited than ever, we wandered down the street. Grief and anxiety were making me weak, and as we joined the outskirts of a large crowd, I began to feel as meek and humble as a penitent child. A gray-haired old man was passing. I caught a glimpse of his face, and it seemed so full of kindness and sorrow that I gently touched his arm, and imploringly asked:

"Will you please, sir, to tell me whether Mr. Lincoln is dead or not?"

"Not dead," he replied, "but dying. God help us!" and with a heavy step he passed on.

"Not dead, but dying! then indeed God help us!"

We learned that the President was mortally wounded—that he had been shot down in his box at the theatre, and that he was not expected to live till morning; when we returned home with heavy hearts. I could not sleep. I wanted to go to Mrs. Lincoln, as I pictured her wild with grief; but then I did not know where to find her, and I must wait till morning. Never did the hours drag so slowly. Every moment seemed an age, and I could do nothing but walk about and hold my arms in mental agony.

Morning came at last, and a sad morning was it. The flags that floated so gayly yesterday now were draped in black, and hung in silent folds at half-mast. The President was dead, and a nation was mourning for him. Every house was draped in black, and every face wore a solemn look. People spoke in subdued tones, and glided whisperingly, wonderingly, silently about the streets.

About eleven o'clock on Saturday morning a carriage drove up to the door, and a messenger asked for "Elizabeth Keckley."

"Who wants her?" I asked.

"I come from Mrs. Lincoln. If you are Mrs. Keckley, come with me immediately to the White House."

I hastily put on my shawl and bonnet, and was driven at a rapid rate to the White House. Everything about the building was sad and solemn. I was quickly shown to Mrs. Lincoln's room, and on entering, saw Mrs. L. tossing uneasily about upon a bed. The room was darkened, and the only person in it besides the widow of the President was Mrs. Secretary Welles, who had spent the night with her. Bowing to Mrs. Welles, I went to the bedside.

"Why did you not come to me last night, Elizabeth—I sent for you?" Mrs. Lincoln asked in a low whisper.

"I did try to come to you, but I could not find you," I answered, as I laid my hand upon her hot brow.

I afterwards learned, that when she had partially recovered from the first shock of the terrible tragedy in the theatre, Mrs. Welles asked:

"Is there no one, Mrs. Lincoln, that you desire to have with you in this terrible affliction?"

"Yes, send for Elizabeth Keckley. I want her just as soon as she can be brought here."

Three messengers, it appears, were successively despatched for me, but all of them mistook the number and failed to find me.

Shortly after entering the room on Saturday morning, Mrs. Welles excused herself, as she said she must go to her own family, and I was left alone with Mrs. Lincoln.

She was nearly exhausted with grief, and when she became a little quiet, I asked and received permission to go into the Guests' Room, where the body of the President lay in state. When I crossed the threshold of the room, I could not help recalling the day on which I had seen little Willie lying in his coffin where the body of his father now lay. I remembered how the President had wept over the pale beautiful face of his gifted boy, and now the President himself was dead. The last time I saw him he spoke kindly to me, but alas! the lips would never move again. The light had faded from his eyes, and when the light went out the soul went with it. What a noble soul was his—noble in all the noble attributes of God! Never did I enter the solemn chamber of death with such palpitating heart and trembling footsteps as I entered it that day. No common mortal had died. The Moses of my people had fallen in the hour of his triumph. Fame had woven her choicest chaplet for his brow. Though the brow was cold and pale in death, the chaplet should not fade, for God had studded it with the glory of the eternal stars.

When I entered the room, the members of the Cabinet and many distinguished officers of the army were grouped around the body of their fallen chief. They made room for me, and, approaching the body, I lifted the white cloth from the white face of the man that I had worshipped as an idol—looked upon as a demi-god. Notwithstanding the violence of the death of the President, there was something beautiful as well as grandly solemn in the expression of the placid face. There lurked the sweetness and gentleness of childhood, and the stately grandeur of god-like intellect. I gazed long at the face, and turned away with tears in my eyes and a choking sensation in my throat. Ah! never was man so widely mourned before. The whole world bowed their heads in grief when Abraham Lincoln died.

Returning to Mrs. Lincoln's room, I found her in a new paroxysm of grief. Robert was bending over his mother with tender affection, and little Tad was crouched at the foot of the bed with a world of agony in his young face. I shall never forget the scene—the wails of a broken heart, the unearthly shrieks, the terrible convulsions, the wild, tempestuous outbursts of grief from the soul. I bathed Mrs. Lincoln's head with cold water, and soothed the terrible tornado as best I could. Tad's grief at his father's death was as great as the grief of his mother, but her terrible outbursts awed the boy into silence. Sometimes he would throw his arms around her neck, and exclaim, between his broken sobs, "Don't cry so, Mamma! don't cry, or you will make me cry, too! You will break my heart."

Mrs. Lincoln could not bear to hear Tad cry, and when he would plead to her not to break his heart, she would calm herself with a great effort, and clasp her child in her arms.

Every room in the White House was darkened, and every one spoke in subdued tones, and moved about with muffled tread. The very atmosphere breathed of the great sorrow which weighed heavily upon each heart. Mrs. Lincoln never left her room, and while the body of her husband was being borne in solemn state from the Atlantic to the broad prairies of the West, she was weeping with her fatherless children in her private chamber. She denied admittance to almost every one, and I was her only companion, except her children, in the days of her great sorrow.

Everton J. Conger

Testimony Before the Military Commission

Booth and Herold rowed across the Potomac on the night of April 22. Claiming to be former Confederate soldiers, they made their way south through the Virginia countryside and crossed the Rappahannock by ferry at Port Royal on April 24. The same day, the War Department received a telegram from southern Maryland reporting that Booth and Herold had escaped across the Potomac eight days earlier. Lafayette Baker, chief of the National Detective Police, the investigative service of the War Department, decided to send a detachment from the 16th New York Cavalry to search for the fugitives between the Potomac and the Rappahannock. He assigned two of his detectives to the cavalry force: his cousin Luther Byron Baker, and in overall command, Everton J. Conger (1834–1918), a former cavalry officer who had been wounded three times in the war. Traveling by boat, Conger, Baker, and twenty-six cavalrymen led by Lieutenant Edward Doherty reached Belle Plain, Virginia, on the night of April 24. Within twenty-four hours witnesses had identified Booth from a photograph and told the detectives that he had crossed the Rappahannock in the company of a former Confederate soldier named Willie Jett. In testimony before the military commission that tried Booth's co-conspirators, Conger related his search for Jett on the night of April 25.

EVERTON J. CONGER
a witness called for the prosecution, being duly sworn, testified as follows:—

By the JUDGE ADVOCATE:

Q. Were you, with others, engaged in the pursuit of the murderers of the President after his assassination?

A. I was.

Q. Will you please take up the narrative of that pursuit at the point where you met with Willie Jett, who has just given his testimony here, and state what occurred afterwards until the pursuit closed?

A. I found him in a room at a hotel in Bowling Green. It will be necessary to premise a little to make myself intelligible. I expected to find somebody else.

Q. Go on, and tell your story in your own way.

A. I went into a room in a hotel at Bowling Green, and found these two men in bed. As I went in, one of them began to get up in the bed.

I said to him, "Is your name Jett?" He said, "Yes, sir." Said I, "Get up: I want you!" He got up, and I told him to put on his clothes. He put on his pants, and came out to where I was in the front part of the room. I asked him, "Where are the two men who came with you across the river at Port Royal?" I was sitting on a chair. He came up towards me, and said, "Can I see you alone?" I said, "Yes, sir: you can." Lieutenant Baker and Lieutenant Doherty were with me. I asked them to go out of the room. After they were gone, he reached out his hand to me, and said, "I know who you want; and I will tell you where they can be found." Said I, "That's what I want to know." Said he, "They are on the road to Port Royal, about three miles this side of that." "At whose house are they?" I asked. "Mr. Garrett's," he replied: "I will go there with you, and show where they are now; and you can get them." I said, "Have you a horse?"— "Yes, sir."—"Get it, and get ready to go!" I said to him, "You say they are on the road to Port Royal?"—"Yes, sir." I said to him, "I have just come from there." He stopped a moment, and seemed to be considerably embarrassed. Said he, "I thought you came from Richmond: if you have come that way, you have come past them. I cannot tell you whether they are there now or not." I said it did not make any difference: we would go back and see. He got up; had his horse saddled. We gathered the party around the house together; went back to Mr. Garrett's house. Just before we got to the house, Jett, riding with me, said, "We are very near now to where we go through: let us stop here, and look around." He and I rode on together. I rode, in the first place, alone forward to find the gate that went through to the house, and rode about as far as I understood him to say it was, and did not see any opening. There was a hedge, or rather a bushy fence, along the side of the road. I turned around, and went back to him; and I told him I did not see any gate,—at any rate, within the distance he named. Then we rode on, I should think three hundred yards farther, and then stopped again. Then we went—Lieutenant Baker and myself—to find it. We opened that gate, and went through. I sent Lieutenant Baker to open another, and I went back for the cavalry; and we rode rapidly up to the house and barn, and stationed the men around the house and quarters. I went to the house, and found Lieutenant Baker at the door, telling somebody to strike a light, and come out. I think the door was open when I got there. The first individual we saw was an old man, whose name was said to be Garrett. I said to him, "Where are the two men who stopped here at your house?"—"They have gone."—"Gone where?"—"Gone to the woods."—"Well, sir, whereabouts in the woods have they gone?" He then commenced to tell me that they came there without his consent; that he did not want them to stay. I said to him, "I do not want any long story out of you: I just want to know where these men have gone." He commenced over again to tell me; and I turned to the door, and said to one of the men, "Bring in a lariat rope here, and I will put that man up to the top of one of those locust-trees." He did not seem inclined to tell. One of his sons then came in, and said, "Don't hurt the old man: he is scared. I will tell you where the men are you want to find." Said I, "That is what I want to know: where are they?" He said, "In the barn." We then left the house immediately, and went to the barn, and stationed the remaining part of the men. As soon as I went to the barn, I heard somebody walking around inside on the hay. I stationed the men around it. There were two Garretts: by that time another one had come from somewhere; and Lieutenant Baker said to one of the Garretts, "You must go in the barn, and get the arms from those men." I think he made some objection to it: I do not know certainly. Baker said, "They know you, and you can go in." Baker said to the men inside, "We are going to send this man, on whose premises you are, in to get your arms; and you must come out, and deliver yourselves up." I do not think there was any thing more said. Garrett went in; and he came out very soon, and said, "This man says, 'Damn you! you have betrayed me!' and threatened to shoot me." I said to him, "How do you know he was going to shoot you?" Said he, "He reached down to the hay behind him to get his revolver, and I came out." I then directed Lieutenant Baker to tell them, that, if they would come out and deliver themselves up, very well; if not, in five minutes we would set the barn on fire. Booth replied, "Who are you? what do you want? whom do you want?" Lieutenant Baker said, "We want you, and we know who you are. Give up your arms, and come out!" I say Booth: I presume it was him. He replied, "Let us have a little time to consider it." Lieutenant Baker said, "Very well;" and some ten or fifteen minutes probably intervened between that time and any thing further being said. He asked again, "Who are you? and what do you want?" I said to Lieutenant Baker, "Do not by any remark made to him allow him to know who we are: you need not tell him who we are. If he thinks we are rebels, or thinks we are his friends, we will take advantage of it. We will not lie to him about it; but we need not answer any question that has any reference to that subject, but simply insist on his coming out if he will." The reply was made to him, "It don't make any difference who we are: we know who you are, and we want you. We want to take you prisoners." Said he, "This is a hard case: it may be I am to be taken by my friends." Some time in the conversation he said, "Captain, I know you to be a brave man, and I believe you to be honorable: I am a cripple. I have got but one leg: if you will withdraw your men in 'line' one hundred yards from the door, I will come out and fight you." Lieutenant Baker replied, that we did not come there to fight; we simply came there to make him a prisoner: we did not want any fight with him. Once more after this he said, "If you'll take your men fifty yards from the door, I'll come out and fight you. Give me a chance for my life!" The same reply was made to him. His answer to that was, in a singularly theatrical voice, "Well, my brave boys, prepare a stretcher for me!"

Some time passed before any further conversation was held with him. In the mean time, I requested one of the Garretts to pile some brush up against the corner of the barn,—pine-boughs. He put some up there, and after a while came to me, and said, "This man inside says, that, if I put any more brush in there, he will put a ball through me."—"Very well," said I: "you need not go there again." After a while, Booth said, "There's a man in here wants to come out." Lieutenant Baker said, "Very well: let him hand his arms out, and come out." Some talk, considerable, passed in the barn: some of it was heard, some not. One of the expressions made use of by Booth to Herold, who was in the barn, was, "You damned coward! will you leave me now? Go, go! I would not have you stay with me." Some conversation ensued between them, which I supposed had reference to the bringing-out of the arms, which was one of the conditions on which Herold was to come out. It was not heard: we could simply hear them talking. He came to the door, and said, "Let me out!" Lieutenant Baker said to him, "Hand out your arms!" The reply was, "I have none." He said, "You carried a carbine; and you must hand it out." Booth replied, "The arms are mine; and I have got them." Lieutenant Baker said, "This man carried a carbine; and he must hand it out." Booth said, "Upon the word and honor of a gentleman, he has no arms: the arms are mine, and I have got them." I stood by the side of the lieutenant, and said to him, "Never mind the arms: if we can get one of the men out, let us do it, and wait no longer." The door was opened. He stuck out his hands: Lieutenant Baker took hold of him, brought him out, and passed him to the rear. I went around to the corner of the barn, pulled some hay out, twisted up a little rope about six inches long, set fire to it, and stuck it back through on top of the hay. It was loose, broken-up hay, that had been—I thought so from seeing it afterwards when I went in the barn—trodden upon the barn-floor. It was trodden down; was very light; and it blazed very rapidly,—lit right up at once. I put my eye up to the crack next to the one the fire was put through, and looked in; and I heard something drop on the floor, which I supposed to be Booth's crutch. He turned around towards me. When I first got a glimpse of him, he stood with his back partly to me, turning towards the front door. He came back within five feet of the corner of the barn. The only thing I noticed he had in his hands when he came was a carbine. He came back, and looked along the cracks one after another rapidly. He could not see any thing. He looked at the fire; and, from the expression of his face, I am satisfied he looked to see if he could put it out, and was satisfied that he could not do it, it was burning so much. He dropped his arm, relaxed his muscles, and turned around, and started for the door for the front of the barn. I ran around to the other side; and, when about half round, I heard the report of a pistol. I went right to the door and went in, and found Lieutenant Baker looking at him, or holding him, raising him up, I do not know which. I said to him, "He shot himself." Said he, "No, he did not, either." Said I, "Where-about is he shot?—in the head or neck?" I raised him then, and looked on the right side of the neck. I saw a place where the blood was running out. Said I, "Yes, sir: he shot himself." Lieutenant Baker replied very earnestly, that he did not. I said to him, "Let us carry him out of here: this will soon be burning." We took him up, and carried him out on to the grass underneath the locust-trees, a little way from the door. I went back into the barn immediately to see if the fire could be put down, and tried somewhat myself to put it down; but I could not, it was burning so fast; and there was no water, and nothing to help with. I turned around, and went back. Before this, I supposed him to be dead. He had all the appearance of a dead man; but, when I got back to him, his eyes and mouth were moving. I called immediately for some water, and put it on his face; and he somewhat revived, and attempted to speak. I put my ear down close to his mouth, and he made several efforts; and finally I understood him to say, "Tell mother, I die for my country." I said to him, "Is that what you say?" repeating it to him. He said, "Yes." They carried him from up there to the porch of Mr. Garrett's house, and laid him on an old straw bed or tick or something. At that time he revived considerably. He could then talk so as to be intelligibly understood, in a whisper: he could not speak above a whisper. He wanted water: we gave it to him. He wanted to be turned on his face. I said to him, "You cannot lie on your face;" and he wanted to be turned on his side. We turned him upon his side three times, I think; but he could not lie with any comfort, and wanted to be turned immediately back. He asked me to put my hand on his throat, and press down, which I did; and he said "Harder." And I pressed down as hard as I thought necessary; and he made very strong exertions to cough, but was unable to do so,—no muscular exertion could be made. I supposed he thought something was in his throat; and I said to him, "Open your mouth, and put out your tongue, and I will see if it bleeds;" which he did. I said to him, "There is no blood in your throat: it has not gone through any part of it there." He repeated two or three times, "Kill me, kill me!" The reply was made to him, "We don't want to kill you: we want you to get well." I then took what things were in his pockets, and tied them up in a piece of paper. He was not then quite dead. He would—once, perhaps, in five minutes—gasp: his heart would almost die out; and then it would commence, and, by a few rapid beats, would make a slight motion again. I left the body and the prisoner Herold in charge of Lieutenant Baker. I told him to wait an hour if he was not dead; if he recovered, to wait there, and send over to Belle Plain for a surgeon from one of the gunships; and, if he died in the space of an hour, to get the best conveyance he could, and bring him on, dead or alive.

Q. You left before he died?

A. No: I staid there some ten minutes after this was said; and the doctor who was there said he was dead.

Boston Corbett

Testimony Before the Military Commission

The man who shot Booth was Sergeant Boston Corbett (b. 1832) of the 16th New York Cavalry. He acted on his own, for, as Everton Conger told his superiors afterwards, the cavalrymen surrounding Booth "had no orders to fire or not to fire." Born in England, Corbett had worked as a hatter in Troy, New York, and may have suffered from mercury poisoning. After the death of his wife and stillborn daughter, Corbett became a street-corner evangelist. When he was tempted one evening by the importuning of two prostitutes, he returned to his room and castrated himself with a pair of scissors. Corbett enlisted in 1861, was taken prisoner in 1864, and survived several months in the hellish prison camp at Andersonville, Georgia. He would eventually receive $1,653.85 of the federal reward money offered for apprehending Booth and Herold (Conger was awarded $15,000). Corbett continued preaching but became increasingly fearful that Confederate sympathizers would kill him. Nearly penniless, he moved to Kansas, worked a homestead, and became a doorkeeper in the state legislature. In February 1887 Corbett drew a revolver and threatened sinful lawmakers with divine retribution until the police disarmed him. Committed to an asylum, "Lincoln's avenger" escaped the following year and disappeared.

SERGEANT BOSTON CORBETT,

a witness called for the prosecution, being duly sworn, testified as follows:—

By the JUDGE ADVOCATE:

Q. Lieutenant-Colonel Conger has just detailed to the Court all the circumstances connected with the pursuit and capture and killing of Booth, in which, I believe, you were engaged. I will ask you what part you took, not in the pursuit, but in the capture and killing of Booth, taking up the narrative at the point when you arrived at the house.

A. When we rode up to the house, my commanding officer, Lieutenant Doherty, as we were standing in the road, rode up to me, and told me that Booth was in that house, saying, "I want you to deploy the men right and left around the house, and see that no one escapes." That was done: the men were deployed around the house. After making inquiries at the house, it was found that Booth was not in the house, but in the barn. A guard was then left upon the house, and the main portion of the

men thrown around the barn, closely investing it, with orders to allow no
one to escape, but previously being cautioned to see that our arms were
in readiness for use. After being ordered to surrender, and told that the
barn would be fired in five minutes if he did not do so, Booth made many
replies. In the first place, he wanted to know who we took him for. He
said that his leg was broken, and what did we want with him? and he was
told that it made no difference. His name was not mentioned at all in the
whole affair; not giving them satisfaction to know whether we knew who
they were or not, any further than he was told that they must surrender,
and give themselves up as prisoners. He wanted to know where we would
take them if they would give themselves up as prisoners. He received no
satisfaction, but was told that he must surrender unconditionally, or else
the barn would be fired. The parley lasted much longer than the time first
set; probably, I should think, a full half-hour. I could not say whether it
was exactly that time, more or less; but it was time for many words to and
fro: he was positively declaring that he would not surrender. At one time
he made the remark, "Well, my brave boys, you can prepare a stretcher
for me;" and at another time, "Well, captain, make quick work of it; shoot
me through the heart!" or words to that effect; and thereby I knew that
he was perfectly desperate, and did not expect that he would surrender.
After a while, we heard the whispering of another person,—although he
[Booth] had previously declared that there was but one there, himself,—
who proved to be the prisoner Herold. Although we could not distinguish
the words, his object seemed to be to persuade Booth to surrender. After
hearing him, probably, a while, he sang out, "Certainly!" seeming to disdain to do it himself. Said he, "Cap., there is a man in here who wants to
surrender mighty bad." Then I suppose words followed inside that we
could not hear. Perhaps Herold thought he had better stand by him, or
something to that effect. Then Booth said, "Oh! go out, and save yourself,
my boy, if you can:" and then he said, "I declare before my Maker that this
man here is innocent of any crime whatever;" seeming willing to take all
the blame on himself, and trying to clear Herold. They were then told,
that, if both would not surrender, the surrender of one of them would be
accepted; and he was told to hand out his arms. Herold declared that he
had no arms; and Booth declared that the arms all belonged to him; that
the other man was unarmed. He was finally taken out without his arms.
Immediately after Herold being taken out, the detective, Mr. Conger,

came from that side of the barn where he had been taken out, around to the side where I was, and, passing me, set fire to the hay through one of the cracks of the boards, at the end of the same side of the barn where I was, a little to my right. I had previously said to Mr. Conger, though, and also to my commanding officer, that the position in which I stood left me in front of a large crack,—you might put your hand through it; and I knew that Booth could distinguish me and others through these cracks in the barn, and could pick us off if he chose to do so. In fact, he made a remark to that effect at one time. Said he, "Cap., I could have picked off three or four of your men already if I wished to do so. Draw your men off fifty yards, and I will come out," or such words. He used such words many times. When the fire was first lit, which was almost immediately after Herold was taken out of the barn, as the flame rose, he was seen. We could then distinguish him, apparently, I think, about the middle of the barn, turning towards the fire, either to put the fire out, or else to shoot the one who started it, I did not know which; but he was then coming right towards me, as it were, a little to my right,—a full front breast view. I could have shot him then much easier than the time I afterwards did; but as long as he was there, making no demonstration to hurt any one, I did not shoot him, but kept my eye upon him steadily. Finding the fire gaining upon him, he turned to the other side of the barn, and got towards where the door was; and, as he got there, I saw him make a movement towards the door. I supposed he was going to fight his way out. One of the men who was watching told me that he aimed the carbine at him. He was taking aim with the carbine, but at whom I could not say. My mind was upon him attentively to see that he did no harm; and, when I became impressed that it was time, I shot him. I took steady aim on my arm, and shot him through a large crack in the barn. When he was brought out, I found that the wound was made in the neck a little back of the ear, and came out a little higher up on the other side of the head. He lived, I should think, until about seven o'clock that morning: I could not say whether after or before, but near seven o'clock, one way or the other; perhaps two or three hours after he was shot. I did not myself hear him speak a word after he was shot, except a cry or shout as he fell. Others, who were near him, and watching him constantly, said that he did utter the words which were published. I did not hear him speak a word audibly after I shot him.

Q.   What time did he die?

A.   I think it was about seven o'clock.

Q.   Will you state whether or not you recognize the prisoner Herold as the man you took out of the barn?

A.   That is the man. [Pointing to David E. Herold, one of the prisoners.]

Q.   Did you know Booth before?

A.   No, sir: I had never seen him before; but I was perfectly satisfied from his first remarks that it was him; for my commanding officer told me, while on the boat coming down to Belle Plain, that his leg was broken; and, when he was summoned to surrender, his first reply was that his leg was broken, and he was alone. I knew also from his desperate replies that he would not be taken alive, and such remarks, that it was Booth. I knew that no other man would act in such a way.

Cross-examined by MR. STONE:

Q.   You say you judged from the conversation in the barn that Herold at first was anxious to surrender?

A.   Yes, sir.

Q.   And upon Booth refusing to surrender, he seemed, you judged, to desire to stay with him?

A.   I rather thought so.

Q.   It was after that that Booth made the declaration that you have mentioned?

A.   I cannot certainly say whether it was after or before; but I am very positive that he made the declaration that the man with him was innocent of any crime whatever; that he declared it before his Maker, using those words. I wish to state here, as improper motives have been imputed to me for the act I did, that I twice offered to my commanding officer, Lieutenant Doherty, and once to Mr. Conger, to go in the barn and take the man, saying that I was not afraid to go in and take him; it was less dangerous to go in and fight him than to stand before a crack, exposed to his fire, where I could not see him, although he could see me: but I was not sent in. Immediately when the fire was lit, our positions were reversed: I could see him, but he could not see me. It was not through fear at all that I shot him, but because it was my impression that it was time the man was shot; for I thought he would do harm to our men in trying to fight his way through that den if I did not.

Louis J. Weichmann

Testimony Before the Military Commission

With Booth dead and John Surratt still a fugitive, the government chose to try eight persons—Lewis Powell; David Herold; George Atzerodt; Mary Surratt; Samuel Mudd, the physician who set Booth's broken leg; Edman (Ned) Spangler, a stagehand at Ford's Theatre; and Samuel Arnold and Michael O'Laughlen, two friends of Booth from Baltimore—out of the hundreds who had been arrested during the assassination investigation. Attorney General James Speed considered the conspirators to be "secret active public enemies" who had committed offenses against the laws of war, and agreed with Stanton that they should be tried by a military tribunal. President Johnson concurred, and ordered the formation of a commission on May 1. Its nine members, all army officers, included Major General David Hunter, whose abolitionism early in the war had made him a hero to the Radical Republicans; Major General Lew Wallace, the future author of *Ben-Hur*, who spent much of his time at the trial drawing expert sketches of the accused; and Brigadier General August Kautz, who had led a division of African-American soldiers into Richmond the previous month. Joseph Holt, the army judge advocate general, headed the prosecution, and was assisted by John Bingham and Henry Burnett. The defendants were represented by seven civilian lawyers, including Reverdy Johnson, a Democratic senator from Maryland, and Thomas Ewing Jr., a former Union general and brother-in-law of William T. Sherman. (Some of the defense lawyers represented more than one defendant.) After rejecting a challenge to its jurisdiction, the commission began hearing testimony on May 12. The following day the prosecution called its most important witness. Louis Weichmann (or Wiechmann, 1842–1902) was a War Department clerk who had moved into Mary Surratt's Washington boardinghouse in November 1864. He had gone to the police on April 15 and subsequently provided testimony that linked Booth to Mary and John Surratt, Mudd, Atzerodt, Herold, and Powell, alias Payne. Under other circumstances, Weichmann might have been charged as a conspirator himself, but under the law as it stood in 1865, a defendant could not testify in a criminal case, and prosecutors needed his testimony. During his direct examination, Weichmann testified regarding Powell's visit to the Surratt house in March 1865, and under cross-examination by Reverdy Johnson, he described coming across a suspicious object belonging to Powell.

Q. Will you state whether you remember, some time in the month of March, of a man calling at Mrs. Surratt's, where you were boarding, and giving himself the name of Wood, and inquiring for John H. Surratt?

A.   Yes, sir: I myself went to open the door; and he inquired for Mr. Surratt. I told him Mr. Surratt was not at home; but I would introduce him to the family if he desired it. He thereupon expressed a desire to see Mrs. Surratt; and I accordingly introduced him, having first asked his name. He gave the name of Wood.

Q.   Do you recognize him among these prisoners?

A.   That is the man (pointing to Lewis Payne, one of the accused).

Q.   He called himself Wood?

A.   Yes, sir.

Q.   How long did he remain with Mrs. Surratt?

A.   That evening, he stopped in the house all night. He had supper served up to him in my own room. I brought him supper from the kitchen.

Q.   When was that?

A.   As near as I can remember, it must have been about eight weeks previous to the assassination. I have no exact knowledge of the date.

Q.   Did he bring any baggage with him to the house?

A.   No, sir. He had a black overcoat on, and a black frock-coat, with gray pants, at that time.

Q.   You say he remained until the next day?

A.   He remained until the next morning, leaving in the earliest train for Baltimore.

Q.   Do you remember whether, some weeks after this, the same man called again?

A.   I should think it was about three weeks afterwards that he called again; and I again went to the door, and again ushered him into the parlor: and, in the mean time, I had forgotten his name, and I asked him his name. That time he gave the name of Payne.

Q.   Was it the same man?

A.   Yes, sir.

Q.   Did he have an interview then with Mrs. Surratt?

A.   He was ushered into the parlor. Mrs. Surratt, Miss Surratt, and Miss Honora Fitzpatrick, were present.

Q.   How long did he remain?

A.   He remained about three days at that time. He represented himself as a Baptist preacher: he also said that he had been in prison in Baltimore for about a week, and that he had taken the oath of allegiance, and was going to become a good and loyal citizen.

Q. Are not the family of Mrs. Surratt and Mrs. Surratt herself Catholics?

A. Yes, sir. Mr. Surratt is himself a Catholic, and was a student of divinity at the same college.

Q. Did you hear any explanation made why a Baptist preacher should go there seeking hospitality?

A. No, sir. They only looked upon it as odd, and laughed at it. Mrs. Surratt herself remarked that he was a great looking Baptist preacher.

Q. Did they not seem to recognize him as the "Wood" of former days who had been there?

A. Yes, sir. In the course of conversation, one of the young ladies called him Wood; and then I recollected, that, on his first visit, he had given the name of Wood.

Q. How was he dressed on the last occasion?

A. He was dressed in gray,—a complete suit of gray.

Q. Did he have any baggage with him on the last occasion?

A. Yes, sir. He had a linen coat, and two linen shirts.

Q. Did you observe any traces of disguise about him, or attempted preparations for disguise?

A. I would say, that one day, returning from my office, I found a false mustache on the table in my room. I took the mustache, and threw it into a little toilet-box I had on the table. This man Payne searched around the table, and inquired for his mustache. I was sitting on the chair, and did not say any thing. I have retained the mustache since, and it was found in my baggage: it was among a box of paints that I had in my trunk.

Q. Did you ever see Payne during that visit, and John H. Surratt, together in their room by themselves?

A. Yes, sir.

Q. What were they occupied with doing?

A. It was on the same day. On returning from my office, I went up stairs to the third story; and I found John H. Surratt and this man Payne seated on a bed, playing with bowie-knives. It was the occasion of Payne's last visit.

Q. Were there any other weapons about them?

A. Two revolvers, and four sets of new spurs.

Q. You say you found upon your own table a false mustache. What was the color of the hair?

A. It was black.

Q. Was it a large or diminutive mustache?

A. It was about a medium-sized mustache. It was not a very small one, nor was it what I would call a very large one.

Q. Was it so large that it would entirely change the appearance of the wearer?

A. Yes, sir.

Q. You think it was?

A. I think so.

Q. You took that off the table where you found it; and you put it in your own box, where you had your paints?

A. Yes, sir: I put it first in my toilet-box, a box standing on the table; and afterwards removed it from that box, and put it in a box of paints which was in my trunk.

Q. And you have kept it ever since?

A. Yes, sir.

Q. When he came home, as I understood you, he seemed to be feeling for something; said he had lost something. Did he not ask for the mustache?

A. Yes, sir: he said, "Where is my mustache?"

Q. Why did you not give it to him? It was not yours.

A. No, sir: it was not mine.

Q. Why did you not give it to him? Did you suspect him at that time of intending any thing wrong?

A. I thought it rather queer that a Baptist preacher should use a mustache; and I did not care about having false mustaches lying around on my table.

Q. But you locked it up?

A. I know I locked it up.

Q. What did you intend to do with it?

A. I did not intend to do any thing with it. I took it, and exhibited it to some of the clerks in the office the day afterwards, and was fooling with it. I put on a pair of spectacles and the mustache, and was making fun of it.

Q. Your only reason for not giving it to him, when he said it was his, was, that you thought it was singular that a Baptist preacher should be fooling with a mustache?

A.   Yes, sir; and I did not want a false mustache about my room.

Q.   It would not have been about your room if you had given it to him, would it?

A.   No, sir.

Q.   That would have taken it out of your room; but, to keep it out of your room, you locked it up in a box, and kept the box with you?

A.   Then, again, I thought no honest person had any reason to wear a false mustache.

John M. Lloyd

Testimony Before the Military Commission

A former policeman in the District of Columbia, John M. Lloyd (1824–1892) had rented the tavern in Surrattsville (now Clinton), Maryland, from Mary Surratt in the fall of 1864. Lloyd was arrested on April 18 by Union officials who suspected that he knew something about the conspiracy. When a detective working for the Washington provost marshal urged him to "make a clean breast of the whole matter" for his family's sake, Lloyd replied, "My God, they will kill me if I implicate them," and then confessed. As in the case of Louis Weichmann, Lloyd was fortunate that the prosecution chose to make him a witness rather than a defendant. Under direct examination on May 13 he told a story that, if left unimpeached, would send Mary Surratt to the gallows.

JOHN M. LLOYD,

a witness called for the prosecution, being duly sworn, testified as follows: —

By the JUDGE ADVOCATE:

Q. Where do you reside?

A. I have been residing at Mrs. Surratt's tavern, Surrattsville.

Q. In what business are you engaged there?

A. Hotel-keeping and farming.

Q. Were you acquainted with John H. Surratt.

A. I have had a very small acquaintance with him since about the 1st of December last; not much previous to that.

Q. Do you know the prisoner Herold?

A. I know Herold. He has been in my house several times.

Q. Do you know the prisoner Atzerodt?

A. Yes, sir.

Q. Will you state whether or not, some five or six weeks before the assassination of the President, any or all of these men about whom I have inquired came to your house?

A. They were there.

Q. All three together?

A. Yes: John H. Surratt, Herold, and Atzerodt were there together.

Q. What did they bring to your house? and what did they do there?

A. When they drove up there in the morning, John H. Surratt and Atzerodt came first: they went from my house, and went towards T. B.,—a post-office kept about five miles below there. They had not been gone more than half an hour when they returned with Herold: then the three were together,—Herold, Surratt, and Atzerodt.

Q. What did they bring to your house?

A. I saw nothing until they all three came into the bar-room. I noticed one of the buggies—the one I supposed Herold was driving or went down in—standing at the front gate. All three of them, when they came into the bar-room, drank, I think; and then John Surratt called me into the front parlor, and on the sofa were two carbines with ammunition. I think he told me they were carbines.

Q. Any thing besides the carbines and ammunition?

A. There was a rope, and also a monkey-wrench.

Q. How long a rope?

A. I cannot tell. It was in a coil,—a right smart bundle,—probably sixteen or twenty feet.

Q. Were those articles left at your house?

A. Yes, sir. Surratt asked me to take care of them, to conceal the carbines. I told him there was no place there to conceal them, and I did not wish to keep such things in the house.

Q. You say that he asked you to conceal those articles for him?

A. Yes, sir: he asked me to conceal them. I told him there was no place to conceal them. He then carried me into a room that I had never been in, which was just immediately above the storeroom, as it were in the back building of the house. I had never been in that room previous to that time. He showed me where I could put them underneath the joists of the house,—the joists of the second floor of the main building. This little unfinished room will admit of any thing between the joists.

Q. Were they put in that place?

A. They were put in there according to his directions.

Q. Were they concealed in that condition?

A. Yes, sir: I put them in there. I stated to Colonel Wells, through mistake, that Surratt put them there; but I put them in there myself. I carried the arms up myself.

Q. How much ammunition was there?

A. One cartridge-box.

Q. For what purpose, and for how long, did he ask you to keep those articles?

A. I am very positive that he said he would call for them in a few days. He said he just wanted them to stay for a few days, and he would call for them.

Q. What kind of carbines were they?

A. I did not examine them: they had covers over them.

Q. Will you state whether or not, on the Monday or Tuesday preceding the assassination of the President, Mrs. Surratt came to your house?

A. I was coming to Washington, and I met Mrs. Surratt at Union-town on the Monday previous.

Q. Did she say any thing to you in regard to those carbines?

A. When she first broached the subject to me, I did not know what she had reference to: then she came out plainer; and I am quite positive she asked me about the "shooting-irons." I am quite positive about that, but not altogether positive. I think she named "shooting-irons," or something to call my attention to those things; for I had almost forgotten about their being there. I told her that they were hid away far back; that I was afraid the house would be searched, and they were shoved far back. She told me to get them out ready: they would be wanted soon.

Q. Was her question to you, first, whether they were still there? or what was it?

A. Really, I cannot recollect the first question she put to me. I could not do it to save my life.

Q. Was it so indistinct, that you did not understand what was meant?

A. It was put in a manner as if she wanted to draw my attention to something so that anybody else could not understand. Finally she came out bolder with it.

Q. And said they would be wanted soon?

A. Yes, sir.

Q. And then she said they would be wanted soon?

A. Yes, sir. I told her at the same time that I had an idea of having them buried; that I was very uneasy about having them there.

Q. Will you state now whether or not, on the evening of the night on which the President was assassinated, Mrs. Surratt came to your house with Mr. Weichmann?

A.   I went to Marlboro' on that day to attend a trial there in court; and in the evening it was probably late when I got home. I found Mrs. Surratt there when I got home. I should judge it was about five o'clock.

Q.   What did she say to you?

A.   She met me out by the wood-pile as I drove in, having fish and oysters in the buggy; and she told me to have those shooting-irons ready that night,—there would be some parties call for them.

Q.   Did she ask you to get any thing else ready for those parties besides the shooting-irons?

A.   She gave me something wrapped up in a piece of paper. I did not know what it was till I took it up stairs; and then I found it to be a field-glass.

Q.   Did she ask you to have any whiskey prepared for them?

A.   She did.

Q.   What did she say about that?

A.   She said to get two bottles of whiskey also.

Q.   And said they were to be called for that night?

A.   Yes: they were to be called for that night.

Q.   State now whether they were called for that night by Booth and Herold.

A.   The carbines and ammunition were called for that night; but the whiskey was not. They drank what whiskey they wanted out of the bottle, and did not carry any bottles of whiskey with them.

Q.   When they came there, did they ask for the carbines?

A.   They did not ask for the carbines. Booth did not come in: Herold came in.

Q.   At what time was that?

A.   Just about midnight, I think, on Friday night: not over a quarter-past twelve o'clock. I did not know Booth; the person was a stranger to me; he remained on his horse. Herold came into the house and got a bottle of whiskey, and took it out to him; and Herold drank some out of a glass, I think, before he went out.

Q.   Do you remember in what terms Booth asked you for that whiskey?

A.   I think he did not ask for the whiskey. He might possibly have asked for something to drink; but he called for the carbines in such terms that I understood what he wanted. He told me, "Lloyd, for God's sake, make haste and get those things!" He might have included whiskey and all for what I know.

Q. He had not before that said to you what "those things" were?

A. He had not.

Q. Did he not seem, from the manner of his language, to suppose that you already understood what he called for?

A. From the way he spoke, he must have been apprised that I already knew what I was to give him.

Q. What did you say?

A. I did not make any reply, but went up stairs and got them.

Q. Did you not give him all the articles, — the field-glass and the monkey-wrench and the rope?

A. No: the rope and monkey-wrench were not what I was told to give him. I gave him such things as I was told to give by Mrs. Surratt.

Q. She told you to give him the carbines and whiskey and field-glass?

A. Yes, sir; and the whiskey they did not take with them.

Q. How long did they remain at your house?

A. I do not think they were over five minutes.

Q. Did they take one or both of the carbines?

A. Only one.

Q. Did they explain why the other was not taken?

A. Booth said that he could not take his, because his leg was broken.

Q. Did he take a drink also?

A. He drank while he was sitting out on his horse.

Q. Did Herold carry the bottle out to him?

A. Yes, sir.

Q. Did they say any thing in regard to the assassination as they rode away?

A. Just as they were about leaving, the man who was with Herold [Booth] said, "I will tell you some news if you want to hear it," or something to that effect. I said, "I am not particular: use your own choice about telling news."—"Well," said he, "I am pretty certain that we have assassinated the President and Secretary Seward." I think that was his language as well as I can recollect: "We have assassinated" or "killed the President and Secretary Seward."

Q. Did he say that in Herold's presence?

A. I am not positive now whether Herold was present at the time he said that, or whether he was across the street. Herold rode across the street towards the stable. I was so much excited and unnerved at it, that I did not know whether it was said in Herold's presence or not. Herold, as soon as he rode back to where we were, got right between me and this other man, and rode off.

Richard C. Morgan

Testimony Before the Military Commission

Mary Surratt avoided arrest in the early hours of April 15 when Washington police came to her boardinghouse looking for her absent son. Acting on a tip from Surratt's African-American servant Susan Mahoney about suspicious visitors on the night of the assassination, investigators from the War Department searched the house and arrested its inhabitants on the night of April 17. During the search Mary Surratt aroused suspicion when Lewis Powell showed up at her home and she claimed not to know him. Her unconvincing assertions quickly led to her detention. Richard C. Morgan, chief clerk to Colonel Henry Olcott, one of Stanton's lead investgators, was a member of the search party.

R. C. MORGAN,

a witness called for the prosecution, being duly sworn, testified as follows:—

By the JUDGE ADVOCATE:

Q. State whether or not, on the 17th or 18th of April last, you were in the service of the Government here, and in what capacity.

A. I was in the service of the War Department, acting under the orders of Colonel Olcott, special commissioner of that department.

Q. Will you state whether, on one or both those days, you had possession of the house of the prisoner, Mrs. Surratt, in this city?

A. Yes, sir.

Q. State where that house is.

A. 541 H Street, in Washington City.

Q. State under what circumstances you took possession of the house, and what occurred while you were there.

A. About twenty minutes past eleven o'clock on the evening of the 17th of April, Colonel Olcott gave me instructions to go to the house, 541 H Street, Mrs. Surratt's, and superintend the seizing of papers and the arrest of the inmates of the house. I proceeded down there; arrived there about half-past eleven o'clock; had been there about ten minutes; found Major Smith, Captain Wermerskirch, and some other officers, who had arrested the inmates of the house; and they were in the parlor: they were about ready to go up. I had sent out an order for a carriage to take up the women found in the house; and I heard a knock and a ring at the door: at the same time, Captain Wermerskirch and myself stepped forward, and opened the door. When we opened the door, the prisoner Payne [pointing to Lewis Payne] came in with a pickaxe over his shoulder, dressed in a gray coat, gray vest, black pants, and a hat made out of, I should judge, the sleeve of a shirt or the leg of a drawer. As soon as he came in, I immediately closed the door. Said he, "I guess I am mistaken." Said I, "Whom do you want to see?" "Mrs. Surratt," said he. "You are right: walk in." He took a seat; and I asked him what he came there at this time of night for. He said he came to dig a gutter: Mrs. Surratt had sent for him. I asked him when. He said, "In the morning." I asked him when she had sent for him; where he last worked. He said, "Sometimes on I Street." I asked him where he boarded. He said he had no boarding-house; he was a poor man, who got his living with the pick. I put my hand on the pickaxe while talking to him. Said I, "How much do you make a day?" — "Sometimes nothing at all, sometimes a dollar, sometimes a dollar and a half." Said I, "Have you any money?" — "Not a cent." I asked him why he came at this time of night to go to work. He said he simply called to find what time he should go to work in the morning. I asked him if he had any previous acquaintance with Mrs. Surratt. He said, "No." Then I asked him why she had selected him. He said she knew he was working around the neighborhood and was a poor man, and came to him. I asked him how old he was. He said, "About twenty." I asked him where he was from. He said he was from Fauquier County, Va. Previous to this, he pulled out an oath of allegiance; and on the oath of allegiance was "Lewis Payne, Fauquier County, Va." I asked him if he was from the South. He said he was. I asked him when he left there. "Some time ago." He said, I think, two months ago; in the month of February, I think he said. I asked him what he left for. He said he would have to go into the army; and he preferred earning his living by the pickaxe. I asked him if he could read. He said, "No." I asked him if he could write. He said, "He could manage to write his name."

Q.   Is that the pickaxe which he had on his shoulder? [Submitting a pickaxe to the witness.]

A.   Yes, sir.

[The pickaxe was offered in evidence without objection.]

I then told him he would have to go up to the Provost Marshal's office, and explain. He moved at that, and did not answer. The carriage had returned then that had taken off the women; and I ordered Thomas Samson and Mr. Rosch to take him up to the Provost Marshal's office. He was taken up by these two officers, and then searched. I then proceeded, with Major Smith and Captain Wermerskirch, to search through the house for papers; and remained there until three o'clock in the morning, searching for papers.

Q.   Had Mrs. Surratt left before he came in, or afterwards?

A.   No: they were all prepared to leave, in the parlor. Mrs. Surratt was directed to get the bonnets and shawls of the rest of the persons in the house, so that they could not communicate with each other. She did so; and they were just ready to go, and had started, as we opened the door, and heard the knock; and we passed them out at the time we let him within. He just got in before they stepped out.

Q.   She did not see him, then, before she left?

A.   Yes, sir: she must have seen him as she passed out; for, just as she was passing out, he passed right in.

Q.   You had no conversation with her in regard to him?

A.   No, sir.

Henry W. Smith

Testimony Before the Military Commission

A staff officer at the headquarters of the Department of Washington, Henry W. Smith (1836–1869) led the party that seized the Surratt house and detained Lewis Powell. Within hours of his arrest, Powell was identified by William Bell, a servant at the Seward residence, and by Augustus Seward as the man who had tried to kill the secretary of state. In the excerpts printed below, Smith answers questions from the prosecution, from Mary Surratt's attorney Frederick A. Aiken, and from both the prosecution and Aiken.

MAJOR H. W. SMITH,
a witness called for the prosecution, being duly sworn, testified as follows:—

By the JUDGE ADVOCATE:

Q. State whether or not, on the night of the 17th of April last, you were at the office of the Provost Marshal of this city, when the prisoner Mrs. Surratt was brought there, and the prisoner Payne.

A. I was not.

Q. Did you see them there afterwards?

A. No, sir.

Q. Were you at Mrs. Surratt's house while it was in the occupation of the authorities?

A. Yes, sir: I was in charge of the party that took possession of the house.

Q. Did you make any inquiry of her in regard to him?

A. After questioning Payne in regard to his occupation, and what business he had at the house that night, he stated that he was a laborer; that he came there to dig a gutter at the request of Mrs. Surratt. I stepped to the door of the parlor, and said, "Mrs. Surratt, will you step here a minute?" Mrs. Surratt stepped there. Said I, "Do you know this man?" She said, raising her right hand, "Before God, sir, I do not know this man; and I have never seen him." I then placed Payne under arrest, and told him he was so suspicious a character, that I would send him to Colonel Wells's or General Augur's headquarters for further examination.

Q. He was standing in full view of her when she said so?

A. Yes, sir; within three paces of her.

Q. That was Mrs. Surratt, the prisoner at the bar?

A. Yes, sir: if the lady will raise her veil, I can be certain. [Mary E. Surratt then raised her veil, which had covered her face.] The prisoner at the bar is the person.

————————

Q. What was transpiring in the house at the time Mrs. Surratt made the asseveration to which you refer in regard to her knowledge of Payne?

A. The man Payne had just come in at the front door; and I was questioning him at the time in regard to what he was; what his profession was, if he had any; and what business he had, at that hour of the night, to come to a private house.

Q. How was Payne dressed at that time?

A. Payne was dressed in a gray coat, black pantaloons, and rather a fine pair of boots. He had on his head a gray shirt-sleeve, hanging over at the side.

Q. A shirt-sleeve on his head?

A. Yes, sir: a cut shirt.

Q. Were his pantaloons tucked into his boots?

A. Yes, sir: they were rolled up over the tops of them, on one leg only, I believe.

Q. He did not strike you at that time as being a gentleman from his looks and appearance?

A. Not particularly so.

Q. His appearance was in no wise genteel?

A. Not at all.

Q. Is it your opinion that any one would recognize a person in that garb, in that dress, who had seen him, if he ever did see him, well dressed, with such a thing as that on his head?

A. That, to the best of my belief, was the thing, the sleeve he had on his head at the time he was arrested, the end similar to a tassel.

Q. Do you think you would recognize a person fixed up in that way, with that shirt-sleeve on his head, and a pickaxe?

A. I most certainly should.

Q. A person you had been in the habit of seeing dressed genteelly?

A. Certainly.

Q. When you called to Mrs. Surratt to come and look at Payne, who had just entered the house, you say she was seated in the parlor?

A. Yes, sir.

Q. Did you ask her directly whether she knew this man, or had seen him before?

A. I did immediately. I said, "Mrs. Surratt, will you please step to the door?" She stepped to the door; and I said, "Do you know this man? and did you hire him to come and dig a gutter for you?" As I said before, she raised her right hand, and said, "Before God, I do not know this man, and have never seen him, and did not hire him to dig a gutter for me."

Q. Did he make any remark?

A. He said nothing; but I immediately arrested him.

By Mr. Aiken:

Q. Mrs. Surratt did not attempt to evade the question in any way?

A. No, sir: her answer was direct.

Q. Was it light in the hall at that time?

A. Yes, sir: very light. The gas was turned on at full head.

James Lusby

Testimony Before the Military Commission

For Mary Surratt to have any hope of acquittal, her defense needed to discredit tavernkeeper John Lloyd's damning testimony about her visit to Surrattsville on April 14 (see pp. 96–101 in this volume). After having failed to effectively challenge him on cross-examination, the defense called four witnesses who variously described Lloyd as having been "drinking right smartly," "pretty tight," "influenced by liquor," and, in the words of James Lusby, "very drunk, I think," on the day in question. In his cross-examination of Lusby, an acquaintance of Lloyd's who had traveled with him from Marlboro to Surrattsville on the evening of the 14th, assistant judge advocate John Bingham sought to establish which of the two men had been drinking the most liquor.

Q. You say Lloyd was drunk?

A. I should call him drunk.

Q. How do you know he was drunk?

A. I have seen him before.

Q. How do you know he was drunk?

A. I thought so from his looks.

Q. Did you see him drink?

A. Yes, sir: I had taken drinks with him.

Q. Which drank the most?

A. I never measured mine.

Q. Do you think you were as tight as he was, or not?

A. Not quite, I think: I do not know.

Q. Do you think you were even with Lloyd after you got up there and got your drink?

A. I never try to keep even with any person when I am drinking.

Q. But you had the advantage: you drank by yourself while he went around by the kitchen.

A. Then I might.

Q. Do you think you got up with him then?

A. I do not know.

Q. You do not know which then was best off?

A. No, sir.

Q. Are you not mistaken altogether as to the man that was drunk on that day?

A. I do not understand you.

Q. Are you sure you know which of you it was, you or Lloyd, that was drunk?

A. I think Lloyd was very drunk, myself.

Q. But you think you were drunk too?

A. No: I do not think I was drunk.

Q. I thought you said you got drunk too?

A. I did not say I was drunk. I said I had been drinking, and that I had taken drinks with Lloyd.

Q. And drank without him?

A. I reckon I drank right smart before I met him, in the course of the day. I was not with him all day long.

Q. You kept drinking all that day?

A. I was summoned on a trial; and, after the Court adjourned, I had taken one or two glasses.

Frederick Stone

Argument for David Herold

It is unlikely that any defense attorney could have delivered a closing argument that would have saved David Herold from a guilty verdict. In the end, Frederick Stone (1820–1899), a prominent lawyer from Charles County, Maryland, did not attend the trial on June 19 and had his statement in Herold's defense read for him by a court reporter. Stone argued that, under martial law, murder charges in the District of Columbia were still tried in civil court, and that the justification for martial law had ended with the surrender of the last Confederate armies. Although he conceded that Herold had assisted Booth in evading arrest, Stone asserted that none of the evidence proved that Herold had aided and abetted in either Lincoln's assassination or the attack on Seward. In the most evocative portion of his plea, Stone sought to portray his client as a simple youth exploited by a master manipulator.

But what guilt in this case is the flight of Herold evidence of? He is found with Booth, and his flight in this case is not only evidence, but constitutes the guilt that he has acknowledged; it constitutes the guilt of his aiding in the escape of Booth, but no more. It by no means follows, because he aided Booth to escape, that he aided him to kill the President. It is bad reasoning to conclude that because he was guilty of one crime he was guilty of others.

But it may be asked, why did he leave in the dead hour of the night with a murderer? A slight glance at the relative character of the two men may explain this difficulty. John Wilkes Booth, as appears from all the evidence in this case, was a man of determined and resolute will, of pleasing, fascinating manners, and one who exercised great influence and control over the lower orders of men with whom he was brought in contact. He was a man of means, quite a prominent actor, fine in personal appearance and manners, and an adept in athletic and manly exercises. All the force of his mind, all his means, and his time in the winter of 1865, were devoted to get agents to aid in his desperate enterprise. In his search he met with Herold, then out of employment, and he at once marked him for his own.

Who is Herold, and what does the testimony disclose him to be? A weak, cowardly, foolish, miserable boy. On this point there is no conflict.

Dr. McKim, who probably knew him best, and in whose employ he had been, declares that his mind was that of a boy of eleven years of age, although his age actually was about 22—not naturally vicious, but weak, light, trifling, easily persuaded, good tempered, ready to laugh and applaud, and ready to do the bidding of those around him. Such a boy was only wax in the hands of a man like Booth.

But though Booth exercised unlimited control over this miserable boy, body and soul, he found him unfit for deeds of blood and violence; he was cowardly; he was too weak and trifling; but still he could be made useful. He knew some of the roads through Lower Maryland, and Booth persuaded him to act as guide, foot-boy, companion. This accounts for their companionship.

There is one piece of evidence introduced by the Government that should be weighed by the Commission. It is the declaration of Booth, made at the time of his capture: "I declare, before my Maker, that this man is innocent." Booth knew well enough, at the time he made that declaration, that his hours, if not his minutes, were numbered. In natures the most depraved, there seems to be left some spark of a better humanity, and this little remnant of a better nature urged Booth to make that declaration while it was yet time to do so. What did he mean by that declaration? Not that Herold was not guilty of the act of aiding and assisting him (Booth) to escape; but what he did mean, and what he tried to convey, was, that Herold was guiltless of the stain of blood being upon his hands, either as an accessory before the fact to the murder of the President, or as an aider and abettor in that murder, or any other deed of violence. That is what he meant.

William E. Doster

Argument for Lewis Powell

A graduate of Harvard Law School who had commanded the 4th Pennsylvania Cavalry during the Gettysburg campaign, William E. Doster (1837–1919) began his closing argument by conceding that Lewis Powell had attacked the secretary of state and that his client was not "within the medical definition of insanity." Doster's attempt to mount an insanity defense had failed when four physicians examined Powell and pronounced him sane, based on his general mental state and on his ability to give similar answers to repeated questions. Unable to plead innocence or insanity, Doster argued that Powell's crimes were the inevitable consequence of his background and experiences. Raised in a slaveowning Florida family, Powell had joined the Confederate army at sixteen and spent two years "in delirious charges, amid shot and shell, amid moaning wounded and stinking dead," before being captured at Gettysburg. In Doster's view, Powell was "the legitimate moral offspring of slavery, State Rights, chivalry, and delusion," and "any American that has been content to be a citizen of a slaveholding republic" was "part father of the assassin in this boy." Doster went even further in his defense, extolling his client's courage and self-sacrifice in a passage containing two quotations from *Julius Caesar*. Whatever slight chance Powell had of receiving mercy from the commission was almost certainly erased by the sudden death of Frances Adeline Seward, the wife of the secretary of state, on June 21.

Courage, then, martyrdom, inextinguishable hate for oppression, are his sins. Now, if courage be a crime, then have you and I, and all of us, who have braved death, been criminals? Then are the emblems of valor, which a grateful country has placed upon your shoulders and breasts, but marks of crime. Is readiness to be sacrificed for the common good a crime? Then are the millions of heroic youths, who have left the plow and girded on the sword for four years, but criminals; then is our banner but the flag of crime; then are our battlefields but loathsome scenes of general fratricidal murder. Is, then, undying hatred for what is believed to be oppression a crime? Then was our Revolution but successful crime. Then were the struggles of Tyrol, of Hungary, of Venice, of Greece, but unsuccessful crimes. Then was Byron a traitor to Greece, Garibaldi a traitor to Austria, Kossuth a traitor to Austria, Hofer a traitor to Austria, and Washington a traitor to England. Mark, throughout the history of the world, there is no lesson taught in clearer language than that the noblest deed of men is to free the world of oppressors. But I hear a student of history reply: True; but they must have been oppressors. Granted; but who is to be the judge? There can be no one but the assassin himself. It is he, and he only, who takes the risk of becoming a deliverer, or a foul and parricidal murderer. Let us, then, see what these people were, against whom he aimed his blow and what they appeared to him. In truth, if you seek for characters in history, you will find none further removed from the oppressors than our late President and the Secretary of State. The one was the great emancipator, the deliverer of a race from bondage, the great *salvator*, the deliverer of a nation from civil war. The other was the great pacificator, the savior from foreign war, the uniter of factions, the constant prophet and messenger of good will and peace. This is how they seemed to us; but such were they not in the eyes of this boy, or of five millions of his fellow-countrymen. To them, the one appeared a usurper of power, a violator of laws, a cruel jester, an invader, a destroyer of life, liberty and property; the other a cunning time-server, an adviser in oppression, and a slippery advocate of an irrepressible conflict. These Southern men had long borne power, and, in their obscurity, felt the envy for greatness which once cried:

> "Ye gods! It doth amaze us,
> A man of such a feeble temper should
> So get the start of the majestic world
> And bear the palm alone."
> * * * * *
> "Why man, he doth bestride the narrow world
> Like a colossus, and we petty men
> Walk under his huge legs, and peep about
> To find ourselves dishonorable graves."

This was his idea of Mr. Lincoln and Mr. Seward. This was what he heard in Florida, among the village politicians. This was what he read in the Richmond papers, in the orders of the generals, in the gossip of the camp-fire, in the letters that he got from home. Every farmer by whose well he filled his canteen told him that; every Southern lass that waved her handkerchief toward him repeated it; his mother in mourning told it; every prisoner returned from Northern prisons told it; every wayside cripple but confirmed it. Lincoln, the oppressor, was in the air, it was in the echo of the drum, it was in the whizzing of the shell, it came on every breeze that floated from the North. Wonderful was his error; strange, indeed, is it that charity and liberty should be thus misconstrued. Let us, then, remember that if he was wrong he erred on the side of courage, on the side of self-sacrifice, and on the side of hatred to what he believed to be oppression; that he differs from the Southern army simply because he surpassed it in courage; that he differed from a patriot and a martyr, simply because he was mistaken in his duty.

If, then, you praise men because they kill such as they believe oppressors, you must praise him; if you praise men who are ready to die for their country, you will praise him; and if you applaud those who show any courage superior to the rest of mankind you will applaud him.

William E. Doster

Argument for George Atzerodt

In the early hours of April 15 John Lee, an army detective sent to Kirkwood House to help protect Vice President Johnson, was told that a suspicious man had checked into the hotel the previous day. When Lee searched George Atzerodt's room, he discovered a revolver, a bowie knife, and a bank book belonging to John Wilkes Booth. Confronted with this evidence, as well as testimony from several witnesses linking Atzerodt to Booth, William E. Doster admitted that Atzerodt had conspired with Booth to capture Lincoln, but denied that his client had tried to kill Johnson. Furthermore, Doster characterized Atzerodt as a "noted," "notorious," and "well-known" coward, someone Booth could never have seriously considered using as an assassin.

———————

Adopting the theory that Atzerodt intended to murder, and lying in wait to murder, we are met at every step with denials. Thus, if he was lying in wait, why did he not stay at the Kirkwood House during the evening? Why did nobody see him lie in wait? Why did he come out of the Kirkwood at about ten minutes after ten without having tried to attack the Vice-President? Why did he not enter the room? Why, at 10:20, was he drinking at the Kimmell House? Why, in short, was he riding about town instead of waiting outside the Vice-President's room? There is only one theory that will make everything agree: Atzerodt backed out. He would have liked the money for capturing, but he did not like to be hung for murder. He never heard of murder before that evening at eight, or he would long before have hid himself. When he did hear it he had firmness enough to object. Coward conscience came to his rescue. But Booth threatened to kill, and he knew well enough he was the man to close the mouth of any one who troubled him. So he went off, driven like a poor frail being between irresolution and fear; took drinks, feigned to be doing his part, talked valiantly while the rum was in his throat, promised gloriously, galloped around fiercely, looked daggers, and when the hour struck did nothing and ran away. This, gentlemen, is the history in a small compass—*venit, videt, fugit*. He tried to become a hero, but he was only a coachmaker.

Look at the face of this impossible Brutus, and see whether you can see therein that he is —

"For dignity composed and high exploits."

Why, gentlemen, this hero, who, under the influence of cocktail courage, would capture Presidents and change the destinies of empires, is the same fleet-footed Quaker, famous in Port Tobacco for jumping out of windows in barroom fights; an excellent leader — of a panic, this son of arms who buries his knife in a gutter and revolves his revolvers into a greenback. Well might it have been said to Booth:

"O, Cassius, you are yoked to a lamb
    That carries anger as the flint bears fire;
    Who much enforced shows a hasty spark,
    And straight is cold again."

He has the courage of vanity and of folly. As long as he could be seen on intimate terms with Booth about hotels, it did his soul good to be so great a confederate; and as long as he could see a bold stroke by which he might suddenly change the coachmaker into a prince, he was, doubtless, brave. But when he heard of murder, conceived to himself his going into the Vice-President's room and stabbing him to the heart, the pigeon-liver asserted itself, the prince was gone, and the habits of the tavern-brawler re-appeared. Nor was he a natural boaster. He was simply the Curius of the conspiracy, who could neither keep his own secrets nor those of others; who was big with the portentous future, although he knew not what it was; who exchanged his wrath for a sudden prudence; and so as he imitated his prototype, "*Repente glorians maria montesque policeri cœpit,*" so he afterward imitated him by pointing out Booth, and informing, under the promise of mercy, upon his fellows. There is, then, no evidence whatever that he was "lying in wait to kill Mr. Johnson, with the intent, unlawfully and maliciously, to kill and murder him." There is only one other clause of the specification that deserves notice — the allegation that the lying in wait was "about the same hour of the night," viz.: Ten o'clock and fifteen minutes, on the evening of the 14th of April. Let us see, again, where the prisoner was at this time, 10:15. Fletcher says he came to Naylor's stable at ten. He then asked him whether he would have a drink. Fletcher said yes. They went down to Thirteen-and-a-half and E street, to the Union Hotel, and took a drink apiece; went back to the stable, and had some conversation about the mare. Meanwhile the boy had got the wrong horse, and had to go back and get the mare. Then they had some conversation about Herold. Then he rode down E, past Thirteen-and-a-half street, and finally came to the Kirkwood House. Fletcher says that he rode so slowly that he kept up with him. Now, believing what is improbable, that Fletcher did keep up with a man on horseback for three squares (for from Naylor's to the corner of Thirteen-and-a-half and E streets is one square, to Twelfth and E two squares, and to Twelfth and Pennsylvania avenue three squares), we are further obliged to believe that, in fifteen minutes, Atzerodt ordered a horse, walked two squares, waited for two drinks, paid for them, held two conversations, mounted, dismounted, had a horse changed, and, afterward, rode three squares so slowly that a hostler could follow him. It is not possible. At 10:15 Atzerodt was either not yet at the Kirkwood House, or else Mr. Fletcher made a mistake in his time. His course after this was as follows: Fletcher says he rode up D in the direction of Tenth; yet at this very time, about ten, McAllister says he came with his mare to the Kimmell House, "rode up to the door, and called the black boy out to hold his horse." Now, the Kimmell is on C street, near Four-and-a-half, and, of course, when he rode down D he went to the Kimmell.

Thus we now know what he was doing at the time Payne was at Mr. Seward's, and at the time Booth shot the President. He was riding round from bar-room to bar-room; and it is very plain he was now in liquor. He was half tight when Fletcher saw him, and yet took another drink with him. He went to the Kirkwood and took another drink; he went to the Kimmell and took another. Certainly, of getting drunk, of riding from tavern to tavern, of guzzling like a Falstaff, of having an inextinguishable thirst—of this he is guilty; but of lying in wait for the Vice-President at 10:15, we are paying him an undeserved compliment.

There is, therefore, no part of the specification proven, but the immediate contrary. During the whole of that evening, as far as the evidence throws any light on his conduct, instead of lying in wait near the Vice-President to murder him, he was standing over the different bars, from the Union House to the Kimmell, with the intent then and there, unlawfully and maliciously, to make Atzerodt drunk. Thus much of the specification.

There is one suggestion I will answer before I leave the specification. Why, if he was so cowardly, so halting, so irresolute a character, did Booth employ him? Booth employed him for an emergency which he was perfectly competent to meet. In the plot of the capture, the part assigned to the prisoner was to furnish the boat to carry the party over the Potomac. For this his experience in a seaport town fitted him. This required no resolution and no courage. For participation in the President's assassination he could never have been intended. Booth, as these men all agree, as his own conduct shows, was ambitious to carry off the glory of this thing. Payne says Booth remarked, he "wanted no botching with the President and Gen. Grant." As for the rest, therefore, of the Cabinet, he probably had no concern; he was far more interested in his own part than in others. When he, therefore, told Atzerodt to take charge of the Vice-President, he must have known that the prisoner had not the courage, and therefore did not care particularly whether he accomplished it or not, only so he himself could attain the desired immortal infamy. He wanted Atzerodt as the *Charon*, the ferryman of the capture, and, *after the failure*, reserved him for greater things, *the duties of Orcus*, which he was incompetent to perform.

Frederick A. Aiken

Argument for Mary Surratt

Senator Reverdy Johnson had joined Mary Surratt's defense early in the trial, but soon withdrew from the proceedings after becoming involved in a dispute over loyalty oaths with Brigadier General Thomas Harris, one of the commission members. The burden of defending Surratt fell on his junior partners John W. Clampitt and Frederick A. Aiken (1832–1878). In his closing statement, Aiken depicted key prosecution witnesses Louis Weichmann and John Lloyd as untrustworthy co-conspirators who were seeking to save themselves by implicating Surratt, and attributed her failure to recognize Lewis Powell on the night of April 17 to her poor eyesight. Aiken closed his argument by portraying his client as "a Christian mother" incapable of committing a heinous crime. Both the attorney and the commission were well aware that if the forty-two-year-old widow was convicted and sentenced to death, she would become the first woman ever to be executed by the federal government.

If any part of Lloyd's statements is true, and Mrs. Surratt did verily bear to his or Mrs. Offutt's hands the field-glass, enveloped in paper, by the evidence itself, we may believe she knew not the nature of the contents of the package; and, *had* she known, what evil could she, or any other, have attached to a commission of so common a nature? No evidence of individual or personal intimacy with Booth has been adduced against Mrs. Surratt; no long and apparently confidential interviews; no indications of a private comprehension mutual between them; only the natural, and not frequent, custom on the part of Booth—as any other associate of her son might and doubtless did do—of inquiring through the mother, whom he would request to see, of the son who, he would learn, was absent from home. No one has been found who could declare any appearance of the nursing or mysteriously discussing of anything like conspiracy within the walls of Mrs. Surratt's house. Even if the son of Mrs. Surratt, from the significancies of associations, is to be classed with the conspirators, if such body existed, it is monstrous to suppose that the son would weave a net of circumstantial evidences around the dwelling of his widowed mother, were he never so reckless and sin-determined; and that they (the mother and the son) joined hands in such dreadful pact, is more monstrous still to be thought.

A mother and son associate in crime! and such a crime as this half of the civilized world never saw matched, in *all* its dreadful bearings! Our judgments can have hardly recovered their unprejudiced poise since the shock of the late horrors, if we can contemplate with credulity such a picture, conjured by the unjust spirits of indiscriminate accusation and revenge. A crime which, in its public magnitude, added to its private misery, would have driven even the Atis-haunted heart of a Medici, a Borgia, or a Madame Bocarme to wild confession before its accomplishment, and daunted even *that* soul, of all the recorded world the most eager for novelty in license, and most unshrinking in sin—the indurated soul of Christina of Sweden; such a crime as profoundest plotters within padded walls would scarcely dare whisper; the words forming the expression of which, spoken aloud in the upper air, would convert all listening boughs to aspens, and all glad sounds of nature to shuddering wails. And *this* made known, even surmised, to a woman! a *mater familias*, the good genius, the *"placens uxor"* of a home where children had gathered all the influences of purity and the reminiscences of innocence, where RELIGION watched, and the CHURCH was MINISTER and TEACHER.

Who—were circumstantial evidence strong and conclusive, such as only time and the slow weaving fates could elucidate and deny—*who* will believe, when the mists of uncertainty which cloud the present shall have dissolved, that a woman born and bred in respectability and competence—a Christian mother, and a citizen who never offended the laws of civil propriety; whose unfailing attention to the most sacred duties of life has won for her the name of "a proper Christian matron;" whose heart was ever warmed by charity; whose door unbarred to the poor, and whose Penates had never cause to veil their faces;—who will believe that she could so suddenly and so fully have learned the intricate arts of sin? A daughter of the South, her life associations confirming her natal predilections, her individual preferences inclined, without logic or question, to the Southern people, but with no consciousness nor intent of *disloyalty* to her *Government*, and causing no exclusion from her friendship and active favors of the people of the loyal North, nor repugnance in the distribution among our Union soldiery of all needed comforts within her command, and on all occasions.

A strong but guileless-hearted woman, her maternal solicitude would have been the first denouncer, even abrupt betrayer, of a plotted crime in which one companion of her son could have been implicated, had cognizance of such reached her. Her days would have been agonized and her nights sleepless, till she might have exposed and counteracted that spirit of defiant hate which watched its moment of vantage to wreak an immortal wrong—till she might have sought the intercession and absolution of the Church, her refuge, in behalf of those she loved. The brains, which were bold, and crafty, and couchant enough to dare the world's opprobrium in the conception of a scheme which held as naught the lives of men in highest places, never imparted it to the intelligence, nor sought the aid nor sympathy of any living woman, who had not, like Lady Macbeth, "unsexed herself"—not though she were wise and discreet as Maria Theresa or the Castilian Isabella. *This woman knew it not.* This woman, who, on the morning preceding that blackest day in our country's annals, knelt in the performance of her most sincere and sacred duty at the confessional, and received the mystic rite of the Eucharist, knew it not. Not only would she have rejected it with horror, but such proposition, presented by the guest who had sat at her hearth as the friend and convive of her son, upon whose arm and integrity her widowed womanhood relied for solace and protection, would have roused her maternal wits to some sure cunning which would have contravened the crime and sheltered her son from the evil influences and miserable results of such companionship.

The mothers of Charles the IX and of Nero could harbor, underneath their terrible smiles, schemes for the violent and unshriven deaths, or the moral vitiation and decadence which would painfully and gradually remove lives sprung from *their own*, were they obstacles to their demoniac ambition. But *they* wrought their awful romances of crime in lands where the sun of supreme civilization, through a gorgeous evening of Syberitish luxury, was sinking, with red tents of revolution, into the night of anarchy and national caducity. In our own young nation, strong in its morality, energy, freedom, and simplicity, assassination can never be indigenous. Even among the desperadoes and imported lazzaroni of our largest cities, it is comparatively an infrequent cause of fear.

The daughters of women to whom, in their yet preserved abodes, the noble mothers who adorned the days of our early independence are vividly remembered realities and not haunting shades—the descendants of earnest seekers for liberty, civil and religious, of rare races, grown great in heroic endurance, in purity which comes of trial borne, and in hope born of conscious right, whom the wheels of Fortune sent hither to transmit such virtues—the descendants of *these* have no heart, no ear for the diabolisms born in hot-beds of tyranny and intolerance. No descendant of these, no woman of this temperate land could have seen, much less *joined*, her son, descending the sanguinary and irrepassable paths of treason and murder, to ignominious death, or an expatriated and attainted life, worse than the punishing wheel and bloody pool of the poets' hell.

In our country, where reason and moderation so easily quench the fires of insane hate, and where *"La Vendetta"* is so easily overcome by the sublime grace of forgiveness, no woman could have been found so desperate as to sacrifice all spiritual, temporal, and social good, self, offspring, fame, honor, and all the *desiderata* of life, and time, and immortality, to the commission, or even countenance, of such a deed of horror as we have been compelled to contemplate the two past months.

In a Christian land, where all records and results of the world's intellectual, civil and moral advancement mold the human heart and mind to highest impulses, the theory of old Helvetius is more probable than desirable.

The natures of all born in equal station are not so widely varied as to present extremes of vice and goodness, but by the effects of rarest and severest experience. Beautiful fairies and terrible gnomes do not stand by each infant's cradle, sowing the nascent mind with tenderest graces or vilest errors. The slow attrition of vicious associations and law-defying indulgences, or the sudden impetus of some terribly multiplied and social disaster, must have worn away the susceptibility of conscience and self respect, or dashed the mind from the height of these down to the deeps of despair and recklessness, before one of *ordinary* life could take counsel with violence and crime. In no such manner was the life of our client marked. It was the parallel of nearly all the competent masses; surrounded by the scenes of her earliest recollections, independent in her condition, she was satisfied with the *mundus* of her daily pursuits, and the maintenance of her own and children's *status* in society and her church.

Remember *your* wives, mothers, sisters and gentle friends, whose graces, purity and careful affection ornament and cherish and strengthen your lives. Not widely different from *their* natures and spheres have been the nature and sphere of the woman who sits in the prisoner's dock to-day, mourning with the heart of Alcestis her children and her lot; by whose desolated hearthstone a solitary daughter wastes her uncomforted life away in tears and prayers and vigils for the dawn of hope; and this wretchedness and unpitied despair have closed like a shadow around one of earth's common pictures of domestic peace and social comfort, by the one sole cause—suspicion fastened and fed upon the facts of acquaintance and mere fortuitous intercourse with that man in whose name so many miseries gather, the assassinator of the President.

Since the days when Christian tuition first elevated womanhood to her present free, refined and refining position, man's power and honoring regard have been the palladium of her sex.

Let no stain of injustice, eager for a sacrifice to revenge, rest upon the reputation of the men of our country and time.

This woman, who, widowed of her natural protectors; who, in helplessness and painfully severe imprisonment, in sickness and in grief ineffable, sues for justice and mercy from your hands, may leave a legacy of blessings, sweet as fruition-hastening showers, for those you love and care for, in return for the happiness of fame and home restored, though life be abbreviated and darkened through this world by the miseries of this unmerited and woeful trial. But long and chilling is the shade which just retribution, slow creeping on with its "*pede claudo*," casts around the fate of him whose heart is merciless to his fellows bowed low in misfortune and exigence.

Let all the fair womanhood of our land hail you with a pæon of joy that you have restored to her sex, in all its ranks, the ægis of impregnable legal justice which circumvallates and sanctifies the threshhold of home and the privacy of home life against the rude irruptions of arbitrary and perhaps malice-born suspicion, with its fearful attendants of arrest and incarceration, which in this case have been sufficient to induce sickness of soul and body.

Let not this first State tribunal in our country's history, which involves a woman's name, be blazoned before the world with the harsh tints of intolerance, which permits injustice. But as the benignant heart and kindly judging mind of the world-lamented victim of a crime which wound, in its ramifications of woe, around so many fates, would himself have counseled you, let the heralds of PEACE and CHARITY, with their wool-bound staves, follow the fasces and axes of JUDGMENT and LAW, and without the sacrifice of any innocent Iphigenia, let the ship of State launch with dignity of unstained sails into the unruffled sea of UNION and PROSPERITY.

John A. Bingham

Argument for the Prosecution

Special judge advocate John A. Bingham (1815–1900) began his closing statement for the government on June 27 with a lengthy legal argument justifying trying the defendants before a military commission. The following day he reviewed the evidence and restated a key element of the law: that all the parties to a conspiracy, whether or not they were present at the execution of a particular act, were "alike guilty of the several acts done by each in the execution of the common design." Bingham denied that there ever had been a plot to capture Lincoln and accused Jefferson Davis and seven Confederate agents in Canada of having conspired with Booth, John Surratt, and the defendants to kill the President. As evidence of the Confederate leader's guilt, Bingham cited the testimony of Lewis Bates, the North Carolina superintendent of the Southern Express Company, who had described Davis's response to the news of Lincoln's death. (Davis later denied that Bates was present when he learned of the assassination.) "When referring to the rebellion," an officer serving in the courtroom recalled, Bingham's "invective burned and seared like a hot iron." But when he spoke of the martyred President, as Bingham did when recalling the fatal moments in Ford's Theatre, "his lips would quiver with emotion, and his voice become as tender and reverent as if he were repeating the Lord's Prayer." In 1866, while serving in Congress as a Republican from Ohio, Bingham would help reshape the Constitution by drafting the first section of the Fourteenth Amendment. Two years later, while he was running for reelection, a heckler sought to unsettle him by shouting Mary Surratt's name. Bingham responded by telling the man to consult the trial record.

――――――――――

But there is one other item of testimony that ought, among honest and intelligent people at all conversant with this evidence, to end all further inquiry as to whether Jefferson Davis was one of the parties, with Booth, as charged upon this record, in the conspiracy to assassinate the President and others. That is, that on the fifth day after the assassination, in the city of Charlotte, North Carolina, a telegraphic dispatch was received by him, at the house of Mr. Bates, from John C. Breckinridge, his rebel Secretary of War, which dispatch is produced here, identified by the telegraph agent, and placed upon your record in the words following:

GREENSBORO', April 19, 1865.

His Excellency, President Davis:
President Lincoln was assassinated in the theater in Washington on

the night of the 14th inst. Seward's house was entered on the same night and he was repeatedly stabbed, and is probably mortally wounded.

"JOHN C. BRECKINRIDGE."

At the time this dispatch was handed to him, Davis was addressing a meeting from the steps of Mr. Bates' house, and after reading the dispatch to the people, he said: "If it were to be done, it were *better* it were well done." Shortly afterward, in the house of the witness, in the same city, Breckinridge, having come to see Davis, stated his regret that the occurrence had happened, because he deemed it unfortunate for the people of the South at that time. Davis replied, referring to the assassination, "Well, General, I don't know; if it were to be done at all, it were *better* that it were well done; and if the same had been done to Andy Johnson, the beast, and to Secretary Stanton, the job would then be *complete*."

Accomplished as this man was in all the arts of a conspirator, he was not equal to the task—as happily, in the good providence of God, no mortal man is—of concealing, by any form of words, any great crime which he may have meditated or perpetrated either against his Government or his fellow-men. It was doubtless furthest from Jefferson Davis' purpose to make confession. His guilt demanded utterance; that demand he could not resist; therefore his words proclaimed his guilt, in spite of his purpose to conceal it. He said, "If it were to be done, it were *better* it were *well done*." Would any man, ignorant of the conspiracy, be able to devise and fashion such a form of speech as that? Had not the President been murdered? Had he not reason to believe that the Secretary of State had been mortally wounded? Yet he was not satisfied, but was compelled to say, "it were *better* it were *well done*"—that is to say, all that had been agreed to be done had not been done. Two days afterward, in his conversation with Breckinridge, he not only repeats the same form of expression—"if it were to be done it were *better* it were *well done*"—but adds these words: "And if the same had been done to Andy Johnson, the beast, and to Secretary Stanton, the *job* would *then be complete*." He would accept the assassination of the President, the Vice-President, of the Secretary of State, and the Secretary of War, as a complete execution of the "job" which he had given out upon contract, and which he had "made all right," so far as the pay was concerned, by the dispatches he had sent to Thompson by Surratt, one of his hired assassins. Whatever may be the conviction of others, my own conviction is that Jefferson Davis is as clearly proven guilty of this conspiracy as is John Wilkes Booth, by whose hand Jefferson Davis inflicted the mortal wound upon Abraham Lincoln. His words of intense hate, and rage, and disappointment, are not to be overlooked—that the assassins had not done their work *well*; that they had not succeeded in robbing the people altogether of their Constitutional Executive and his advisers; and hence he exclaims, "If they had killed Andy Johnson, the beast!" Neither can he conceal his chagrin and disappointment that the War Minister of the Republic, whose energy, incorruptible integrity, sleepless vigilance, and executive ability had organized day by day, month by month, and year by year, victory for our arms, had escaped the knife of the hired assassins. The job, says this procurer of assassination, was not well done; it had been *better* if it had been well done! Because Abraham Lincoln had been clear in his great office, and had saved the nation's life by enforcing the nation's laws, this traitor declares he must be murdered; because Mr. Seward, as the foreign Secretary of the country, had thwarted the purposes of treason to plunge his country into a war with England, he must be murdered; because, upon the murder of Mr. Lincoln, Andrew Johnson would succeed to the Presidency, and because he had been true to the Constitution and Government, faithful found among the faithless of his own State, clinging to the falling pillars of the Republic when others had fled, he must be murdered; and because the Secretary of War had taken care by the faithful discharge of his duties, that the Republic should live and not die, he must be murdered. Inasmuch as these two faithful officers were not also assassinated, assuming that the Secretary of State was mortally wounded, Davis could not conceal his disappointment and chagrin that the work was not "well done," that the "job was not complete!"

Booth proceeded to the theater about nine o'clock in the evening, at the same time that Atzerodt, Payne and Herold were riding the streets, while Surratt, having parted with his mother at the brief interview in her parlor, from which his retreating steps were heard, was walking the avenue, booted and spurred, and doubtless consulting with O'Laughlin. When Booth reached the rear of the theater, he called Spangler to him (whose denial of that fact, when charged with it, as proven by three witnesses, is very significant), and received from Spangler his pledge to help him all he could, when with Booth he entered the theater by the stage door, doubtless to see that the way was clear from the box to the rear door of the theater, and look upon their victim, whose exact position they could study from the stage. After this view, Booth passes to the street, in front of the theater, where, on the pavement with other conspirators yet unknown, among them one described as a low-browed villain, he awaits the appointed moment. Booth himself, impatient, enters the vestibule of the theater from the front, and asks the time. He is referred to the clock, and returns. Presently, as the hour of ten approached, one of his guilty associates called the time; they wait; again, as the moments elapsed, this conspirator upon watch called the time; again, as the appointed hour draws nigh, he calls the time; and finally, when the fatal moment arrives, he repeats in a louder tone, "Ten minutes past ten o'clock." Ten minutes past ten o'clock! The hour has come when the red right hand of these murderous conspirators should strike, and the dreadful deed of assassination be done.

Booth, at the appointed moment, entered the theater, ascended to the dress-circle, passed to the right, paused a moment, looking down, doubtless to see if Spangler was at his post, and approached the outer door of the close passage leading to the box occupied by the President, pressed it open, passed in, and closed the passage door behind him. Spangler's bar was in its place, and was readily adjusted by Booth in the mortise, and pressed against the inner side of the door, so that he was secure from interruption from without. He passes on to the next door, immediately behind the President, and there stopping, looks through the aperture in the door into the President's box, and deliberately observes the precise position of his victim, seated in the chair which had been prepared by the conspirators as the altar for the sacrifice, looking calmly and quietly down upon the glad and grateful people whom by his fidelity he had saved from the peril which had threatened the destruction of their government, and all they held dear this side of the grave, and whom he had come upon invitation to greet with his presence, with the words still lingering upon his lips which he had uttered with uncovered head and uplifted hand before God and his country, when on the 4th of last March he took again the oath to preserve, protect and defend the

Constitution, declaring that he entered upon the duties of his great office "with malice toward none—with charity for all." In a moment more, strengthened by the knowledge that his co-conspirators were all at their posts, seven at least of them present in the city, two of them, Mudd and Arnold, at their appointed places, watching for his coming, this hired assassin moves stealthily through the door, the fastenings of which had been removed to facilitate his entrance, fires upon his victim, and the martyr spirit of Abraham Lincoln ascends to God.

> "Treason has done his worst; nor steel nor poison,
> Malice domestic, foreign levy, nothing
> Can touch him further."

The New York Times

End of the Assassins

On June 29 the nine-man military commission began its deliberations after adopting rules that made five votes necessary for a conviction and six for a death sentence. The next day they sent their verdicts under seal to President Johnson, who approved them on July 5. Stagehand Ned Spangler was found guilty of helping Booth escape from Ford's Theatre and was sentenced to six years in prison. Samuel Arnold and Michael O'Laughlen were found guilty of conspiracy and sentenced to life terms. (Both men had plotted with Booth to abduct Lincoln, but played no role in the attacks of April 14, although the government claimed that O'Laughlen had unsuccessfully stalked Ulysses S. Grant.) Samuel Mudd, whom the prosecution charged with being an active participant in the conspiracy who had met with Booth several times before the assassination, also received a life sentence. George Atzerodt, David Herold, Lewis Powell, and Mary Surratt were convicted and sentenced to death. Although five members of the commission signed an appeal asking for clemency for Surratt, it was not granted. (Johnson later claimed that Judge Advocate Holt never showed him the clemency request, a charge Holt vehemently denied.) Ten days after the executions, the surviving defendants were sent to Fort Jefferson, a military prison in the Dry Tortugas in the Gulf of Mexico, where O'Laughlen would die of yellow fever in 1867. Arnold, Mudd, and Spangler were pardoned by Johnson in 1869 shortly before he left the White House. In 1866 John Surratt was discovered serving in the papal guard in Rome under an assumed name. He fled to Egypt, but was arrested and returned to the United States. Surratt was tried in a civil court in the District of Columbia for the murder of President Lincoln. His lawyers presented evidence that Surratt had been in Elmira, New York, at the time of the assassination, having left Washington ten days before. The trial ended in a hung jury in August 1867, and Surratt was never retried.

Execution of Mrs. Surratt, Payne,
Herrold and Atzeroth.

Their Demeanor on Thursday Night and
Friday Morning.

Attempt to Release Mrs. Surratt
on a Writ of Habeas Corpus.

Argument of Counsel—Order of
the President.

SCENES AT THE SCAFFOLD.

The Four Hang Together and Die Simultaneously.

Interesting Incidents—Excitement in Washington—Order and Quiet in the City.

Special Dispatch to the New-York Times.

WASHINGTON, Friday, July 7, 1865.

The conspirators have gone to their long home, the swift hand of justice has smitten them, and they stand before the judgment seat. Electrified—saddened as the country was by the terrible calamity brought upon it by the damnable deeds of these deep-dyed villains, astounded as it has been by the daily revelations of the trial of the criminals, it was doubtless unprepared, as were all here, for the quick flash of the sword of power, whose blade to-day fell upon the guilty heads of the assassins of our lamented President.

Tried, convicted and sentenced, they stood this morning upon the threshold of the house of death, all covered with the great sin whose pall fell darkly upon the land. Young and old, equal in crime, they spent the night as is told hereafter, and when the first grey pencillings of the early morning traced the dawning day upon the sky, the city was all agog for the coming scene of retribution and of justice.

THE HABEAS CORPUS.

Mrs. SURRATT's friends have been constant and faithful. They have manipulated presses and created public sentiment. The papers received here to-day were singularly unanimous in the supposition that the President would commute the sentence of Mrs. SURRATT to imprisonment for life. Such a sentiment found no echo here. It was well known that the counsel, family and friends of the culprit were determined to make every exertion, to strain every nerve in a strong pull and tug at the tender heart of the President in her behalf. She was a woman, and a sick woman at that. Her daughter was with her, and her cowardly son, with secrets in his possession that might mitigate her guilt—these and like arguments, it was said, would be brought to bear upon the President, backed with certain political strength which could not fail to succeed. But such talk has seemed idle from the first. Woman as she was, she knew her business well; sick as she was, she had strength sufficient for her fearful purpose, and stern as the sentence was, its justice was absolute, its execution certain. We have heard many express the desire that the woman's life might be spared and its weary hours passed in the quiet of the prison, but no one who knew the President and his unmoveable nature supposed for an instant that the sentence would be changed in jot or tittle.

The hotels were thronged on Thursday. The streets were filled with restless, impatient people. The headquarters were surrounded by crowds of anxious men, who desired above all things to witness the execution, and who were willing to spend hundreds of dollars for that poor privilege. All day long the trains came in loaded with people from the North; all night long the country roads were lined with pedestrians, with parties hurrying on to the city, where they might at least participate in the excitements of the occasion.

Officials of every grade and name, with or without influence, were pestered by applications for tickets; the subordinate officers of the department were approached in every conceivable way, and by every possible avenue, by those whose idle or morbid curiosity impelled them to come to this hot and sweltering city in search of food for gossip and remembrance. Of course all endeavor was futile. Major-Gen. HANCOCK, who had charge of everything, had carefully prepared the list of people entitled to admission, and beyond those thereon named, no one was permitted to be present. The

SCENES AT THE OLD CAPITOL

Prison on Thursday night were by no means so harrowing in intensity as the public doubtless imagine. So far as the authorities were concerned, there was possibly an increased vigilance, and extra precautions were taken with Mrs. SURRATT; but beyond that, matters went along quite in accordance with the general custom.

MRS. SURRATT,

about whose fearful participation in the murder of the President there has been thrown so much mystery, was a very remarkable woman, and, like most remarkable women, had an undertone of superstition which served her in place of true religion, and enabled her to sleep peacefully even while cognizant of such a crime as that for which she has now suffered. She was fifty years of age, but, although since her illness of the past two weeks she has grown old and looked pale and thin, she would be called rather forty-two or three. Firmness and decision were part and parcel of her nature. A cold eye, that would quail at no scene of torture; a close, shut mouth, whence no word of sympathy with suffering would pass; a firm chin, indicative of fixedness of resolve; a square, solid figure, whose proportions were never disfigured by remorse or marred by loss of sleep—these have ever marked the *personnel* of MARY SURRATT—these, her neighbors say, were correct indices of her every-day and every-year life.

Those who have watched her through the whole of this protracted trial have noticed her utter indifference to anything and everything said or suggested about her. The most terrible flagellation produced no effect upon her rocky countenance, stolid, quiet, entirely self-possessed, calm as a May morning, she sat, uninterested from the opening to the close.

Her guardians say she anticipated an acquittal, she alone knew why. When, therefore, she was informed of the finding of the court, the sentence, and its near execution, she might well be roused from the state of utter listlessness she had thitherto maintained. Weakened by continued illness, with head stunned by the sudden blow, she for a moment forgot the Surratt in the woman, and felt the keenness of her position. Fainting, she cried aloud in the bitterness of her woe, wailing forth great waves of sorrow, she fell upon the floor and gave vent to a paroxysm of grief, partially hysterical, and wholly nervous. This was so unlike her, so entirely different from any conduct previously noticed, that the officer and her attendants were alarmed for her life. They went at once for the regular physician of the arsenal, who pronounced her system deranged and dangerously prostrated. Wine of valerian and other quieting drink was given her, and she revived, but no longer was she the Mrs. SURRATT of the court-room. She desired to see her spiritual advisers, and they were sent for. The sacred vail of ghostly comfort should not be rudely rent nor lightly lifted, but we may state with entire propriety that the miserable woman expressed the most emphatic desire for prayer and holy consolation. Desirous of clearing her mind first of all worldly affairs, she indicated the disposition she wished made of her property, and talked long and earnestly of her children and their future prospects. Toward her cowardly son JOHN she quite naturally entertained feelings of deep-seated bitterness. This she in a measure overcame after having relieved her mind about him and his conduct, and finally appeared reconciled to his desertion. What the feelings of the scoundrel must be to-day we cannot well imagine. If, as Mrs. SURRATT's friends more than intimated, his testimony would save her, if, as his own offer proved, his revelations would keep her from a death of infamy, we cannot believe he will dare survive her. Suicide and the unknown possibilities of the future, would seem preferable to life and the certain remorse and disgrace attending it here.

As the night wore on Mrs. SURRATT, who had been removed from the larger room where she has been confined since her illness, began to toss uneasily on her narrow bed. She was really ill and the kind offices of the physician were frequently needed. Conscious of the approach of day, she betook herself again to the preparation of her soul for its infinite journey. She rallied mentally and physically and determined evidently to bear and brave the scaffold. Her daughter, whose faithful service has been most touching in its constancy, had done all she could. The President had been seen, Judge HOLT had been visited. To both of them the most fervent appeals, inspired by a filial love as devoted as it was disinterested, had been presented, but in vain. Five of the members of the court had joined in a recommendation for commutation to imprisonment for life, and it was understood that the entire court concurred in the same, but this too was in vain. These facts the heartbroken daughter had communicated to her sentenced mother, and as she bent her head upon her neck she bathed her shoulders with tears of unfeigned grief and sympathy.

Seemingly convinced of the utter hopelessness of her situation, and apparently desirous of quieting the exceedingly demonstrative outbursts of her daughter, Mrs. SURRATT rose from her bed and again betook herself to her devotional exercises. It may seem strange that this woman, who was proven to know all about the projected assassination, who kept open house for the scoundrels who planned and the villains who did the deed, who insisted that she had never seen and never knew PAYNE, and who said, when informed of her sentence, "I had no hand in the murder of the President," should seem so calm and consistent in her preparation for death. Nevertheless the fact is that after turning her back upon hope, she gave herself with apparent sincerity and with heartiness to prayer and communion, the effect of which it is not for us to judge.

This morning, however, the counsel of Mrs. SURRATT, Messrs. AIKEN and CLAMPITT, who had determined to leave no stone unturned to effect her release, or if not that a detention in the execution of sentence, went at an early hour before Judge WYLIE, of the Supreme Court of this

city, and applied for a writ of habeas corpus, directed to Maj.-Gen. HAN-COCK, who had charge of the prison and control of the prisoners, commanding him to bring into Court the body of MARY E. SURRATT. The
WORDING OF THE PETITION
is as follows:
To the Hon. Andrew Wylie, one of the Justices of the Supreme Court of the District of Columbia:

The petition of MARY E. SURRATT by her counsel, F. A. AIKEN and JNO. W. CLAMPITT, most respectfully represents unto your Honor that, on or about the 17th day of April, A. D. 1865, your petitioner was arrested by the military authorities of the United States, under the charge of complicity with the murder of ABRAHAM LINCOLN, late President of the United States, and has ever since that time been, and is now confined on said charge, under and by virtue of the said military power of the United States, and is in the especial custody of Major-Gen. W. S. HANCOCK, commanding Middle Military Division, that since her said arrest, your petitioner has been tried against her solemn protest, by a military commission, unlawfully and without warrant, convened by the Secretary of War, as will appear from paragraph nine, Special Orders No. 211, dated War Department. Adjutant-General's Office, Washington, May 6, 1865: and by said commission notwithstanding her formal plea to the jurisdiction of the said commission is now unlawfully and unjustifiably detained in custody, and sentenced to be hanged on to-morrow, July 7, 1865, between the hours of 10 A.M. and 2 P.M., your petitioner shows unto your Honor that at the time of the commission of the said offence she was a private citizen of the United States, and in no manner connected with the military authority of the same, and that said offence was committed within the District of Columbia, said District being at the time within the lines of the armies of the United States, and not enemy's territory or under the control of a military commander for the trial of civil causes, but on the contrary, your petitioner alleges that the said crime was an offence simply against the peace of the United States, properly and solely cognizable, under the constitution and laws of the United States, by the Criminal Court of this District, and which said court was and is now open for the trial of such crimes and offences. Wherefore, inasmuch as the said crime was only an offence against the peace of the United States, and not an act of war, inasmuch as your petitioner was a private citizen of the same, and not subject to military jurisdiction, or in any wise amenable to military law, inasmuch as said District was the peaceful territory of the United States, and that all crimes committed within such territory are under the constitution and laws of the United States, to be tried only before its criminal tribunals with the right of public trial by jury. Inasmuch as said commission was a military commission, organized and governed by the laws of military court-martial, and unlawfully convened without warrant or authority, and when she had not the right of public trial by jury as guaranteed to by the constitution and laws of the United States; that therefore her detention and sentence are so without warrant against positive law and unjustifiable, wherefore, she prays your Honor to grant unto her the United States most gracious writ of habeas corpus, commanding the said Major-Gen. W. S. HANCOCK to produce before your Honor the body of your said petitioner, with the cause and day of her said detention to abide, &c., and she will ever pray.

(Signed,)   MARY E. SURRATT.
By FREDERICK A. AIKEN, JNO. W. CLAMPITT.

After hearing the argument, the Judge indorsed upon the petition:

Let the writ issue as prayed, returnable before the Criminal Court of the District of Columbia, now sitting, at the hour of ten o'clock A.M., this seventh day of July, 1865.

(Signed,)   ANDREW WYLIE,
A Justice of the Supreme Court of the District of Columbia.
JULY 7, 1865, AT 3 O'CLOCK A.M.

The writ was then formally issued, and the Marshal of the District was directed to serve it. The news spread like wildfire, and all sorts of reports were circulated throughout the city. The hotels swarmed with talkative people, every one of whom had the latest news, and was only too ready to communicate it to his neighbor. "Mrs. SURRATT is pardoned,"

"She is not expected to live," "Her sentence has been commuted." Every one had his pet theory, but it concerned Mrs. SURRATT alone—the fate of the others seemed certain.

THE RETURN

was ordered at 10 o'clock, and at that hour the court room was thronged with people interested to know the result. The Marshal, in response to a question by the court, stated that Major-Gen. HANCOCK had not yet appeared, although it was past the hour.

After sundry criticisms and objections to the proceedings by the District-Attorney, the counsel for Mrs. SURRATT stated that if his client was guilty of any crime, she was amenable to this court, a court which was competent to take cognizance of the same, and not to a military tribunal.

The District Attorney Mr. CARRINGTON, after reading the certificate of the Marshal, stating that he had served the writ on Gen. HANCOCK, at 8:30 o'clock, said that he appeared to defend the action of the Marshal by direction of the court, and he desired to report to the court, that the Marshal had done his duty.

The Court:

The case is not now here on its merits. On the petition of the party this morning at an early hour, I directed this writ of *habeas corpus* to issue. The writ was issued and was served upon Gen. HANCOCK, who has the custody of Mrs. SURRATT, the party on whose behalf the writ was obtained. The writ required him to have the body of Mrs. SURRATT with the cause of her detention before this court this morning at 10 o'clock, he has neglected to obey the order of the court, and the question now before us is what is the court to do under the circumstances. That is the only question before the court at this time. Any discussion on the merits involved would now be out of place. The court acknowledges that its powers are inadequate to meet the military power possessed by Gen. HANCOCK. If the court were to decide at this moment that Gen. HANCOCK was in contempt, the only process which it would issue, would be an attachment for the disregard of its authority; but why issue an attachment against the whole military power of the United States? This Court acknowledges that the laws are silent, and that it is without power in the premises, and therefore declines to make any order whatever. If there be a disposition on the part of the military power to respect the authority of the civil courts, they will respect the writ which has already been served: if on the other hand it is their determination to treat the authority of this court with contempt, in this matter they have the power, and will treat with equal contempt any other process which the court might order. The court therefore must submit to the supreme physical power which now holds the custody of petitioner, and declines to issue an attachment or to make any other order in this case.

After these remarks the court proceeded with the trial of Miss HARRIS, which was continued until 11:30 o'clock, when

GEN. HANCOCK APPEARED,

accompanied by Attorney-General SPEED. The trial was at once suspended, and the Attorney-General addressed the court as follows:

May it please the Court in regard to the writ of *habeas corpus* directed to Gen. HANCOCK, I desire to say by way of apology for his not sooner making a return, that the process was not served on him until about breakfast time this morning, and that, owing to his having a great many persons to see, a great many important matters requiring immediate attention, and his distance from the court-house, he was not able to get here at an earlier hour, I wish to assure the court that no disrespect was intended to it by delay to which it has been unavoidably subjected.

The Court declined to make any order in the case.

ATTORNEY-GENERAL—Gen. HANCOCK, in obedience to the writ, makes the following return:

HEADQUARTERS MIDDLE MILITARY DIVISION,
WASHINGTON, D. C., July 7, 1865.
To Hon. Andrew Wylie, Justice of the Supreme Court of the District of Columbia:

I hereby acknowledge the service of the writ hereto attached, and return the same, and respectfully say that the body of MARY E. SURRATT is in my possession under and by virtue of an order of

ANDREW JOHNSON, President of the United States and Commander-in-Chief of the Army and Navy, for the purposes in said order expressed, a copy of which is hereto attached and made part of this return. And that I do not produce said body by reason of the order of the President of the United States indorsed upon said writ to which reference is hereby respectfully made. Dated July 7, 1865.

    (Signed,)   WINFIELD S. HANCOCK,
                      Major-Gen. United States Vols., Commanding.

PRESIDENT'S INDORSEMENT.
                EXECUTIVE OFFICE, July 7, 1865—1 o'clock A.M.
To Major-Gen. W. S. Hancock, Commander, &c.:

I, ANDREW JOHNSON, President of the United States, do hereby declare that the writ of habeas corpus has been heretofore suspended in such cases as this, and I do hereby especially suspend this writ, and direct that you proceed to execute the order heretofore given upon the judgement of the Military Commission, and you will give this order in return to this writ.

    Signed,   ANDREW JOHNSON, President.

THE COURT—This court finds itself powerless to take any further action in the premises, and therefore declines to make orders which would be vain for any practical purpose. As regards the delay, it having been fully accounted for, the court has no fault to attach to the respondents in that respect.

ATTORNEY-GENERAL SPEED.—It may not be out of order for me to say here that this whole subject has of course had the most earnest and anxious considerations of the Executive, and of the war-making power of the government. Every man, upon reflection, and particularly every lawyer knows that war cannot be fought by due process of law, and armies cannot be maintained by due process of law; there must be armies, there must be battles of war; of war comes the law of war, and usage permits battles to be fought, permits human life to be taken without the judgment of the court, and without the process of the court it permits prisoners to be taken and prisoners to be held; and your Honor will not undertake to discharge them although the constitution says that human life shall not be taken, or man be deprived of his liberty or property without due process of law. Conflict of necessity comes up when war comes between the Executive and the judicial. If the war power in war does not transcend the civil, war is made for the maintenance of the civil power, that is, when peace comes, for the purpose of giving us the benefit of the civil. This country is now in the midst of a great war, and the Commander-in-Chief of the armies of the United States was slain in the discharge of his duties, and if the armies of the United States cannot, under the laws of war, protect its Commander-in-Chief from assassination, and if the laws and usages of war cannot protect by military law, its Commander-in-Chief from assassination and destruction. What has the government come to? The thing appears to me to be too plain for consideration, but as your Honor has disposed of the case, I only make these remarks for the purpose of satisfying your Honor that we have anxiously, and, I think, most naturally considered this matter, giving your Honor credit for having done what you regard to be your duty in this matter, and are very glad to hear that your Honor gives us credit for having done what we have done, and regarded to be our duty to the court. The writ was applied for and I had no authority to refuse to grant it. It is a writ dear and sacred to every lover of liberty, indispensable to the protection of citizens, and can only be constitutionally set aside in times of war and insurrection, when the public safety requires it, and in regard to offences committed in connection with the army or the militia when called into active service. With reference to the merits of this case, which has occupied so much of the attention of the public, and in fact of the whole civilian world. It would be out of place for the court to express any opinion; the case is not before it. The court can only say that it has no doubt the gentlemen connected with the government who have had the duty of conducting this trial are truly convinced in their own minds as to the manner in which they have performed their duties. I do not feel at liberty—I could not, I dared not refuse to grant the writ. The return which has been made to the writ is from the President of the United States, and declares the writ of *habeas corpus* to be suspended in this case, as has been in other and similar cases, the Court has no further authority in the case. If the government desires to carry out its purpose in regard to the petitioner, the Court cannot prevent it, and I do not know that it would be possible ever hereafter to bring the case up for argument on this court, for if the petitioner be executed as designed, the body cannot be brought into court, and, therefore, there is an end of the case. The jurisdiction of this court yields to the suspension of the writ of habeas corpus from the President of the United States.

Gen. HANCOCK then asked leave to retire, which was granted, and he left in company with Attorney-General SPEED.

This settled the case, so far as Mrs. SURRATT was concerned, and word was at once sent to her that all hope was gone.

Concerning PAYNE or POWELL, as he called himself, there has been a great deal of unnecessary mystery and foolish surmisings. His name, so far as the public is concerned, is

LEWIS PAYNE,

and if behind that he hid the honest name of a respectable family, the fact is one to his credit; but of that no one cares. He is dead; gone before the bar of a higher tribunal than that which last judged him, and with his future we have naught to do. The cool villainy, the absolute savagery of the fellow, has been consistent with the atrocity of his crime, until, with singular emotion, he became the apologist for his fellow-criminal, and the assailer of her son. By no means handsome, or of the romantic scoundrel stamp, PAYNE seems to have been a very common kind of person, with an exceedingly hard head and apparently no heart. No mere man would or could have deliberately cut and slashed the face of a sick and dying sufferer; it required the instinct of a demon and the temper of a brute to suggest and execute such a project. He was a species of idiot, an intelligent beast, with wit enough to understand his duty, sense enough to do it thoroughly, but unable to talk or maneuvre himself out of such a scrape as he fell into at the door of Mrs. SURRATT's house.

Throughout the trial he has been unmoved. Never sullen nor morose, he kept his eyes about him, seeing everybody and everything, but never for an instant admitting by sign or gesture that he recognized anything. The confinement didn't annoy him at all. Quite likely he would have enjoyed a night in the town, and been as ready for a spree or a murder as ever; but he rarely opened his mouth, and as rarely closed his eyes, which wandered around and around, as if in continual search for an object of rest.

In his cell, PAYNE manifested no different appearance. His conduct was the same everywhere and at all times. He was a fit tool for the hand that used him—a reliable blade for a bloody purpose. At night he slept; in the morning he awoke early; his appetite was always good, and when the time for the meeting of the court was announced, he went along quietly as a lamb, as docile as an ox in yoke. When, therefore, his sentence was read to him, it was to be expected that his dont-care-ativeness, or stupidity, or *sang froid*, or whatever it may be termed, would still characterize him. He neither appeared surprised nor disappointed. Had he been pronounced "not guilty," it would have been the same—until he was freed; then he might have developed differently, though that is mere conjecture, baseable upon no reliable data.

Doubly ironed, doubly guarded, PAYNE spent the day and night before his death. No future presented aught of hope or fear for him; no God or devil stared him in the face with searching scrutiny or tantalizing punishment. He simply felt nothing, and yet in the midst of apathy and indifference, we find him explaining that Mrs. SURRATT had nothing to do with the murder, inveighing against JOHN SURRATT as a coward and scoundrel who had deserted his mother, leaving her to die when he should fill her place, and expressing tenderest regret that any act of his should have brought her into trouble and put her life in jeopardy. It is difficult to reconcile these two phases of character, so entirely different. Common sense forbids the belief that he feigned stupidity and was in reality a man of birth and breeding, and it likewise scouts the theory that he was entitled to sympathy on account of idiocy. Declining to participate in any religious mummery, and wholly averse to any religious reality, he passed his last hours in quiet stupidity, exerting himself to please no one, caring apparently nothing, either for the people here or the probabilities of the hereafter. His body was a source of no earthly consideration. Until he died it was not his—his keepers had it; after his death it was not his, and he did not care who had it. His friends, he said, lived in Florida. Before they could come, if they would, he would be gone, and the senseless clod which tenemented his seared soul would be en route to corruption. Why should he care? He didn't care.

One redeeming feature stood prominent. Noticing the kind consideration of Miss SURRATT toward her mother, PAYNE expressed regret that they should be compelled to part. He said he would do anything, say anything which could help Mrs. SURRATT, who was an innocent woman. He emerged from his brutism and became humane; he left his carelessness behind him and asserted the case of the mother against her recreant son; he forgot the idiot and resumed for the moment the attitude and intelligence of a man. With the clergymen he had but little to say. He seemed entirely careless as to his future, and down to the very last maintained his stolid, indifferent, hang-dog manner.

Perhaps there was more sympathy expressed for

DAVID E. HERROLD

than for any of the prisoners. He was young, thoughtless, light and trivial. He probably had never known a serious moment nor a sober thought. His following of BOOTH was very much such a companionship as a dog affords, and it seemed as if he might have been so thoroughly under the influence of that fascinating fiend as to be entirely *non compos*. The legal evidence against him was, however, clear and conclusive. As early as February last he was found to have been in confidential relations with the assassin, and was proved to have been present on several occasions at secret meetings with BOOTH, ATZEROTH and others of the conspirators. Once he was at Mrs. SURRATT's in company with them. He called with SURRATT and ATZEROTH at the tavern in Surratsville, and left the two carbines and ammunition which were taken away from the tavern by him and BOOTH on the night of the assassination. During their flight he acknowledged to WILLIE JETT and other rebel soldiers that he and BOOTH were the assassins of Mr. LINCOLN, and he was captured in the barn with Booth. His personal appearance was that of a boy of nineteen, dressed in a faded blue suit, in height about five feet four inches, dusky black, neglected hair, lively, dark hazel eyes, slight tufts of beard along the chin and jaws, and faintly surrounding the mouth, rather round face, full but not prominent nose, full lips, foolish, weak, confiding countenance, indicating but little intelligence, and not the faintest trace of ferocity. His sisters, who are apparently very estimable young women, labored with him, hoping to make some serious impression upon him, but in vain. He was full of levity almost to the very hour of his death. At the announcement of the finding of the court, HERROLD was unmoved. Indeed, none of the prisoners at first manifested any great concern—HERROLD and PAYNE least of any. PAYNE was sullen and indifferent, HERROLD careless and free. After a little, when the later hours of the night were passing silently by, he became more tractable and for the time left his habit of joking and gossiping, and when asked if he had any requests to make, desired that his body might be given to his family. With the clergyman he was ever respectful, but beyond a routine repetition of words and phrases seemed to know and care little more about the coming than the present world. Impressible to a remarkable degree, but equally elastic, he talked and wept with the ministers, but was as ready for a quib or a joke immediately after as ever. It is difficult to say he was not a responsible person, and yet he seemed more like a butterfly than a man. He was at no time manly in deportment, and his exit from this world, was in accordance with his variable temperament while in it.

GEORGE A. ATZEROTH

was a coward, mentally, morally and physically. He failed to grasp the magnitude of the conspiracy as unfolded to him by the leaders; he failed to accomplish his part of the assassination scheme, and he failed to make any one care a rap whether he lived or died. During the trial he was unconcerned; since his imprisonment, was peevish and full of complaints, and on the night before his death he was restless and uneasy. He couldn't sleep at all, and, unlike PAYNE, had no appetite. He was a poor, miserable fellow, and his death amounted to no more than did his life.

THE MORNING OF THE DAY

appeared, and with it came thousands of people from afar to witness the execution. They might as well have come to see GEORGE WASHINGTON, the one as easy as the other. As above stated, every person in any way connected with the government, was tortured and annoyed by applications for passes to the prison. This morning the crowd of besiegers again appeared before 7 o'clock, and most of them failing to receive the desired pass, the curious wended their way to the arsenal grounds, two miles distant, in the hot sun, there to renew their importunities. When we arrived at the latter place, about 10 o'clock, the streets and avenues were blocked up by hundreds of vehicles, and probably 2,000 lookers-on, whose only reward for their exposure and labor was a peep at the prison walls in the distance. Four and One-half-street, the thoroughfare leading directly to the arsenal, was strongly and thickly guarded from Pennsylvania-avenue to the arsenal lot, and at the entrance to the latter, and completely surrounding it, were numerous soldiers on guard. Entering the inclosure, we found several regiments on duty—in all, two brigades of HANCOCK's corps—scattered here and there between the gates and the prison.

Pedestrians were flocking rapidly toward the building, and when we entered the latter, we found already several hundred persons—a mixed assembly of civilians and military men. We learned that none of the prisoners had slept during the past night save PAYNE and HERROLD, both of whom had a sound, quiet rest of about two hours. None of them had eaten anything scarcely except PAYNE, who partook heartily of breakfast. During the night opiates had been given Mrs. SURRATT to produce rest, but without avail. The spiritual advisers and friends of the condemned left the prison shortly after 11 o'clock last night, and none returned until this morning, except Miss SURRATT, who remained with her mother from about midnight until 5 o'clock A.M. No confessions had been made. None, indeed, could have been expected from either PAYNE, HERROLD or ATZEROTH, who had already from time to time, given in the main, probably, the truthful account of their relations to the bloody tragedy in which they were participants. Mrs. SURRATT was the only one remaining who had not acknowledged the full measure of her guilt. She, it was rumored, had made a full confession to her confessor, but on inquiry we found her confession in preparation for receiving the sacrament, was confounded with an acknowledgment of guilt for publicity. She had hope up to almost the hour of her execution that her sentence would be respited, if not commuted, and she had apparently lost sight of her own interest in deep solicitude for her daughter, of whom she constantly talked, and repeatedly, frantically and with wringing of hands asked: "What will become of her—what will be ANNA's fate?"

STATEMENTS OF PAYNE.

PAYNE, last evening, informed Col. DODD, who has special charge of the prisoners, that so far as he knew, Mrs. SURRATT had nothing to do with the plot for assassination. Certainly she had never said a word to him on the subject, nor had any of his co-conspirators mentioned her in connection with the matter. She may have known what was going on, but to him she never disclosed her knowledge by word or act. That immediately after he had made the murderous attack upon Mr. SEWARD, he felt he had done wrong, and he had wandered around and slept in the woods that night, frequently feeling inclined to come to the city and give himself up. That when, finally, he was by hunger and loss of rest driven to Mrs. SURRATT's house he had doubts about his reception there and whether she would not deliver him to the officers of the law for punishment. Col. DODD, who has been constantly in conversation with PAYNE, recently says the latter has never varied from one straightforward, consistent story, claiming at all times that he was informed and believed that he was acting under an order from the rebel authorities, and did not, therefore, originally view his act as a murderous one. HERROLD says in the original plot to him was assigned the duty of shutting off the gas in the theatre, and he had once rehearsed the work with BOOTH; that, however, on the night of the assassination, he was only required to be in waiting near the Navy-yard Bridge to assist BOOTH in his escape.

These statements embrace substantially all the prisoners have given in the nature of confessions, other than what is found in the proofs and admissions on the trial.

DEMEANOR OF THE CONDEMNED.

We were permitted to look in upon the cells on several occasions during the forenoon, and up to a few minutes before the execution. The four prisoners condemned to death were removed yesterday from the upper floor of the prison to a tier of cells on the first floor South. ATZEROTH occupied the eastern apartment, No. 151, Mrs. SURRATT the next West, No. 153, HERROLD, No. 155, and PAYNE, No. 157, thus leaving a vacant cell between each of the prisoners.

Our first observation of ATZEROTH, found him in company with the Rev. Mr. RUTLER, a Lutheran minister of the gospel. The prisoner was lying upon his bed an intent and quiet listener to the whisperings of the minister. At another time ATZEROTH seemed utterly unnerved and tossed about, frequently clasping his hands together and wringing them as in hopelessness and dispair. At noon and thereafter he became calmer and scarcely spoke or moved.

Mrs. SURRATT throughout the day continued in physical prostration, but grew calmer as the hour approached for execution. The parting between herself and daughter was borne with more fortitude than was expected of her, and whilst the latter swooned away, and was carried to an adjoining apartment senseless, Mrs. SURRATT appeared to rally in strength for the moment. Soon again, however, she lost strength, and when taken from her cell to the scaffold, she had to be almost literally lifted and borne along by the officers.

HERROLD's demeanor was somewhat after the manner he has shown from the commencement of the trial—listlessness and lack of appreciation of his fearful position, with alternatives of serious reflection.

PAYNE was, throughout the day, quiet and firm, occasionally joining the Rev. Dr. GILLETTE in earnest prayer.

THE SCAFFOLD.

In the lot south of the prison, and surrounded by a wall thirty feet high, the scaffold was erected. The structure is about seventy feet from the prison near by, say thirty feet distant, were four freshly dug graves, and beside them four large pine coffins coarsely constructed.

The scaffold was so arranged that the four condemned could be hung at the same time.

The enclosure was much larger than was stated in my dispatch of last night, and there must have been present within the lot and upon the top of the wall, which was literally packed with soldiers, quite 3,000 spectators, three-fourths of whom were soldiers.

About 12:30 o'clock, Gen. HANCOCK arrived, and remained personally inspecting all the official acts.

THE PROCESSION OF DEATH.

At 1:15 the procession proceeded from the prison to the scaffold in the following order, preceded by Gen. HARTRANFT:

Mrs. SURRATT, supported by an officer and a noncommissioned officer, and attended by Rev. Fathers WALTER and WIGETT.

ATZEROTH, attended by an officer, with whom walked his spiritual advisers, Rev. J. G. BUTLER, of the Lutheran Church, and Chaplain WINCHESTER.

HERROLD came next, attended by Rev. Dr. OLDS, of Christ Church; Episcopal.

PAYNE, attended by Rev. Dr. GILLETTE, of the First Baptist Church, of this city, and Rev. Dr. STRIKER, of Baltimore.

Mrs. SURRATT, attended by two soldiers. Her waist and ankles were ironed; she was attired in a plain black alpacca dress, with black bonnet and thin veil. Her face could be easily seen. She gazed up at the horrid instrument of death, and her lips were moving rapidly as in prayer. She was assisted upon the scaffold and seated in a chair near the drop. She gazed upon the noose, which dangled in the wind before her face, and again her lips moved as if in prayer.

ATZEROTH followed, with a glaring, haggard look. He seemed to have changed in appearance greatly since his incarceration. He, also, was assisted by two soldiers, and seemed very feeble, but appeared to rally when on the scaffold, and took an evident interest in the proceedings.

HERROLD came next, supported on each side. He seemed very feeble, but revived a little subsequently. He realized his position now, if he never did before. He was very pale and careworn. He examined the scaffold closely, upon approaching it, and especially the drop.

PAYNE came next, with his usual bold, straight attitude, looking with seeming indifference upon the instrument of death. He wore a blue shirt and straw hat. There was not firmness in his step as he marched to the scaffold.

REMARKS AND PRAYERS OF THE ATTENDING CLERGY.

The Catholic priest in attendance upon Mrs. SURRATT declined making any public remark. Dr. GILLETTE stepped forward and said:

> The prisoner, LEWIS THORNTON POWELL, known as PAYNE, requests me on this occasion, to say for him, that he thanks, publicly and sincerely thanks, Gen. HARTRANFT, all the officers and soldiers who had charge of him, and all persons who have ministered to his wants, for their unwavering kindness to him in this trying hour. Not an unkind word nor an ill-feeling act has been made toward him.
>
> Almighty God, our Heavenly Father, we pray thee to permit us to commit this soul into thy hands, not for any claim we have to make for it in ourselves, but depending as we do upon the merits of our Lord Jesus Christ, grant, O Heavenly Father, we beseech thee, that his spirit may be accorded an easy passage out of this world, and, if consistent with thy purposes of mercy, and thou delightest in mercy, receive him. This we humbly ask, through Jesus Christ, our Lord and our Redeemer. Amen.

Dr. OLDS, in behalf of HERROLD, followed, saying:

DAVID E. HERROLD, who is here about to undergo the extreme penalty of offended law, desires me to say that he hopes your prayers may be offered up to the Most High God for him; that he forgives all who may at any time have wronged him, and asks of all forgiveness for all the wrong or supposed wrong he has done unto them, that he thanks the officers who have had charge of him during his confinement in prison for their deeds of kindness toward him, he hopes that he dies in charity with all the world and is convinced that his soul is in the hands of God. Amen.

Rev. Mr. BUTLER, the spiritual adviser of ATZEROTH, then rose and said:

GEORGE A. ATZEROTH requests me thus publicly to return his unfeigned thanks to Gen. HARTRANFT, and all associated with him in this prison, for their uniform courtesy and kindness during his imprisonment. And now, GEORGE A. ATZEROTH, may God have mercy upon you. The ways of the transgressor is hard. The wages of sin is death; but if we freely confess our sins, God will in mercy pardon them. Christ came into the world to save sinners—even the chief of sinners. Believe in the Lord Jesus Christ, and thou shalt be saved. The blood of the blessed Redeemer, Jesus Christ, cleanseth from all sin. You profess to have thus believed to have peace in your heart; and may God be with you in this hour of trial and suffering; and may you be enabled so to commend your soul to the Creator of it that you may have peace in this last moment of life. The Lord God Almighty, Father of Mercy, have mercy upon you, and receive you into His heavenly keeping. Lord God, Redeemer of the world, have mercy upon this man. Lord God, Holy Spirit of the Father and the Son, have mercy upon him and grant him thy peace. Amen.

THE LAST PAINFUL SCENE.

Gen. HARTRANFT read the order of the War Department, embracing the President's Executive Order, for the execution.

The limbs of each of the prisoners were now pinioned. The caps were drawn over their heads, Mrs. SURRATT exclaiming in a faint voice, "Don't let me fall; hold on!"

ATZEROTH exclaimed in a loud tone: "Gentlemen, take warning;" then, after an interval of about two minutes he said: "Good-by, gentlemen who are before me; may we all meet in the other world."

It was now twenty-five minutes past 1 o'clock. The officer in charge of the scaffold here made some preconcerted motions to the attendant soldiers to step back from the drop, and then, with a motion of his hand, the drop fell and the bodies of the criminals were suspended in the air.

The bodies fell simultaneously, and swayed backward and forward for a few minutes. Mrs. SURRATT, appeared to suffer very little. PAYNE and HERROLD, on the contrary, writhed in apparent agony, the first for about two minutes, and the latter for about five minutes. The muscles of their feet and hands were visibly contracted. PAYNE's hands, which were more exposed than the others, became purpled, as did his neck near where the rope was fastened. ATZEROTH's agony seemed, like Mrs. SURRATT's, to be of but very short duration.

After the lapse of ten minutes, the medical officers, Surgeon WOODWARD, U. S. A., Dr. OTIS, U. S. V., and Dr. PORTER, U. S. A., and Surgeon of the post examined severally the bodies, and pronounced life extinct. The ropes were cut, the bodies lowered, stretched upon the tops of the coffins, and a further and more minute examination made by the Surgeons, who state that the necks of each were instantly broken.

At about 4 o'clock the bodies were placed in the coffins and buried.

The soldiers who were required to let fall the trap of the scaffold, are of Company F, Fourteenth Veteran Reserves. They were chosen by the Commander of that regiment who, without making known what was his purpose, required four able bodied men of the regiment to be selected from the left of the line, to perform a special and important duty. The selection was accordingly made before the service to be performed became known to the members of the regiment.

MUDD, ARNOLD, O'LAUGHLIN and SPANGLER will probably be sent to the Penitentiary to-morrow.

MOURNING AND
REMEMBERING LINCOLN

Manton Marble

FROM *The New York World*

For three years, beginning with its takeover by prominent anti-administration Democrats in 1862, the *New York World* issued an avalanche of splenetic editorials assailing Lincoln, emancipation, and the draft. Relations between the White House and the newspaper reached their nadir on May 18, 1864, when the *World* published—accidentally and innocently, it maintained—a bogus presidential proclamation calling for 400,000 new troops to be raised by enlistment or conscription. Convinced by Stanton that the hoax was an attempt to undermine Union morale and give aid and comfort to the rebels, Lincoln ordered the paper shut down and its proprietor, Manton Marble (1834–1917), arrested. When the bogus proclamation proved to be the financially, and not politically, motivated brainchild of a reporter for the *Brooklyn Eagle*, Marble regained his liberty and his presses and escalated his attacks on the administration during the 1864 presidential campaign. As recently as April 13, 1865, the *World* had denounced Lincoln's speech on reconstruction for its "vagueness," "indecision," "emptiness," "timidity," and "vacuity." But in response to the assassination, the paper did an about-face. Not a trace of Manton Marble's longtime antipathy to Lincoln could be found in its coverage of, and commentary on, the president's death.

But yesterday the nation was at the height of joyful exultation over the decisive victories which seemed to promise peace and a restored Union to a long-suffering people.

To-day every loyal heart must suffer the terrible shock, and swell with overburdening grief at the calamity which has been permitted to befall us, in the assassination of the Chief Magistrate.

The flags that flaunted their glittering colors in the sunshine of yesterday, and bespoke the re-established supremacy of the government, to-day must hang suspended at half-mast, for its chosen chief lies low in death.

The splendor of our triumph is robbed of half its luster. It is deeper loss than if our first soldier had fallen by a hostile bullet as the gallant SEDGWICK fell; more than if an army had perished in the shock of battle. For it is the commander-in-chief of our armies and navies who has fallen; and he has fallen, not by the natural course of disease, nor in the accepted peril of war, but by the foul stroke of some unknown assassin.

Our history has no parallel to this. Such grief as ours to-day is new to this nation's heart. Other Presidents have died while holding the same high place—HARRISON and TAYLOR; but both died in the ordinary course of nature, and the nation's grief then had no such pang in it as this which is now given by the shot of an assassin.

The cry of the murderer as he leaped from the President's box and ran across the stage, "sic semper tyrannis," betrays no madman's frenzy. The plot included the murder of Secretary SEWARD also, and all the circumstances show that the same political fury and hate which lit the flames of the great rebellion inspired these hellish deeds; and by so much as these detract from the splendor of our triumph in its utter subjugation, by so much do they brand with a deeper and more damning infamy its plotters, its leaders, its abettors, its sympathizers, its character in impartial history.

Let every city, town, and street and lane and house and farm of the whole North become to-day but the wards of an infinite prison to shut in and secure the villains who have done this thing. Let every man be an officer of the law to search them out and bring them to summary and condign justice. The machinery of government has already been set in motion: but let there be no escape for them if that should fail.

Into what proportions this calamity will yet develop, no human eye can now foresee. Its effect upon the political future of the nation will, at least, not be such as when a dynasty is overthrown. Our laws provide for the succession to such remote degrees that even assassination cannot leave the nation without a visible leader and head.

ANDREW JOHNSON to-day becomes the President of the United States, and the chief political consequences which will follow from this tragedy will be mainly such as his personal character and political opinions, especially on the subject of reconstruction, shall determine. May GOD give him wisdom to discharge worthily the duties of his great office.

April 15, 1865

Never before in history has there been an occasion so fraught with public consequences that was, at the same time, so like an overwhelming domestic affliction. This portentous national calamity, conscious as we all are of its weighty and inscrutable significance in the future politics of the country, is also so full of affecting pathos and tragic horror that a smitten people are overborne by a flood of sensibility, like a bereaved family who have no heart to think on their estate and prospects when the tide of sudden affliction has swept away the supporting prop of the household. By no other single achievement could death have carried such a feeling of desolation into every dwelling, and have caused this whole land to mourn as over the sundering of some dear domestic tie.

The terrible deed which has filled the national heart with grief and consternation, lacks no conceivable accessory of tragic horror. When the storm which has gone over us seemed to have spent its force, there is suddenly shot from an unexpected quarter, without warning or prepara-tion, a swift thunderbolt which strikes away the chief pillar of the state and shakes the whole edifice to its foundations. Death, always affecting, becomes horrible when dealt by the hand of an assassin; even though the victim be but a private individual, the deed of violence spreads a feeling of uneasiness and alarm through an excited community. The demise of the chief magistrate of a great nation, even though he die calmly in his bed, in the most tranquil times, is an awful and affecting event; when an assassin deals the blow, the surcharge of horror is naturally as great in proportion as in the case of a murdered individual; but if the calamity comes in a crisis when that particular life is unusually felt to be of su-preme value to a nation's hopes and prospects, the awfulness of the trag-edy is heightened by all the considerations that can give overwhelming poignancy to a nation's grief. Even the unimportant circumstances and surroundings of this foul deed have a tragic complexion. Perpetrated on the anniversary of the opening of the war; in a place of public amuse-ment; in the presence of a paralyzed multitude who had come cluster-ing together to witness a spectacle; the murderer an actor by profession, trained to an exaggerated admiration of certain historic characters whose suggestive names had become prefixes in his family; his escape from a crowded assembly by leaping upon the stage and disappearing behind the scenes with a Latin motto in his mouth, while the consort of his illustrious victim was swooning in an agony of which no imagination can measure the depth;—and then the cry that arose at midnight in all the cities of this afflicted land, and the horror and consternation that fell upon all hearts as the sun heaved up his orb into the morning sky,—all this together completes a spectacle for the horror-struck imagination such as history, even with the trappings of the tragic muse to set it off, has seldom or never approached. What has the Eternal Mind that presides over and shapes out the course of human history in store for us, that He has thus permitted to be spread upon the canvas allotted to this country and this century a scene so affecting and awful that none of its colors can fade till both continents are ingulfed in the all-effacing ocean?

Whatever a wise and unsearchable Providence may bring out of this appalling visitation, we can, as yet, see nothing in it but calamity. It is a terrible proof of the depth, intensity and danger of those passions which have been wakened into such fearful vigor by the events of the war. An ardent young man, not personally predisposed to crime; brought up to an art which stands aloof from political associations; accustomed to view the events of history only on their pathetic or their scenic side; trained to regulate every gesture and mold every lineament of his face to court public admiration; this young man with this imaginative training is not transformed into an assassin by the vulgar impulses of an ordinary murderer. In this terrible deed, as in the ordinary exercise of his profession, he has been a candidate for sympathy and approbation. It was his instinctive and sympathetic knowledge of what lurks in the hearts of the baffled secessionists, which made him see that this unavailing act of vengeance would enshrine him in their affections, and make his a dear and canonized name. His dreadful act is an awful commentary on the consequences of party passions when they are fanned into such rage that they strip the most odious crimes of their horror and clothe them in the seductive drapery of public virtue. While the disabled half of the country is yet a caldron of unsubdued and seething passions, it is lamentable that there should be taken from us a mild and paternal chief magistrate who was preparing to pour over these agitated passions the soothing influence of his natural clemency. As soon as the war-cloud visibly lifted, he set himself to the performance of acts which commanded the approval even of his former opponents; and the day which preceded his death was passed in employments more full of promise than any other in the calendar of this momentous era. There will fall into his opening and honored grave no warmer or more plentiful tribute of honest sensibility than is shed by those of his loyal fellow-citizens who did not contribute to his re-election.

Of the career brought thus suddenly to this tragic close it is yet too early to make any estimate that will not require revision. It is probable that the judgment of history will differ in many respects from that of Mr. LINCOLN's contemporaries; and in no respect, perhaps, more than in reversing the current tenor of the public thinking on what has been considered the vacillation of his character. It must never be overlooked that Mr. LINCOLN was elevated to the presidency without previous training; that he was a novice in the discharge of high executive functions. Confronted at the very threshold with problems of a novelty, magnitude, and difficulty which would have caused the most experienced statesmen to quail, beset on all sides by the most conflicting advice, it would not have been wisdom, but shallow and foolhardy presumption, indicating unseemly levity of character, if he had affected a display of the same kind of confident decision with which an old sailor manages a cock-boat in fair weather. If, under such circumstances, he had played the *role* of a man of decision, he would have forfeited all title to be considered a man of sense. When the most experienced and reputable statesmen of the country came to opposite conclusions, it is creditable to the strength, solidarity, and modesty of Mr. LINCOLN's mind, that he acted with a cautious and hesitating deliberation proportioned rather to a sense of his great responsibilities, than to a theatrical notion of political stage effect.

Had the country, previous to Mr. LINCOLN's first election, foreseen what was coming, it would not have chosen for President a man of Mr. LINCOLN's inexperience and peculiar type of character. But if his party was to succeed, we doubt whether foresight and deliberation would have made so good a choice. With the Republican party in power, this terrible struggle was inevitable; and with a man of fixed views and inflexible purpose at the head of the government it would probably have resulted either in a dissolution of the Union or civil war in the North. In either event, we should have lost our institutions. The stability of a republican government, and indeed of any form of free government, depends upon its possessing that kind of flexibility which yields easily to the control of public opinion. In this respect, the English government is more pliable than our own, the administration being at all times subject to immediate change by losing the confidence of the representatives of the people; whereas under our Constitution, an iron inflexibility can maintain itself in office for the full period of four years without any possibility of

displacing it, except by revolution. In ordinary times, this works well
enough; for the growth of opinion in any ordinary four years, could not
be so rapid as to indispose the people to await the presidential election. But when there was let loose upon us, at the beginning of the last
administration, the wild outbreakings of turbulence and treason, the
development of opinion went forward with gigantic strides corresponding, in some degree, to the violence and magnitude of the contest. *Any*
policy which a Republican President might have adopted with decision
in the spring of 1861, and adhered to with steadiness during the four
years, would have exposed the government to be shivered into fragments
by the shocks of changing opinion. What was wanting in the flexibility
of our political system was made up in the character of Mr. LINCOLN.
Whatever may be thought of the absolute merits of the late President's
administration—on which it would not be decorous to express our views
on this occasion—it cannot well be denied that it has been, throughout,
a tolerably faithful reflex of the predominant public opinion of the country. Whether that opinion was, at any particular stage, right and wise,
is a different question; but it cannot be doubtful that the predominant
opinion carries with it the predominance of physical strength. A government against which this is arrayed in gathering force, must yield to it or
go to pieces. Had Mr. LINCOLN started with his emancipation policy in
the spring of 1861, his administration would have been wrecked by the
moral aid which would have been given the South by the northern conservatives, including a large part of the Republican party. Had he refused
to adopt the emancipation policy much beyond the autumn of 1862, the
Republican party would have refused public support to the war, and the
South would have gained its independence by their aid. With a stiff Republican Senate, the government would have been at a dead-lock, and
the violence of opinion would have wrenched its conflicting parts asunder. Regarding the growth of opinion simply in the light of a *fact*, we
must concede that Mr. LINCOLN's slowness, indecision, and reluctant
changes of policy have been in skillful, or at least fortunate, adaptation
to the prevailing public sentiment of the country. Some have changed
more rapidly, some more slowly than he; but there are few of his countrymen who have not changed at all.

If we look for the elements of character which have contributed to
the extraordinary and constantly growing popularity of Mr. LINCOLN,

they are not far to seek. The kindly, companionable, jovial turn of his disposition, free from every taint of affectation, puerile vanity, or *parvenu* insolence, conveyed a strong impression of worth, sense, and solidity, as well as goodness of heart. He never disclosed the slightest symptom that he was dazzled or elated by his great position, or that it was incumbent upon him to be any body but plain ABRAHAM LINCOLN. This was in infinitely better taste than would have been any attempt to put on manners that did not sit easily upon training and habits, under the false notion that he would be supporting the dignity of his office. No offense in manners is so intolerable as affectation; nor anything so vulgar as a soul haunted by an uneasy consciousness of vulgarity. Mr. LINCOLN's freedom from any such upstart affectations was one of the good points of his character; it betokened his genuineness and sincerity.

The conspicuous weakness of Mr. LINCOLN's mind on the side of imagination, taste, and refined sensibility, has rather helped him in the estimation of the multitude. Except so far as they contribute something to dignity of character, these qualities have little scope in the pursuits of a statesman; and their misplaced obtrusion is always offensive. They are a great aid, to be sure, in electric appeals to the passions; but in times like these through which we have been living, the passions have needed sedatives, not incentives; and the cool mastery of emotion has deserved to rank among the chief virtues. Mr. LINCOLN had no need of this virtue because the sluggishness of his emotional nature shielded him against the corresponding temptation; but this defect has served him as well as the virtue amid the more inflammable natures with which he has been in contact. His character was entirely relieved from repulsive matter-of-fact hardness by the unaffected kindliness of his disposition and the flow of his homely and somewhat grotesque mother-wit—the most popular of all the minor mental endowments.

The total absence from Mr. LINCOLN's sentiments and bearing of anything lofty or chivalric, and the hesitating slowness of his decisions, did not denote any feebleness of character. He has given a signal proof of a strong and manly nature in the fact that although he surrounded himself with the most considerable and experienced statesmen of his party, none of them were able to take advantage of his inexperience and gain any conspicuous ascendency over him. All his chief decisions have been his own; formed indeed, after much anxious and brooding consultation, but, in the final result, the fruit of his own independent volition. He has changed or retained particular members of his cabinet, and indorsed or rejected particular dogmas of his party, with the same ultimate reliance on the decisions of his own judgment. It is this feature of his character, which was gradually disclosed to the public view, together with the cautious and paternal cast of his disposition, that gave him his strong and increasing hold on the confidence of the masses.

Among the sources of Mr. LINCOLN's influence, we must not omit to mention the quaint and peculiar character of his written and spoken eloquence. It was as completely his own, as much the natural outgrowth of his character, as his personal manners. Formed on no model, and aiming only at the most convincing statement of what he wished to say, it was terse, shrewd, clear, with a peculiar twist in the phraseology which more than made up in point what it sometimes lost by its uncouthness. On the multitude, who do not appreciate literary refinement, and despise literary affectation, its effect was as great as the same ideas and arguments could have produced by any form of presentation. His style had the great redeeming excellence of that air of straightforward sincerity which is worth all the arts of the rhetorician.

The loss of such a man, in such a crisis; of a man who possessed so large and growing a share of the public confidence, and whose administration had recently borrowed new luster from the crowning achievements of our armies; of a ruler whom victory was inspiring with the wise and paternal magnanimity which sought to make the conciliation as cordial as the strife has been deadly; the loss of such a President, at such a conjuncture, is an afflicting dispensation which bows a disappointed and stricken nation in sorrow more deep, sincere, and universal than ever before supplicated the compassion of pitying Heaven.

April 17, 1865

Franklin Pierce

Speech at Concord, New Hampshire

No chief executive ever had to contend with as many vexatious, living former presidents as Lincoln—among them John Tyler (who served in the Confederate Congress) and Franklin Pierce (1804–1869), whom Lincoln had accused in 1858 of conspiring with Chief Justice Roger B. Taney and U.S. Senator Stephen A. Douglas to spread slavery throughout the nation. Understandably, the elegant New England Democrat bore no affection for the informal western Republican, and publicly blamed him for secession and war. Their relationship softened in 1862, when Pierce—whose eleven-year-old son had been killed in a railroad accident nine years earlier—learned that Lincoln's own child Willie had died of disease in Washington at the same age. "Even in this hour, so full of danger to our Country," sympathized the former President, "your thoughts, will be, of your cherished boy, who will nestle at your heart, until you meet him in that new life, when tears and toils and conflict will be unknown." Still, when news of Lincoln's murder reached New Hampshire, a furious crowd surrounded Pierce's home and demanded that he denounce the assassins. His carefully structured—and, by all accounts, brilliantly performed—response defused the mob's anger.

FELLOW-TOWNSMEN—I come to ascertain the motives of this call. What is your desire?

[Some person in the crowd replied, "We wish to hear some words from you on this sad occasion." General Pierce proceeded.]

I wish I could address you words of solace. But that can hardly be done. The magnitude of the calamity, in all aspects, is overwhelming. If your hearts are oppressed by events more calculated to awaken profound sorrow and regret than any which have hitherto occurred in our history, mine mingles its deepest regrets and sorrows with yours.

It is to be hoped that the great wickedness and atrocity was confined, morally and actually, to the heads and hearts of but two individuals of all those who still survive on this continent; and that they may speedily, and in obedience to law, meet the punishment due to their unparalleled crimes. It is well that you—it is well that I—well that all men worthy to be called citizens of the United States, make manifest in all suitable forms the emotions incident to the bereavement and distress which have been brought to the hearths and homes of the two most conspicuous families of the Republic. I give them my warm, outgushing sympathy, as I am sure all persons within the hearing of my voice must do.

But beyond personal grief and loss, there will abide with us inevitably the most painful memories. Because, as citizens obedient to law, revering the Constitution, holding fast to the Union, thankful for the period of history which succeeded the Revolution in so many years of peaceful growth and prosperity, and loving with the devotion of true and faithful children all that belongs to the advancement and glory of the nation, we can never forget or cease to deplore the great crime and deep stain.

[A voice from the crowd—"Where is your flag?"]

It is not necessary for me to show my devotion for the stars and stripes by any special exhibition, or upon the demand of any man or body of men. My ancestors followed it through the Revolution—one of them, at least, never having seen his mother's roof from the beginning to the close of that protracted struggle. My brothers followed it in the war of 1812, and I left my family in the spring of 1847, among you, to follow its fortunes and maintain it upon a foreign soil.

But this you all know. If the period during which I have served our State and country in various situations, commencing more than thirty-five years ago, have left the question of my devotion to the flag, the Constitution and Union, in doubt, it is too late now to remove it by any such exhibition as the inquiry suggests. Besides, to remove such doubts from minds where they may have been cultivated by a spirit of domination and partisan rancor, if such a thing were possible, would be of no consequence to you, and it is certainly of none to me. The malicious questionings would return to re-assert their supremacy and pursue the work of injustice.

Conscious of the infirmities of temperament which, to a greater or less extent, beset us all, I have never felt or found that violence or passion was ultimately productive of beneficent results. It is gratifying to perceive that your observation, briefer than mine, has led your minds to the same conclusion. What a priceless commentary upon this general thought is the final reported conversation between the late President and his Cabinet! and with that dispatch comes news to warrant the cheering hope, that in spite of the knife of the assassin, the life and intellect of the Secretary of State may, through Providence, be spared to us in this appalling emergency.

I thank you for the silent attention with which you have listened to me, and for the manifestations of your approval as my neighbors, and will not detain you in this storm longer than to add my best wishes for you all, and for what, individually and collectively, we ought to hold most dear—our country—our whole country. Good night.

George Templeton Strong

Diary, April 15–17, 1865

A successful lawyer in New York City, George Templeton Strong (1820–1875) served during the Civil War as the treasurer of the U.S. Sanitary Commission, a civilian organization that cared for sick and wounded Union soldiers. One of the most prodigious diarists of the nineteenth century, he recorded nearly every day of his adult life in a journal that ultimately bulged with 4.5 million words. After meeting Lincoln in January 1862 for the second time, Strong wrote that the President was a "yahoo, or gorilla in respect of outside polish," but also "sensible, straightforward, honest," and the best chief magistrate since Andrew Jackson. A steadfast Republican, Strong enthusiastically supported Lincoln's reelection in 1864. The assassination unleashed in him a torrent of emotions, including abject horror, boundless grief, and a burning desire for vengeance.

April 15, Saturday. Nine o'clock in the morning. *LINCOLN AND SEWARD ASSASSINATED LAST NIGHT!!!!*

The South has nearly filled up the measure of her iniquities at last! Lincoln's death not yet certainly announced, but the one o'clock despatch states that he was then dying. Seward's side room was entered by the same or another assassin, and his throat cut. It is unlikely he will survive, for he was suffering from a broken arm and other injuries, the consequence of a fall, and is advanced in life. Ellie brought this news two hours ago, but I can hardly *take it in* even yet. *Eheu* A. Lincoln!

I have been expecting this. I predicted an attempt would be made on Lincoln's life when he went into Richmond; but just now, after his generous dealings with Lee, I should have said the danger was past. But the ferocious malignity of Southerners is infinite and inexhaustible. I am stunned, as by a fearful personal calamity, though I can see that this thing, occurring just at this time, may be overruled to our great good. Poor Ellie is heartbroken, though never an admirer of Lincoln's. We shall appreciate him at last.

Up with the Black Flag now!

Ten P.M. What a day it has been! Excitement and suspension of business even more general than on the 3rd instant. Tone of feeling very like that of four years ago when the news came of Sumter. This atrocity has invigorated national feeling in the same way, almost in the same degree. People who pitied our misguided brethren yesterday, and thought they had been punished enough already, and hoped there would be a general amnesty, including J. Davis himself, talk approvingly today of vindictive justice and favor the introduction of judges, juries, gaolers, and hangmen among the dramatis personae. Above all, there is a profound, awe-stricken feeling that we are, as it were, in immediate presence of a fearful, gigantic crime, such as has not been committed in our day and can hardly be matched in history.

Faulkner, one of our Kenzua directors, called for me by appointment at half-past nine, and we drove to the foot of Jane Street to inspect apparatus for the reduction of gold ore by amalgamation, which he considers a great improvement on the machinery generally used for that purpose. Returned uptown and saw Bellows to advise about adjournment of our Sanitary Commission meeting next week. Thence to Wall Street. Immense crowd. Bulletins and extras following each other in quick, contradictory succession. Seward and his Fred had died and had not. Booth (one of the assassins, a Marylander, brother of Edwin Booth) had been taken and had not. So it has gone on all day. Tonight the case stands thus:

Abraham Lincoln died at twenty-two minutes after seven this morning. He never regained consciousness after the pistol ball fired at him from behind, over his wife's shoulder, entered his brain. Seward is living and may recover. The gentleman assigned to the duty of murdering him did his butchery badly. The throat is severely lacerated by his knife, but it's believed that no arteries are injured. Fred Seward's situation is less hopeful, his skull being fractured by a bludgeon or sling shot used by the same gentleman. The attendant who was stabbed, is dead. (Is not.)

The temper of the great meeting I found assembled in front of the Custom House (the old Exchange) was grim. A Southerner would compare it with that of the first session of the Jacobins after Marat's death. I thought it healthy and virile. It was the first great patriotic meeting since the war began at which there was no talk of concession and conciliation. It would have endured no such talk. Its sentiment seemed like this: "Now it is plain at last to everybody that there can be no terms with the woman-flogging aristocracy. Grant's generous dealing with Lee was a blunder. The *Tribune's* talk for the last fortnight was folly. Let us henceforth deal with rebels as they deserve. The rosewater treatment does not meet their case." I have heard it said fifty times today: "These madmen have murdered the two best friends they had in the world!" I heard of three or four men in Wall Street and near the Post Office who spoke lightly of the tragedy, and were instantly set upon by the bystanders and pummelled. One of them narrowly escaped death. It was Charles E. Anderson, brother of our friend Professor Henry James Anderson, father of pretty Miss Louisa. Moses H. Grinnell and the police had hard work to save him. I never supposed him a secessionist.

To Trinity Church vestry meeting, specially called, at half-past three at the rebuilt vestry office, corner Fulton and Church. A series of resolutions was read, drawn by the Rector. They were masculine and good, and they were passed *nem. con.*, though Verplanck and Tillou were in their seats—Copperheads both. I looked at the record of our action when Washington died sixty-six years ago. It was a mere resolution that the church and chapels be put in mourning. Our resolutions of today went, naturally, much further. I record to the credit of Gouverneur Ogden, whom I have always held cold-hearted and selfish, that he broke down in trying to read these resolutions, could not get beyond the first sentence, and had to hand them back to the Rector. There was a little diversity of opinion whether we should put our chancel into mourning tomorrow, being Easter Sunday, or postpone it a day longer. We left it to the Rector's discretion. No business was done today. Most shops are closed and draped with black and white muslin. Broadway is clad in "weepers" from Wall Street to Union Square. At 823 with Agnew, Bellows, and Gibbs. George Anthon dined here; with him to Union League Club. Special meeting and dense, asphyxiating crowd. Orations by George Bancroft and by the Rev. (Presbyterian) Thompson of the Tabernacle. Both good; Thompson's very good. "When A. Johnson was sworn in as President today," said the Rev. Thompson, "the Statue of Liberty that surmounts the dome of the Capitol and was put there by Lincoln, looked down on the city and on the nation and said, 'Our Government is unchanged—it has merely passed from the hands of one man into those of another. Let the dead bury their dead. Follow thou Me.'" Burnside tells me this morning that he ranks Johnson very high.

Jeff Davis has at last issued a manifesto. It is from Danville, before Lee's surrender and is full of fight.

April 16. An Easter Sunday unlike any I have seen. Drove downtown very early with Ellie, Johnny, and Temple. Nearly every building in Broadway and in all the side streets, as far as one could see, festooned lavishly with black and white muslin. Columns swathed in the same material. Rosettes pinned to window curtains. Flags at half mast and tied up with crape. I hear that even in second and third class quarters, people who could afford to do no more have generally displayed at least a little twenty-five cent flag with a little scrap of crape annexed. Never was a public mourning more spontaneous and general. It is like what we read of the demonstrations that followed Princess Charlotte's death, but with feelings of just wrath and aspirations for vengeance that had no place there.

Trinity was never filled so full, not even last Tuesday. The crowd packed the aisles tight and even occupied the choir steps and the choir itself nearly to the chancel rails. The outer doors, by the by, were in mourning, and the flag on the spire edged in black pursuant to my suggestion yesterday. Within the church, the symbols of public sorrow properly gave place to those of Easter. When we came to the closing prayers of the litany, Vinton proclaimed, "I bid you all unite with me in prayer for all the bereaved and afflicted families of this land, and especially for that of Abraham Lincoln, late President of the United States, recently destroyed by assassination," and read the proper prayer for those in affliction. He then prefaced the usual prayer for a sick person by a like bidding "for the Secretary of State and the Assistant Secretary of State, now in peril of death from wounds inflicted on them by an assassin." The effect of these formulas introduced into the service was telling. The anthem (Hallelujah Chorus) represented the ecclesiastical aspect of the day and was admirably well done. Vinton's sermon, or rather address, was far the best I have heard him deliver; extemporaneous, as he told us afterwards, when Ellie asked him for a copy. He blended the Easter sentiment with that of public grief most skillfully, or I should rather say by presenting suggestions of deep-lying truths that harmonized them. He brought out clearly the thought that had occurred to me and to many others: Perhaps Lincoln had done his appointed work; his honesty, sagacity, kindliness, and singleness of purpose had united the North and secured the suppression of rebellion. Perhaps the time has come for something beside kindliness, mercy, and forbearance, even for vengeance and judgment. Perhaps the murdered President's magnanimity would have been circumvented and his generosity and goodness abused by rebel subtlety and falsehood to our lasting national injury. Perhaps God's voice in this tragedy is "Well done, good and faithful servant. Thou hast done thy work of mercy. To others is given the duty of vengeance. Thy murder will help teach them that duty. Enter thou, by a painless process of death, into the joy of the Lord."

Southern barbarism has largely promoted our ethical education. What should we have said four years ago of Vinton earnestly enforcing on us the duty of hewing the (Southern) Agag in pieces before the Lord, not from personal animosity, but as a sacred obligation to be neglected only at peril of divine punishment, public and private? The whole service was a new experience to me. Men and women (poor Ellie among them) were sobbing and crying bitterly all around. My own eyes kept filling, and the corners of my mouth would twitch now and then in spite of all I could do.

Tonight Osten-Sacken, little Kate and her papa, George Anthon, and Colonel Howe, with a pocket full of telegrams from Washington. Seward and his son seem doing well. Sorry to say that neither assassin has yet been caught. There are reports that our policy at Richmond is to be changed, that the proposed convocation of Virginia rebels will be dispersed, and that some of them will be held as hostages against further attempts at assassination of presidents and cabinet officers.

There is intense exasperation. I hear of a dozen households whose Celtic handmaidens have been summarily discharged for some talk rejoicing at Abe Lincoln's death. The New York Hotel was protected by policemen last night and today on its proprietor's petition. The President's funeral is to be Thursday next. Gramercy Park House dismissed a batch of waiters today, at Howe's instigation, for blind, foolish, Celtic talk approving Lincoln's murder. Horace Greeley, the advocate of pacification and amnesty, is as unpopular as General Lee. I directed my waiter to stop the *Tribune*. There are hopeful signs that the community may be ready at last for action against its Barlows, LaRocques, Belmonts, and Duncans.

April 17. Very busy in Wall Street, and at two to Columbia College meeting. A little progress made in the ancient undertaking of the "new statutes." Did any one of the pyramids take so much time to build? Also we passed and ordered published a series of resolutions on the assassination. Barnard drew them. They are plain-spoken and radical enough, declaring this atrocity, like the attempted incendiarism of last November and the systematic starvation of 60,000 prisoners of war, due to the brutalizing influences of slavery. They seemed diffuse, and too abundantly peppered with vehemence of adjectives, but it is hard to find words too strong for this case. Betts and Zabriskie recalcitrated, of course; doubted, demurred, and did not like the resolutions a bit. But they passed without a division. Thence to No. 823, making arrangements for the Sanitary Commission session at Washington, for which I expect to leave town tomorrow.

All over the city, people have been at work all day, draping street fronts, so that hardly a building on Wall Street, Broadway, Chambers Street, Bowery, Fourth Avenue is without its symbol of the profound public sorrow. What a place this man, whom his friends have been patronizing for four years as a well-meaning, sagacious, kind-hearted, ignorant, old codger, had won for himself in the hearts of the people! What a place he will fill in history! I foresaw most clearly that he would be ranked high as the Great Emancipator twenty years hence, but I did not suppose his death would instantly reveal—even to Copperhead newspaper editors—the nobleness and the glory of his part in this great contest. It reminds one of the last line of Blanco White's great sonnet, "If Light can thus deceive, wherefore not Life?" *Death* has suddenly opened the eyes of the people (and I think of the world) to the fact that a hero has been holding high place among them for four years, closely watched and studied, but despised and rejected by a third of this community, and only tolerated by the other two-thirds.

1865

George W. Julian

Diary, April 15–19, 1865

A Radical Republican congressman from Indiana, George W. Julian (1817–1899) had hailed the passage of the Thirteenth Amendment by Congress in January 1865 as the "greatest event of this century." On the evening of April 14 Julian returned to the capital after visiting Richmond with fellow members of the congressional Joint Committee on the Conduct of the War. His frank description of the "hostility" and "contempt" for Lincoln's leadership expressed the next day in an informal caucus held by Radical senators Benjamin F. Wade and Zachariah Chandler, former congressman John Covode, Chief Justice David Cartter of the District of Columbia Supreme Court (who was assisting Stanton in the assassination investigation), and Samuel Wilkinson of the *New York Tribune* illustrates the bitter divisions that remained in the Republican Party after Appomattox. The immediate cause for Radical disdain for Lincoln was his decision after the fall of Richmond to allow the secessionist Virginia legislature to meet for the sole purpose of withdrawing their state troops from the Confederate army. When Lincoln learned that the rebel legislators hoped to negotiate peace terms, he rescinded his earlier order. The Radicals' hopes for remaking the cabinet under the new president soon came to naught, and over the next year Andrew Johnson's political maladroitness and commitment to preserving white supremacy would set him firmly on the path that culminated with his impeachment.

SATURDAY EVENING, April 15.

Reached here at seven o'clock yesterday evening, as glad to get back as I was sorry to have missed Charleston. Went to bed about 10:30 and was soon roused from a deep sleep by someone knocking at my door. Mr. Woods entered and told me Lincoln was murdered, and Seward and son probably, and that assassins were about to take the town. I was still half asleep and in my fright grew suddenly cold, heartsick, and almost helpless. On going out on the street a little later I found the whole town in a blaze of excitement and rage. About 7:30 the church bells tolled the President's death. The weather was as gloomy as the mood of the people. All sorts of rumors were afloat about Seward and his sons, who are still living, but with doubtful chance of recovery. They are said to be dreadfully gashed and bruised. Booth is the murderer of Lincoln, but the other assassins are not yet known.

Johnson was inaugurated today at 11 A.M., and took the oath, and he has already been in the hands of Chase, the Blairs, Halleck, General Scott, etc. Chase has again gone crazy about the presidency, and it is said is now plotting for the State Department as a stepping stone. Vain thought! The War Committee today sent a request for an interview with the President and will probably secure it tomorrow. Have spent most of the afternoon in caucus with Wade, Chandler, Covode, Judge Carter and Wilkinson, correspondent of *The Tribune*, who is determined to put Greeley on the war-path. In this caucus we agreed upon a new cabinet, which we are tomorrow to urge upon Johnson, among other things placing Butler in the State Department, Stebbins, of New York, in the navy, and Covode Postmaster General. I like the radicalism of the members of this caucus, but have not in a long time heard so much profanity. It became intolerably disgusting. Their hostility towards Lincoln's policy of conciliation and contempt for his weakness were undisguised; and the universal feeling among radical men here is that his death is a godsend. It really seems so, for among the last acts of his official life was an invitation to some of the chief rebel conspirators to meet in Richmond and confer with us on the subject of peace. The dastardly attack upon Lincoln and Seward, the great leaders in the policy of mercy, puts to flight utterly every vestige of humanitarian weakness, and makes it seem that justice shall be done and the righteous ends of the war made sure. The government could not have survived the policy upon which it had entered.

SUNDAY NIGHT, April 16.

This morning went with our committee by appointment to meet the new President at his headquarters in the Treasury Department. He received us with decided cordiality. Wade said: "Johnson, we have faith in you. By the Gods, there will be no trouble now in running the government." He replied, "I am very much obliged to you gentlemen, and I can only say you can judge of my policy by the past. Everybody knows what that is. I hold this: Robbery is a crime; rape is a crime; murder is a crime; *treason* is a crime; and *crime* must be punished. The law provides for it and the courts are open. Treason must be made infamous and traitors must be impoverished. We applauded his declarations and parted. From him and others I learn that General Weitzel's order before referred to was issued by direction of Lincoln, who yielded to the pressure against him so far as to acquiesce in Stanton's order removing Weitzel for having acted without authority. This was outrageously unjust to Weitzel. It seems from the *Intelligencer* this morning that Lincoln had ordered that Thompson and Letcher should be allowed to escape out of the country as one of his last public acts. On our way from the Treasury we called on General Butler at Willard's, who had just reached the city. He is in fine spirits and is to see the President this evening. A caucus of the radical members of the War Committee is to meet the President tomorrow morning at 9 o'clock to confer about a new cabinet. Butler says the President must not administer on the estate of Lincoln but on that of the government, and select new men to do it. I am now more than rejoiced that we did not go to Charleston. The conservatives of the country are not here, and the presence and influence of the War Committee with Johnson, who is an ex-member, will powerfully aid the new administration in getting onto the right track.

Grant's terms with Lee were too easy, and the force surrendered was too small to be of great consequence.

MONDAY EVENING, April 17.

Last night went to the African Baptist church on Fourth street and was much interested. This morning went as per appointment to see the President. We talked very frankly and the symptoms seemed favorable. This evening attended the meeting of Senators and Representatives to make arrangements as to the funeral of the President. I am on the committee of escort to convey the remains to Illinois, but I cannot leave my duties here. The excitement growing out of the President's murder increases.

TUESDAY EVENING, 18th.

Wrote a long letter home for the *Republican*. Great crowds are pouring in to attend the funeral tomorrow. Went to the east room of the White House this evening and saw the remains of the President. Great crowds have been struggling for admission all day, and more than 100,000 must have gazed at his remains since morning. Made a very pleasant call on Father Pierrepont this evening.

WEDNESDAY NIGHT.

Attended the funeral in the east room. The procession has no parallel.

The funeral of General Taylor, which I attended, was nothing in comparison. The negroes appeared finely in the procession, and the President's hold on them is wonderful, and indeed on the whole country, including even those who regarded his death as a providential means of saving the country. He was a plain man of the people, indeed *one* of them, and hence their devotion to him.

Henry J. Raymond

FROM *The New York Times*

Among New York's many politically connected newspaper editors, Henry J. Raymond (1820–1869), founder of *The New York Times*, stood out for his closeness to the Lincoln administration. A prominent voice among moderate Republicans in the North, Raymond enjoyed considerable influence on presidential patronage, served as chairman of the National Union (Republican) party executive committee during the 1864 election, and in his spare time produced a massive Lincoln campaign biography. Known among his peers as a calm and gifted writer, especially under pressure, Raymond expressed the grief and sorrow felt by millions in a series of editorials. They suggest that the unemotional editor, named the "Little Villain" by his rival Horace Greeley, had lost not only a benefactor, but a friend.

THE MURDER OF PRESIDENT LINCOLN.

The heart of this nation was stirred yesterday as it has never been stirred before. The news of the assassination of ABRAHAM LINCOLN carried with it a sensation of horror and of agony which no other event in our history has ever excited. In this city the demonstrations of grief and consternation were without a parallel. Business was suspended. Crowds of people thronged the streets—great gatherings sprung up spontaneously everywhere seeking to give expression, by speeches, resolutions, &c., &c., to the universal sense of dismay and indignation which pervaded the public mind.

Perhaps the paramount element in this public feeling was evoked by personal regard for ABRAHAM LINCOLN. That a man so gentle, so kind, so free from every particle of malice or unkindness, every act of whose life has been so marked by benevolence and goodwill, should become the victim of a cold-blooded assassination, shocked the public heart beyond expression. That the very moment, too, when he was closing the rebellion which had drenched our land in blood and tears—by acts of magnanimity so signal as even to excite the reluctant distrust and apprehensions of his own friends—should be chosen for his murder, adds a new element of horror to the dreadful tragedy.

But a powerful element of the general feeling which the news aroused was a profound concern for the public welfare. The whole nation had come to lean on ABRAHAM LINCOLN in this dread crisis of its fate with a degree of confidence never accorded to any President since GEORGE WASHINGTON. His love of his country ardent and all-pervading, — swaying every act and prompting every word, — his unsuspected uprightness and personal integrity, — his plain, simple common sense, conspicuous in everything he did or said, commending itself irresistibly to the judgment and approval of the great body of the people, had won for him a solid and immovable hold upon the regard and confidence even of his political opponents. The whole people mourn his death with profound and sincere appreciation of his character and his worth.

ANDREW JOHNSON, of Tennessee, is now the President of the United States. We have no doubts and no misgivings in regard to the manner in which he will discharge the duties which devolve so suddenly upon him. This country has no more patriotic citizen than he — no one among all her public men who will bring to her service a higher sense of his responsibilities, a sounder judgment in regard to her interests, or a firmer purpose in the maintenance of her honor and the promotion of her welfare. He has suffered, in his person, his property and his family relations, terribly from the wicked rebellion which has desolated the land; but he is not the man to allow a sense of personal wrong to sway his judgment or control his action in a great national emergency. Traitors and rebels have nothing to expect at his hands, but strict justice, tempered with such mercy only as the welfare of the nation may require.

In this hour of mourning and of gloom, while the shadow of an awful and unparalleled calamity hangs over the land, it is well to remember that the stability of our government and the welfare of our country do not depend upon the life of any individual, and that the great current of affairs is not to be changed or checked by the loss of any man however high or however honored. In nations where all power is vested in single hands, an assassin's knife may overthrow governments and wrap a continent in the flames of war. But here the PEOPLE rule, and events inevitably follow the course which *they* prescribe. ABRAHAM LINCOLN has been their agent and instrument for the four years past; ANDREW JOHNSON is to be their agent for the four years that are now to come. If the people have faith, courage and wisdom, the result will be the same.

YESTERDAY.—It would be presumptuous to attempt to express in words the deep sorrow with which the death of our noble President has filled all hearts. To the honor of our people be it said, that, with a few unimportant exceptions, the nation's heart throbs with the profoundest grief, and the utterances of the nation's voice are all in accord in lamentation. The great calamity was scarcely known, and where known, was hardly believed, at the late hour of its announcement on Friday night. But early yesterday morning we were assured of the mournful truth. As one man the people put on the habiliments of mourning, and the glad songs of triumph over the anticipated advent of peace were subdued to the wail of such grief as only a nation can feel. All day the stunned and bewildered citizens were putting forth the emblems of mourning. Business was almost entirely suspended. Sorrow was visible on every face, not seldom varied with an expression that partook of revenge. The low, earnest conversation of friends, the almost fearful greetings of acquaintances, the entire absence of the ordinary hum and bustle of business, fittingly marked the people's appreciation of their bereavement. It was a day never paralleled, and never to be forgotten.

April 16, 1865

THE NATION'S BEREAVEMENT.

Death, as the Northmen imaged him, is no dart-brandishing skeleton, but a gigantic shape, that inwraps mortals within the massive folds of its dark garment. Long has it been since those dread robes closed upon a mightier victim than President LINCOLN. It is like the earth's opening and swallowing up a city. The public loss is so great, the chasm made in our national councils so tremendous, that the mind, not knowing how to adjust itself to such a change, shrinks back appalled. It comes home to every bosom with the force of a personal affliction. There is not a loyal family in the land that does not mourn. It is as when there "was a great cry in Egypt, for there was not a house where there was not one dead."

No public man has ever died in America invested with such responsibilities, and the mark of so much attention, as ABRAHAM LINCOLN. The unprecedented manner of his death has shocked inexpressibly; but it is not that which most harrows with anguish. It is the loss of the man himself—the privation of him when he seemed peculiarly necessary to the country, and when the heart of the people was bound to him more than ever. Had he been taken by a natural death, the public grief would have been just as profound, though unaccompanied with the other emotions which his assassination has excited. All true men feel that they have lost a man of wondrous fitness for the task he had to execute. Few Americans have lived who had such a faculty of discovering the real relations of things, and shaping his thoughts and actions strictly upon them without external bias. In his own independent, and perhaps we may say very peculiar way, he invariably got at the needed truths of the time. Without anything like brilliancy of genius, without any great breadth of information or literary accomplishment, he still had that perfect balance of thoroughly sound faculties which gives an almost infallible judgment. This, combined with great calmness of temper, great firmness of purpose, supreme moral principle, and intense patriotism, made up just that character which fitted him, as the same qualities fitted WASHINGTON, for a wise and safe conduct of public affairs in a season of great peril.

Political opponents have sometimes denied that Mr. LINCOLN was a great man. But if he had not great faculties and great qualities, how happens it that he has met the greatest emergencies that ever befell a nation in a manner that so gained for him the confidence of the people? No man ever had greater responsibilities, and yet never were responsibilities discharged with greater acceptance. All disparagement sinks powerless before this one fact, that the more ABRAHAM LINCOLN was tried, the more he was trusted. Nobody can be so foolish as to impute this to the arts and delusions which sometimes give success to the intriguer and demagogue of the hour. It would be the worst insult to the American people to suppose them capable of being so cajoled when the very life of their country was at stake. Nor was it in the nature of Mr. LINCOLN to act a part. He was the least pretentious of men. He never sought to win confidence by any high professions. He never even protested his determination to do his duty. Nor, after he had done his duty, did he go about seeking glory for his exploits, or asking thanks by his presence for the great benefits he had conferred. Sampson-like, he could rend a lion and tell neither father nor mother of it. He was a true hero of the silent sort, who spoke mostly by his actions, and whose action-speech was altogether of the highest kind, and best of its kind. He was not an adventurer, aiming at great things for himself and courting the chances of fortune; nor was he a great artist in any sense, undergoing passions and reflecting them; but he was a great power, fulfilling his way independently of art and passion, and simple, as all great powers are. No thought of self—no concern for his own repute—none of the prudish sensitiveness for his own good name, which is the form selfishness often assumes in able and honorable men, ever seemed to enter his mind. To him it was but the ordinary course of life to do that which has made him illustrious. He had a habit of greatness. An intense, all-comprehensive patriotism, was a constant stimulus of all his public exertions. It grew into the very constitution of his soul, and operated, like a natural function, continuously, spontaneously and almost as it were unconsciously. It pervaded and vivified all that he said, and formed the prime incentive of all that he did. If he had ambition, it was to serve his country, and in that sphere where he might do it most effectually. In no way did he ever fail his country in the time of need. He was independent, self-poised, steadfast. You always knew where to find him; you could calculate him like a planet. A public trust was to him a sacred thing. Sublimer moral courage, more resolute devotion to duty, cannot be found in the history of man than he has displayed for the salvation of the American Union. It was the sublime performance of sublime duties that made him so trusted, and which has given him a fame as solid as justice, and as genuine as truth.

ABRAHAM LINCOLN had a heart full of all gentle and pure affections —a heart not prone to strong passion or tumultuous emotion, but ever glowing with a steady, warm, all-comprehensive sympathy. It was a large, equable, genial, tender heart, none the less delicately strung because its chords were deep laid. It was a heart that could not retain a single bitter or vindictive feeling. Public life has a tendency to chill the kindly and generous affections, and blight the sweet charities of life; but of President LINCOLN it may be said as was said of Mr. FOX, that his heart was as little hardened as if he had lived and died in a farm-house. No public power, no public care, no public applause could spoil him; he remained ever the same plain man of the people. It was this which peculiarly endeared him to the people, and makes the sorrow for him so tender as a personal feeling, apart from the sense of a national calamity. It is not simply because "he hath been so clear in his great office," but because "he hath borne his faculties so meek"

> "that his virtues
> Will plead like angels, trumpet-tongued, against
> The deep damnation of his taking off."

THE EFFECT OF PRESIDENT LINCOLN'S DEATH ON NATIONAL AFFAIRS.

The death of President LINCOLN naturally excites universal and profound solicitude as to the immediate future of the country. He has been so marked a figure in the terrible events of the last four years, the action of the government in its contest with the rebellion has been so stamped by the impress of his personal character, and he had come to have so strong a hold upon the confidence and love of the whole people, without distinction of party, that his sudden removal from the stage of events naturally excites anxiety and apprehension in the public mind. He does, indeed, seem to have been needed to close the great work of pacification which he had so well begun.

Nevertheless, it is well to remember that the peculiar nature of our institutions makes it impossible that any one man should be absolutely indispensable to their preservation and successful working. Our government is of the people. They not only elect our rulers, but their spirit, their temper, their will pervade and control all the acts and all the measures of the government. Whoever dies, the people live, and the government lives also. If the Emperor NAPOLEON had been assassinated, all France would have been in revolution before twenty-four hours had passed away. President LINCOLN's death, sudden and awful as it was — though it removes him in an instant from the most important and conspicuous position held by any living man, — does not interrupt for an instant the grand movement of our republican government. So far from exciting revolution, it only unites the whole people, more thoroughly than ever, in a common sentiment of devotion to the country and of profound grief for the great calamity that has fallen upon it. All party rancor is hushed.

Political strife has ceased. All men of all parties, feeling a common interest and a common grief, stand together in support of the nation and of the man thus suddenly charged with the execution of the people's will.

The current of events will continue to dictate the policy of the government, as it has done hitherto. The rebellion is already substantially crushed. The war, to all intents and purposes, is closed. There is nothing in the death of Mr. LINCOLN which can raise new armies for the rebel service or inspire new hopes for the rebel cause. No portion of the Southern people will be stimulated by it to renew the struggle. The same great Generals who have given our flag victory are still at the head of our armies and the act of an assassin has so fired the loyal heart of the nation, that those armies can be doubled in number if the necessity should arise. But it will not arise. The blow which has aroused the North will paralyze the South. The rebels will see in it nothing encouraging to their cause, nothing inciting them to new exertions on its behalf.

In President JOHNSON, moreover, the country has a man of courage, of sound judgment and of a patriotism which has stood the test of the most terrible trials. His sympathies are with the people, and all his action will be for their good. He will respond to their sentiments and will execute their will. Nor will he be unmindful of the fact that the general line of policy which ABRAHAM LINCOLN was carrying out, when arrested by the murderer's blow, commanded the hearty and universal approbation of the great mass of the American people. No man ever came suddenly to power with a plainer path before him than that which lies before the new President. And no one need fear for a moment that the rebellion is to gain anything by the death of President LINCOLN or by the accession to power of ANDREW JOHNSON as his successor.

April 17, 1865

Horace Greeley

The Nation's Loss

The nation's most prominent newspaper editor, Horace Greeley (1811–1872) of the *New York Tribune*, shared the President's antipathy toward slavery, but was as unpredictable and emotional as Lincoln was steady and resolute. From 1860 on the two men had a tempestuous relationship, disagreeing over political patronage, secession, war, emancipation, and other issues. In July 1864 Greeley had involved Lincoln in an ill-fated attempt to open peace negotiations with Confederate envoys at Niagara Falls. When the overture's failure further jeopardized the President's already dire reelection prospects, Greeley encouraged fellow Republicans to find a new presidential candidate. An exasperated Lincoln told his cabinet that the "not truthful" editor reminded him of a rotten shoe "that nothing can be done with." During the final months of the war the icy relationship between the two men never really thawed. In the immediate aftermath of the assassination Greeley offered an assessment of Lincoln's legacy.

The immediate presence of the horrible crime which has stricken the Republic to the heart, in the hour of its transcendent and long-awaited triumph, is unfavorable to a full and clear conception of its importance and its consequences. It must necessarily appear to different observers under different aspects, and each will especially lament it for some reasons which will have less force and weight with others.

For our own part, it intensifies our regret, while it is nevertheless our abiding consolation, that the lamented Head of the Republic now sleeping in his bloody shroud was never provoked to the exhibition of one trace of hate or even wrath toward those against whom he was compelled to battle for the life of the Nation. From the hour, now eleven years past, when, in view of the treacherous repudiation of the Missouri compact, he enunciated the axiomatic yet startling truth: "The Union cannot permanently exist half slave and half free," down to that of his assassination, he uttered no syllable of retort to the hideous vomitings of abuse and slander wherewith he was incessantly covered by the partisans of the doomed but still vital and venomous "institution." Perpetually represented to the Southern people as a libel on Humanity and a tiger ravenous for blood, he not only put forth no speech, no paper, no manifesto, that gave the least countenance to these calumnies, but he never, in his most intimate and confidential moments, indicated a hope, a wish, that evil should befall one of these enemies, save as it should be necessary for the salvation of the country. And this fact, hitherto suppressed and distorted, will now make itself felt and respected. The blow that struck down Abraham Lincoln bereft the Union's misguided and criminal assailants of the firmest and most powerful opponent of all avoidable severity, all not indispensable harshness, in suppressing their Rebellion. His very last public utterance—the speech of the Tuesday night prior to his assassination—was conceived in this spirit, and had no other purpose than to reconcile the North to the most gentle and magnanimous treatment of the discomfited insurgents. If ever man made war in a Christian spirit, Mr. Lincoln was that man. His first Inaugural is the most affecting appeal ever made to a disaffected party against the madness and crime of plunging their country into an abyss of blood and horror. His last Inaugural, so solemn and religious in its tone, and now seeming to have been written under the shadow of impending death, is pervaded by the same spirit. His failings as a leader in such a crisis were prompted by a nature slow to anger and shrinking from any but the most indispensable shedding of blood. No portion of the American people have greater reason to deplore his murder than those in whose presumed interest or to glut whose malignity it was perpetrated.

President Lincoln fell a sacrifice to his country's salvation as absolutely, palpably, as though he had been struck down while leading an assault on the ramparts of Petersburg. The wretch who killed him was impelled by no private malice, but imagined himself an avenger of that downcast idol which, disliking to be known simply as Slavery, styles itself "the South." He was murdered, not that Slavery might live, but that it might bring down its most conspicuous enemy in its fall. His death sets the seal of Fate to the decree that dooms Slavery speedily to perish, not in this country only, but in all its remaining lurking-places throughout the civilized world.

The Republic is saved forever from its giant curse and shame. It will not be divided; it will all be Free. If there had been doubt of this last week, as there was not, there is doubt no longer. Our abiding and serious peril is a transfusion into the veins of the Loyal Millions of some portion of the blood of the monster they have slain. The public feeling aroused by the double assassination at Washington needs to be calmed and directed, not inflamed and aggravated. There is depravity but no danger in the babble of the mad fool who says he is glad Lincoln is killed; there is food for graver thought, there is a call for sterner reprobation, in the pious suggestion that our good President has been Providentially called hence in order that the leading Rebels may receive that condign punishment which his kindness of heart would have averted.

For nothing can be further from the truth than the current notion that Mr. Lincoln was a man easily deflected from his course. He was slow to reach conclusions; but, once attained, they were immovable. He was among the last to perceive that the struggle into which we have been plunged could only be fought to a successful issue by openly recognizing the fact that Slavery had challenged the Union to mortal encounter and that the gage must be taken up as it was thrown down; but, once convinced of that fact, he was convinced forever. There was not in all America one man more inflexible in his resolve that Slavery should die and the Union be restored than was Abraham Lincoln. And whoever imagines that he could have been duped, or cajoled, or wheedled, out of his purpose on this head, does gross injustice to his memory. We venture to add that no man perceived more readily or repelled more sternly than he the error of Gen. Weitzel in consenting to the convocation under our flag at Richmond of Extra Billy Smith and his presumptively impenitent confederates on the assumption that they are to-day the Governor and Legislature of Virginia.

To human vision, it would seem that Mr. Lincoln has fallen at the very moment when his loss would be most keenly and justly felt. The soldier had done his work: the hour of the statesman had fully struck: and the President was ready and eager for the task. Had he lived a very few days longer, we believe he would have issued a Proclamation of Amnesty which would have dissolved all that remains of the Rebellion, leaving its leaders no choice but between flight and unconditional surrender. We have no special knowledge of the purposes of his successor, but we will not doubt that the good Providence which has borne our country so nobly through her past trials will continue her guide and guardian through whatever may be still before her, and that the storm and gloom of the present will speedily be effaced by the sunshine of Peace, Union and Impartial Freedom.

April 7, 1865

Edmund Clarence Stedman

Abraham Lincoln Assassinated Good Friday, 1865

Born in Hartford, Connecticut, Edmund Clarence Stedman (1833–1908) covered the opening months of the Civil War as a battlefield correspondent for the then pro-Republican *New York World*. He then became a successful stockbroker and popular figure in New York literary circles. Stedman's swift and angry call for vengeance appeared in the *New York Tribune* on April 17, 1865, the same day as Horace Greeley's editorial, "The Nation's Loss."

"Forgive them, for they know not what they do!"
　　HE said, and so went shriven to his fate—
　　Unknowing went, that generous heart and true.
　　Even while he spoke the slayer lay in wait,
　　And when the morning opened Heaven's gate
　　There passed the whitest soul a nation knew.
　　Henceforth all thoughts of pardon are too late;
　　They, in whose cause that arm its weapon drew,
　　Have murdered MERCY. Now alone shall stand
　　Blind JUSTICE, with the sword unsheathed she wore.
　　Hark, from the eastern to the western strand,
　　The swelling thunder of the people's roar:
　　What words they murmur—FETTER NOT HER HAND!
　　SO LET IT SMITE, SUCH DEEDS SHALL BE NO MORE!

EDMUND C. STEDMAN.

April 15, 1865.

Taylor Peirce

Letter to Catharine Peirce

Taylor Peirce (1822–1901) grew corn and operated a sawmill before enlisting in the 22nd Iowa Infantry in August 1862. A steadfast admirer of "old Abe," Peirce resolved "to try and be one of the many that God has raised to put down this rebellion and blot out the institution of slavery." He fought in the Vicksburg campaign and at Winchester and Cedar Creek in the Shenandoah Valley before being posted in March 1865 to the Union supply depot at Morehead City, North Carolina. Peirce wrote to his wife in Des Moines after learning of the assassination.

———————

Head Quarters 22 Iowa Infty
Morehead City NC April 17th 65

Dear Catharine and all the rest

I wrote you last night full of hope and bright anticipations for the future. But ah how Soon is the brightest prospects clouded. Truly is it said that we know not what a day will bring forth. Amid the general joy and anticipations of an early peace joy a sad and prolonged wail comes from the North and tell us of the death by the assassins hand of one of Earths best men. Lincoln is dead.

Oh what crime has our country been guilty of that it requires that Such men as he must fall. I had thought or hoped at least the sin of slavery had been washed out in the blood of the thousands of the best and bravest of the land but it seems not. The magnitude of the national Sin must nescessarily require proportionate attonement. And when one comes to contemplate it, it only creates wonder that the destruction of life and property has not been greater. We have no particulars of the murder here yet. We have only heard that Lincoln was murdered in the "Theatre" and that Stanton and his son was killed in their own house. This is only in keeping in the principles of the Southeren People. Slavery has divested them of every principle of humanity. They are more like barbarians than civilized beings. While we were in Savannah our Lt Col was invited to a party at the house of a prominent Rebel Lady or at least she called herself a lady when the conversation turned on the relics retained by persons as a momento of the war. When she addressed the Col and told him She had a letter from an admirer of hers sent from the battle field of Chickamanga that She thought a great deal of. He said that it was written with the blood of a dead yankee. Her admirer wrote her that he dipped the pen in the blood as it ran from the wound that caused the yankees death and she was going to preserve it as an evidence of the heroeism of the Chivalry. Another one of the chivalry was captured last fall in the Valley, the Nephew of Gov Letcher who used the jaw bone of a Yankee for a spur. Another lady had a yankee skull for a drinking cup. Now when we think of these things I do not wonder at them assasinating any one that they can get to without being caught.

I would not be surprised to learn that our northern Cops had a hand in it too for men of their avowd principle would stop at nothing to carry out their ends.

I would be in favour of letting the niggers go in now and make a clean shucking of the South. I am in favour of having the South Settled with a better breed of dogs and therefore let the negroes take it. For I beleve they are as much better than the Southeren Whites that they might bear the same comparison to them that the Jews did to the Gentiles. I want you to write to me how the cops behave over the news. If they seem to rejoice over it I am of the opinion that the thing has had its inception in the north among the traitors and Cowards. My lord if I ever hear a man justify or even hint at a justification of such a thing I would send him to hell quicker than ever a cat killed a mouse. What is to become of us now? I have no confidence in Johnson. Seward is not likely to recover and who is there now to manage things to keep us out of the hands of a Military Dictator? I am sure I can not tell. All looks gloomy. I want Cyrus to write and tell me how the cops in Des Moins take the news. And also let me know what the feelings is in the North in regard to the future. We get so little news here that I do not find out much but the war News.

I must close. Kiss the little ones for me and give my love to Mary and Cyrus and all the friends.

Thine affectionately
Taylor

April 19th. I am well and am going out to hunt Shells on the beach with the Rev Mr Roach of Des Moines to-day.

I received thy letter of the 4 of April yesterday. Glad to hear hope C will not have any more of his bad spells.

James Madison Bell

Poem in Commemoration of Lincoln

Born a free man in Ohio, the poet James Madison Bell (1826–1902) earned his living as a plasterer and brick mason. Bell moved to Chatham, Canada West, in 1854 and became a friend and supporter of John Brown. In 1860 he settled in San Francisco, where he became known as a poet, orator, and leader of the black community in northern California. One of his best known poems, "The Day and the War," dedicated to Brown and written to commemorate the first anniversary of the Emancipation Proclamation, concluded with praise for Lincoln: "And tribes and peoples yet unborn, / Shall hail and bless his natal morn." When the news reached California by telegraph that the President had been murdered, Bell wrote a tribute in a matter of days.

———————

In commemoration of the death of Abraham Lincoln, delivered at the great public meeting of colored citizens on Tuesday evening, April 18, 1865, Sacramento, Cal.

> Wherefore half-mast and waving sadly
> And seeming ill-disposed to move,
> Are those bright emblems which so gladly
> Were wont to wave our homes above?
> And why is all this lamentation?
> And why those outward signs of woe?
> And why is this all-glorious nation
> Thus in her hour of hope bowed low?
>
> Wherefore those marks of grief and sorrow
> So visible on every face?
> To what foul deed of bloody horror
> Do all those gloomy signs retrace?
> Aback to the walls and lofty spire!
> Back to the Nation's Halls of State!
> Back to our country's bleeding sire!
> Back to our dying Magistrate!

We know not why God has permitted
  This tragic scene, this bloody deed;
An act so seemingly unfitted,
  In this auspicious hour of need.
Though none perhaps may the intention,
  Or the wonderous purpose tell,
Of this direful life-suspension—
  Yet God, the Lord, doeth all things well!

Our Nation's Father has been murdered!
  Our Nation's Chieftain has been slain!
By traitorous hands most basely ordered;
  And we, his children, feel the pain.
Our pain is mixed with indignation,
  Our sorrow is not purely grief,
And nothing short of a *libation*
  From *Treason's* heart can bring relief.

And we, in sight of earth and heaven,
  On bended knee, with lifted hand,
Swear as we hope to be forgiven,
  To drive foul Treason from the land!
And that fair land so long polluted
  By the sweat of unpaid toil,
Shall be by liberty uprooted,
  And thickly spread with freedom's soil.

Thus we'll avenge the death of Lincoln,
  His noble principles maintain,
Till every base inhuman falcon
  Is swept from freedom's broad domain;
Until from tower and from turret,
  From mountain height and prairie wide,
One flag shall wave—and freedom's spirit
  In peace and love o'er all preside.

William O. Stoddard

Recollection of the Lincoln Assassination

The co-editor of the *Central Illinois Gazette*, William Osborn Stoddard (1835–1925) eagerly sought a White House position after the 1860 election based on only the briefest acquaintance with the new President-elect. Initially hired by the Interior Department to sign Lincoln's name to land patents, Stoddard was assigned to the White House in July 1861 and became the so-called third secretary after John G. Nicolay and John Hay. He eventually took charge of the incoming correspondence, which sometimes approached an overwhelming 500 letters and parcels daily. When his health faltered in 1864, Stoddard asked Lincoln to appoint him as the U.S. marshal for eastern Arkansas. In a memoir completed in 1907 that remained unpublished in his lifetime, he recounted how the news of the assassination reached him in Little Rock. (In his manuscript, Stoddard describes hearing about the attempt on Seward's life several hours before news arrived of Lincoln's murder. It is possible that he conflated learning about the attempted assassination of the secretary of state with hearing about Seward's serious carriage accident on April 5.)

———————

There came a night in the Spring of 1865 when Henry and myself lay down as usual upon our camp beds in the Marshal's office in the old Statehouse building. The night was warm and one of the windows was open. The previous evening we had heard of the attempt upon the life of Mr. Seward and of his dangerous condition, and had been talking about him, for to myself he had been always a kindly friend for whom I had a strong personal regard. It was in the early dawn, or a little after sunrise, that I found myself suddenly sitting up in bed, listening. In a moment more I knew why, for there came booming in through the window the sound of a heavy gun. Henry was also now awake and the first exclamation made by either of us was, in some form, "What? An attack by the Confederate army? That's from a fort!" "Impossible!" I exclaimed. "None of them are near enough. Hark!"

One minute, another gun, one minute more, another ominous report, and I was on my feet at the window.

"Minute guns, Harry," I said. "Seward is dead. Get up. We must go out and get the news." Just then there was a loud bang at the door and when I opened it the bewildered, excited face of Captain Redmond looked into mine as he shouted:

"Marshal Stoddard, President Lincoln is assassinated!"

Away he went and we were left to stare at each other as bewildered and as excited as he had been. We began to dress and it happened that the only black clothes we had were our dress suits. These were put on, therefore, without discussion, and we walked out into the Main Street. The first man we met was Mr. Jacks, the newly elected Union Congressman from the northeast district. He was a short, sturdy, rough-looking man, but he walked along, swinging his hands, weeping bitterly and swearing like a pirate. He did not speak a word to us for he went by, staring at the ground. Not many yards further, we met a tall, portly man, well dressed, who had been Confederate District Attorney and an intense Rebel. In one hand he was carrying a tremendous bowie knife and in the other a huge red silk handkerchief with which he was mopping his face, for he too was weeping—and swearing furiously—exclaiming:

"Damn them! This is the worst blow that could have fallen upon the South at this hour!"

We passed him without speaking and at no great distance beyond we were near a row of small houses occupied by the colored people. Men, women, and children were swarming out of them but all appeared to have been struck dumb. They were busily tying bits of black cloth, of any sort they could obtain, upon the doors and windows of their houses.

A little further and I saw a squad of angry men in blue with their knives out, pursuing a fellow who took refuge in a dwelling when I called them to "Halt!" receiving from husky voices the explanation:

"Why, Colonel, he ought to be killed! He said it was good enough for him! Good enough for him!"

Killed he would have been if they had not been halted, but hardly had that incident passed before another squad of volunteers came running to me to shout at me that "Old Bernays is opening his liquor store. We told him not to but he's taking down his shutters."

"Go and tell Bernays to shut up," I replied. "No stores will be open in Little Rock today. Tell him he will get his orders from the Provost Marshal pretty soon. Every bar must close."

I had no real authority but took for granted the sure action of General Reynolds and the soldiers took care of the obedience, for if "Old

Bernays" had not obeyed they would have cleaned him out. I myself went on to headquarters to obtain the facts of the matter. It was the third or fourth day after the assassination, I think, owing to the delay in getting telegraph despatches from Memphis to Little Rock. The quarters were thronged with military men and prominent civilians and before long a surprise came to me that somehow or other did not surprise me, perhaps because nothing on earth could have done so, just then. Little Rock had been a great headquarters of the Masonic Fraternity. They had there a "Masonic College" and nearly all the old citizens, of any good standing were members of the order, including neighboring planters, etc. Somehow or other, the leading Lodge had won for itself the title of "The Reb Masons" and it had the finest hall in the town. It was from this body that I received an invitation to attend a "Lodge of Sorrow," to be held in the hall at noon, and to deliver an oration.

I went and found the hall crowded. I made an address which was received with evidently sincere and intense interest by an intelligent body of men who saw and felt that in the murder of Abraham Lincoln the really best friend and protector of the future interests of the defeated South had been taken away. I finished my address and walked away to my office, weary and sick at heart.

The loyal state officers and representatives and senators had been only nominally friendly for it was in the air that I might be in their way in any subsequent political operations. I can even suppose that they suspected me of ambition and of being on too good terms with the old secesh element which I failed to condemn as they did. Therefore, in preparing for a tremendous public meeting at the State Representative chamber, that evening, a long list of speakers was selected and announced and my name was not upon it. I was not wanted and other men were to avail themselves of the political occasion. I did not at all care to attend but went and lay down, after supper, to grieve for Lincoln. I had not yet had time to consider how great a change this loss of my best friend was making in my own position and in my future course in life. I was not asleep, nevertheless, when several men, one of them a U.S. Senator, came hurriedly in to stir me up. The hall, they said, was packed to suffocation, but "the boys" would not allow any other man to speak until they had heard from me.

Every effort of any orator on the list had been angrily shouted down, for the boys in blue had no political aspirations and knew their own minds. I arose, wearily enough, and with some difficulty I was wedged through the crowd to a place on the platform. Behind me were flags in crape and many men. Before me was a sea of mournful faces, and a kind of inspiration came upon me. Just what I said, during the hour that followed I never tried to recall but when I at last sank back upon my chair it was of no use for the chairman of the meeting to announce another orator. The boys had heard what they wanted to hear and with one accord they marched slowly, thoughtfully, out of the hall, leaving it almost empty. It was a most impressive sight to see those bowed heads go—a greater tribute to Lincoln's memory than anything that I or any other man could have uttered in words.

The next morning, to my next surprise, Judge Caldwell came and asked me to write upon the Court records the memorial tribute he deemed the event to require and there it is to this day. So the death of Lincoln became a thing of the past but his memory hardly seems so, he has left behind him so much that still is living in the history of his country.

Sarah Morgan

Diary, April 19, 1865

Sarah Morgan (1842–1909) fled her home in Baton Rouge, Louisiana, in August 1862 after Confederate forces unsuccessfully attempted to retake the town. Morgan, her sister, and their widowed mother lived near Port Hudson for eight months before food shortages and the prospect of renewed fighting reluctantly drove them to seek refuge with Morgan's half brother in Union-occupied New Orleans. "O if I was only a man!" Morgan wrote shortly after her arrival in the city. "Blood, fire, desolation, I feel ready to invoke all, on these Yankees." In January 1864 two of her brothers died from illness, one while serving with Lee's army in Virginia and the other in a Union prison camp in Ohio. (Her brother James, a midshipman in the Confederate navy, survived the war.) Morgan began her diary entry for April 19, 1865, with a quotation from Tennyson's "The Lotos-Eaters."

April 19th. 1865. No. 211. Camp St.

"All things are taken from us, and become portions and parcels of the dreadful past."

My life change, changes. I let it change as God will, feeling he doeth all things well. Sister has gone to Germany with Charlotte, Nellie, and Lavinia to place them at school, probably at Brussels. Mother and I have taken her place with the five remaining children. I am nominally housekeeper; that is to say I keep the keys in my pocket, and my eyes on the children, and sit at the head of the table. But I dont order dinner, for which I am thankful; for I would not be able to name a single article, if my reputation depended on the test. Of course I have a general idea that soup, roast, baked and boiled meats are eaten, but whether all the same day, or which to be chosen, I could not decide, nor as to the kind of animal or fish. So the cook does that, though I am trying to observe every day what he provides, in order to perfect myself in the mystery.

In five days, I have twice been heart-broken about making Brother's coffee too strong. He will not complain, and I would still be ignorant of the error if I had not accidently observed the untouched cup after he left the table, and discovering the mistake by tasting punished myself by drinking every drop of the bitter draught. Mem. To-morrow if I fail, drink it until I learn the exact proportion.

Thursday the 13th, came the dreadful tidings of the surrender of Lee and his army on the 9th. Every body cried, but I would not, satisfied that God will still save us, even though all should apparently be lost. Followed at intervals of two or three hours by the announcement of the capture of Richmond, Selma, Mobile, and Johnson's army, even the staunchest Southerners were hopeless. Every one proclaimed Peace, and the only matter under consideration was whether Jeff. Davis, all politicians, every man above the rank of Captain in the army, and above that of Lieutenant in the navy, should be hanged immediately, or *some* graciously pardoned. Henry Ward Beecher humanely pleaded mercy for us, supported by a small minority. Davis and all leading men *must* be executed; the blood of the others would serve to irrigate the country. Under this lively prospect, Peace! blessed Peace! was the cry. I whispered "Never! let a great earthquake swallow us up first! Let us leave our land and emigrate to any desert spot of the earth, rather than return to the Union, even as it Was!"

Six days this has lasted. Blessed with the silently obstinate disposition, I would not dispute, but felt my heart swell repeating "God is our refuge and our strength, a very present help in time of trouble," and could not for an instant believe this could end in our overthrow.

This morning when I went down to breakfast at seven, Brother read the announcement of the assassination of Lincoln and Secretary Seward. "Vengence is mine; I will repay, saith the Lord." This is murder! God have mercy on those who did it! A while ago, Lincoln's chief occupation was thinking what death, thousands who ruled like lords when he was cutting logs, should die. A moment more, and the man who was progressing to murder countless human beings, is interrupted in his work by the shot of an assassin. Do I justify this murder? No! I shudder with horror, wonder, pity and fear, and then feeling that it is the salvation of all I love that has been purchased by this man's crime, I long to thank God for those spared, and shudder to think that that is rejoicing against our enemy, being grateful for a fellow-creature's death. I am not! Seward was ill—dying—helpless. This was dastard murder. His throat was cut in bed. Horrible!

Charlotte Corday killed Marat in his bath, and is held up in history as one of Liberty's martyrs, and one of the heroines of her country. To me, it is all Murder. Let historians extol blood shedding; it is woman's place to abhor it. And because I know that they would have apotheosized any man who had crucified Jeff Davis, I abhor this, and call it foul murder, unworthy of our cause—and God grant it was only the temporary insanity of a desperate man that committed this crime! Let not his blood be visited on our nation, Lord!

Across the way, a large building undoubtedly inhabited by officers is being draped in black. Immense streamers of black and white hang from the balcony. Down town, I understand all shops are closed, and all wrapped in mourning. And I hardly dare pray God to bless us, with the crape hanging over the way. It would have been banners, if our president had been killed, though! Now the struggle will be desperate, awful, short. Spare Jimmy, dear Lord! Have mercy on us as a people!

And yet what was the song of Deborah, when she hammered a nail in the head of the sleeping Sisera? Was she not extolled for the treacherous deed? What was Miriam's song over the drowning Egyptian? "Our enemies are fallen, fallen!" Was not Judith immortalized for delivering her people from the hands of a tyrant? "Pour le salut de ma patree—!"

Where does patriotism end, and murder begin? And considering that every one is closely watched, and that five men have been killed this day for expressing their indifference on the death of Mr Lincoln, it would be best to postpone this discussion.

Louisville Journal

President Lincoln's Death—The Spirit and Comments of the Press

In the mid-nineteenth century it was common for American newspapers to compile and reprint commentary published in other journals. Four days after the President's death the *Louisville Journal*, a conservative Unionist publication that had opposed Lincoln's reelection in 1864, provided its readers with a selection of editorial reactions from throughout the East and Midwest.

———————

To-day the burial ceremonies over the remains of Hon. Abraham Lincoln, late President of the United States, will take place in Washington City. The whole nation is humbled at his untimely grave, and as a befitting tribute to his memory we forego the discussion of ordinary events, and surrender our usual editorial space to extracts from various public journals touching the sudden and terrible calamity which has overtaken the nation.

The New York World, of Saturday morning last, in the course of the leading editorial on the Presidential assassination, says:

"Our history has no parallel to this. Such grief as ours to-day is new to this nation's heart. Other Presidents have died while holding the same high place—Harrison and Taylor; but both died in the ordinary course of nature, and the nation's grief then had no such pang in it as this which is now given by the shot of an assassin.

"The cry of the murderer as he leaped from the President's box and ran across the stage, 'sic semper tyrannis,' betrays no madman's frenzy. The plot included the murder of Secretary Seward also, and all the circumstances show that the same political fury and hate which lit the flames of the great rebellion inspired these hellish deeds; and by so much as these detract from the splendor of our triumph in its utter subjugation, by so much do they brand with a deeper and more damning infamy its plotters, its leaders, its abettors, its sympathizers, its character in impartial history.

"Let every city, town, and street, and lane, and house, and farm of the whole North become to-day but the wards of an infinite prison to shut in and secure the villains who have done this thing. Let every man be an officer of the law to search them out and bring them to summary and condign justice. The machinery of government has already been set in motion, but let there be no escape for them if that should fail.

"Into what proportions this calamity will yet develop, no human eye can now foresee. Its effect upon the political future of the nation will at least not be such as when a dynasty is overthrown. Our laws provide for the succession to such remote degrees that even assassination cannot leave the nation without a visible leader and head.

"Andrew Johnson to-day becomes the President of the United States, and the chief political consequences which will follow from this tragedy will be mainly such as his personal character and political opinions, especially on the subject of reconstruction, shall determine. May God give him wisdom to discharge worthily the duties of his great office."

The New York Times, on the morning succeeding the fatal evening when the intelligence of the deed reached that city, and as if too full of grief for utterance, contains only the following brief allusion to it:

"The events of last night in Washington will strike with profound horror the whole American people. At this moment of writing, we have only a partial announcement of the facts, and have neither the data nor the spirit for comment."

The following is an extract from the leading editorial of the Philadelphia American and Gazette of the 17th inst.:

"There is a singular array of circumstances connected with this murder which are well calculated to confound us—the manner in which it was executed, the strange impunity enjoyed by the assassin in his escape, as though the plan had been deeply laid and skilfully carried into effect. Perhaps the most painful feature of the event is that the murder took place in the presence of Mrs. Lincoln. The exclamation of the wretch after the deed was done, indicates that he is a Virginian, the Latin quotation being the motto of that State. It seems unaccountable that the assassination should not have been attempted during Mr. Lincoln's sojourn in Richmond, and still more so that it occurs at the moment when Virginia has submitted to the authority of the Union, and her armies have all surrendered or been dispersed.

"The act will, unfortunately, have the tendency to create a widespread and determined desire to put a stop at once to any disposition to deal leniently with rebels and traitors. This manifestation of reckless and insane malignity will engender a prevalent belief that with such a spirit abroad in the South magnanimity is a crime and a blunder. The result, therefore, will be not less a terrible calamity to the South than to the nation.

"The Hon. Andrew Johnson, of Tennessee, the Vice-President, who becomes President by the death of Abraham Lincoln, is a man of whom no fear need be entertained in regard to his firm and unyielding devotion to the great cause. He stood true in the Senate when all around were false, and in the hour when treason seemed to be an epidemic among the Representatives of the South. Throughout the whole of the war he has never for a moment hesitated to give his cordial support to the measures and policy of the Administration. By those who have known him longest at home he is regarded with attachment of the most remarkable description. We, therefore, entertain no fears for him whatever, and believe that he will be just as stanch a man as we need in this emergency."

The following touching reference to the melancholy event is from the Chicago Journal:

"We cannot write with composure or speak without emotion. And it were vain to attempt to convey, in human words, any conception of the grief that is devouring our human hearts.

"The bells, toll they ever so solemnly, are totally inadequate to express the solemnity of the hour—a vain attempt to utter the unutterable woe. The weeds of sombre and white that clothe the city do not, cannot give any but a very trifling intimation of the city's sorrow.

"The tolling bells, the weeds of mourning, the bowed heads, the streaming eyes, the choked speech, the silent salutation—how idle, after all, are all these to tell the story of our affliction, and to speak what we feel, as we sink overcome, overmastered, overwhelmed by this, the Republic's unprecedented bereavement.

"We can but lay our faces on the earth in recognition of Him who holds the nations in the hollow of His hand, and turning an eye upward, mean the words that we cannot speak. Farewell to the good and faithful servant, to the second Father of his country, 'with all kind love, good thoughts, and reverence.' Farewell, Abraham Lincoln!

"Sleep in dust, with kindred ashes
Of the noble and the true,
Hand that never failed its country,
Heart that bareness never knew."

The Philadelphia Age, the Democratic organ of that city says:

"The country will be more than startled—it will be appalled—by the announcement that President Lincoln was last night mortally wounded. Such an event would have been deplorable at any time, but at this juncture it is, humanly speaking, the greatest misfortune that could befall the country. He had shown recently so manifest a desire and intention to act with magnanimity and moderation in adjusting our difficulties, that there was good reason to look for the speedy advent of a just and lasting peace; and it is the possible frustration of this hope that will at once suggest itself to every patriot. We are assured that there is every reason to fear that the wound may prove fatal. May Heaven avert such a calamity!"

The Buffalo (New York) Courier says:

"We have no words in which to speak of the awful crime, the appalling calamity, of which the telegraph brought us news last night. President Lincoln is murdered; Secretary Seward has, in all probability, received his death wound at the assassin's hand. We need not here recount the slender details given elsewhere.

"This is a horror unspeakable, and the mind staggers in the attempt to contemplate either the fact itself or its possible results. Not this country alone but civilization receives a shock from the blow by which our President has fallen. To find a parallel for the hideous event we must go back a thousand years, and seek for it in the annals of the most barbarous nations. It must needs be a calmer moment than this in which the people shall attempt an observation of their new and sorrowful situation. Let it suffice for the present to say that the hand of the fiend incarnate who smote down President Lincoln last night has been guided by a hellish inspiration of sagacity. God save the Republic in this its dark hour."

The St. Louis (Missouri) Democrat says:

"Of all the occurrences within the range of possibility, the assassination of our President in Washington, at this triumphant stage of the war, and while he was devoting himself in the most liberal spirit to an adjustment with the rebels, was perhaps the one event never thought of, still less looked for. The intelligence of it came with a force the more astounding and appalling because the land was just then decking herself in the richest regalia of joy—a joy in which gratitude and esteem toward the President were largely mingled. The intense and universal expression of profoundest mourning testifies how deeply, in the hour of our country's deliverance, the personal and official worth of Abraham Lincoln have enshrined him in the hearts of his countrymen.

"He is dead. It is now a poor satisfaction to pour curses on the head of the wretch who perpetrated the strange crime. The severest punishment would avail little to repair the immense mischief wrought, and nothing to assuage the nation's sorrow. The assassin may well be left to a calm investigation of the motives which influenced him, and to dispassionate justice. There is too much deep grief for rage. The heroic statesman to whom has been twice confided the ark of our political salvation, on whom all eyes have been fixed, whose form and lineaments, and character have become indelibly engraven upon the popular mind, and endeared to the popular heart, is suddenly cut down at the helm of affairs. Worthy honors are to be paid to his high merit and historic name. This is a great work, but it is one which the hearts of the people and the genius of the nation will well perform. His patriotic influence will continue and become invested with a moral power which it never before possessed. The holy cause of the Union will only be the holier and dearer because Mr. Lincoln has crowned his labors for it with his blood. The popular devotion to liberty and nationality was never lessened, and never will be, by the martyrdom of their champions. From his official and personal influence over his countrymen, he has passed to a grander and loftier sphere, from which, with Washington and Jackson, he will wield a more potent scepter through all coming time. If doomed rebellion could have added a final seal to its infamy and damnation, it has affixed that seal in the assassination of the nation's twice chosen ruler."

The Chicago Times (Democratic) says on the 17th inst.:

"It is yet to be known whether Mr. Lincoln and Mr. Seward were the victims of a rebel conspiracy or of drunken insanity. We can understand why they should have been the former. We can understand why desperate rebel leaders should wish to strike *them* down. Events of the two days prior to the occurrence of the tragedy disclosed the adoption by Mr. Lincoln of a conciliatory policy toward the rebellion, under which

Virginia, by the action of her leading public men, had inaugurated a movement toward reconciliation; and it is very well known that this policy had something more than Mr. Seward's concurrence. Virginia thus withdrawn from the rebellion, what ground of hope would remain for it? What, in the minds of desperate rebel leaders, more likely to change this conciliatory policy and defeat the Virginia movement than the death of Mr. Lincoln and Mr. Seward? If the assassinations were the result of a conspiracy, this is the solution. If they were the work of insanity only—and it is to be hoped, for the credit of human nature, that they were—then rebellion has not crowned its crimes with an unpardonable sin.

"There are not on this day mourners more sincere than the Democracy of these Northern States. Widely as they have differed with Mr. Lincoln —greatly as their confidence in him had been shaken—they yet saw in the indications of the last few days of his life that he might command their support in the close of the war, as he did in its beginning. These indications inspired them with hope, and confidence, and joy, which are now dashed to the ground. The Democracy may well mourn the death of Abraham Lincoln.

"The country may be happily disappointed in his successor. This is a possibility, though not a probability. At this writing, the intelligence is that Mr. Seward is still living, and that he may recover. We pray God that he will. His life has a new value now, since the chief command has fallen into so uncertain hands."

The Chicago Tribune (Republican) says:

"No man but Abraham Lincoln could restrain the American people from visiting righteous wrath upon the heads of the wicked leaders of the accursed rebellion. No living man possessed the confidence and affection of the people and army as he. To the judgment of no other man would they defer so cheerfully and willingly. He possessed a marvellous power over the minds of the people; they reposed unlimited faith in his sagacity, integrity, honesty, and soundness of judgment. He could do almost whatever he pleased, because he never abused the confidence of the people, never betrayed their trust—because he was solely actuated by a sense of duty and patriotism. He ever tried to do what he conscientiously believed to be *right*. Right was his polar star; conscience was his monitor, and he tempered all his dealings with the rebels with forbearance and mercy. He harbored no particle of animosity. He never felt the sensation of revenge in his life; he never hated a human being. His millions of admirers and friends never found but one fault, and that was with his excess of lenity and kindness toward public enemies. It made his heart bleed to sign the death warrant of the worst guerilla assassin or rebel spy; he thought no evil; he wished no human being harm; he was the embodiment of Christian precepts and virtues. The Chair of State, made vacant by his death, there is none in the land—no, not one, able to fill it as he filled it. An age produces but one Washington. Abraham Lincoln was the Washington of this generation—the second Father of his Country. In his untimely death a heavy calamity has fallen upon the American people."

The Chicago Post (Democratic) expresses itself in the following appropriate terms:

"The American people have cause for grief such as no other people have ever had. A nation mourns not alone for her Executive and her Minister of State, but for the shame that any one who has ever borne the name of American should sully the pages of history with such an atrocious deed.

"The rebellion has added another to its long record of bloody crimes. Treason stalked with fire and sword through the land, carrying desolation and ruin in its progress. Its four years of existence have been four years of blood—of blood spilled under the flimsy pretext of belligerent rights, and under the forms of war. But now, when its armies have been overcome, and its powers of armed resistance destroyed, it resorts to the assassin's pistol and the knife. Woe be to that man who took upon himself the bloody office of assassin! Woe be to those men, North or South, who may be found counsellors, advisers, or approvers of the deed! Woe be to that rebellion in whose behalf and in whose interest this fearful tragedy has been enacted. When the present profound grief shall have in some degree lost its intensity, the American people will demand a retribution equal in magnitude to the calamity that has been wrought. Where that retribution will end, and where it will be visited, it is not difficult to imagine.

"The present and future effect of this horrible affair upon the country it is impossible to predict. It may revolutionize for a while the country, or, more properly speaking, may paralyze it temporarily; but let us hope that the awful occurrence will duly impress the public mind with the fearful character of the present condition of affairs.

"Mr. Andrew Johnson has already been inaugurated as President. Let us hope that the country will unitedly give him that support and that encouragement that will enable him to bring the country forth from the fearful and appalling circumstances which now surround it.

"We have faith that Andrew Johnson will prove equal to the duty before him. If he be weak, the greater the reason for supporting him. Let us forget the past, and clinging to the one great end, the rescue of our country, let us stand by the Government, because that Government is all that stands between us and utter ruin, desolation, anarchy, and assassination."

The Cincinnati Commercial of the 17th says:

"The bullet that pierced the head of President Lincoln touched the heart of the nation. No event since the death of Washington has so filled the land with sorrow.

"Added to the grief that would have been felt at the death of one so well respected as President Lincoln, is the unspeakable indignation and horror at the manner of his taking off, which we cannot help ascribing to a fanatical sympathy with the blackest and bloodiest treason that the world ever saw.

"Then it is a reflection, full of mournfulness that words are weak to tell, that after a life of such hard labor, and years of such harassing anxieties, seasons of the deepest gloom, and no intermission in the heaviest cares, President Lincoln should be struck down just as he had gained the public confidence and appreciation—in the blaze of victory and the dawn of peace.

"We can only trust that in his case, as in that of the assassination of William of Orange, the passionate grief of the people will strengthen their public spirit, animate every bosom to serve the country with a higher devotion than ever; and that thus, under Divine Providence, whose mysterious ways to perform wonders the ages testify, as the poet sings, good may be wrought out of a calamity, that, to the finite senses, seems almost unbearable."

The Cincinnati Times, in the course of a very fine editorial, speaks as follows:

"Booth—a name henceforward to be mentioned in hours of darkness as a sound of terror—to be whispered for all ages in the ears of children, as hideous gnomes and ghouls are whispered—to be our Guy of Faux, with hues of murder for the old traditional picture under the vaults of the Commons which stills the babes of England—was but an instrument, such as his pistol and his dagger. The real ruffian is the rebel chief.

Place his features upon the shoulders of his emissary, and we shall have an epitome of the great tragedy.

"The world will read it so. Ever will men see a double figure stalk at midnight, with blood upon its garments. Ever will they shrink before the brandished steel held by the burly hand of Booth, bearing the countenance of Davis. Ever will their hearts chill at the thought of a little sharp report, a cruel puff of smoke, and the prostrate form of a great and good man, who would not have harmed a fellow-being in the world. And ever will they cry for vengeance. Vengeance! Why, what have these to pay for their dark deed? Can they render back his pure life by their's of perjury and murder? Can such as they pay down the price of the treasure they have stolen, or mend the golden bowl that's broken at the fountain, or twist again the silver cord that's loosed?

> "Yet retribution is a goodly thing,
>   And it were well to wring the payment from them
>   Even to the utmost drop of their heart's blood."

"They cannot escape. The gyves are already on their wrists. The earth dare not conceal them. They may not hide themselves upon the multitudinous seas incarnadine. The very rays of light, the stars, the quiet beams of the moon will point them out; and speedily the cause which this vile murder was meant to prop will sink into the bowels of that sacred soil which will never cast it up again."

The Baltimore American says:

"The President has been murdered. At the time when he had become most endearing to the nation, at the moment when the war was of the past, and he was bending the energies of his mind and the kindly feelings of a character more than usually forgiving toward the pacification of the country, Mr. Lincoln has been basely, cowardly and traitorously assassinated. Whilst surrounded by hundreds who would have given their lives to save his, with his wife by his side and his friends around him, the ball of the assassin, directed by that foul and traitorous spirit which has brought so many woes upon the country, reached his brain, and the President of the nation, the friend of the people, is no more.

"We have no words to express the feelings which this terrible event will excite. Its awful suddenness has overwhelmed us as it will overwhelm the country to-day. No language can adequately depict the sadness with which our people will turn from their rejoicings to mourning over an event that will stir up their deepest and most mournful feelings. Abraham Lincoln is dying. What more can we say."

The Cincinnati Enquirer (Democratic) says:

"This is one of the most awful pages in the dread history of the last four years, stained as it is with horrors, and rendered bloody with crime. The hand of affliction has indeed been laid heavily upon our people, and we have been visited with the most dreadful ills that can scourge a nation, or render its tenure of existence painful and insecure.

"Fondly do we express a hope that the history is near its conclusion, and that the murder of our chief rulers in high places is the culminating leaf of an atrocious record, and that our darkest hour has passed, soon to be succeeded by a brighter dawn.

"In this connection we regret to hear or see any political allusions, for we scorn the thought that there is or can be any politics that will not detest and abhor the act of private murder, or any party that will not vie with its antagonists in condemning the first and great primal crime of our nature. It is the duty, as it should be the aim, of all to use their influence in calming passion, to oppose hatred and prejudice, and to exercise the simple act of believing, without the strongest proof to the contrary, that there are men among us so base that they deplore with all their heart and soul this dark shadow of death that now rests upon the land."

The Nashville Union says on the 16th inst.:

"Abraham Lincoln was a great and good man, and his administration of the Government, whatever may be the future career of our nation, will ever be regarded as one of extraordinary sagacity, vigor, and efficiency. And he will always be regarded as a public benefactor, our second Washington.

"Penetrated with grief by the nation's great affliction, we have no heart to go into an investigation of the probable motives which impelled the assassin to fire the fatal shot. We bow in deep humiliation, amazed that any one with a human heart could be found to perpetrate so dastardly a crime, and trust to the justice of God for its punishment."

The above extracts from the press, both Democratic and Republican, indicate to the reader the profound public grief which the death of Abraham Lincoln has carried to the nation's heart.

Ralph Waldo Emerson

Remarks at the Services Held in Concord, Massachusetts

As the funeral rites for the martyred President began in the White House on April 19, services were simultaneously occurring in churches and synagogues throughout the North. When mourners gathered at the Unitarian Church in Concord, Massachusetts, the obvious candidate to deliver the principal oration was the town's most celebrated resident, Ralph Waldo Emerson (1803–1882). Emerson, along with many members of his audience, had considered Lincoln to be lacking in both polish and his zeal for emancipation, and in his eulogy the philosopher focused instead on the late President's inspiring, and quintessentially American, rise from obscurity to world fame.

We meet under the gloom of a calamity which darkens down over the minds of good men in all civil society, as the fearful tidings travel over sea, over land, from country to country, like the shadow of an uncalculated eclipse over the planet. Old as history is, and manifold as are its tragedies, I doubt if any death has caused so much pain to mankind as this has caused, or will cause, on its announcement; and this, not so much because nations are by modern arts brought so closely together, as because of the mysterious hopes and fears which, in the present day, are connected with the name and institutions of America.

In this country, on Saturday, every one was struck dumb, and saw at first only deep below deep, as he meditated on the ghastly blow. And perhaps, at this hour, when the coffin which contains the dust of the President sets forward on its long march through mourning States, on its way to his home in Illinois, we might well be silent, and suffer the awful voices of the time to thunder to us. Yes, but that first despair was brief: the man was not so to be mourned. He was the most active and hopeful of men; and his work had not perished: but acclamations of praise for the task he had accomplished burst out into a song of triumph, which even tears for his death cannot keep down.

The President stood before us as a man of the people. He was thoroughly American, had never crossed the sea, had never been spoiled by English insularity or French dissipation; a quite native, aboriginal man, as an acorn from the oak; no aping of foreigners, no frivolous accomplishments, Kentuckian born, working on a farm, a flatboatman, a captain in the Black Hawk war, a country lawyer, a representative in the rural Legislature of Illinois;—on such modest foundations the broad structure of his fame was laid. How slowly, and yet by happily prepared steps, he came to his place. All of us remember,—it is only a history of five or six years,—the surprise and the disappointment of the country at his first nomination by the Convention at Chicago. Mr. Seward, then in the culmination of his good fame, was the favorite of the Eastern States. And when the new and comparatively unknown name of Lincoln was announced, (notwithstanding the report of the acclamations of that Convention,) we heard the result coldly and sadly. It seemed too rash, on a purely local reputation, to build so grave a trust in such anxious times; and men naturally talked of the chances in politics as incalculable. But it turned out not to be chance. The profound good opinion which the people of Illinois and of the West had conceived of him, and which they had imparted to their colleagues that they also might justify themselves to their constituents at home, was not rash, though they did not begin to know the riches of his worth.

A plain man of the people, an extraordinary fortune attended him. He offered no shining qualities at the first encounter; he did not offend by superiority. He had a face and manner which disarmed suspicion, which inspired confidence, which confirmed good-will. He was a man without vices. He had a strong sense of duty, which it was very easy for him to obey. Then, he had what farmers call a long head; was excellent in working out the sum for himself; in arguing his case and convincing you fairly and firmly. Then, it turned out that he was a great worker; had prodigious faculty of performance; worked easily. A good worker is so rare; everybody has some disabling quality. In a host of young men that start together and promise so many brilliant leaders for the next age, each fails on trial; one by bad health, one by conceit, or by love of pleasure, or lethargy, or an ugly temper,—each has some disqualifying fault that throws him out of the career. But this man was sound to the core, cheerful, persistent, all right for labor, and liked nothing so well.

Then, he had a vast good-nature, which made him tolerant and accessible to all; fair-minded, leaning to the claim of the petitioner; affable, and not sensible to the affliction which the innumerable visits paid to him when President would have brought to any one else. And how this good-nature became a noble humanity, in many a tragic case which the events of the war brought to him, every one will remember; and with what increasing tenderness he dealt when a whole race was thrown on his compassion. The poor negro said of him, on an impressive occasion, "Massa Linkum am eberywhere."

Then his broad good-humor, running easily into jocular talk, in which he delighted and in which he excelled, was a rich gift to this wise man. It enabled him to keep his secret; to meet every kind of man and every rank in society; to take off the edge of the severest decisions; to mask his own purpose and sound his companion; and to catch with true instinct the temper of every company he addressed. And, more than all, it is to a man of severe labor, in anxious and exhausting crises, the natural restorative, good as sleep, and is the protection of the overdriven brain against rancor and insanity.

He is the author of a multitude of good sayings, so disguised as pleasantries that it is certain they had no reputation at first but as jests; and only later, by the very acceptance and adoption they find in the mouths of millions, turn out to be the wisdom of the hour. I am sure if this man had ruled in a period of less facility of printing, he would have become mythological in a very few years, like Æsop or Pilpay, or one of the Seven Wise Masters, by his fables and proverbs. But the weight and penetration of many passages in his letters, messages and speeches, hidden now by the very closeness of their application to the moment, are destined hereafter to wide fame. What pregnant definitions; what unerring common sense; what foresight; and, on great occasion, what lofty, and more than national, what humane tone! His brief speech at Gettysburg will not easily be surpassed by words on any recorded occasion. This, and one other American speech, that of John Brown to the court that tried him, and a part of Kossuth's speech at Birmingham, can only be compared with each other, and with no fourth.

His occupying the chair of State was a triumph of the good-sense of mankind, and of the public conscience. This middle-class country had got a middle-class President, at last. Yes, in manners and sympathies, but not in powers, for his powers were superior. This man grew according to the need. His mind mastered the problem of the day; and, as the problem grew, so did his comprehension of it. Rarely was man so fitted to the event. In the midst of fears and jealousies, in the Babel of counsels and parties, this man wrought incessantly with all his might and all his honesty, laboring to find what the people wanted, and how to obtain that. It cannot be said there is any exaggeration of his worth. If ever a man was fairly tested, he was. There was no lack of resistance, nor of slander, nor of ridicule. The times have allowed no state secrets; the nation has been in such ferment, such multitudes had to be trusted, that no secret could be kept. Every door was ajar, and we know all that befell.

Then, what an occasion was the whirlwind of the war. Here was place for no holiday magistrate, no fair-weather sailor; the new pilot was hurried to the helm in a tornado. In four years,—four years of battle-days,—his endurance, his fertility of resources, his magnanimity, were sorely tried and never found wanting. There, by his courage, his justice, his even temper, his fertile counsel, his humanity, he stood a heroic figure in the centre of a heroic epoch. He is the true history of the American people in his time. Step by step he walked before them; slow with their slowness, quickening his march by theirs, the true representative of this continent; an entirely public man; father of his country, the pulse of twenty millions throbbing in his heart, the thought of their minds articulated by his tongue.

Adam Smith remarks that the axe, which in Houbraken's portraits of British kings and worthies is engraved under those who have suffered at the block, adds a certain lofty charm to the picture. And who does not see, even in this tragedy so recent, how fast the terror and rain of the massacre are already burning into glory around the victim? Far happier this fate than to have lived to be wished away; to have watched the decay of his own faculties; to have seen,—perhaps even he,—the proverbial ingratitude of statesmen; to have seen mean men preferred. Had he not lived long enough to keep the greatest promise that ever man made to his fellow-men,—the practical abolition of slavery? He had seen Tennessee, Missouri and Maryland emancipate their slaves. He had seen Savannah, Charleston and Richmond surrendered; had seen the main army of the rebellion lay down its arms. He had conquered the public opinion of Canada, England and France. Only Washington can compare with him in fortune.

And what if it should turn out, in the unfolding of the web, that he had reached the term; that this heroic deliverer could no longer serve us; that the rebellion had touched its natural conclusion, and what remained to be done required new and uncommitted hands,—a new spirit born out of the ashes of the war; and that Heaven, wishing to show the world a completed benefactor, shall make him serve his country even more by his death than by his life? Nations, like kings, are not good by facility and complaisance. "The kindness of kings consists in justice and strength." Easy good-nature has been the dangerous foible of the Republic, and it was necessary that its enemies should outrage it, and drive us to unwonted firmness, to secure the salvation of this country in the next ages.

The ancients believed in a serene and beautiful Genius which ruled in the affairs of nations; which, with a slow but stern justice, carried forward the fortunes of certain chosen houses, weeding out single offenders or offending families, and securing at last the firm prosperity of the favorites of Heaven. It was too narrow a view of the Eternal Nemesis. There is a serene Providence which rules the fate of nations, which makes little account of time, little of one generation or race, makes no account of disasters, conquers alike by what is called defeat or by what is called victory, thrusts aside enemy and obstruction, crushes everything immoral as inhuman, and obtains the ultimate triumph of the best race by the sacrifice of everything which resists the moral laws of the world. It makes its own instruments, creates the man for the time, trains him in poverty, inspires his genius, and arms him for his task. It has given every race its own talent, and ordains that only that race which combines perfectly with the virtues of all shall endure.

April 19, 1865

Isaac Mayer Wise

Sermon at Cincinnati

The evening of April 14, 1865, was the fifth night of Passover, and at services on the sacred seventh and eighth days, many American rabbis were moved to eulogize Lincoln as an American Moses who had led the nation out of bondage and within sight of a promised land that he himself was fated not to enter. Born in Bohemia, Isaac Mayer Wise (1819–1900) immigrated to the United States in 1846 and served as a rabbi in Albany, New York, before moving to Cincinnati in 1854. A prolific writer, Wise used the pages of his weekly newspaper *The Israelite* to become arguably the nation's most influential Reform rabbi. He blamed the Republican Party for the outbreak of the Civil War, and rarely commented on the conflict once it began. In January 1863 Wise met Lincoln as part of a delegation seeking the revocation of Grant's notorious order expelling Jews "as a class" from his military department. When Lincoln overturned the order, Wise praised him for knowing "no distinction between Jew and Gentile." In his sermon he compared the slain president to his biblical namesake and reflected on the sins of the nation at large.

The day when the people of the United States were called upon to perform the painful duty of showing the last honors to the assassinated Chief Magistrate, was the gloomiest and most lamentable one in the history of this country. The people, without exception almost, felt profoundly this lamentable truth.

The synagogues of Cincinnati were densely crowded on this occasion, the services solemn beyond description, and the draperies of mourning fully appropriate.

We reproduce two sermons preached in the synagogues on that memorable day, as they appeared in the Cincinnati *Commercial*, April 20; one this week and one next week:

LODGE STREET TEMPLE.

After the introductory hymns and ceremonies, Dr. Wise preached the following sermon:

"And the Lord said unto Abram, Get thee out of thy country, and out of thy birth-place, and from thy father's house, unto the land that I will show thee. And I will make of them a great nation, and I will bless thee, and make thy name great; and thou shalt be a blessing. And I will bless those that bless thee, and him that curseth thee will I curse; and in thee shall all families of the earth be blessed. So Abram departed, as the Lord had spoken to him."

Abraham Lincoln departed, as the Lord had spoken to him. Abraham Lincoln, whose biography is too well known to be repeated here, the President of the United States, from March 4, 1861, to the day of his assassination, April 14, 1865; the generous, genial and honest man, who stood at the head of our people in this unprecedented struggle for national existence and popular liberty; whose words and deeds speak alike and aloud of his unsophisticated mind, purity of heart, honesty of purpose, confidence in the great cause, and implicit faith in the justice of Providence, which inspired him to consistency, courage and self-denial; this Abraham Lincoln, who endeared himself to so many millions of hearts, and gained the admiration of other millions of people, both at home and abroad; whom the myriads of freedmen consider their savior, and tens of thousands esteem as high as George Washington, and feel as sincerely and affectionately attached to as Israel to her David, Rome to her Augustus, and France to her Napoleon I; this Abraham Lincoln, whose greatness was in his goodness, and whose might was in his unshaken faith, was assassinated. Blush, humanity!—he was assassinated. This is the lamentable fact which to-day bends so many stout hearts with sorrow and grief—speaks by the tears of countless myriads, and the dark clouds of mourning which envelop the great Republic. Hark! listen to the voice of grievous lamentation, of woeful complaint, filling the very air of this vast country. "The elders of the daughter of Zion sit upon the ground; they are silent; they have thrown dust upon their heads; they have girt themselves with sackcloth; the virgins of Jerusalem have brought down low their head to the ground. My eyes do fail with tears, my bowels are heated, my liver is poured upon the earth, because of the breach of the daughter of my people. * * How shall I cheer thee, to whom compare thee, O daughter of Jerusalem?—to what shall I liken thee, to console thee,—O virgin daughter of Zion?—for great like the sea is thy breach, who can heal thee?" Hark, listen to the doleful voice of woe, echoing from thousands of hearts: "Fallen is the crown of our head; woe to us, for we have sinned; therefore our heart is woe-stricken; therefore are our eyes dimmed." This is the lamentable cause of our meeting to-day before God, to weep with the nation, to mourn with our country, to show the last honors to Abraham Lincoln.

[Here the burial hymn was sung.]

Why? Wherefore must it be so? you ask: Silent, mortals! Upon your knees, sons of the dust! "And the Lord said unto Abram, get thee out of thy country, out of thy birthplace, and from thy father's house, unto the land that I will show thee. * * So Abram departed as the Lord had spoken to him." Who of the finite and perishable creatures will unravel the mysterious ways of infinite and everlasting Providence? The drop comprehends not the seas, the mote understands not the sun; man, whose life is like a passing shadow, can not penetrate the counsels of the eternal and allwise God. Worship with humiliation, bow down with awe at the throne of glory, and proclaim anew the sacred words: "The Lord hath given, the Lord hath taken away, the name of the Lord be blessed." We can only look in and about ourselves to find the proper answer to the question: How can we honor best the memory of Abraham Lincoln.

Repent your sins. "Return, Israel, to the Lord thy God, for thou hast stumbled in thine iniquity," this deplorable event cries, with a loud voice. God has punished us grievously. His mighty hand inflicted a deep and burning wound upon the heart of the nation, and He is just. "The Rock, his work is perfect, for all His ways are just. The God of truth and without iniquity, just and upright is He." The Lord has revealed His powerful arm to remind us of our iniquity, and move us to repentance. Behold the man at whose command the mightiest armies of this world moved, and whose name is associated with the dearest affections of so many millions of men; the man upon whom the whole civilized world looked, and whom, to protect and shield, a great nation was ready, was destroyed by one mad villain. Must not this rouse us from our sinful lethargy to a consciousness of our weakness? All the power, wisdom, goodness and affection of man can not protect us when the Lord decrees to call us hence. Must not this rouse us from our sinful lethargy to a consciousness of our guilt? Abraham Lincoln was a good man; the millions testify, and history, with her impartial pencil, will record it. Not in his sins, in ours, he died; "for before wickedness, the righteous is taken away." He is the sin-offering for our iniquities. His death cries aloud, "Repent, repent your sins."

Verily, we need not inquire deeply to find our sins, when we know that an assassin was born and raised in our midst; the assassin of Abraham Lincoln brooded over his diabolic schemes in the very capital of our country. Where shall we begin to speak of the enormity of our sins? Must we speak first of the precepts of revenge which poison so many hearts and pervert so many minds to consider murder and assassination a matter of honor—assassination for offensive words—murder in duels? Or must we mention first the barbarous habit of bearing concealed arms to hide cowardice under the garb of crime? Or must we speak of the mercenary passions, which know of no intrinsic values of either persons or duties, honor or pride, art or science; which weigh or measure all persons and things alike by the standard of the market? Or must we mention the frigid hypocrisy which seeks refuge on the cushioned pews of fashionable churches; the haughtiness of little creatures embelished in costly garments and beglittered with gems, or such other dust; the scorn to which religion is subjected, the smile of pity cast on old-fashioned virtue, or the numerous and costly means to silence the crying conscience? There is no necessity for mentioning either of them, which are the mere fountains of our national sins, when we may look at once upon the broad and mad streams, with their impetuous billows and thousand whirlpools. Remember the frauds which were committed on the nation when hundred thousands of her noblest sons rushed to arms and offered their lives in vindication of her holy cause. Remember the legion of traitors and spies who surrounded our armies and penetrated into the most secret recesses of our Government. Or if that is too vast, too much to be remembered at once, then remember, simply, that our very President, the chosen banner-bearer of our people, the Messiah of this country, was slain by the assassin's hand in the midst of his people; and we must cry with Cain, "Mine iniquity is greater than I can bear."

Repentance is the great lesson which this deplorable event should teach us. Away with your idols of silver and your idols of gold; away with haughtiness, selfishness, delusion, deception and barbarism; prostrate yourselves with humble spirits and contrite hearts before God; confess and repent your sins; be healed of your diseases, distill the Balm of Gilead in the wounds of your conscience; cry for mercy and forgiveness to your God, then rise better men, better citizens, true children of the living God—and you have honored the memory of him who died in our national sins; you have erected a durable and grand monument to that martyr of liberty whose untimely departure we lament. Let him live in your virtues, resurrect in your patriotism; let him glow and shine in your aspirations, for the benefit of humanity, and the triumph of justice and liberty, of light over night, and right over might; and Abraham Lincoln lives as he wished to live—the benefactor of his people; and Abraham Lincoln departed as the Lord had spoken unto him that God might fulfill his divine promise: "And I will make of thee a great nation." So let us do honor to the memory of the departed martyr of liberty.

Honor brethren, honor the deceased President of the United States, by securing to him a perpetual reign, and a dominion everlasting. How? The dead should reign, the deceased one have dominion everlasting? Yes, even so shall you do.

The photographer or lithographer, the painter or sculptor, can not eternalize a man; he can not give you more of him than a faint delineation of the outside, shape and features, the most unimportant portion, the mere case of a person. Monuments, however lofty and extensive, crowded with inscriptions and symbols, tell very little, after all, of the man himself, to whose honor they may be erected. The passions, feelings, struggles, victories, motives and thoughts of a great mind, and each of them is a real fraction of his existence, are so innumerably manifold and change so often, that no artist can represent a considerable portion of them. This is the case especially with the deceased, Abraham Lincoln. The best representation of his figure will not tell posterity who he was. His outside appearance bore no resemblance even to his real nature. The most skillful philosopher will fail in describing the man who stood at the head of affairs during this gigantic struggle, his cares and troubles, his sleepless nights and days of anxiety, his thoughts and his schemes, his triumphs and mortifications, his hopes and fears, and ten thousand more sentiments, feelings and thoughts, which moved his mind in the stormy period of his Presidential term. He will be obliged to satisfy himself with the focus in which all these rays of the mind center, with the actions of the deceased. Let these actions be our political creed, and Lincoln reigns perpetually, his is the "covenant of an everlasting priesthood," he is immortal in his people.

"I will restore the Union," he promised us, and twice he took the solemn oath to protect and enforce the Constitution of the United States.

Let these two points be forever the beginning and end of our political creed. He gave liberty to an oppressed race, "And ye shall proclaim freedom to all the inhabitants of the land." Let us adhere to this great principle. All shall be free, all equal before the law. He was kind, charitable, and lenient toward the enemies of his country, longed and hoped for peace.—Let also these be cardinal points of our creed. Let us not be led astray by blind passions, hatred, a spirit of revenge; let us act entirely and conscientiously in the very spirit of the departed man, and we honor him. He reigns in death, and holds his dominion as though he was living still.

Let us carry into effect and perpetuate the great desires which heaved the breast of Abraham Lincoln; let us be one people, one, free, just and enlightened; let us be the chosen people to perpetuate and promulgate liberty and righteousness, the union and freedom of the human family; let us break asunder, wherever we can, the chains of the bondsman, the fetters of the slave, the iron rod of despotism, the oppressive yoke of tyranny; let us banish strife, discord, hatred, injustice, oppression from the domain of man, as far as our hands do reach, and we secure to Abraham Lincoln a perpetual reign and dominion everlasting; we set him the most durable monument in the hearts of the human family; then he is not dead, not removed even, from our midst, and will live forever. If his person was called from our midst, that we be guarded against the follies of apotheosis, which numerous admirers already approximated, to teach us again the great lesson, "Trust not in the noblest ones, in the son of man with whom there is no salvation," or as the prophet Isaiah expressed it, "Withdraw yourselves from man, whose breath is in his nostrils; because, for what is he to be esteemed?" If God permitted it that we learn the great lesson of the firmness and fitness of our Government, which is the people's Government, depending on no man or party; or to wake us to a sense of duty to our Government, to unite and fraternize us more in mourning and the common sympathy with the deceased President and his mourning family, the abused and ill-treated Secretary of State and his sons; if God has permitted the sudden removal of THE PERSON of Abraham Lincoln from our midst, for any or all of these reasons, or for reasons unknown to us, (but just and wise they certainly must be); his personality, his essence and substance, his mind, his soul, his principles, may forever remain with us and be our guiding stars. So we may secure to him a perpetual reign, and a dominion everlasting; for the ideas of union, justice, liberty, peace, kindness, charity, forbearance and goodness are everlasting, like God himself.

Murmur not against the justice and wisdom of Providence. God is just. Abraham Lincoln fought the battles for great ideas, and his enemies, of necessity, must be numerous and violent. He was a man, and where is the mortal one without his measure of faults and infirmities; with a great man, in a great period of time, they only become, with his virtues, more conspicuous. Every man has his mission, his destiny on earth; with men of eminent positions it only becomes more conspicuous. Whenever our mission is fulfilled God calls us hence. Abraham Lincoln fulfilled a great mission; he led the country through this glorious struggle to glorious victory, and bequeathed to us the ideas which, when fully developed and realized, not only will bring upon us the great blessing, "And I will make of thee a great nation;" but will also fulfill that sacred and most glorious promise, "And in thee all families of the earth shall be blessed." All families of the earth shall be blessed by freedom, as the chain of the negro was broken; by Union, peace, justice, equality, charity and kindness. So Abraham Lincoln shall reign perpetually and have an everlasting dominion. Therefore, "Abram departed, as the Lord had spoken to him."

Brethren, the lamented Abraham Lincoln, believed to be bone from our bone and flesh from our flesh. He supposed to be a descendant of Hebrew parenting. He said so in my presence. And, indeed, he preserved numerous features of the Hebrew race, both in countenance and character.

He was a man of many noble virtues, which may be our heritage; and God may forgive him his sins, and accept his soul in grace among the righteous men of all nations, and the martyrs of every sacred cause. May the Lord send consolation to his bereft widow and children, and heal the burning wound of this country which his departure afflicted on her. Brethren, let us read the funeral service for the soul of departed Abraham Lincoln.

[Here followed the burial service.]

PRAYER.

O, God and father! with bleeding hearts we submit to Thy paternal decrees, and acknowledge the justice and wisdom of Thy providence, although our eyes are too dim to penetrate the designs of Thy paternal goodness. Thou art God, and we are dust and ashes. Thou art the Great Cause of all causes, the Eternal Reality, the Infinite Substance, and we are small and perishable effects, whose life lasts but a few hours, and whose wisdom is too insignificant to be brought in account before Thee. Thou art the Father—the benign, merciful and gracious Father—and we are Thy children, Thine image; we submit, with childlike confidence and faith, to the decrees of Thy holy will. O, God! turn Thy correcting hand from us, consume us not in our sinfulness; let us behold days of joy and happiness, as we have seen time of calamity, affliction and distress. Behold, O, Lord! this bleeding, mourning, weeping land; heal us, for we are wounded; sustain us with Thy Heavenly manna, for we are sick and woe-stricken. Guard us, that we may see war and rebellion no more; let us behold Thy blessing of peace. Protect us and preserve our Union, our Government, our freedom, to the blessing of all Thy children. Shield the administrators of our Government, inspire them with Thy wisdom, justice and goodness, that Thy will be done on earth.

We beseech Thee, O Lord, to heal the wounds of Thy servant, William H. Seward, and bless him with many years of prosperity and happiness. We entreat thee, O Father, to console the widow and children of Thy deceased servant, Abraham Lincoln. Thou art the Father of orphans and the Protector of widows; with mercy Thou regardest the helpless and feeble ones. We pray Thee, O Lord, to vouchsafe Thy blessing to this city, this country, and to all lands where Thy children abide. Grant peace, justice, freedom and truth to all the sons of man.

Blessed Father, bless this congregation; fulfill upon us Thy sacred promise: "For if the mountains move and the hills totter, My grace shall not be moved from thee, and the covenant of My peace shall not change, saith Thy merciful God." Amen.

Whitelaw Reid

Dispatch from Washington

The Washington correspondent for the Radical Republican *Cincinnati Gazette*, Whitelaw Reid (1837–1912), writing as "Agate," was a keen observer of both the military and political aspects of the Civil War. His dispatch from the capital on the day of Lincoln's funeral quotes from (and alters) Alfred Lord Tennyson's "Ode on the Death of the Duke of Wellington."

WASHINGTON, April 19.

Historic Nineteenth of April! This day, four years ago, in the streets of Baltimore, the first blood was shed in the War for the Union; this day, after four years of terrible war, amid bulletins of falling cities and surrendering armies, the Rebellion ends, and the authorities of the Nation, in all the pomp and circumstance of funereal grief, bear from the White House to the Capitol, with crape-enshrouded banners, and muffled drums, and arms reversed, and cannon shrouded, and mournful martial music, and a long, long procession,

"As fits an universal woe,"

the murdered martyr, whose tragic death closes the War, and opens the Reconstruction.

"Bury the great man
    With an empire's lamentation,
Let us bury the great man
    To the noise of the mourning of a mighty nation."

"Mourning when its leaders fall;
While sorrow adornes hamlet and hall
            *   *   *   *   *   *   *
Mourn for the man of amplest influence,
Yet clearest of ambitious crime,
Our foremost, yet with least pretense;

219

*   *   *   *   *   *   *

Rich in saving common sense,
And, as the greatest only are,
In his simplicity sublime."

The New York Times

The Obsequies

The funeral ceremony held at the White House on April 19 was reported in detail by *The New York Times*, which printed in full the sermon given by the Reverend Phineas D. Gurley (1816–1868). Gurley was the pastor of the New York Avenue Presbyterian Church in Washington, which the Lincolns had attended regularly, although they never became members of the congregation. In 1862 Gurley had presided at the funeral of eleven-year-old Willie Lincoln, and had also attended the President on his deathbed in the Petersen house.

FUNERAL OF ABRAHAM LINCOLN

Solemn and Imposing Ceremonies.

A Day of Deep and Impressive Sadness.

THE FUNERAL SERMON.

Just Tribute to the Virtues and National Services of the Late President.

[OFFICIAL.]

FROM SECRETARY STANTON TO GEN. DIX

WAR DEPARTMENT, WASHINGTON,
April 19 — 1:30 P.M.

Maj.-Gen. Dix:

The arrangement for conveying the President's remains to Springfield, Ill., has been changed this morning. They will go direct from Washington to Philadelphia, Harrisburgh, Pittsburgh, Fort Wayne, and thence to Springfield.

EDWIN M. STANTON, Secretary of War.

SECOND DISPATCH.

WAR DEPARTMENT,
WASHINGTON, April 19 — 11 P.M.

Maj.-Gen. John A. Dix, New-York:

It has been finally concluded to conform to the original arrangements made yesterday for the conveyance of the remains of the late President,

ABRAHAM LINCOLN, from Washington to Springfield, viz. By way of Baltimore, Harrisburgh, Philadelphia, New-York, Albany, Buffalo, Cleveland, Columbus, Indianapolis and Chicago to Springfield.

EDWIN M. STANTON, Secretary of War.

THE FUNERAL.
Special Dispatch to the New-York Times.

WASHINGTON, D. C., Wednesday, April 19.

THE FUNERAL CEREMONIES.

The solemn and imposing funeral ceremonies of the day are over, and in point of sad sublimity and moral grandeur, the spectacle has been the most impressive ever witnessed in the national capital. The unanimity and depth of feeling, the decorum, good order, and complete success of all the arrangements, and the solemn dignity which pervaded all classes, will mark the obsequies of ABRAHAM LINCOLN as the greatest pageant ever tendered to the honored dead on this continent. The day has been delightfully warm and pleasant, and thus contributed to swell the throng of spectators, which was by far the greatest that ever filled the streets of the city.

As early as 8 o'clock, people began to throng the avenue, and by 11 o'clock many thousands were assembled in the vicinity of the departments and the Executive mansion. The avenue, between Fifteenth and Seventeenth streets, was kept clear by a strong guard of cavalry, for the purpose of forming the procession, though many of the societies had to wait on the side streets for hours. The arrangements made by the committee were carried out with a far greater degree of accuracy and comfort than is usual on occasions of this magnitude. No one was allowed to enter the grounds of the Executive mansion save such as had been provided with tickets, which included enough, however, to fill the great east room, where the body laid in state. It was intended that the attendance upon the funeral services should be of a highly representative character, and the intention was carried out with great success.

At about 11 o'clock the various distinguished bodies and committees began to arrive, and to be ushered into their appropriate positions in the east room. This room has already been described in the TIMES, but since yesterday several tiers of low seats, or standing places, elevated one above another, just sufficient to give all a good view, had been erected on the east side and both ends of the room, and all covered with black muslin. On the west side of the room, against the door leading to the main corridor, were placed fifteen chairs, all draped, which were especially reserved by Secretary HARRINGTON, of the Arrangement Committee, for the use of the press, a courtesy which was so completely arranged as to draw forth the commendation of every representative there. This grand east room presented a solemn appearance. It was hung with black everywhere. All glitter and gay color, save in the carpet beneath our feet, had been covered with the emblem of grief. The only relief from the mournful shade which met the eye everywhere were the white silk sashes of the marshals and committees, the rich silver ornamentation of the coffin, and the beautiful white japonicas, roses and green leaves which shed their perfume as incense over the dead.

The first to enter were the officiating clergymen, Rev. Dr. HALL, Rector of the Epiphany, Bishop SIMPSON, of the Methodist Episcopal Church, Rev. P. D. GURLEY, of the New-York Avenue Presbyterian Church, the President's Pastor, and Rev. E. H. GRAY, Chaplain of the Senate and Pastor of the E street Baptist Church. Soon after came the Merchant's Committee of New-York, whose names I sent you yesterday, followed by the Committee of the Union League. They took position on the platform at the north end of the room.

At 11:25, the Mayor of Washington and the Common Council entered, escorting the Committee of the New-York Common Council, of which Alderman BRICE is Chairman; also, Mayor LINCOLN and a committee from Boston, and a like committee from Philadelphia. Then came the officers of the Senate and House of Representatives, who took appropriate stations; the officers and members of the Christian and Sanitary Commissions, the Assistant Secretaries, the Delegations from Kentucky and Illinois, the States of the President's birth and residence, who were designated as mourners, Govs. Fenton of New-York, Andrew of Massachusetts, Parker of New-Jersey, Brough of Ohio, Oglesby of Illinois, Buckingham of Connecticut, and their staffs; the diplomatic corps in full court dress, the members of the Senate and House of Representatives, Admirals Gregory, Porter, Shubrick and Goldsborough, the Supreme Court in the persons of Chief Justice Chase, Nelson, Davis and Swayne, Ex-Vice-President Hamlin, the pall-bearers, twenty-two in number, then Grant and Farragut, arm in arm, Burnside and Hunter, Gen. Dyer of the

Ordnance Department, six lady mourners, the only ladies present, save one or two of the nurses of the household, Mrs. Sprague, Miss Nettie Chase, Mrs. Stanton, Mrs. Usher, Mrs. Welles and Mrs. Dennison.

At just 12 o'clock President JOHNSON, escorted by the venerable PRESTON KING and the members of the Cabinet, entered and took their places on the right of the coffin. Private Secretaries NICOLAY and HAY, and Capt. ROBERT LINCOLN, the President's oldest son, and only member of the family present, then Gen. TODD, of Dakotah, and relative of the family, who were seated near the foot of the catafalque.

The room was now full, but no crowding, no disorder of any kind. The attendants upon the ceremonies had all arrived, and the scene in the room was of a very imposing character. A gentleman who had attended the funerals of three Presidents, assures me that this was the most imposing of all. The pall of black which met the eye everywhere, was suggestive of grandeur rather than gloom. The representative men from every part of the country impressed the beholder with the vastness of the power and influence of the form that lay cold in death, and the services which followed, the earnest prayer and eloquent sermon impressed upon all minds the virtues and great national services of ABRAHAM LINCOLN.

At ten minutes past 12, Rev. Mr. HALL opened the services by reading from the Episcopal burial service from the dead as follows:

"I am the resurrection and the life, saith the Lord; he that believeth in me, though he were dead, yet shall he live, and whosoever liveth and believeth in me shall never die. John 11th chap. 25th and 26th verses.

I know that my Redeemer liveth, and that He shall stand at the latter day upon the earth, and though after my skin worms destroy this body, yet in my flesh shall I see God, whom I shall see for myself, and mine eyes shall behold, and not another.—Job, chap. xix., 25th, 26th and 27th verses.

We brought nothing into this world, and it is certain we can carry nothing out. The Lord gave and the Lord hath taken away. Blessed be the name of the Lord."—First Timothy, chap. vi., 7th verse, and Job, chap. i, 21st verse.

"Lord, let me know my end and the number of my days, that I

may be certified how long I have to live. Behold Thou hast made my days as it were but a span long, and mine age is even as nothing in respect of Thee. And verily every man living is altogether vanity; for man walketh in a vain shadow, and disquieteth himself in vain. He heapeth up riches, and cannot tell who shall gather them. And now, Lord, what is my hope? Truly my Hope is ever in Thee; deliver me from all my offences, and make me not a rebuke unto the foolish. When Thou, with rebukes, doth chasten man for sin, Thou makest his beauty to consume away, like as it were a moth fretting a garment. Every man is, therefore, but vanity. Hear my prayer, O Lord, and with Thine ears consider my calling. Hold not Thy peace at my tears, for I am a stranger with Thee, and a sojourner, as all my fathers were. O, spare me a little, that I may recover my strength before I go hence and be no more seen. Lord, Thou hast been our refuge from one generation to another. Before the mountains were brought forth or even the earth and the world were made, thou art God from everlasting and world without end. Thou turnest man to destruction; again thou sayest, come again ye children of men, for a thousand years in thy sight are but as yesterday, seeing that it is past as a watch in the night. As soon as thou scatterest them, they are even as sheep and fade away suddenly like the grass. In the morning it is green and groweth up, but in the evening it is cut down, dried up and withered. For we consume away in Thy displeasure, and are afraid at Thy wrathful indignation. Thou hast set our misdeeds before Thee, and our secret sins in the light of Thy countenance; for when Thou art angry all our days are gone. We bring our years to an end as it were a tale that is told. The days of our age are threescore years and ten, and though men be so strong that they come to fourscore years, yet is their strength then but labor and sorrow, so soon passeth it away, and we are gone. So teach us to number our days that we may apply our hearts unto wisdom. Glory be to the Father and to the Son and to the Holy Ghost; as it was in the beginning, is now, and ever shall be, world without end. Amen."

Then was read the lesson from the 15th chapter of St. Paul to the Corinthians, beginning with the 20th verse.

Right Rev. Bishop SIMPSON, of the Methodist Episcopal Church, then delivered a most eloquent and affecting prayer, after which Rev. Dr. GURLEY, of the New-York-avenue Presbyterian Church, in which the deceased President had worshiped, delivered the following funeral sermon:

DR. GURLEY'S SERMON.

As we stand here to-day mourners around this coffin and around the lifeless remains of our beloved Chief Magistrate, we recognize and we adore the sovereignty of God. His throne is in the heavens, and His kingdom ruleth over all. He hath done and He hath permitted to be done whatsoever he pleased. Clouds and darkness are round about him; righteousness and judgment are the habitation of His throne. His way is in sea and His path in the great waters, and His footsteps are not known. Canst thou by searching find out God? Canst thou find out the Almighty unto perfection? It is as high as Heaven—what canst thou do? Deeper than Hell—what canst thou know? The measure thereof is longer than the earth and broader than the sea. If He cut off and shut up, or gather together, then who can hinder him—for He knoweth vain men, He seeth wickedness: also will he not then consider it? We bow before His Infinite Majesty—we bow, we weep, we worship. Where reason fails with all her powers—there faith prevails and love adores. It was a cruel, cruel hand, that dark hand of the assassin, which smote our honored, wise and noble President, and filled the land with sorrow. But above and beyond that hand there is another, which we must see and acknowledge. It is the chastening hand of a wise and faithful Father. He gives us this bitter cup, and the cup that our Father has given us shall we not drink it?

> God of the just, thou givest us the cup,
> We yield to thy behest and drink it up.

Whom the Lord loveth he chasteneth. Oh, how these blessed words have cheered and strengthened and sustained us through all these long and weary years of civil strife, while our friends and brothers on so many ensanguined fields were falling and dying for the cause of liberty and Union. Let them cheer and strengthen and sustain us to-day. True, this new sorrow and chastening has come in

such an hour and in such a way as we thought not, and it bears the
impress of a rod that is very heavy, of mystery that is very deep,
that such a life should be sacrificed at such a time, by such a foul
and diabolical agency that the man at the head of the nation, whom
the people had learned to trust with a confiding and loving confidence, and upon whom more than upon any other were centered
under God our best hopes for the true and speedy pacification of
the country, the restoration of the Union and the return of harmony and love—that he should be taken from among us, and taken
just as the prospect of peace was brightly opening upon our torn
and bleeding country, and just as he was beginning to be animated
and gladdened with the hope of ere long enjoying with the people
the blessed fruit and reward of his and their toils, care and patience
and self-sacrificing devotion to the interests of liberty and the
Union. Oh, it is a mysterious and a most afflicting visitation. But it
is our Father in Heaven, the God of our fathers and our God, who
permits us to be so suddenly and sorely smitten, and we know that
his judgments are right, and that in faithfulness he has afflicted us
in the midst of our rejoicings. We needed this stroke, this dealing,
this discipline, and therefore he has sent it. Let us remember our
affliction has not come forth of the dust, and our trouble has not
sprung out of the ground. Through and beyond all second causes,
let us see the sovereign permissive agency of the great First Cause.
It is His prerogative to bring light out of darkness and good out of
evil. Surely the wrath of man shall praise Him, and the remainder
of wrath He will restrain. In the light of a clearer day, we may yet
see that the wrath which planned and perpetrated the death of the
President was overruled by Him whose judgments are unsearchable and His ways past finding out, for the highest welfare of all
those interests which are so dear to the Christian patriot and
philanthropist, and for which a loyal people have made such an unexampled sacrifice of treasure and of blood. Let us not be faithless,
but believing. "Blind unbelief is prone to err and scan His work in
vain. God is His own interpreter, and he will make it plain." We will
wait for His interpretation; and we will wait in faith, nothing
doubting. He who has led us so well, and defended and prospered
us so wonderfully during the last four years of toil and struggle and

sorrow, will not forsake us now. He may chasten, but he will not destroy. He may purify more and more in the furnace of trial, but he will not consume us. No, no. He has chosen us, as He did his people of old, in the furnace of affliction, and he has said of us, as he said of them, this people have reformed. For myself they shall show forth my praise. Let our principal anxiety now be that this new sorrow may be a sanctified sorrow, that it may lead us to deeper repentance, to a more humbling sense of our dependence upon God, and to the more unreserved consecration of ourselves and all that we have to the cause of truth and justice, of law and order, of liberty and good government, of pure and undefiled religion. Then, though weeping may endure for a night, joy will come in the morning. Blessed be God. Despite of the great, and sudden, and temporary darkness, the morning has begun to dawn, the morning of a bright and glorious day such as our country has never seen. That day will come, and not tarry and the death of a hundred Presidents and their Cabinets can never, never prevent it. While we are thus hopeful, however, let us also be humble. The occasion calls us to prayerful and tearful humiliation. It demands of us that we lie low, very low, before him who has smitten us for our sins. O! that all our rulers, and all our people, may bow in the dust to-day beneath the chastening hand of God, and may their voices go up to Him as one voice, and their hearts go up to Him as one heart, pleading with Him for mercy, for grace to sanctify our great and sore bereavement, and for wisdom to guide us in this our time of need. Such a united cry and pleading will not be in vain. It will enter into the ear and heart of Him who sits upon the throne, and He will say to us, as to His ancients, "In a little wrath, I hid my face from thee for a moment, but with everlasting kindness will I have mercy upon thee, saith the Lord, thy Redeemer." I have said that the people confided in the late lamented President with a full and a loving confidence. Probably no man since the days of WASHINGTON was ever so deeply and firmly imbedded and enshrined in the very hearts of the people as ABRAHAM LINCOLN. Nor was it a mistaken confidence and love. He deserved it; deserved it well; deserved it all. He merited it by his character, by his acts, and by the tenor and tone and spirit of his life. He was simple and sincere, plain and

honest, truthful and just, benevolent and kind. His perceptions
were quick and clear, his judgments were calm and accurate, and
his purposes were good and pure beyond a question, always and
everywhere. He aimed and endeavored to be right and to do right.
His integrity was thorough, all-pervading, all controlling and incorruptible. It was the same in every place and relation, in the consideration and control of matters great or small, the same firm and
steady principle of power and beauty, that shed a clear and crowning lustre upon all his other excellencies of mind and heart, and
recommended him to his fellow-citizens as the man who, in a time
of unexampled peril, when the very life of the nation was at stake,
should be chosen to occupy in the country, and for the country, its
highest post of power and responsibility. How wisely and well, how
purely and faithfully, how firmly and steadily, how justly and successfully, he did occupy that post and meet its grave demands, in
circumstances of surpassing trial and difficulty, is known to you
all—known to the country and the world; he comprehended from
the first the perils to which treason had exposed the freest and
best government on the earth—the vast interests of liberty and
humanity that were to be saved or lost forever in the urgent impending conflict. He rose to the dignity and momentousness of the
occasion, saw his duty as the Chief Magistrate of a great and im-
periled people, and he determined to do his duty, and his whole
duty, seeking the guidance and leaning upon the arm of Him of
whom it is written—He giveth power to the faint, and to them that
have no might He increaseth the strength. Yes, he leaned upon His
arm. He recognized and received the truth that the kingdom is the
Lord's, and He is the governor among the nations. He remembered
that God is in history, and he felt that nowhere had His hand and
His mercy been so marvelously conspicuous as in the history of
this nation. He hoped and he prayed that that same hand would
continue to guide us, and that same mercy continue to abound to
us in the time of our greatest need. I speak what I know and testify
what I have often heard him say, when I affirm that guidance and
mercy were the props on which he humbly and habitually leaned.
That they were the best hope he had for himself and for his country. Hence when he was leaving home in Illinois and coming to this

city to take his seat in the Executive Chair of a disturbed and troubled nation, he said to the old and tried friends who gathered tear-
fully around him, and bade him farewell, I leave you with this
request—pray for me. They did pray for him, and millions of others
prayed for him. Nor did they pray in vain. Their prayers were heard,
and the answer appears in all his subsequent history. It shines forth
with a heavenly radiance in the whole course and tenor of his administration from its commencement to its close. God raised him
up for a great and glorious mission, furnished him for his work, and
aided him in its accomplishment. Nor was it merely by strength of
mind and honesty of heart and purity and pertinacity of purpose,
that He furnished him. In addition to these things He gave him a
calm and abiding confidence in the overruling providence of God,
and in the ultimate triumph of truth and righteousness through
the power and the blessing of God. This confidence strengthened
him in all his hours of anxiety and toil, and inspired him with calm
and cheering hope when others were inclined to despondency and
gloom. Never shall I forget the emphasis and the deep emotion
with which he said in this very room, to a company of clergymen
and others who called to pay him their respects in the darkest day
of our civil conflict: "Gentlemen, my hope of success in this great
and terrible struggle rests on that immutable foundation, the justice and goodness of God, and when events are very threatening
and prospects very dark, I still hope that in some way which man
cannot see, all will be well in the end, because our cause is just and
God is on our side. "Such was his sublime and holy faith, and it was
an anchor to his soul both sure and steadfast. It made him firm and
strong. It emboldened him in the pathway of duty, however rugged
and perilous it might be. It made him valiant for the right, for the
cause of God and humanity, and it held him in steady, patient and
unswerving adherence to a policy of administration which he
thought and which we all now think, both God and humanity required
him to adopt. We admired and loved him on many accounts, for
strong and various reasons. We admired his child-like simplicity;
his freedom from guile and deceit; his staunch and sterling integrity; his kind and forgiving temper; his industry and patience; his
persistent, self-sacrificing devotion to all the duties of his eminent

position, from the least to the greatest; his readiness to hear and consider the cause of the poor and humble, suffering and oppressed; his charity; His inflexible purpose, that what freedom had gained in our terrible civil strife should never be lost, and that the end of the war should be the end of slavery, and as a consequence of rebellion, his readiness to spend and be spent for the attainment of such a triumph, a triumph, the blessed fruits of which should be as wide-spreading as the earth, and as enduring as the sun. All these things commanded and fixed our admiration, and the admiration of the world, and stamped upon his character and life the unmistakable impress of greatness. But more sublime than any or all of these, more holy and influential, more beautiful and strong and sustaining was his abiding confidence in God and in the final triumph of truth and righteousness through Him and for His sake. This was his noblest virtue, his grandest principle, the secret alike of his strength, his patience and his success. This, it seems to me, after being near him steadily and with him often for more than four years, is the principle by which more than by any other, he being dead yet speaketh. Yes, by his steady enduring confidence in God, and in the complete ultimate success of the cause of God, which is the cause of humanity, more than in any other way does he now speak to us and to the nation he loved and served so well. By this he speaks to his successor in office, and charges him to have faith in God. By this he speaks to the members of his Cabinet, the men with whom he counciled so often and associated with so long, and he charges them to have faith in God. By this he speaks to all who occupy positions of influence and authority in these sad and tumultuous times, and he charges them all to have faith in God. By this he speaks to this great people as they sit in sackcloth to-day, and weep for him with a bitter wailing, and refuse to be comforted, and he charges them to have faith in God, and by this he will speak through the ages, and to all rulers and people in every land, and His message to them will be, Cling to liberty and right, battle for them, bleed for them, die for them if need be, and have confidence in God. O, that the voice of this testimony may sink down into our hearts to-day and every day, and into the heart of the nation, and exert appropriate influence upon our feelings, our faith, our patience and our devotion to the cause, now dearer to us than ever before, because consecrated by the blood of its conspicuous defender, its truest and most fondly trusted friend. He is dead. But the God in whom he trusted lives, and He can guide and strengthen his successor as He guided and strengthened him. He is dead. But the memory of his virtues; of his wise and patriotic counsels and labors; of his calm and steady faith in God, lives as precious, and will be a power for good in the country quite down to the end of time. He is dead. But the cause he so ardently loved; so ably, patiently, toward those who questioned the correctness of his opinions and the wisdom of his policy; his wonderful skill in reconciling differences among the friends of the Union, leading them away from abstractions and inducing them to work together and harmoniously for the common weal; his true and enlarged philanthropy, that knew no distinction of color or race, but regarded all men as brethren, and endowed alike by their creator with certain inalienable rights, amongst which are life, liberty, and the pursuit of happiness; faithfully represented and defended, not for himself only, not for us only, but for all people in all their coming generations till time shall be no more. That cause survives his fall and will survive it. The light of its brightening prospects flashes cheeringly to-day athwart the gloom occasioned by his death, and the language of God's united providences is telling us that though the friends of liberty die liberty itself is immortal. There is no assassin strong enough and no weapon deadly enough to quench its inexhaustible life or arrest its onward march to the conquest and empire of the world. This is our confidence and this is our consolation, as we weep and mourn to-day; though our beloved President is slain our beloved country is saved; and so we sing of mercy as well as of judgment. Tears of gratitude mingle with those of sorrow, while there is also the dawning of a brighter, happier day upon our stricken and weary land. God be praised that our fallen chief lived long enough to see the day dawn, and the day star of joy and peace arise upon the nation. He saw it and was glad. Alas! alas! He only saw the dawn when the sun has risen full orbed and glorious, and a happy reunited people are rejoicing in its light. It will shine upon his grave, but that grave will be a precious and a consecrated spot. The friends of Liberty and of the Union will repair to it in years and ages to come, to pronounce the memory of its occupant blessed, and gathering from his very ashes, and from the rehearsal of his deeds and virtues, fresh incentives to patriotism, they will there renew their vows of fidelity to their country and their God. And now I know not that I can more appropriately conclude this discourse, which is but a sincere and simple utterance of the heart, than by addressing to our departed President, with some slight modification, the language which TACITUS, in his Life of AGRICOLA, addresses to his venerable and departed father-in-law. With you we may now congratulate. You are blessed not only because your life was a career of glory, but because you were released when your country was safe, it was happiness to die. We have lost a parent, and in our distress it is now an addition to our heartfelt sorrow that we had it not in our power to commune with you on the bed of languishing and receive your last embrace. Your dying words would have been ever dear to us. Your commands we should have treasured up, and graven them on our hearts. This sad comfort we have lost, and the wound, for that reason, pierces deeper. From the world of spirits behold your disconsolate family and people. Exalt our mind from fond regret and unavailing grief to the contemplation of your virtues. Those we must not lament. It were impiety to sully them with a tear. To cherish their memory, to embalm them with our praises, and so far as we can to emulate your bright example, will be the truest mark of our respect, the best tribute we can offer. Your wife will thus preserve the memory of the best of husbands; and thus your children will prove their filial piety; by dwelling constantly on your works and actions, they will have an illustrious character before their eyes; and not content with the bare image of your mortal frame, they will have what is more valuable—the form and features of your mind. Busts and statues, like their originals, are frail and perishable. The soul is formed of finer elements, and its inward form is not to be expressed by the hand of an artist. With unconscious matter our manners and our morals may, in some degree, trace the resemblance. All of you that gained our love and raised our admiration still subsist, and will ever subsist, preserved in the minds of men, the register of ages; and the records of fame of others who figured in the stage of life, and were the worthiest of a former day, will sink for want of a faithful historian into the common lot of oblivion, inglorious and unremembered. But you, our lamented friend and head, delineated with truth and fairly consigned to posterity, will survive yourself and triumph over the injuries of time.

Rev. E. H. GRAY, D. D. pastor of the E-street Baptist Church, closed the solemn services with prayer.

The corpse was then removed to the hearse, which was in front of the door of the Executive Mansion, and at 2 o'clock the procession was formed. It took the line of Pennsylvania-avenue. The streets were kept clear of all incumbrances, but the sidewalks were densely lined with people from the White House to the Capitol, a distance of a mile and a half. The roofs, porticos, windows and all elevated points were occupied by interested spectators. As the procession started minute-guns were fired near St. John's Church, the City Hall and the Capitol. The bells of all the churches in the city and of the various engine-houses were tolled.

First in the order of procession was a detachment of colored troops, then followed white regiments of infantry and bodies of artillery and cavalry, navy, marine and army officers on foot; the pall-bearers in carriages next; the hearse, drawn by six white horses—the coffin prominent to every beholder. The floor on which it rested was strewn with evergreens, and the coffin covered with white flowers. Then followed Physicians of the late President, then the grand hearse and the guard of honor and the pall-bearers, Capt. ROBERT LINCOLN and little TAD, the President's favorite son, in a carriage, and TOMMY behind. Mrs. LINCOLN was not present at either the ceremony or in the procession, she not having left her bed since Saturday last. The mourners, the delegations from Illinois and Kentucky, came next in order, and then President JOHNSON in a carriage, with Hon. PRESTON KING and the Cabinet Ministers. The carriages on this part of the line were flanked by a strong cavalry guard, with drawn sabres. Then came more carriages, with the Diplomatic Corps, Judges, Senators, and others; then members of the House of Representatives, on foot; the officers of the House; the New-York delegations; the Massachusetts delegation, with Gen. BUTLER, in civilian's dress, prominently in the line, delegations from other States, Masons, Knight

Templars, Perseverance Fire Company of Philadelphia, Catholic clergy, nine delegations, department clerks two thousand strong, Gen. MEIGS and staff and the Quartermasters department brigade, a regiment of Fenians, the Treasury regiment. Gen. McCALLUM and staff, and a brigade of the employes of the United States military railroads, all wearing an appropriate badge. Next a large delegation from Alexandria, with a car on which was painted, "Alexandria mourns the national loss." Then came one of the saddest scenes in the entire column, a battalion of scarred and maimed veterans, with bandaged limbs and heads, with an arm or leg gone, but hobbling along on crutches, determined that their homage to their great chief should be as sincere as that of their companions. Then more firemen and Sons of Temperance, with a battalion of soldiers, in full regalia of these excellent Sons; then Colored Benevolent Associations, with their banners draped and their walk and mien the very impersonation of sorrow.

The procession finally ended, but was almost two hours in passing a given point, and the head of it had actually begun to disperse at the Capitol before the rear of the column had passed beyond the Treasury Department.

On the arrival at the eastern gate of the Capitol, the remains were conveyed into the rotunda, where a catafalque like that in the Executive Mansion had been erected to receive them. Here the attendants assembled, and amid profound silence Rev. Dr. GURLEY read the burial service.

The vast assemblage then began to disperse, and the obsequies of the lamented dead were over. During the entire afternoon the bells in the city and in Georgetown and Alexandria were tolled, and minute guns fired from the fortifications. So may we lament with TENNYSON:

> Let the bell be toll'd.
> And a deeper knell in the heart be knoll'd.
> And the sound of the sorrowing anthem roll'd
> Through the dome of the golden cross
> And the volleying cannon thunder his loss.

The remains lie in state at the capitol until Friday morning, at 8 o'clock, when they will proceed northward. The route has been shortened somewhat from the published programme of this morning at the earnest request of Mrs. LINCOLN, but she has finally consented that they may proceed to Philadelphia and New-York, and they will lie in state at Philadelphia during Sunday, and arrive in New-York on Monday morning, at 7 o'clock, remaining there until Tuesday.

Wilbur Fisk

Letter to The Green Mountain Freeman

A schoolteacher and farm laborer, Wilbur Fisk (1839–1914) enlisted in the 2nd
Vermont Infantry in September 1861 and began contributing regular letters to *The
Green Mountain Freeman* of Montpelier under the name "Anti-Rebel." Fisk fought
in the Seven Days' Battles and at Chancellorsville, the Wilderness, Spotsylvania,
Petersburg, and in the Shenandoah Valley before being detached for guard duty at
the Sixth Corps hospital at City Point, Virginia, in January 1865. In a letter to the
Freeman, Fisk described the President's visit to the hospital on April 8 shortly before Lincoln returned to Washington: "When the President came all the men that
were able arranged themselves by common consent into line, on the edge of the
walk that runs along by the door of the stockades, and Mr. Lincoln passed along in
front, paying personal respect to each man. 'Are you well, sir?' 'How do you do to-
day?' 'How are you, sir?' looking each man in the face, and giving him a word and
a shake of the hand as he passed. He went into each of the stockades and tents, to
see those who were not able to be out. 'Is this Father Abraham?' says one very sick
man to Mr. Lincoln. The President assured him, good naturedly, that it was. Mr.
Lincoln presides over millions of people, and each individual share of his attention
must necessarily be very small, and yet he wouldn't slight the humblest of them
all." He concluded: "The men not only reverence and admire Mr. Lincoln, but they
love him. May God bless him, and spare his life to us for many years."

Sixth Corps Hospital
City Point, Va.
April 20, 1865

The sad calamity which the nation has suffered, here, as elsewhere, is
the all absorbing topic of conversation and of thought. The fountains of
feeling have been so deeply stirred by this horrid event, that other events
scarcely stir them at all. Scarcely anything else seems worth talking about,
and all other news has lost its interest beside this. Less than two weeks
ago Mr. Lincoln came here and shook hands with us, and we all wished
that for many long years yet "Father Abraham" might be spared to this
nation, which he, humanly speaking, has saved. But President Lincoln
has been murdered—murdered by the same fiendish spirit, begotten in
hell, and fed by slavery on earth, that has brought forth this rebellion.
If I write a letter to-day I must write of this event. I should mock my

own feelings if I did not. Never has sadder news been brought to us than this. It seemed as if we had lost a father. Mr. Lincoln was different from everybody; so sagacious, so straight-forward in all that he did, so apt in all that he said, and withal so kind-hearted and honest, he was winning the admiration of the whole world. When he was here a week ago last Saturday, some of the surgeons told him that to attempt to shake hands with so many thousand men would be more than he ought to endure, but he overruled them, for he said he wanted to shake hands with the brave boys who had won the great victories which gave him, with all the rest of the nation, so much cause to rejoice, and had been wounded, many of them, in so doing. The President appeared to take delight in it. I believe he took almost as much pleasure in honoring the boys, as the boys did in receiving the honor from him. But Abraham Lincoln is dead. As we think of this mournful calamity we can hardly keep from asking, Oh why did a just and merciful Providence permit this thing to happen? Why was not the assassin's hand stayed before it had stricken down the man we all so much loved to honor, and the leader in whom we could place our fullest confidence. But we must quote, in view of this event, the same words that Mr. Lincoln quoted in his second inaugural, "The judgements of the Lord are true and righteous altogether."

Last Sunday was a day of mourning here at City Point. The people were startled when the news came. Abraham Lincoln dead! oh no, it could not be. Rumor had outdone itself. We could not believe it. The doctors saddled their horses and rode to the Point, before waiting for the official news to come to the hospital. Alas, the news was confirmed. Not only the ladies wept, but the soldiers many of them shed tears tenderly like women, for all felt this to be no common grief. We felt as you did, dear reader, too much grief and indignation for words to express. For four long years we had been at work fighting the rebellion, that our lawfully chosen Chief Magistrate might administer the laws in every one of our United States, and now just as the war was about to close, and our object be accomplished, the hand that has led us and the heart that has beat in sympathy for us in all the struggle, are still and cold in death. A rebel has done it—a stealthy cowardly rebel. The boys swore eternal enmity against everything in sympathy with that spirit of secession that has committed this crime, unequalled in atrocity in the history of the world. I have seen the men look grave and sad before when we have heard of defeats, of losses in battle, of comrades killed, but I have never seen that which moved every one with sorrow as did this. I remember last May at Spotsylvania, when the brave and much loved commander of our corps was killed, and what a feeling of depression there was when it was told us that our almost idolized general was shot and mortally wounded; but General Sedgwick was killed in the accepted danger of honorable warfare, and we bowed to fate's decree. Mr. Lincoln was killed by an assassin, and it seemed almost impossible to submit to it as a dispensation of Divine Providence. A man from the front told me that he never saw such a feeling manifested among the troops, as there was when the news of the President's murder was received. The indignation of the men knew no bounds. Had there been fighting going on, and more rebel prisoners captured, he thought that it would have been difficult to have restrained them from indiscriminate carnage. They swore if it came in their power to take a rebel's life they would take it, no matter what the risk might be to their own.

Over in the Fifth Corps Hospital a wounded rebel indiscreetly dropped a word expressing his satisfaction that Abe. Lincoln was murdered, and his indiscretion liked to have cost him his life. The boys in his ward would have torn him to pieces had not the authorities arrested and confined him. Even then he would hardly have been safe if the officers had not assured them that he should be sent to the Point in the morning and taken care of—taken care of being supposed to imply a punishment of a magnitude commensurate with his crime, as they regarded it.

There was a singular rumor afloat here Sunday evening, which shows how easy it is to catch at and believe what we wish to believe. It was reported that the whole story was a hoax. Some rebels had tapped the telegraph between here and Fortress Monroe and sent us up this news just for a sensation. Some of the men doubted this, but others believed it fully, and laughed at their former fears. "A pretty big fright we have had to-day," says one. "Yes," is the reply, "I never felt so bad in my life." But this rumor stilled our fears only for a brief moment. The booming salute in the morning gave us no longer any room to hope.

I believe I have never seen newspapers in such demand as they have been since Sunday. The details of this appalling tragedy, and the movements of the authorities to arrest the perpetrators, excite more interest now than the details of the last battles, or the movements of our armies in pursuit of the foe. Every other interest is swallowed up in this. We want by all means that the remainder of the rebels should be caught, but to-day we feel a livelier interest that Mr. Lincoln's murderer shall be brought to justice.

Just now, however, there isn't much of interest going on. There are all sorts of rumors as to the disposal that is going to be made of us. The Ninth Corps Hospital here commenced to break up yesterday. They were to take transports for some place, but they had no certain idea where, though the most of them supposed it would be to Washington. Part of the Ninth Corps itself passed here to-day to go on board the boats waiting for them at the wharf. They seem to think, the most of them, that they shall be sent to Washington, and from there sent home on discharged furloughs, that is, they are to be left to shift for themselves in the world without Uncle Sam's pay or his rations, but to be ready at any time, if needed, to fall in and enter active service. The Government is not quite willing to let go of us, nor quite able to bear the burden of our support, and hence this compromise. However, the boys will be abundantly willing to accept their liberty on these terms, if they are the best the Government can give. If this is true of the Ninth Corps it will probably be true of ours. The surgeon in charge expects the whole thing to be cleared out here in a short time. A fellow applied to the surgeon for a furlough, the surgeon told him in three weeks we would all have furloughs. He might have been in earnest or in fun, but his remarks made an excellent foundation for a camp story, and it has been given a pretty wide circulation.

Our Corps they say is in camp out to Burkeville Station. I understand our boys have got them a fine camp out there in a pine woods, and are resting on their laurels. They have but little to do now, and nothing to hinder them from enjoying themselves to their utmost. There is no enemy in front of them, and they have no picketing of any consequence to do. The boys think it a little odd, for it is something new in the experience of the Sixth Corps. We shall be expecting them this way now soon. Rumor has had them on the way every day since the surrender of Lee.

The hospitals here have been filled to their greatest capacity since the late battles, and many new tents added, but they are sending off to the general hospital every day, almost, many of the worst cases. None are sent to their regiments. I suppose they are waiting for the regiments to be sent here. There can be no doubt but that we shall be on our way to Washington before many days, and then *home*, we hope.

Emma LeConte

Diary, April 21, 1865

The daughter of a professor of chemistry and geology at South Carolina College in Columbia, Emma LeConte (1847–1932) was tutored in Greek, Latin, French, German, and mathematics. On the morning of February 17, 1865, troops from William T. Sherman's army entered Columbia as residents looted warehouses and stores and started fires among the cotton bales stockpiled in the streets. While some Union soldiers fought the fires, others lit new ones. Spread by high winds, the flames eventually burned almost half the city. LeConte witnessed the inferno from her house, which survived the conflagration, and wrote: "This is the way in which the 'cultured' Yankee nation wars upon women and children." Two months after the burning of Columbia, she lamented the news of Lee's surrender: "The South lies prostrate—their foot is on us—there is no help." The next entry in LeConte's diary recorded her reaction to Lincoln's assassination. Her quotation in French is from the fourth verse of "La Marseillaise": "Tremble tyrants, and you traitors / The shame of all parties / Tremble! your parricidal schemes / Will finally receive their reward."

———————

Friday, April 21st.

—Hurrah! Old Abe Lincoln has been assassinated! It may be abstractly wrong to be so jubilant, but I just can't help it. After all the heaviness and gloom of yesterday this blow to our enemies comes like a gleam of light. We have suffered till we feel savage. There seems no reason to exult, for this will make no change in our position—will only infuriate them against us. Never mind, our hated enemy has not the just reward of his life. The whole story may be a Yankee lie. The despatch purports to be from Stanton to Sherman—It says Lincoln was murdered in his private box at the theatre on the night of the 14th—(Good Friday—at the *theatre*) The assassin brandished a dagger and shouting, "*Sic semper tyrannis*—Virginia is avenged", shot the president through the head. He fell senseless and expired next day a little after ten. The assassin made his escape in the crowd. No doubt it was regularly planned and he was surrounded by Southern sympathizers. "*Sic semper tyrannis.*" Could there have been a fitter death for such a man? At the same hour nearly Seward's house was entered—he was badly wounded as also his son. Why could not the assassin have done his work more thoroughly? That *vile* Seward—he it is to whom we owe this war—it is a shame he should escape.

I was at Mrs. Leland's saying my German when Mrs. Snowden brought in the news. We were all so excited and talked so much that Wilhelm Tell was quite forgotten. Our spirits had been so low that the least good news elevated them wonderfully and this was so utterly onlooked-for—took us so completely by surprise. I actually *flew* home and for the first time in oh, so long I was trembling and my heart beating with excitement. I stepped in at Aunt Josie's to talk it over.

As soon as I reached the head of the stairs they all cried—"What do you think of the news?"—"Isn't it splended—" etc.

We are all in a tremor of excitement. At home it was the same. If it is *only* true! The first feeling I had when the news was announced was simply gratified revenge. The man we hated has met his proper fate. I thought with exultation of the howl it had by that time sent through the North, and how it would cast a damper on their rejoicings over the fall of our noble Lee. The next thought was how it would infuriate them against us—and that was pleasant too. After talking it over the hope presented itself that it might produce a confusion that would be favorable but there is scarcely any likelihood of that—he is hardly important enough for that. Andy Johnson will succeed him—the rail-splitter will be succeeded by the drunken ass. Such are the successors of Washington and Jefferson—such are to rule the South. "*Sic semper tyrannis*"—it has run in my head all day,

> "*Trembles tyrans! et vous perfides*
> *L'opprobres de toutes les parties—*
> *Tremblez! vos projets parricides*
> *Mont enfin recevoir leur prix!*"

What exciting, what eventful times we are living in.

Mary Chesnut

Diary, April 22–23, 1865

Mary Chesnut (1823–1886) had spent much of the war in Richmond, where her husband, a former U.S. senator from South Carolina, served as a military aide to Jefferson Davis. Although Chesnut privately deplored "this hated institution" of slavery—"ours is a *monstrous* system & wrong & iniquity"—she became an ardent supporter of Confederate independence, writing in 1861: "We have risked all, & we must play our best for the stake is life or death." She learned of Lincoln's assassination in Chester, South Carolina, where she had found refuge after fleeing Columbia earlier in the year. During the 1860s Chesnut kept a diary that she would later revise and expand from 1881 to 1884. Her original diary for April 1865 is not known to have survived, and the selections printed here are taken from the revised version.

Colonel Cad Jones came with a dispatch, a sealed secret dispatch. It was for General Chesnut. I opened it.

Lincoln—old Abe Lincoln—killed—murdered—Seward wounded!

Why? By whom? It is simply maddening, all this.

I sent off messenger after messenger for General Chesnut. I have not the faintest idea where he is, but I know this foul murder will bring down worse miseries on us.

Mary Darby says: "But they murdered him themselves. No Confederates in Washington."

"But if they see fit to accuse us of instigating it?"

"Who murdered him?"

"Who knows!"

"See if they don't take vengeance on us, now that we are ruined and cannot repel them any longer."

Met Mr. Heyward. He said: "Plebiscitum it is. See, our army are deserting Joe Johnston. That is the people's vote against a continuance of the war. And the death of Lincoln—I call that a warning to tyrants. He will not be the last president put to death in the capital, though he is the first."

"Joe Johnston's army that he has risked his reputation to save from the very first year of the war—*deserting*. Saving his army by retreats, and now they are deserting *him*."

"Yes, Stonewall's tactics were the best—hard knocks, blow after blow in rapid succession, quick marches, surprises, victories quand même. That would have saved us. Watch, wait, retreat, ruined us. Now look out for bands of marauders, black and white, lawless disbanded soldiery from both armies."

An armistice, they say, is agreed on.

Taking stock, as the shopkeepers say. Heavy debts for the support of negroes during the war—and before, as far as we are concerned. No home—our husbands shot or made prisoners.

"Stop, Mrs. C. At best, Camden for life—that is worse than the galleys for you."

April 22, 1865

————

"Oh!" said Mary Darby vengefully one night, as Burton Harrison had left us after telling all manner of wrongs done Mr. Davis. "Oh! One thing is so respectable in those awful Yankees. If they did choose a baboon to reign over them, they were true to him, they stuck to him through weal and through woe. Oh! they were sharp Yankees and saw in his ugly hide the stuff to carry them through, and he saved them—if he could not save himself."

"That mad man that killed him! Now he will be Saint Abe for all time, saint and martyr."

"When they print his life I wonder if they put in all of the dirty stories his soul delighted in."

"Faugh!" said Mary Darby, whose darling D had enlightened her in many ways. "Now most of the anecdotes, funny as they were told me as coming from Lincoln, were so eminently calculated to raise a blush upon a young person's cheek that I had never been able to repeat them."

April 23, 1865

Wendell Phillips

The Lesson of President Lincoln's Death

The renowned abolitionist orator Wendell Phillips (1811–1884) had denounced Lincoln in 1860 as "the Slave-Hound of Illinois" for his willingness to enforce the fugitive slave clause of the Constitution. In 1864 Phillips had supported the radical splinter candidacy of John C. Frémont, and continued to attack the administration's emancipation and reconstruction policies after Frémont withdrew from the race. Before a hometown audience at the Tremont Temple in Boston in October 1864, Phillips declared that he had "no faith in Abraham Lincoln" and "dare not trust him with our future." Six months later he returned to the same hall and offered a measured eulogy for the slain president.

THESE are sober days. The judgments of God have found us out. Years gone by chastised us with whips; these chastise us with scorpions. Thirty years ago, how strong our mountain stood, laughing prosperity on all its sides! None heeded the fire and gloom which slumbered below. It was nothing that a giant sin gagged our pulpits; that its mobs ruled our streets, burnt men at the stake for their opinions, and hunted them like wild beasts for their humanity. It was nothing, that, in the lonely quiet of the plantation, there fell on the unpitied person of the slave every torture which hellish ingenuity could devise. It was nothing that as husband and father, mother and child, the negro drained to its dregs all the bitterness that could be pressed into his cup; that, torn with whip and dogs, starved, hunted, tortured, racked, he cried, "How long! O Lord, how long!" In vain did a thousand witnesses crowd our highways, telling to the world the horrors of this prison-house. None stopped to consider, none believed. Trade turned away its deaf ear; the Church gazed on them with stony brow; Letters passed by with mocking tongue. But what the world would not look at, God has set to-day in a light so ghastly bright, that it almost dazzles us blind. What the world refused to believe, God has written all over the face of the continent, with the sword's point, in the blood of our best and most beloved. We believe the agony of the slave's hovel, the mother, and the husband, when it takes its seat at our board. We realize the barbarism that crushed him in the sickening and brutal use of the relics of Bull Run, in the torture and starvation of Libby

245

Prison, where idiocy was mercy, and death was God's best blessing; and now, still more bitterly, we realize it in the coward spite which strikes an unarmed man, unwarned, behind his back; in the assassin fingers which dabble with bloody knife at the throats of old men on sick pillows. O, God! let this lesson be enough! Spare us any more such costly teaching!

This deed is but the result, and fair representative, of the system in whose defence it was done. No matter whether it was previously approved at Richmond, or whether the assassin, if he reaches the confederates, be received with all honor, as the wretch Brooks was, and as this bloodier wretch will surely be, wherever rebels are not dumb with fear of our cannon. No matter for all this. God shows this terrible act to teach the nation, in unmistakable terms, the terrible foe with which it has to deal. But for this fiendish spirit, North and South, which holds up the rebellion, the assassin had never either wished or dared such a deed. This lurid flash only shows us how black and wide the cloud from which it sprung.

And what of him in whose precious blood this momentous lesson is writ? He sleeps in the blessings of the poor, whose fetters God commissioned him to break. Give prayers and tears to the desolate widow and the fatherless; but count him blessed far above the crowd of his fellow-men. [Fervent cries of "Amen!"] He was permitted himself to deal the last staggering blow which sent rebellion reeling to its grave; and then, holding his darling boy by the hand, to walk the streets of its surrendered capital, while his ears drank in praise and thanksgiving which bore his name to the throne of God in every form piety and gratitude could invent; and finally, to seal the sure triumph of the cause he loved with his own blood. He caught the first notes of the coming jubilee, and heard his own name in every one. Who among living men may not envy him? Suppose that, when a boy, as he floated on the slow current of the Mississippi, idly gazing at the slave upon its banks, some angel had lifted the curtain, and shown him, that, in the prime of his manhood, he should see this proud empire rocked to its foundation in the effort to break those chains; should himself marshal the hosts of the Almighty in the grandest and holiest war that Christendom ever knew, and deal, with half-reluctant hand, that thunderbolt of justice which would smite the foul system to the dust; then die, leaving a name immortal in the sturdy pride of our race and the undying gratitude of another,—would any credulity, however sanguine, any enthusiasm, however fervid, have enabled him to believe it? Fortunate man! He has lived to do it! [Applause.] God has graciously withheld him from any fatal misstep in the great advance, and withdrawn him at the moment when his star touched its zenith, and the nation needed a sterner hand for the work God gives it to do.

No matter now, that, unable to lead and form the nation, he was contented to be only its representative and mouthpiece; no matter, that, with prejudices hanging about him, he groped his way very slowly and sometimes reluctantly forward; let us remember how patient he was of contradiction, how little obstinate in opinion, how willing, like Lord Bacon, "to light his torch at every man's candle." With the least possible personal hatred; with too little sectional bitterness, often forgetting justice in mercy; tender-hearted to any misery his own eyes saw; and in any deed which needed his actual sanction, if his sympathy had limits, recollect he was human, and that he welcomed light more than most men, was more honest than his fellows, and with a truth to his own convictions such as few politicians achieve. With all his shortcomings, we point proudly to him as the natural growth of democratic institutions. [Applause.] Coming time will put him in that galaxy of Americans which makes our history the day-star of the nations,—Washington, Hamilton, Franklin, Jefferson and Jay. History will add his name to the bright list, with a more loving claim on our gratitude than either of them. No one of those was called to die for his cause. For him, when the nation needed to be raised to its last dread duty, we were prepared for it by the baptism of his blood.

What shall we say as to the punishment of rebels? The air is thick with threats of vengeance. I admire the motive which prompts these; but let us remember, no cause, however infamous, was ever crushed by punishing its advocates and abettors. All history proves this. There is no class of men base and coward enough, no matter what their views and purpose, to make the policy of vengeance successful. In bad causes, as well as good, it is still true that "the blood of the martyrs is the seed of the Church." We cannot prevail against this principle of human nature. And, again, with regard to the dozen chief rebels, it will never be a practical question whether we shall hang them. Those not now in Europe will soon be there. Indeed, after paroling the bloodiest and guiltiest of all, Robert Lee [loud applause], there would be little fitness in hanging any lesser wretch.

The only punishment which ever crushes a cause is that which its leaders necessarily suffer in consequence of the new order of things made necessary to prevent the recurrence of their sin. It was not the blood of two peers and thirty commoners, which England shed after the rebellion of 1715, or that of five peers and twenty commoners, after the rising of 1745, which crushed the House of Stuart. Though the fight had lasted only a few months, those blocks and gibbets gave Charles his only chance to recover. But the confiscated lands of his adherents, and the new political arrangement of the Highlands,—just, and recognized as such, because necessary,—these quenched his star forever.

Our Rebellion has lasted four years. Government has exchanged prisoners and acknowledged its belligerent rights. After that, gibbets are out of the question. A thousand men rule the Rebellion,—are the Rebellion. A thousand men! We cannot hang them all. We cannot hang men in regiments. What, cover the continent with gibbets! We cannot sicken the nineteenth century with such a sight. It would sink our civilization to the level of Southern barbarism. It would forfeit our very right to supersede the Southern system, which right is based on ours being better than theirs. To make its corner-stone the gibbet would degrade us to the level of Davis and Lee. The structure of Government which bore the earthquake shock of 1861 with hardly a jar, and which now bears the assassination of its Chief Magistrate, in this crisis of civil war, with even less disturbance, needs, for its safety, no such policy of vengeance; its serene strength needs to use only so much severity as will fully guarantee security for the future.

Banish every one of these thousand rebel leaders,—every one of them, on pain of death if they ever return! [Loud applause.] Confiscate every dollar and acre they own. [Applause.] These steps the world and their followers will see are necessary to kill the seeds of *caste*, dangerous State rights and secession. [Applause.] Banish Lee with the rest. [Applause.] No Government should ask of the South which he has wasted and the North which he has murdered such superabundant Christian patience as to tolerate in our streets the presence of a wretch whose hand upheld Libby Prison and Andersonville, and whose soul is black with sixty-four thousand deaths of prisoners by starvation and torture.

What of our new President? His whole life is a pledge that he knows and hates thoroughly that *caste* which is the Gibraltar of secession. *Caste*, mailed in State rights, seized slavery as its weapon to smite down the Union. Said Jackson, in 1833; "Slavery will be the next *pretext* for rebellion." PRETEXT! That pretext and weapon we wrench from the rebel hands the moment we pass the anti-slavery amendment to the Constitution. Now kill *caste*, the foe who wields it. Andy Johnson is our natural leader for this. His life has been pledged to it. He put on his spurs with this vow of knighthood. He sees that confiscation, land placed in the hands of the *masses*, is the means to kill this foe.

Land and the ballot are the true foundations of all Governments. Intrust them wherever loyalty exists, to all those, black and white, who have upheld the flag. [Applause.] Reconstruct no State without giving to every loyal man in it the ballot. I scout all limitations of knowledge, property or race. [Applause.] Universal suffrage for me. That was the Revolutionary model. Every freeman voted, black or white, whether he could read or not. My rule is, any citizen liable to be hanged for crime is entitled to vote for rulers. The ballot insures the school.

Mr. Johnson has not yet uttered a word which shows that he sees the need of negro suffrage to guarantee the Union. The best thing he has said on this point, showing a mind open to light, is thus reported by one of the most intelligent men in the country, the Baltimore correspondent of the Boston *Commonwealth:* —

"The Vice-President was holding forth very eloquently in front of Admiral Lee's dwelling, just in front of the War-Office in Washington. He said he was willing to send every negro in the country to Africa to save the Union. Nay, he was willing to cut Africa loose from Asia, and sink the whole black race ten thousand fathoms deep to effect this object. A loud voice sang out in the crowd, 'Let the negro stay where he is, governor, and give him the ballot, and the Union will be safe forever!' 'And I am ready to do that, too!' [loud applause] shouted the governor, with intense energy, whereat he got three times three for the noble sentiment. I witnessed this scene, and was pleased to hear our Vice-President take this high ground, for up to this point must the nation quickly advance, or there will be no peace, no rest, no prosperity, no blessing, for our suffering and distracted country."

The need of giving the negro a ballot is what we must press on the

President's attention. Beware the mistake which fastened McClellan on us, running too fast to indorse a man while untried, determined to manufacture a hero and leader at any rate. The President tells us that he waits to announce his policy till events call for it,—a wise, timely, and statesman-like course. Let us imitate it. Assure him in return that the government shall have our support like good citizens. But remind him that we will tell him what we think of his policy when we learn what it is. He says, "Wait: I shall punish; I shall confiscate. What more I shall do, you will know when I do it."

Let us reply: "Good! So far, good! Banish the rebels. See to it that, beyond all mistake, you strip them of all possibility of doing harm. But see to it also that before you admit a single State to the Union, you oblige it to give every loyal man in it the ballot,—the ballot, which secures education; the ballot, which begets character where it lodges responsibility; the ballot, having which, no class need fear injustice or contempt; the ballot, which puts the helm of the Union into the hands of those who love and have upheld it. Land,—where every man's title-deed, based on confiscation, is the bond which ties his interest to the Union; ballot,— the weapon which enables him to defend his property and the Union. These are the motives for the white man: the negro needs no motive but his instinct and heart. Give him the bullet and ballot, he needs them; and while he holds them the Union is safe. To reconstruct now without giving the negro the ballot would be a greater blunder, and, considering our better light, a greater sin than our fathers committed in 1789; and we should have no right to expect from it any less disastrous results."

This is the lesson God teaches us in the blood of Lincoln. Like Egypt, we are made to read our lesson in the blood of our first-born, and the seats of our princes left empty. We bury all false magnanimity in this fresh grave, writing over it the maxim of the coming four years: "Treason is the greatest of crimes, and not a mere difference of opinion." That is the motto of our leader to-day,—that the warning this atrocious crime sounds throughout the land. Let us heed it, and need no more such costly teaching. [Loud applause.]

George Bancroft

Oration in Union Square, New York City

After ceremonies in Baltimore, Harrisburg, and Philadelphia, Lincoln's body arrived in New York City on the morning of April 24 and was conveyed to City Hall, where it lay in state overnight. The next day a lavish funeral procession witnessed by hundreds of thousands of mourners moved up Broadway past Union Square to the Hudson River depot, where the slain president's remains were placed on a train bound for Albany. As the procession made its way uptown, the historian George Bancroft (1800–1891) addressed a large public meeting held in Union Square. Best known for his popular and influential multivolume work *A History of the United States*, Bancroft had served as secretary of the navy and minister to Great Britain during the James Polk administration and backed Stephen A. Douglas in the 1860 presidential election. Unlike many of Lincoln's eulogists, Bancroft maintained a secular tone, commending him for his role in preserving the Union and emancipating the slaves without engaging in sanctification. His oration also recorded some of the passions of the moment: the "state in our vicinity" Bancroft reproaches for refusing to ratify the abolitionist Thirteenth Amendment is New Jersey, and the unnamed general he criticizes is William T. Sherman, who had signed an overly lenient surrender agreement with Confederate General Joseph E. Johnston in North Carolina on April 18 that was quickly repudiated by President Johnson and the cabinet.

Our grief and horror at the crime which has clothed the continent in mourning, find no adequate expression in words, and no relief in tears. The President of the United States of America has fallen by the hands of an assassin. Neither the office with which he was invested by the approved choice of a mighty people, nor the most simple-hearted kindliness of nature, could save him from the fiendish passions of relentless fanaticism. The wailings of the millions attend his remains as they are borne in solemn procession over our great rivers, along the seaside, beyond the mountains, across the prairie, to their resting place in the valley of the Mississippi. His funeral knell vibrates through the world, and the friends of freedom of every tongue and in every clime are his mourners.

Too few days have passed away since Abraham Lincoln stood in the flush of vigorous manhood, to permit any attempt at an analysis of his character or an exposition of his career. We find it hard to believe that his large eyes, which in their softness and beauty expressed nothing but benevolence and gentleness, are closed in death; we almost look for the pleasant smile that brought out more vividly the earnest cast of his features, which were serious even to sadness. A few years ago he was a village attorney, engaged in the support of a rising family, unknown to fame, scarcely named beyond his neighborhood; his administration made him the most conspicuous man in his country, and drew on him first the astonished gaze, and then the respect and admiration of the world.

Those who come after us will decide how much of the wonderful results of his public career is due to his own good common sense, his shrewd sagacity, readiness of wit, quick interpretation of the public mind, his rare combination of fixedness and pliancy, his steady tendency of purpose; how much to the American people, who, as he walked with them side by side, inspired him with their own wisdom and energy; and how much to the overruling laws of the moral world, by which the selfishness of evil is made to defeat itself. But after every allowance, it will remain that members of the government which preceded his administration opened the gates to treason, and he closed them; that when he went to Washington the ground on which he trod shook under his feet, and he left the republic on a solid foundation; that traitors had seized public forts and arsenals, and he recovered them for the United States, to whom they belonged; that the capital, which he found the abode of slaves, is now the home only of the free; that the boundless public domain which was grasped at, and, in a great measure, held for the diffusion of slavery, is now irrevocably devoted to freedom; that then men talked a jargon of a balance of power in a republic between slave states and free states, and now the foolish words are blown away forever by the breath of Maryland, Missouri, and Tennessee; that a terrible cloud of political heresy rose from the abyss, threatening to hide the light of the sun, and under its darkness a rebellion was growing into indefinable proportions; now the atmosphere is purer than ever before, and the insurrection is vanishing away; the country is cast into another mould, and the gigantic system of wrong, which had been the work of more than two centuries, is dashed down, we hope forever. And as to himself, personally: he was then scoffed at by the proud as unfit for his station, and now against the usage of later years and in spite of numerous competitors he was the unbiased and the undoubted choice of the American people for a second term of service. Through all the mad business of treason he retained the sweetness of a most placable disposition; and the slaughter of myriads of the best on the battle field, and the more terrible destruction of our men in captivity by the slow torture of exposure and starvation, had never been able to provoke him into harboring one vengeful feeling or one purpose of cruelty.

How shall the nation most completely show its sorrow at Mr. Lincoln's death? How shall it best honor his memory? There can be but one answer. He was struck down when he was highest in its service, and in strict conformity with duty was engaged in carrying out principles affecting its life, its good name, and its relations to the cause of freedom and the progress of mankind. Grief must take the character of action, and breathe itself forth in the assertion of the policy to which he fell a victim. The standard which he held in his hand must be uplifted again higher and more firmly than before, and must be carried on to triumph. Above everything else, his proclamation of the first day of January, 1863, declaring throughout the parts of the country in rebellion, the freedom of all persons who had been held as slaves, must be affirmed and maintained.

Events, as they rolled onward, have removed every doubt of the legality and binding force of that proclamation. The country and the rebel government have each laid claim to the public service of the slave, and yet but one of the two can have a rightful claim to such service. That rightful claim belongs to the United States, because every one born on their soil, with the few exceptions of the children of travellers and transient residents, owes them a primary allegiance. Every one so born has been counted among those represented in Congress; every slave has ever been represented in Congress; imperfectly and wrongly it may be—but still has been counted and represented. The slave born on our soil always owed allegiance to the general government. It may in time past have been a qualified allegiance, manifested through his master, as the allegiance of a ward through its guardian, or of an infant through its parent. But when the master became false to his allegiance, the slave stood face to face with his country; and his allegiance, which may before have been a qualified one, became direct and immediate. His chains fell off, and he rose at once in the presence of the nation, bound, like the rest of us, to its defence. Mr. Lincoln's proclamation did but take notice of the already existing right of the bondman to freedom. The treason of the master made it a public crime for the slave to continue his obedience; the treason of a state set free the collective bondmen of that state.

This doctrine is supported by the analogy of precedents. In the times of feudalism the treason of the lord of the manor deprived him of his serfs; the spurious feudalism that existed among us differs in many respects from the feudalism of the middle ages, but so far the precedent runs parallel with the present case; for treason the master then, for treason the master now, loses his slaves.

In the middle ages the sovereign appointed another lord over the serfs and the land which they cultivated; in our day the sovereign makes them masters of their own persons, lords over themselves.

It has been said that we are at war, and that emancipation is not a belligerent right. The objection disappears before analysis. In a war between independent powers the invading foreigner invites to his standard all who will give him aid, whether bond or free, and he rewards them according to his ability and his pleasure, with gifts or freedom: but when at a peace, he withdraws from the invaded country, he must take his aiders and comforters with him; or if he leaves them behind, where he has no court to enforce his decrees, he can give them no security, unless it be by the stipulations of a treaty. In a civil war it is altogether different. There, when rebellion is crushed, the old government is restored, and its courts resume their jurisdiction. So it is with us; the United States have courts of their own, that must punish the guilt of treason and vindicate the freedom of persons whom the fact of rebellion has set free.

Nor may it be said, that because slavery existed in most of the states when the Union was formed, it cannot rightfully be interfered with now. A change has taken place, such as Madison foresaw, and for which he pointed out the remedy. The constitutions of states had been transformed before the plotters of treason carried them away into rebellion. When the federal Constitution was framed, general emancipation was thought to be near; and everywhere the respective legislatures had authority, in the exercise of their ordinary functions, to do away with slavery. Since that time the attempt has been made in what are called slave states, to render the condition of slavery perpetual; and events have proved with the clearness of demonstration, that a constitution which seeks to continue a caste of hereditary bondmen through endless generations is inconsistent with the existence of republican institutions.

So, then, the new President and the people of the United States must insist that the proclamation of freedom shall stand as a reality. And, moreover, the people must never cease to insist that the Constitution shall be so amended as utterly to prohibit slavery on any part of our soil for evermore.

Alas! that a state in our vicinity should withhold its assent to this last beneficent measure; its refusal was an encouragement to our enemies equal to the gain of a pitched battle; and delays the only hopeful method of pacification. The removal of the cause of the rebellion is not only demanded by justice; it is the policy of mercy, making room for a wider clemency; it is the part of order against a chaos of controversy; its success brings with it true reconcilement, a lasting peace, a continuous growth of confidence through an assimilation of the social condition.

Here is the fitting expression of the mourning of to-day.

And let no lover of his country say that this warning is uncalled for. The cry is delusive that slavery is dead. Even now it is nerving itself for a fresh struggle for continuance. The last winds from the south waft to us the sad intelligence that a man who had surrounded himself with the glory of the most brilliant and most varied achievements, who but a week ago was counted with affectionate pride among the greatest benefactors of his country and the ablest generals of all time, has initiated the exercise of more than the whole power of the Executive, and under the name of peace has, perhaps unconsciously, revived slavery, and given the hope of security and political power to traitors, from the Chesapeake to the Rio Grande. Why could he not remember the dying advice of Washington, never to draw the sword but for self-defence or the rights of his country, and when drawn, never to sheath it till its work should be accomplished? And yet, from this ill-considered act, which the people with one united voice condemn, no great evil will follow save the shadow on his own fame, and that also we hope will pass away. The individual, even in the greatness of military glory, sinks into insignificance before the resistless movements of ideas in the history of man. No one can turn back or stay the march of Providence.

No sentiment of despair may mix with our sorrow. We owe it to the memory of the dead, we owe it to the cause of popular liberty throughout the world, that the sudden crime which has taken the life of the President of the United States shall not produce the least impediment

in the smooth course of public affairs. This great city, in the midst of unexampled emblems of deeply-seated grief, has sustained itself with composure and magnanimity. It has nobly done its part in guarding against
the derangement of business or the slightest shock to public credit. The
enemies of the republic put it to the severest trial; but the voice of fac-
tion has not been heard; doubt and despondency have been unknown.
In serene majesty the country rises in the beauty and strength and hope
of youth, and proves to the world the quiet energy and the durability of
institutions growing out of the reason and affections of the people.

Heaven has willed it that the United States shall live. The nations of
the earth cannot spare them. All the wornout aristocracies of Europe
saw in the spurious feudalism of slaveholding, their strongest outpost,
and banded themselves together with the deadly enemies of our national
life. If the Old World will discuss the respective advantages of oligarchy
or equality; of the union of church and state, or the rightful freedom
of religion; of land accessible to the many, or of land monopolized by an
ever-decreasing number of the few, the United States must live to control
the decision by their quiet and unobtrusive example. It has often and truly
been observed, that the trust and affection of the masses gather naturally
round an individual; if the inquiry is made, whether the man so trusted and
beloved shall elicit from the reason of the people enduring institutions of
their own, or shall sequester political power for a superintending dynasty,
the United States must live to solve the problem. If a question is raised
on the respective merits of Timoleon or Julius Cæsar, of Washington or
Napoleon, the United States must be there to call to mind that there were
twelve Cæsars, most of them the opprobrium of the human race, and to
contrast with them the line of American presidents.

The duty of the hour is incomplete, our mourning is insincere, if,
while we express unwavering trust in the great principles that underlie
our government, we do not also give our support to the man to whom
the people have entrusted its administration.

Andrew Johnson is now, by the Constitution, the president of the
United States, and he stands before the world as the most conspicuous
representative of the industrial classes. Left an orphan at four years old,
poverty and toil were his steps to honor. His youth was not passed in the
halls of colleges; nevertheless he has received a thorough political education in statesmanship, in the school of the people and by long experience

of public life. A village functionary; member successively of each branch of the Tennessee legislature, hearing with a thrill of joy, the words, "The Union, it must be preserved;" a representative in Congress for successive years; governor of the great state of Tennessee; approved as its governor by re-election; he was at the opening of the rebellion a senator from that state in Congress. Then at the Capitol, when senators, unrebuked by the government, sent word by telegram to seize forts and arsenals, he alone from that southern region told them what the government did not dare to tell them, that they were traitors, and deserved the punishment of treason. Undismayed by a perpetual purpose of public enemies to take his life, bearing up against the still greater trial of the persecution of his wife and children, in due time he went back to his state, determined to restore it to the Union, or die with the American flag for his winding sheet. And now, at the call of the United States, he has returned to Washington as a conqueror, with Tennessee as a free state for his trophy. It remains for him to consummate the vindication of the Union.

To that Union Abraham Lincoln has fallen a martyr. His death, which was meant to sever it beyond repair, binds it more closely and more firmly than ever. The blow aimed at him, was aimed not at the native of Kentucky, not at the citizen of Illinois, but at the man, who, as President, in the executive branch of the government, stood as the representative of every man in the United States. The object of the crime was the life of the whole people; and it wounds the affections of the whole people. From Maine to the southwest boundary on the Pacific, it makes us one. The country may have needed an imperishable grief to touch its inmost feeling. The grave that receives the remains of Lincoln, receives the costly sacrifice to the Union; the monument which will rise over his body will bear witness to the Union; his enduring memory will assist during countless ages to bind the states together, and to incite to the love of our one undivided, indivisible country. Peace to the ashes of our departed friend, the friend of his country and his race. He was happy in his life, for he was the restorer of the republic; he was happy in his death, for his martyrdom will plead for ever for the Union of the states and the freedom of man.

April 25, 1865

William Cullen Bryant

Ode

On February 27, 1860, the poet William Cullen Bryant (1794–1878), who had edited the antislavery *New York Evening Post* for thirty years, introduced Lincoln to an audience of 1,500 at Cooper Union in New York City. Lincoln's well-received lecture on slavery and the founders, which Bryant printed and praised in his influential newspaper, helped propel the Illinois Republican toward his party's presidential nomination three months later. During the Civil War, Bryant sometimes criticized Lincoln for being indecisive, but supported his reelection in 1864. His ode to the slain President was recited at the Union Square memorial meeting by the Unitarian minister Samuel Osgood and later published as "The Death of Lincoln."

Oh, slow to smite and swift to spare,
    Gentle and merciful and just!
Who, in the fear of God, didst bear
    The sword of power—a nation's trust.

In sorrow by thy bier we stand,
    Amid the awe that hushes all,
And speak the anguish of a land
    That shook with horror at thy fall.

Thy task is done—the bond are free,
    We bear thee to an honored grave,
Whose proudest monument shall be
The broken fetters of the slave.

Pure was thy life; its bloody close
    Hath placed thee with the sons of light,
Among the noble host of those
    Who perished in the cause of right.

New York Tribune

Editorial on the New York Funeral Procession

Lincoln's New York funeral was held in a city haunted by the horrific draft riots of July 1863 in which as many as 119 people had been killed. At least eleven African-American men were lynched by white mobs during the violence, while the Colored Orphans Asylum on Fifth Avenue was looted and burned. Two years later the civic establishment sought to maintain peace by excluding black New Yorkers from public events. While black troops had marched in the inaugural parade in Washington on March 4, the grand procession held in New York two days later to celebrate recent Union victories had been open to whites only. Similarly, the New York City council sought to exclude black mourners from the funeral ceremonies for the late President. An editorial in the *New York Tribune* on April 24, the day Lincoln's body reached the city, addressed the controversy.

———————

We understand that the Colored Men of our City have been practically refused a place in the grand procession to-morrow in honor of the services and memory of President Lincoln. The grief of this class is probably deemed too real and hearty to bear any part in a mourning pageant devised and engineered by men who always opposed and never even professed to honor and respect our late President until they were quite sure he was dead.

We trust the Blacks will not take this refusal to heart. So long as a draft impended over our City, they were vouchsafed the amplest opportunities to fill the ranks of that quite earnest procession which was constantly moving hence on Richmond and Charleston in response to the President's calls for defenders of the National integrity. Should more soldiers be wanted, we warrant that a large share of those who parade to-morrow will stand back and give every negro a fair chance to go in. And, as the Blacks of our City do not need any display of banners, mottoes, regalia, &c., to convince anybody that *they* grieve for the loss of our good President, we suggest that they need not take to heart their exclusion from the parade of to-morrow.

James W. C. Pennington

The Funeral of President Lincoln and the Colored People

A Presbyterian minister and leader in New York City's black community, James W. C. Pennington (1807–1870) had successfully challenged the segregation of the city's streetcars in the 1850s. Born into slavery on the Eastern Shore of Maryland, Pennington had escaped to Pennsylvania in 1828; published *The Origin and History of the Colored People* (1841) and an autobiographical narrative, *The Fugitive Blacksmith* (1849); and served for several years as pastor of Shiloh Church in New York City. His letter about the funeral procession appeared in *The Anglo-African* on May 13, 1865.

MR. EDITOR: The Common Council of New York had certainly no more right to rule the societies of colored men out of the funeral procession than they would have to decide that a certain part of a man's family should not attend his funeral through the street.

One story is that the Common Council was influenced in their action by an intimation that the Irish societies had determined not to join in the procession if colored societies were assigned a place.

This is simply ridiculous. Was Mr. Lincoln the President of the Irish only? Of all other classes, was he not emphatically the President of the colored man? Have we not had it thrown in our teeth by the Irish that our father was dead? The spirit that would exclude colored men from the President's funeral, is the same that murdered him, from whomsoever it may come.

Another story is that the objection came from the white Free Masons, based upon their jealousy of colored bodies of that Order. Well, pray what has the Common Council to do with colored Free Masons any more than any other order? They had no more right to rule them out of the procession than they have to prohibit their having lodges in the city.

The President of the United States is the commander-in-chief of the armies and navy of the same; and also the chief Civil Magistrate of the Nation; and, as such, the President's funeral was a military funeral. And as the Civil Magistrate's it is public to the nation of all classes.

The action of the Common Council was an insult to the memory of the President; and had they gone one step further, and caused a single person, or a class of persons, to be removed from, or hindered from entering that procession, they would have been liable to arrest and trial for impeding the President's funeral procession. The streets, parks and squares through which the procession passed were for the time military highways, and not under the control of the Common Council.

To ask the colored men "not to take the action of the Common Council to heart," is only adding insult to injury.

A story goes the round that the article on the subject in which this request occurs was written at the instance of two clergymen of the city— one of them colored.

If this be true, these gentlemen should, as teachers, certainly, be well enough versed in the philosophy of human nature to know that colored men have no right to stultify the finest feelings of their brethren to accommodate the stupidity of a Copperhead Mayor and Common Council of New York, and a host of common scoundrels at their backs.

A story is also told that the sage editor regrets having published the article. There is no man of the editorial corps of this country more read by us than the editor of the *Tribune*, and he has a fair chance to know us. Pity the article ever appeared because it looks as if the first impulse of the white man is to sacrifice the colored man; and that justice always comes second handed. The rights of individual colored men were not affected by the notion of societies. Those connected with the Custom House had a perfect right to walk in that section; those belonging to certain wards had a right in such sections; colored clergymen had a right to be with those of their profession. These, sir, are my views of the whole matter; and I hope that should a thing of this kind occur again, which is not impossible, we shall know how to act. I was at first opposed to the turnout; but upon reflection I conceived it well to try the case so as to settle the precedent or to a bad precedent being made.

The Common Council has been defeated and disgraced. The point has been gained. The smallness of the number out, compared to what might have been out, does not change the principle at issue: that colored men have a right in the funeral procession of a President of these United States, the objections of the Common Council of New York, the Irish societies, or the white Free Masons to the contrary notwithstanding.

J. W. C. PENNINGTON.

April 27th, 1865.

The Anglo-African

Caste Hate at the Great Funeral

One of the most influential black newspapers during the Civil War, *The Anglo-African* was edited by Robert Hamilton (1819–1870), a music teacher and abolitionist, and published weekly in New York City. The newspaper's first editorial on the funeral controversy, probably written by Hamilton, appeared on April 29. It was followed on May 5 by "The Common Council's Caste," an extensive report on the incident that included a statement by a city councilman claiming that it would have been "injudicious and improper" to assign "the colored people" a place in the procession "to the exclusion of the thirty odd other associations of white men" who had also applied at a late hour.

WE have no indignation to waste on the Committee of the Common Council for their refusal to admit colored citizens into the line of the procession. On the contrary, we should have been greatly surprised had we found sufficient favor in their eyes to have obtained from them this deeply coveted privilege. Had the Committee said frankly "yes," we would instinctively felt our persons to discover whether we had met the fate of Midas, or our pockets to discover whether they were swelled up and foaming over with greenbacks. In either of these incidents, or had we "struck ile" in any visible direction, we would have understood the "assent" of a Committee representing a body so famous as the Common Council of New York City. As it was, they adjourned stating that they had referred our request to a sub-Committee. We hope we may never meet that sub-Committee, nor hear its report; if rendered when such Committees of our Common Council will make their reports—neither in the heavens above, nor the earth beneath—we are not at all anxious to be present.

As it is, the Committee has consigned itself and its principles to a deeper infamy than has yet befallen to their lot, which is saying a great deal. At Washington no less than three thousand colored troops, and members of benevolent societies formed part of the funeral procession of ABRAHAM LINCOLN; in Baltimore and in Philadelphia, colored societies in like manner formed part of the great pageant. This was as it should be; and afforded a sincere tribute to the well-known feelings of the departed hero, who, in the language of Gerrit Smith, "kept open house for the poor." O shame! shame! on our great metropolis which insulted the martyred dead through those who bear living witness to the noblest attributes of his nature.

A statement in regard to this affair was prepared for this number of the paper, but crowded out.

National Anti-Slavery Standard

Obsequies of the Martyred President

Published weekly in New York City, the *National Anti-Slavery Standard* was the official newspaper of the American Anti-Slavery Society, founded in 1833 by William Lloyd Garrison. On April 29 it reported on the outcome of the attempt to exclude black mourners from the New York City funeral procession—and on Secretary of War Stanton's order barring discrimination at the events.

WE shall not attempt an extended account of the honors paid to the memory of ABRAHAM LINCOLN by the people of this city on Tuesday last. The display, we venture to affirm, was the most imposing and impressive ever witnessed in the country. Our whole population, except only those who were too old or sick to leave their homes appeared to be in the streets, while thousands upon thousands came hither from adjoining cities and towns and far-off places. The decorous and dignified demeanor of the great multitude testified their high appreciation of the solemn spectacle they were all so eager to witness.

The remains of the illustrious dead arrived in this city from Philadelphia on Monday morning at 10 o'clock, and were at once taken under military escort to the City Hall. From noon of Monday till noon of Tuesday, not even excepting a single hour of the night, the body lay in state, the face exposed to view. It is estimated that not less than 150,000 people—men, women and children—availed themselves of the opportunity to look at the face of the martyred dead. The multitude took their places in line, four deep, in the street on either side of the Park, many of them at first so far away from the City Hall that they were four or five hours in reaching the coffin. The line on Broadway, on Tuesday morning, extended as far as Liberty street. Women and children rose from their beds at midnight to take places in the line, and others, who were in the line at an earlier hour, were out nearly the whole night.

One o'clock was the hour appointed for the procession to move from the City Hall to the Hudson River Railroad station in Thirtieth St. The route of the procession was through Broadway to Fourteenth St., Fourteenth St. to Fifth Avenue, Fifth Avenue to Thirty-fourth Street, etc. Just before that hour the coffin was placed on the funeral car, and thus raised high enough to be plainly seen by the crowds who thronged the streets through which the procession was to pass. The military part of the procession numbered not less than 15,000 men. The array, in double line, before filing into procession, extended over four miles. The civic part of the procession, embracing Governors of States, Judges, members of the City government in all its departments, U.S. officers, and a large number of associations, clubs, etc., numbered, it is estimated, from 40,000 to 50,000 people. Of the banners borne by these multitudes and the decorations of the buildings along the line of the procession, we have not space to speak. We must refer those who are curious in respect to these and other details to the daily journals. The funeral car was drawn by sixteen gray horses, each horse led by a colored groom in mourning. As it passed slowly and solemnly on its way, the people seemed to be profoundly moved, and many testified their emotion by tears.

The arrangements for the occasion were under the direction of the city authorities, and in every respect save one were creditable to them and honorable to the city. The exception to which we allude was the disgraceful refusal of the Committee of Arrangements to permit the colored people of the city to join in the demonstration. They asked for a place in the procession, but it was refused! On Monday evening, Mr. Acton, Commissioner of Police, went before the Common Council and urged that the Committee should reverse their obnoxious and insulting regulation. They refused compliance with his request, whereupon he notified them that the colored people would, by his order, be assigned a place in the procession, and that the police would protect them from molestation. On the same evening the following telegram came from Washington:

WASHINGTON, April 24, 1865.

Major General JOHN A. DIX:

It is the desire of the Secretary of War that no discrimination respecting color should be exercised in admitting persons to the funeral procession to-morrow. In this city a black regiment formed part of the escort.

C. A. DANA, Assistant Secretary of War.

It was then too late, however, for the colored people to make adequate preparation to take part in the demonstration; and besides, they were not inclined to do so upon any other invitation than that of the Common Council, the body which had the management of the affair. Grateful as they were to Commissioner Acton, they thought it not best, by accepting his invitation, to relieve the Common Council, in any degree, from the odium likely to accrue from their exclusion.

Still, a few colored men, most of them from Brooklyn, responded to Commissioner Acton's invitation, and were assigned a place at the rear. They bore a banner, inscribed on the front—

"Abraham Lincoln our Emancipator."

On the other side were these words:

"To millions of Bondmen he Liberty gave."

The *Tribune* says:

"The banner was made on Monday by the ladies of Mr. Beecher's Church, and was carried by four freedmen just from the South, who had never before seen a white audience, and were perfectly astounded to know that there were so many more 'Yankees' than blacks! Behind the banner were nearly or quite two hundred colored men, some recently from the benefits of the 'divine institution,' but most of them presenting an appearance not to be surpassed, we say (in our own opinion and that of many bystanders) certainly by any body of men in the rear of the Educational bodies themselves. The venerable Dr. Pennington, walked in front, with a white clergyman connected with the care of freedmen in this vicinity: and we take pleasure in adding that two other gentlemen of the Caucasian race were proud to take position in this line of sincere mourners. One of them remarked that he had waited for this portion of the procession, to walk with the blacks through the Fifth avenue.

"Two entire platoons of police preceded, and the same number followed the colored men, securing to them, in the fullest degree, all the rights of place and respect.

"But the police were not needed to enforce respect. Along the line of march as far as Fourteenth street, ever and anon cheers and waving of handkerchiefs greeted the blacks. Particularly when passing the New York Hospital, Taylor's International Hotel, the St. Nicholas, the

Metropolitan and Wallack's, they were greeted with the warmest sympathy; and in front of Van Amburgh's the assembled crowd so far forgot themselves in the gratitude of the moment as to give way to cheers that sounded to our ears very much like praise to God. But from the moment that they turned at Union Square the ovation ceased not. If even the residents of the New York Hotel forgot the past and cheered them on, those on the avenue and beyond were no less zealous. One naval officer particularly was noticeable standing at Twenty-second street, with a handkerchief tied to his sword, waiving his sentiments. On all the line—we speak from personal observation—only *one hiss* was audible."

James M. Mason

Letter to The Index

Stanton's letter informing Charles Francis Adams of the assassination reached London on April 26 and was printed in the English press the next day. It elicited an immediate response from James M. Mason (1798–1871), a former U.S. senator from Virginia who had served as a Confederate envoy in England since 1862. Mason's letter appeared in *The Index*, a pro-Confederate London weekly, and was reprinted in *The New York Times* on May 11.

From the London Index.

Time will develop the mystery as yet attending the assassination of ABRAHAM LINCOLN, late President of the United States, and the attempted assassination of Mr. SEWARD, his Secretary of State. I desire only to repel at once the calumnious assertion of EDWIN M. STANTON, the Secretary of War, in his letter to Mr. ADAMS, printed in the London journals of this morning, that these acts were "planned and set on foot by rebels, under pretence of avenging the South and aiding the rebel cause," and of which he says there is "evidence obtained." Mr. STANTON'S letter is dated on the 15th of April, and states that Mr. LINCOLN was assassinated in the theatre at half-past 10 the previous night, and died at 20 minutes past 7 on the morning of the day that he wrote. I adduce this to show how unlikely it is, in the hurried excitement, and the necessary occupations attending such events, that any but the wildest theories would prevail in regard to the cause of the event, or the objects of the perpetrators. Mr. STANTON adopts that which he deemed would be the most useful before the public of his country. Should the "evidence" to which he refers support his calumny ever see the light, it will be scanned with the experience derived in regard to other evidence, unscrupulously fabricated in the same quarter, during the present war, for base political effect. It is the crudest conception, too, that the murder of ABRAHAM LINCOLN was planned and executed for the purpose of "aiding the rebel cause;" but I can well understand that it may have material influence in aiding the cause of that overpowering party in the United States of which Mr. STANTON is the type, and ANDREW JOHNSON, who succeeds as President, with BUTLER, of the notorious prefix, are the exponents and leaders—a party in whose path the late President and his Secretary were acknowledged obstacles in their projected schemes of plunder and rapine to follow their dominion over the Southern States. For the rest, I learn from a well-informed source in London that "WILKES BOOTH," who is accused of the deed, is a son of the celebrated English actor of that name, was of his father's profession, which he pursued principally in the Northern States, and was generally understood as inheriting those traits significant of his father's name, JUNIUS BRUTUS BOOTH, by whom he was named JOHN WILKES, after the great English Radical—an origin and mental training little likely to engender the slightest sympathy with the great cause of the conservative South. As to the crime which has been committed, none will view it with more abhorrence than the people of the South, but they will know, as will equally all well-balanced minds, that it is the necessary offspring of those scenes of bloodshed and murder in every form of unbridled license, which have signalised the invasion of the South by Northern armies, unrebuked certainly, and therefore instigated, by their leaders, and those over them.

Pardon the length of this note. I desired only instantly to repel the atrocious calumnies in the letter of Mr. STANTON.

Very respectfully yours,

J. M. MASON.

No. 24 Upper Seymour-street, Portman-square, London, April 27, 1865.

The Morning Star

Editorial

During the Civil War most of the British press had been openly sympathetic to the Confederate cause and hostile to Lincoln and the Union. *The Times* of London, the most influential daily newspaper in the country, had responded in October 1862 to news of the preliminary Emancipation Proclamation by accusing Lincoln of exciting "a servile war" and appealing to "the black blood of the African" to engage in "the pleasures of spoil" and "the gratification of yet fiercer instincts." A notable exception to this pro-Confederate bias was *The Morning Star*, a London daily founded in 1856 by Richard Cobden and John Bright, the leaders of the Radical reform wing of the Liberal Party and prominent advocates for the Union cause. *The Morning Star* eulogized Lincoln on April 27 in an untitled editorial.

The appalling tragedy which has just been perpetrated at Washington is absolutely without historical precedent. Not in the records of the fiercest European convulsion, in the darkest hour of partisan hatreds, have we an example of an assassin plot at once so foul and so senseless, so horrible and so successful, as that to which Abraham Lincoln has already fallen a victim, and from which William H. Seward can hardly escape. Only in such instances as the murder of William of Orange, of Henri Quatre, or of Capodistria, have we any deed approaching in hideous ferocity to that which has just robbed the United States of one of the greatest of their Presidents. But from the fanatic's hateful point of view there was at least something to be said for men like Balthazar Gerard and Ravaillac. They at least might have believed that they saw embodied in their victims the whole living principle and motive power of that religious freedom which they detested. They might have supposed that with the man would die the great hopes and the great cause he inspired and guided. So, too, of Orsini. That unfortunate and guilty being believed, at least, that in Napoleon the Third there stood an embodied and concentrated system. But Abraham Lincoln was no dictator and no autocrat. He represented simply the resolution and the resources of a great people. The miserable excuse which fanaticism might attempt to plead for other political assassins has no application to the wretch whose felon hand dealt death to the pure and noble magistrate of a free nation.

One would gladly, for the poor sake of common humanity, have caught at the idea that the crime was but the work of some maniacal partisan. But the mere nature of the deeds, without any additional evidence whatever, bids defiance to such an idea. While the one murderer was slaying the President of the republic, the other was making his even more dastardly attempt upon the life of the sick and prostrate Secretary. It does not need even the disclosures which have now, too late for any good purpose, reached official quarters to prove that two madmen cannot become simultaneously inspired with the same monstrous project and impelled at the one moment to do their several parts of the one bloody business. The chivalry of the South has had much European compliment of late. It has been discovered to be the fount and origin of all the most noble and knightly qualities which the world heretofore had principally known through the medium of mediæval romance. Let it not be forgotten that southern brains lately planned the conflagration of a peaceful city. It never can be forgotten while history is read that the hands of southern partisans have been reddened by the foulest assassin plot the world has ever known, that they have been treacherously dipped in the blood of one of the best citizens and purest patriots to whom the land of Washington gave birth.

For Abraham Lincoln one cry of universal regret will be raised all over the civilized earth. We do not believe that even the fiercest partisans of the confederacy in this country will entertain any sentiment at such a time but one of grief and horror. To us Abraham Lincoln has always seemed the finest character produced by the American war, on either side of the struggle. He was great not merely by the force of genius—and only the word genius will describe the power of intellect by which he guided himself and his country through such a crisis—but by the simple, natural strength and grandeur of his character. Talleyrand once said of a great American statesman that without experience he "divined" his way through any crisis. Mr. Lincoln thus divined his way through the perilous, exhausting, and unprecedented difficulties which might well have broken the strength and binded the prescience of the best trained professional statesman. He seemed to arrive by instinct—by the instinct of a noble, unselfish, and manly nature—at the very ends which the highest of political genius, the longest of political experience, could have done no more than reach. He bore himself fearlessly in danger, calmly in difficulty, modestly in success. The world was at last beginning to know how good, and, in the best sense, how great a man he was. It had long indeed learned that he was as devoid of vanity as of fear, but it had only just come to know what magnanimity and mercy the hour of triumph would prove that he possessed. Reluctant enemies were just beginning to break into eulogy over his wise and noble clemency when the dastard hand of a vile murderer destroyed his noble and valuable life. We in England have something to feel ashamed of when we meditate upon the true greatness of the man so ruthlessly slain. Too many Englishmen lent themselves to the vulgar and ignoble cry which was raised against him. English writers degraded themselves to the level of the coarsest caricaturists when they had to tell of Abraham Lincoln. They stooped to criticise a foreign patriot as a menial might comment on the bearing of a hero. They sneered at his manners, as if Cromwell was a Chesterfield; they accused him of ugliness, as if Mirabeau was a beauty; they made coarse pleasantry of his figure, as if Peel was a posture-master; they were facetious about his dress, as if Cavour was a D'Orsay; they were indignant about his jokes, as if Palmerston never jested. We do not remember any instance since the wildest days of British fury against the "Corsican Ogre," in which a foreign statesman was ever so dealt with in English writings as Mr. Lincoln. And when we make the comparison we cannot but remember that while Napoleon was our unscrupulous enemy, Lincoln was our steady friend. Assailed by the coarsest attacks on this side the ocean, tried by the sorest temptations on that, Abraham Lincoln calmly and steadfastly maintained a policy of peace with England, and never did a deed, never wrote or spoke a word, which was unjust or unfriendly to the British nation. Had such a man died by the hand of disease in the hour of his triumph the world must have mourned for his loss. That he has fallen by the coward hand of a vile assassin exasperates and imbitters the grief beyond any power of language to express.

Had Lincoln been a vain man he might almost have ambitioned such a death. The weapon of the murderer has made sure for him an immortal place in history. Disappointment, failure, political change, popular caprice, the efforts of rivals, the malice of enemies, can touch him no more. He lived long enough to accomplish his great patriotic work, and then he became its martyr. It would be idle to speculate as yet upon the effect which his cruel death will produce upon the political fortunes of his country; but the destinies of that country will be cared for. Its hopes are too well sustained to faint and fall even over the grave of so great a patriot and so wise a leader as Abraham Lincoln. There are still clear and vigorous intellects left to conduct what remains of Lincoln's work to a triumphant conclusion; nor must we allow one day's unhappy misconduct to make us forget the undoubted abilities and patriotic purpose of the man so suddenly and strangely called to fill Lincoln's place. Dramatic justice has, indeed, been marvellously wreaked thus far upon the criminal pride of the South. A negro regiment was the first to enter Richmond, and now one of the poor whites, the "white trash" of a southern State, is called to receive from the South its final submission. We trust and feel assured that even in this hour of just indignation and natural excitement the North may still bear itself with that magnanimous clemency which thus far has illumined its triumph. But it may be that the conquered South has yet to learn that it too must mourn over the bloody grave to which Abraham Lincoln has been consigned by a southern assassin's hand.

Queen Victoria

Letter to Mary Lincoln

President Lincoln had sent a lengthy formal message of condolence to Queen Victoria after the death of her beloved consort, Prince Albert, in December 1861. Drafted by Secretary of State Seward, the letter praised the "cordial friendship and sympathy" between the United States and Great Britain and assured the Queen that the "American People" sympathized in "Your Majesty's irreparable bereavement with an unaffected sorrow" that "emanated from only virtuous motives and natural affection." In contrast, the condolence note Victoria (1819–1901) wrote within days of learning of Lincoln's assassination not only offered personal sympathy, but explicitly referred to her own bereavement, using phrases—"the *Light* of my Life,—my Stay—my *All*"—that Mary Lincoln would adapt and use in her own correspondence throughout the remaining seventeen years of her life.

Osborne.

April 29. 1865.

Dear Madam,

Though a stranger to you I cannot remain silent when so terrible a calamnity has fallen upon you & your Country & most personally express my *deep* & *heartfelt* sympathy with you under the shocking circumstances of your present dreadful misfortunes.

No one can better appreciate than *I* can, who am myself *utterly brokenhearted* by the loss of my own beloved Husband, who was the *Light* of my Life,—my Stay—*my All*,—what your sufferings must be; and I earnestly pray that you may be supported by Him to whom alone the sorely stricken can look for comfort, in this hour of heavy affliction.

With the renewed expression of true sympathy,

I remain,

dear Madam,

Your sincere

friend

Victoria Rg

Benjamin Disraeli

Remarks in the House of Commons

On May 1 Sir George Grey, home secretary in the Liberal government headed by Lord Palmerston, moved that the House of Commons adopt an address to the crown expressing its "deep sorrow and indignation" over the assassination. Grey reminded the House that the government had "maintained a strict and impartial neutrality" during the American conflict. He then said that while opinion in the country had been divided, he believed the "sympathies of the majority" had been with the Union—a statement that was met with cries of both "No, no!" and "Hear, hear!" from his audience. Whatever the opinions of the nation as a whole, it was undeniable that for a variety of reasons—dislike of Northern democracy and egalitarianism, sympathy for the Southern planter class, fear of the long-term threat an undivided United States posed to British power—the landowning classes that dominated Parliament had generally favored Confederate independence. It fell to the engaging Conservative leader in the Commons, the future prime minister Benjamin Disraeli (1804–1881), to find the words that would smooth over discordant realities and allow the motion to be unanimously adopted.

Mr. DISRAELI said: There are rare instances when the sympathy of a nation approaches those tenderer feelings which are generally supposed to be peculiar to the individual, and to be the happy privilege of private life, and this is one. Under any circumstances we should have bewailed the catastrophe at Washington; under any circumstances we should have shuddered at the means by which it was accomplished. But in the character of the victim, and even in the accessories of his last moments, there is something so homely and innocent, that it takes the question, as it were, out of all the pomp of history and the ceremonial of diplomacy; it touches the heart of nations, and appeals to the domestic sentiment of mankind. [Cheers.] Whatever the various and varying opinions in this House, and in the country generally, on the policy of the late President of the United States, all must agree that in one of the severest trials which ever tested the moral qualities of man he fulfilled his duty with simplicity and strength. [Cheers.] Nor is it possible for the people of England at such a moment to forget that he sprung from the same fatherland, and spoke the same mother tongue. [Cheers.] When such crimes are perpetrated the public mind is apt to fall into gloom and perplexity, for it is ignorant alike of the causes and the consequences of such deeds. But it is one of our duties to reassure them under unreasoning panic and despondency. Assassination has never changed the history of the world. I will not refer to the remote past, though an accident has made the most memorable instance of antiquity at this moment fresh in the minds and memory of all around me. But even the costly sacrifice of a Cæsar did not propitiate the inexorable destiny of his country. If we look to modern times, to times at least with the feelings of which we are familiar, and the people of which were animated and influenced by the same interests as ourselves, the violent deaths of two heroic men, Henry IV, of France, and the Prince of Orange, are conspicuous illustrations of this truth. In expressing our unaffected and profound sympathy with the citizens of the United States on this untimely end of their elected chief, let us not, therefore, sanction any feeling of depression, but rather let us express a fervent hope that from out of the awful trials of the last four years, of which the least is not this violent demise, the various populations of North America may issue elevated and chastened, rich with the accumulated wisdom and strong in the disciplined energy which a young nation can only acquire in a protracted and perilous struggle; then they will be enabled not merely to renew their career of power and prosperity, but they will renew it to contribute to the general happiness of mankind. [Cheers.] It is with these feelings that I second the address to the Crown. [Loud cheers.]

William T. Coggleshall

FROM *The Journeys of Abraham Lincoln*

"I now leave, not knowing when, or whether ever, I may return," Lincoln had said in his farewell address before departing from Springfield on February 11, 1861. His remains returned to his hometown on the morning of May 3, 1865, after a journey of twelve days and more than 1,600 miles that had seen the funeral train stop for ceremonies in Baltimore, Harrisburg, Philadelphia, New York, Albany, Buffalo, Cleveland, Columbus, Indianapolis, Michigan City, and Chicago. William T. Coggleshall (1824–1867), editor of the *Ohio State Journal*, described the ceremonies held in Springfield in his book *The Journeys of Abraham Lincoln: from Springfield to Washington, 1861, as President Elect; and from Washington to Springfield, 1865, as President Martyred* (1865).

The principal decorations of the city were confined to the buildings on the four sides of the Capitol Square. At the First National Bank a wreath of evergreen and a portrait of the deceased President surmounted the motto:

> "He left us upheld by our prayers,
> He returns embalmed in our tears."

Over Wolf & Bergmann's was a portrait, and the motto:

> "An honest man now lies at rest,
> As ever God with his image blest;
> Few hearts like his with virtue warmed,
> Few heads with knowledge so informed."

Hammerslough Brothers displayed a portrait of Mr. Lincoln, with the motto: "*Millions bless thy name.*" The store of J. H. Holfer & Co. was decorated with drapery and a bust of Lincoln trimmed with evergreens. John McGriery's store was decorated with drapery and flags, and the motto: "*Revere his Memory.*" The headquarters of the Paymaster's Department were appropriately draped, and displayed the flag at half mast. L. Steiners & Co.'s store had the following motto: "*Weep, sweet country weep, let every section mourn; the North has lost its champion, the South its truest friend. Let every patriot halt at our country's altar, and drop a passing tear for departed worth.*" The Court House and the rooms of the State Agricultural Society were very beautifully draped. Little's store had the motto: "*He still lives in the hearts of his countrymen.*" G. W. Chatterton's store displayed the most elegant and tasteful decoration in the city. The building was profusely draped, and had on its front a monument against a black background, inscribed: "LINCOLN." "*With malice towards none, with charity for all.*" In the large window, which was heavily set in black, was an eagle holding in his beak a beautiful wreath of evergreens and immortelles, the whole surmounting a bust of the departed President, at the base of which was the motto: "*Ours in life—the nation's in death.*" Robinson & Banman's store had the motto: "*Our nation mourns.*" Smith & Bros.' store displayed a bust wreathed in evergreens, with the motto: "*How we loved him.*" J. H. Adams' store had a bust in the window, with the motto: "*A sigh the absent claim, the dead a tear;*" also, a portrait with the motto: "*Our martyred chief.*" The Odd Fellows' Hall displayed a portrait beautifully trimmed with evergreens. Other places of business and many of the private residences in the city were beautifully draped, among them the Executive Mansion, and the residences of ex-Governor Matteson and Colonel Baker of the *State Journal*.

The old residence of Mr. Lincoln was the center of mournful interest. The house, which was occupied by Lucien Tilton, was very heavily draped in mourning. The windows were curtained with black and white, the corner posts wreathed with evergreens, the cornice hidden by festoons of black and white looped up at intervals, and the space between the cornice of the door and the central window filled with the American flag gracefully trimmed. The law office which Mr. Lincoln had occupied in a block of three-story brick buildings, was draped in mourning, and at the door hung a portrait of the deceased.

The State House was decorated with superior taste and skill. The outside of the dome was deep black, and, together with the cornice and pillars on which it rests, was elaborately festooned with white and black. Similar drapery fell from the eves and columns; the pediments, both on the north and south entrances, were corrugated with evergreens, and the capitals draped with white and black muslin. All the windows were partially curtained with black-white trimmings at the top and black falling at the base; from the crown of the dome was a staff, on which was the national flag at half-mast with black streamers. The entrance to the Capitol and the rotunda was heavily draped, and festoons of evergreens hung from the dome.

In the Representatives Hall the general arrangement made the decorations correspond with the room, which is a semi-circular colonade of eleven Corinthian columns, supporting a half dome, the straight side being toward the west, at the centre of which was the Speaker's chair, which had been removed for the occasion. At the apex of the dome was a rising sun, radiant to the circumference. On the floor a dais was erected, ascended by three steps. On the dais a hexagon canopy, supported on columns twelve feet high, the shaft covered with black velvet; the capitals wrought in white velvet, with silver bands, filled the canopy, tent-shaped, rising seven feet in the centre, covered with heavy black broadcloth in radiating slack folds, surmounted at the apex and at each angle with black plumes having white centres. A draped eagle was perched on the middle of each crown-mould. The cornice was of Egyptian pattern, corresponding with the capitals covered with black velvet; the bands and mouldings were of silver; the lining of the canopy was white crape in radiating folds over blue, thickly set with stars of silver, and terminating at the cornice inside in a band of black velvet with silver fillets. Between the columns was a rich valance in folds, with heavy silver fringe, from under which depended velvet curtains extending from each column two-thirds of the distance from the capitals to the centre of the cornice, looped with silver bands—the whole so disposed as to exhibit both columns and capitals, inside and out. The effect of the canopy and its supports and the drapery was very imposing, the whole being unique and elegant, combining lightness with massiveness in harmony. Twelve brilliant jets of gas burning in ground glass globes springing from the columns, lighted the interior and reflected from the folds of double lining an opuline atmosphere to the whole.

The catafalque was covered with black velvet, trimmed with silver and satin, and adorned with thirty-six burnished silver stars, twelve at the head and twelve on each side. The floor of the dais was covered with evergreens and white flowers. The steps of the dais were covered with broadcloth drapery, banded with silver lace. The columns of the room were hung with black crape, and the capitals festooned and entwined with the same, so as to display the architecture to good advantage, without detriment to the effect. The cornice was appropriately draped, and, in large antique letters on a black ground, were the words of President Lincoln at Independence Hall, Philadelphia, Feb. 22, 1861: — "Sooner than surrender these principles, I would be assassinated on the spot." In front of the gallery were black panels nine feet by two and a half, having silver bands and centres of crossed olive branches; above the gallery looped curtains of black crape extended around the semi-circle; below the gallery white crape curtains overhung with black crape festoons. Each column was ornamented with a beautiful wreath of evergreens and white flowers, the gift of Mrs. Gehlman, of Springfield. On the top of the gallery, extending the entire length, was a festoon of evergreens. The Corinthian cornice was festooned on the west at each side, twenty-four feet forward of the centre, supported by pilasters of the same order, the space between being surmounted by an obtuse arch reaching within one foot of the apex, and projecting six inches, leaving, after the removal of the speaker's chair, a depression resembling a panel, thirty-three feet wide by thirty-seven feet high. At the extreme height, in the upper portion of this was placed a blue semi-circular field, sixteen feet across, studded with thirty-six stars six inches in diameter, and from which radiated the thirteen stripes on the American flag in delicate crape, two feet wide at the circumference of the blue field, increasing to the extreme lower angle, breaking on the dais below and the pilasters on either side; the whole crowned with blue and black crape, and so disposed as to correspond with the blue field, the stars, and radiated panels of the ceiling; the central red stripe fell opposite the opening in the curtains at the head of the catafalque. On the cornice, each side of the flag work, were placed two mottoes, corresponding with that on the semi-circular freese, forming together these words: *"Washington the Father and Lincoln the Saviour."* A life-sized portrait of Washington, the frame draped in blue crape, stood at the head of the dais. In the northwest and southwest corners living evergreen trees and flowers were arranged. The interior decorations were perfected under the direction of the Chairman of the committee, Mr. G. F. Wright, formerly from Hartford, Conn.

The catafalque was designed by Col. Schwarts. The exterior decorations and those of all other public buildings, were entirely under the superintendence of E. E. Myers, architect at Springfield.

Immediately after the body had been placed upon the catafalque, the waiting people were admitted to the State House. They were obliged to ascend a winding staircase into the Representatives' Hall, and return by the same route; and the passage was often obstructed, but the people were sad and patient, and rarely did confusion interrupt the stream of mourners, which continued in almost unbroken line from about ten o'clock on the morning of the 3d of May till ten o'clock on the morning of the 4th. It was estimated that at least seventy-five thousand persons visited the remains. All beholders were impressed with awe by the mournfulness of the surroundings, and by the solemn reminders of the grave which met their gaze, and moved through the Hall in silence. They approached at the left hand of the corpse, passed around the head, and out on the opposite side. At midnight a train of cars came in on the Great Western Railroad, and the whole body of passengers filed at once down to the Capitol, and passed through. Trains were continually arriving, bringing thousands more, and at three o'clock on the morning of the 3d, hundreds were walking the streets, unable to find any accommodation, although the citizens generally threw open their houses. A little before midnight the ladies of the Soldiers' Aid Society laid on the coffin a cross of evergreen and white flowers, and unknown persons placed on it three wreaths of the same. Some, as they passed the corpse, exhibited little emotion; but so soon as they were removed from the awe-inspiring scene, and fully realized that they had looked for the last time on earth, on the features of the great and good man, once their familiar neighbor, wept with a touching sorrow.

On the 4th of May the crowds which filled the streets of Springfield were greatly augmented by each train which arrived on the several railways. According to the advertised arrangements, heavy guns were fired, solemn dirges were played, and bells were tolled. All places of business were closed. The weather was propitious. At eight o'clock a vast assemblage of people had collected about the State House grounds, and, while the funeral preparations were being completed, a choir of 250 singers, grouped on the Capitol steps, sang, with great sweetness and impressiveness, a hymn called "Peace, peace, troubled soul." The singers were under the direction of Mr. Messner, of Springfield, assisted by Mr. Palmer, of St. Louis. While the eight sergeants were carrying the coffin out on their shoulders, they sang, after a prelude by the band, Pleyl's beautiful hymn:

> "Children of the Heavenly King,
> As ye journey sweetly sing;
> Sing our Saviour's worthy praise,
> Glorious in His works and ways."

The military were drawn up on Washington street, north of the Capitol, and when the coffin was placed in the hearse they marched east along the street, allowing it to come in the rear. The procession was then formed in the order which had been announced. The pall-bearers were: Hon. Jesse K. Dubois, Hon. S. T. Logan, Hon. G. P. Kœrner, James L. Lamb, Esq., Hon. S. H. Treat, Col. John Williams, Erastus Wright, Esq., Hon. J. N. Brown, Jacob Bunn, Esq., C. W. Matheny, Esq., Elijah Iles, Esq., Hon. J. T. Stuart.

At half-past eleven the cortege began to move, a band playing at the moment of its departure "Lincoln's Funeral March." On the route to the cemetery the bands played the "Dead March in Saul," with solemn and mournful effect. The route led by the former house of Mr. Lincoln, on the corner of Eighth and Jefferson streets, and from thence west to Fourth, and thence on Fourth to Oak Ridge Cemetery, which is a mile and a half north of the city, near the line of the Chicago and St. Louis Railroad. But a small portion of the people who had assembled to witness the ceremonies took position in the procession, but hastened by shorter routes through its line to the cemetery, which very appropriately takes its name from two high ridges, running east and west, covered principally with large oak trees. Between these is a valley about seventy-five feet in depth, winding with pleasing irregularity, and watered by a little brook of clear water. The gate of the cemetery is at the head of this valley, and for several rods it descends quite rapidly, though near the tomb it is nearly level. The tomb stands on the south side in a little cove in the bank, where it is quite steep, so that the roof of it is but a few feet in length. It is built of Joliet limestone, the architecture of the main arch being rustic. The upper range of the arch projecting a few inches from the main wall, is of rubbed stone, and rests on Doric pilasters. The whole is about twelve feet high, and ten wide. The brick walls inside were covered with evergreen; and in the centre stood a foundation bearing a marble slab, on which the coffin was deposited. The remains of "Little Willie" were deposited in the same tomb.

The scene was most solemn, and, beyond the power of language to express, impressive, when in the presence of nearly all the citizens of the city which had so long been the home of Mr. Lincoln, and of a vast throng assembled from all the States of the Northwest, the imposing procession entered the cemetery under an evergreen arch, and filed toward the tomb to the music of dirges performed by many powerful bands.

L. M. Dawn

Farewell Father, Friend and Guardian

After Lincoln's body was carried into its tomb, a choir sang a dirge, "Farewell Father, Friend and Guardian," with music by George F. Root (the popular composer of "Battle Flag of Freedom" and "Just Before the Battle, Mother") and words by L. M. Dawn (or "Dawes," in some accounts). The sheet music for the song contains a chorus not performed at the funeral: "Farewell father, friend and guardian / Thou hast joined the martyr band, / But thy glorious work remaineth, / Our redeemed beloved land."

———————

All our land is draped in mourning,
   Hearts are bowed and strong men weep;
For our loved, our noble leader
   Sleeps his last, his dreamless sleep—
Gone for ever, gone for ever,
   Fallen by a traitor's hand,
Though preserved his dearest treasure,
   Our redeem'd, beloved land.
      Rest in peace.

Through our night of bloody struggle
   Ever dauntless, firm, and true,
Bravely, gently, forth he led us,
   Till the morn burst on our view—
Till he saw the day of triumph,
   Saw the field our heroes won;
Then his honor'd life was ended,
   Then his glorious work was done.
      Rest in peace.

When from mountain, hill, and valley,
   To their homes our brave boys come,
When with welcome notes we greet them,
   Song, and cheer, and pealing drum;
When we miss our lov'd ones fallen,

When to weep we turn aside,
Then for him our tears shall mingle,
   He has suffered—he has died.
      Rest in peace.

Honor'd leader, long and fondly
   Shall thy mem'ry cherished be;
Hearts shall bless thee for their freedom,
   Hearts unborn shall sigh for thee;
He who gave thee might and wisdom,
   Gave thy spirit sweet release;
Farewell father, friend and guardian,
   Rest forever, rest in peace.
      Rest in peace.

Matthew Simpson

Funeral Address at the Burial of President Lincoln

Bishop Matthew Simpson (1811–1884) of the Methodist Episcopal Church delivered both the opening prayer at Lincoln's White House funeral and the main address at his Springfield burial. Simpson and Lincoln had first become friends in the winter of 1860–61, when Simpson was serving as president of a Methodist seminary in Evanston, Illinois. A popular preacher and orator, Simpson traveled and spoke widely in support of the Union cause during the war and frequently visited the White House to discuss current issues with the President. "He has no axe to grind," Lincoln reportedly said of the bishop, "and, therefore, I can depend upon him for such information as I need." Despite all the time he had spent with him, Simpson could not definitively characterize the late President's religious experience. "My acquaintance with him," the clergyman admitted, "did not give me the opportunity to hear him speak on those topics." (In his eulogy, Simpson quotes Lincoln at length speaking about "the slave power" in 1839, but the quoted passage actually appeared in a speech Lincoln gave that year in opposition to President Martin Van Buren's sub-treasury plan.)

FELLOW-CITIZENS OF ILLINOIS, AND OF MANY PARTS OF OUR ENTIRE UNION:

Near the capitol of this large and growing State of Illinois, in the midst of this beautiful grove, and at the open mouth of the vault which has just received the remains of our fallen chieftain, we gather to pay a tribute of respect and to drop the tears of sorrow around the ashes of the mighty dead. A little more than four years ago he left his plain and quiet home in yonder city, receiving the parting words of the concourse of friends who in the midst of the dropping of the gentle shower gathered around him. He spoke of the pain of parting from the place where he had lived for a quarter of a century, where his children had been born, and his home had been rendered pleasant by friendly associations; and, as he left, he made an earnest request, in the hearing of some who are present at this hour, that, as he was about to enter upon responsibilities which he believed to be greater than any which had fallen upon any man since the days of Washington, the people would offer up prayers that God would aid and sustain him in the work which they had given him to do. His company left your quiet city, but as it went snares were in waiting for the chief magistrate. Scarcely did he escape the dangers of the way or the hands of the assassin as he neared Washington; and I believe he escaped only through the vigilance of officers and the prayers of the people, so that the blow was suspended for more than four years, which was at last permitted, through the providence of God, to fall.

How different the occasion which witnessed his departure from that which witnessed his return! Doubtless you expected to take him by the hand, and to feel the warm grasp which you had felt in other days, and to see the tall form walking among you which you had delighted to honor in years past. But he was never permitted to come until he came with lips mute and silent, the frame encoffined, and a weeping nation following as his mourners. Such a scene as his return to you was never witnessed. Among the events of history there have been great processions of mourners. There was one for the patriarch Jacob, which went up from Egypt, and the Egyptians wondered at the evidences of reverence and filial affection which came from the hearts of the Israelites. There was mourning when Moses fell upon the heights of Pisgah, and was hid from human view. There have been mournings in the kingdoms of the earth when kings and warriors have fallen. But never was there in the history of man such mourning as that which has accompanied this funeral procession, and has gathered around the mortal remains of him who was our loved one, and who now sleeps among us. If we glance at the procession which followed him, we see how the nation stood aghast. Tears filled the eyes of manly, sun-burnt faces. Strong men, as they clasped the hands of their friends, were not able in words to find vent for their grief. Women and little children caught up the tidings as they ran through the land, and were melted into tears. The nation stood still. Men left their plows in the fields and asked what the end should be. The hum of manufactories ceased, and the sound of the hammer was not heard. Busy merchants closed their doors, and in the exchange gold passed no more from hand to hand. Though three weeks have elapsed, the nation has scarcely breathed easily yet. A mournful silence is abroad upon the land; nor is this mourning confined to any class or to any district of country. Men of all political parties, and of all religious creeds, have united in paying this mournful tribute. The archbishop of the Roman Catholic Church in New York and a Protestant minister walked side by side in the sad procession, and a Jewish rabbi performed a part of the solemn services.

Here are gathered around his tomb the representatives of the army and navy, senators, judges, governors, and officers of all the branches of the government. Here, too, are members of civic processions, with men and women from the humblest as well as the highest occupations. Here and there, too, are tears as sincere and warm as any that drop, which come from the eyes of those whose kindred and whose race have been freed from their chains by him whom they mourn as their deliverer. More persons have gazed on the face of the departed than ever looked upon the face of any other departed man. More have looked on the procession for sixteen hundred miles, by night and by day, by sunlight, dawn, twilight, and by torchlight, than ever before watched the progress of a procession.

We ask why this wonderful mourning, this great procession? I answer, first, a part of the interest has arisen from the times in which we live, and in which he that has fallen was a principal actor. It is a principle of our nature that feelings once excited turn readily from the object by which they are excited to some other object which may for the time being take possession of the mind. Another principle is, the deepest affections of our hearts gather around some human form in which are incarnated the living thoughts and ideas of the passing age. If we look then at the times, we see an age of excitement. For four years the popular heart has been stirred to its inmost depth. War had come upon us, dividing families, separating nearest and dearest friends, a war the extent and magnitude of which no one could estimate; a war in which the blood of brethren was shed by a brother's hand. A call for soldiers was made by this voice now hushed, and all over the land, from hill to mountain, from plain to valley, there sprung up thousands of bold hearts, ready to go forth and save our national Union. This feeling of excitement was transformed next into a feeling of deep grief because of the dangers in which our country was placed. Many said, "Is it possible to save our nation?" Some in our country, and nearly all the leading men in other countries, declared it to be impossible to maintain the Union; and many an honest and patriotic heart was deeply pained with apprehensions of common ruin; and many, in grief and almost in despair, anxiously inquired, What shall the end of these things be? In addition to this, wives had given their husbands, mothers their sons, the pride and joy of their hearts. They saw them put on the uniform, they saw them take the martial step, and they tried to hide their deep feeling of sadness. Many dear ones slept upon the battle-field never to return again, and there was mourning in every mansion and in every cabin in our broad land. Then came a feeling of deeper sadness as the story came of prisoners tortured to death or starved through the mandates of those who are called the representatives of the chivalry, and who claimed to be the honorable ones of the earth; and as we read the stories of frames attenuated and reduced to mere skeletons, our grief turned partly into horror and partly into a cry for vengeance.

Then this feeling was changed to one of joy. There came signs of the end of this rebellion. We followed the career of our glorious generals. We saw our army, under the command of the brave officer who is guiding this procession, climb up the heights of Lookout Mountain, and drive the rebels from their strongholds. Another brave general swept through Georgia, South and North Carolina, and drove the combined armies of the rebels before him, while the honored Lieutenant-General held Lee and his hosts in a death-grasp.

Then the tidings came that Richmond was evacuated, and that Lee had surrendered. The bells rang merrily all over the land. The booming of cannon was heard; illuminations and torchlight processions manifested the general joy, and families were looking for the speedy return of their loved ones from the field of battle. Just in the midst of this wildest joy, in one hour, nay, in one moment, the tidings thrilled throughout the land that Abraham Lincoln, the best of presidents, had perished by the hands of an assassin. Then all the feelings which had been gathering for four years in forms of excitement, grief, horror, and joy, turned into one wail of woe, a sadness inexpressible, an anguish unutterable.

But it is not the times merely which caused this mourning. The mode of his death must be taken into the account. Had he died on a bed of illness, with kind friends around him; had the sweat of death been wiped from his brow by gentle hands, while he was yet conscious; could he have had power to speak words of affection to his stricken widow, or words of counsel to us like those which we heard in his parting inaugural at Washington, which shall now be immortal, how it would have softened or assuaged something of the grief! There might at least have been preparation for the event. But no moment of warning was given to him or to us. He was stricken down, too, when his hopes for the end of the rebellion were bright, and prospects of a joyous life were before him. There was a cabinet meeting that day, said to have been the most cheerful and happy of any held since the beginning of the rebellion. After this meeting he talked with his friends, and spoke of the four years of tempest, of the storm being over, and of the four years of pleasure and joy now awaiting him, as the weight of care and anxiety would be taken from his mind, and he could have happy days with his family again. In the midst of these anticipations he left his house never to return alive. The evening was Good Friday, the saddest day in the whole calendar for the Christian Church, henceforth in this country to be made sadder, if possible, by the memory of our nation's loss; and so filled with grief was every Christian heart that even all the joyous thought of Easter Sunday failed to remove the crushing sorrow under which the true worshiper bowed in the house of God.

But the great cause of this mourning is to be found in the man himself. Mr. Lincoln was no ordinary man. I believe the conviction has been growing on the nation's mind, as it certainly has been on my own, especially in the last years of his administration, that by the hand of God he was especially singled out to guide our government in these troublesome times, and it seems to me that the hand of God may be traced in many of the events connected with his history. First, then, I recognize this in the physical education which he received, and which prepared him for enduring herculean labors. In the toils of his boyhood and the labors of his manhood, God was giving him an iron frame. Next to this was his identification with the heart of the great people, understanding their feelings because he was one of them, and connected with them in their movements and life. His education was simple. A few months spent in the school-house gave him the elements of education. He read few books, but mastered all he read. Pilgrim's Progress, Æsop's Fables, and the Life of Washington, were his favorites. In these we recognize the works which gave the bias to his character, and which partly moulded his style. His early life, with its varied struggles, joined him indissolubly to the working masses, and no elevation in society diminished his respect for the sons of toil. He knew what it was to fell the tall trees of the forest and to stem the current of the broad Mississippi. His home was in the growing West, the heart of the republic, and, invigorated by the wind which swept over its prairies, he learned lessons of self-reliance which sustained him in seasons of adversity.

His genius was soon recognized, as true genius always will be, and he was placed in the legislature of his state. Already acquainted with the principles of law, he devoted his thoughts to matters of public interest, and began to be looked on as the coming statesman. As early as 1839 he presented resolutions in the legislature asking for emancipation in the District of Columbia, when, with but rare exceptions, the whole popular mind of his state was opposed to the measure. From that hour he was a steady and uniform friend of humanity, and was preparing for the conflict of later years.

If you ask me on what mental characteristic his greatness rested, I answer, On a quick and ready perception of facts; on a memory unusually tenacious and retentive; and on a logical turn of mind, which followed sternly and unwaveringly every link in the chain of thought on every subject which he was called to investigate. I think there have been minds more broad in their character, more comprehensive in their scope, but I doubt if ever there has been a man who could follow step by step, with more logical power, the points which he desired to illustrate. He gained this power by the close study of geometry, and by a determination to perceive the truth in all its relations and simplicity, and when found, to utter it.

It is said of him that in childhood when he had any difficulty in listening to a conversation, to ascertain what people meant, if he retired to rest he could not sleep till he tried to understand the precise point intended, and when understood, to frame language to convey in it a clearer manner to others. Who that has read his messages fails to perceive the directness and the simplicity of his style? And this very trait, which was scoffed at and decried by opponents, is now recognized as one of the strong points of that mighty mind which has so powerfully influenced the destiny of this nation, and which shall, for ages to come, influence the destiny of humanity.

It was not, however, chiefly by his mental faculties that he gained such control over mankind. His moral power gave him pre-eminence. The convictions of men that Abraham Lincoln was an honest man led them to yield to his guidance. As has been said of Cobden, whom he greatly resembled, he made all men feel a *sense of himself;* a recognition of individuality; a self-relying power. They saw in him a man whom they believed would do what is right, regardless of all consequences. It was this moral feeling which gave him the greatest hold on the people, and made

his utterances almost oracular. When the nation was angered by the per-
fidy of foreign nations in allowing privateers to be fitted out, he uttered
the significant expression, "One war at a time," and it stilled the national heart. When his own friends were divided as to what steps should
be taken as to slavery, that simple utterance, "I will save the Union, if
I can, with slavery; if not, slavery must perish, for the Union must be
preserved," became the rallying word. Men felt the struggle was for the
Union, and all other questions must be subsidiary.

But after all, by the acts of a man shall his fame be perpetuated. What
are his acts? Much praise is due to the men who aided him. He called able
counselors around him, some of whom have displayed the highest order
of talent united with the purest and most devoted patriotism. He summoned able generals into the field, men who have borne the sword as
bravely as ever any human arm has borne it. He had the aid of prayerful
and thoughtful men everywhere. But, under his own guiding hands, wise
counsels were combined and great movements conducted.

Turn toward the different departments. We had an unorganized militia, a mere skeleton army, yet, under his care, that army has been enlarged into a force which, for skill, intelligence, efficiency, and bravery,
surpasses any which the world had ever seen. Before its veterans the
fame of even the renowned veterans of Napoleon shall pale, and the
mothers and sisters on these hillsides, and all over the land, shall take to
their arms again braver sons and brothers than ever fought in European
wars. The reason is obvious. Money, or a desire for fame, collected those
armies, or they were rallied to sustain favorite thrones or dynasties; but
the armies he called into being fought for liberty, for the Union, and
for the right of self-government; and many of them felt that the battles
they won were for humanity everywhere, and for all time; for I believe
that God has not suffered this terrible rebellion to come upon our land
merely for a chastisement to us, or as a lesson to our age.

There are moments which involve in themselves eternities. There are
instants which seem to contain germs which shall develop and bloom
forever. Such a moment came in the tide of time to our land, when a
question must be settled which affected all the earth. The contest was
for human freedom, not for this republic merely, not for the Union simply, but to decide whether the people, as a people, in their entire majesty,
were destined to be the government, or whether they were to be subjects

to tyrants or aristocrats, or to class-rule of any kind. This is the great question for which we have been fighting, and its decision is at hand, and the result of the contest will affect the ages to come. If successful, republics will spread, in spite of monarchs, all over this earth.

I turn from the army to the navy. What was it when the war commenced? Now we have our ships-of-war at home and abroad, to guard privateers in foreign sympathizing ports, as well as to care for every part of our own coast. They have taken forts that military men said could not be taken; and a brave admiral, for the first time in the world's history, lashed himself to the mast, there to remain as long as he had a particle of skill or strength to watch over his ship, while it engaged in the perilous contest of taking the strong forts of the rebels.

Then again I turn to the treasury department. Where should the money come from? Wise men predicted ruin, but our national credit has been maintained, and our currency is safer to-day than it ever was before. Not only so, but through our national bonds, if properly used, we shall have a permanent basis for our currency, and an investment so desirable for capitalists of other nations that, under the laws of trade, I believe the center of exchange will speedily be transferred from England to the United States.

But the great act of the mighty chieftain, on which his fame shall rest long after his frame shall moulder away, is that of giving freedom to a race. We have all been taught to revere the sacred characters. Among them Moses stands pre-eminently high. He received the law from God, and his name is honored among the hosts of heaven. Was not his greatest act the delivering of three millions of his kindred out of bondage? Yet we may assert that Abraham Lincoln, by his proclamation, liberated more enslaved people than ever Moses set free, and those not of his kindred or his race. Such a power, or such an opportunity, God has seldom given to man. When other events shall have been forgotten; when this world shall have become a network of republics; when every throne shall be swept from the face of the earth; when literature shall enlighten all minds; when the claims of humanity shall be recognized everywhere, this act shall still be conspicuous on the pages of history. We are thankful that God gave to Abraham Lincoln the decision and wisdom and grace to issue that proclamation, which stands high above all other papers which have been penned by uninspired men.

Abraham Lincoln was a good man. He was known as an honest, temperate, forgiving man; a just man; a man of noble heart in every way. As to his religious experience, I cannot speak definitely, because I was not privileged to know much of his private sentiments. My acquaintance with him did not give me the opportunity to hear him speak on those topics. This I know, however, he read the Bible frequently; loved it for its great truths and its profound teachings; and he tried to be guided by its precepts. He believed in Christ the Saviour of sinners; and I think he was sincere in trying to bring his life into harmony with the principles of revealed religion. Certainly if there ever was a man who illustrated some of the principles of pure religion, that man was our departed president. Look over all his speeches; listen to his utterances. He never spoke unkindly of any man. Even the rebels received no word of anger from him; and his last day illustrated in a remarkable manner his forgiving disposition. A dispatch was received that afternoon that Thompson and Tucker were trying to make their escape through Maine, and it was proposed to arrest them. Mr. Lincoln, however, preferred rather to let them quietly escape. He was seeking to save the very men who had been plotting his destruction. This morning we read a proclamation offering $25,000 for the arrest of these men as aiders and abettors of his assassination; so that, in his expiring acts, he was saying, "Father, forgive them, they know not what they do."

As a ruler I doubt if any president has ever shown such trust in God, or in public documents so frequently referred to Divine aid. Often did he remark to friends and to delegations that his hope for our success rested in his conviction that God would bless our efforts, because we were trying to do right. To the address of a large religious body he replied, "Thanks be unto God, who, in our national trials, giveth us the Churches." To a minister who said he hoped the Lord was on our side, he replied that it gave him no concern whether the Lord was on our side or not, "For," he added, "I know the Lord is always on the side of right;" and with deep feeling added, "But God is my witness that it is my constant anxiety and prayer that both myself and this nation should be on the Lord's side."

In his domestic life he was exceedingly kind and affectionate. He was a devoted husband and father. During his presidential term he lost his second son, Willie. To an officer of the army he said, not long since, "Do you ever find yourself talking with the dead?" and added, "Since Willie's death I catch myself every day involuntarily talking with him, as if he were with me." On his widow, who is unable to be here, I need only invoke the blessing of Almighty God that she may be comforted and sustained. For his son, who has witnessed the exercises of this hour, all that I can desire is that the mantle of his father may fall upon him.

Let us pause a moment in the lesson of the hour before we part. This man, though he fell by an assassin, still fell under the permissive hand of God. He had some wise purpose in allowing him so to fall. What more could he have desired of life for himself? Were not his honors full? There was no office to which he could aspire. The popular heart clung around him as around no other man. The nations of the world had learned to honor our chief magistrate. If rumors of a desired alliance with England be true, Napoleon trembled when he heard of the fall of Richmond, and asked what nation would join him to protect him against our government under the guidance of such a man. His fame was full, his work was done, and he sealed his glory by becoming the nation's great martyr for liberty.

He appears to have had a strange presentiment, early in political life, that some day he would be president. You see it indicated in 1839. Of the slave power he said, "Broken by it I too may be; bow to it I never will. The probability that we may fail in the struggle ought not to deter us from the support of a cause which I deem to be just. It shall not deter me. If ever I feel the soul within me elevate and expand to those dimensions not wholly unworthy of its Almighty architect, it is when I contemplate the cause of my country, deserted by all the world besides, and I standing up boldly and alone and hurling defiance at her victorious oppressors. Here, without contemplating consequences, before high Heaven, and in the face of the world, I swear eternal fidelity to the just cause, as I deem it, of the land of my life, my liberty, and my love." And yet, recently, he said to more than one, "I never shall live out the four years of my term. When the rebellion is crushed my work is done." So it was. He lived to see the last battle fought, and dictate a dispatch from the home of Jefferson Davis; lived till the power of the rebellion was broken; and then, having done the work for which God had sent him, angels, I trust, were sent to shield him from one moment of pain or suffering, and to bear him from this world to the high and glorious realm where the patriot and the good shall live forever.

His career teaches young men that every position of eminence is open before the diligent and the worthy. To the active men of the country his example is an incentive to trust in God and do right. To the ambitious there is this fearful lesson: Of the four candidates for presidential honors in 1860, two of them—Douglas and Lincoln—once competitors, but now sleeping patriots, rest from their labors; Bell abandoned to perish in poverty and misery, as a traitor might perish; and Breckinridge is a frightened fugitive, with the brand of traitor on his brow.

Standing, as we do to-day, by his coffin and his sepulcher, let us resolve to carry forward the policy which he so nobly begun. Let us do right to all men. Let us vow, in the sight of Heaven, to eradicate every vestige of human slavery; to give every human being his true position before God and man; to crush every form of rebellion, and to stand by the flag which God has given us. How joyful that it floated over parts of every state before Mr. Lincoln's career was ended! How singular that, to the fact of the assassin's heels being caught in the folds of the flag, we are probably indebted for his capture. The flag and the traitor must ever be enemies.

Traitors will probably suffer by the change of rulers, for one of sterner mould, and who himself has deeply suffered from the rebellion, now wields the sword of justice. Our country, too, is stronger for the trial. A republic was declared by monarchists too weak to endure a civil war; yet we have crushed the most gigantic rebellion in history, and have grown in strength and population every year of the struggle. We have passed through the ordeal of a popular election while swords and bayonets were in the field, and have come out unharmed. And now, in an hour of excitement, with a large minority having preferred another man for President, when the bullet of the assassin has laid our President prostrate, has there been a mutiny? Has any rival proffered his claims? Out of an army of near a million, no officer or soldier uttered one note of dissent; and, in an hour or two after Mr. Lincoln's death, another leader, under constitutional forms, occupied his chair, and the government moved forward without one single jar. The world will learn that republics are the strongest governments on earth.

And now, my friends, in the words of the departed, "with malice toward none," free from all feelings of personal vengeance, yet believing that the sword must not be borne in vain, let us go forward even in painful duty. Let every man who was a senator or representative in Congress, and who aided in beginning this rebellion, and thus led to the slaughter of our sons and daughters, be brought to speedy and to certain punishment. Let every officer educated at the public expense, and who, having been advanced to high position, perjured himself and turned his sword against the vitals of his country, be doomed to a traitor's death. This, I believe, is the will of the American people. Men may attempt to compromise, and to restore these traitors and murderers to society again. Vainly may they talk of the fancied honor or chivalry of these murderers of our sons—these starvers of our prisoners—these officers who mined their prisons and placed kegs of powder to destroy our captive officers. But the American people will rise in their majesty and sweep all such compromises and compromisers away, and will declare that there shall be no safety for rebel leaders. But to the deluded masses we will extend the arms of forgiveness. We will take them to our hearts, and walk with them side by side, as we go forward to work out a glorious destiny.

The time will come when, in the beautiful words of him whose lips are now forever sealed, "The mystic cords of memory, stretching from every battlefield and patriot grave to every living heart and hearthstone all over this broad land, will yet swell the chorus of the Union, when again touched, as surely they will be, by the better angels of our nature."

Chieftain, farewell! The nation mourns thee. Mothers shall teach thy name to their lisping children. The youth of our land shall emulate thy virtues. Statesmen shall study thy record and learn lessons of wisdom. Mute though thy lips be, yet they still speak. Hushed is thy voice, but its echoes of liberty are ringing through the world, and the sons of bondage listen with joy. Prisoned thou art in death, and yet thou art marching abroad, and chains and manacles are bursting at thy touch. Thou didst fall not for thyself. The assassin had no hate for thee. Our hearts were aimed at, our national life was sought. We crown thee as our martyr, and humanity enthrones thee as her triumphant son. Hero, Martyr, Friend, FAREWELL!

Tom Taylor

Abraham Lincoln Foully Assassinated April 14, 1865

The author of *Our American Cousin* was the prolific British playwright and journalist Tom Taylor (1817–1880). Taylor was also a senior contributor to the weekly comic magazine *Punch*, which, like most of the English press, had spent years mocking Lincoln. As recently as December 1864, *Punch* had printed an engraving by John Tenniel depicting the recently reelected president as a fierce-looking phoenix taking flight from a bonfire fueled by burning logs labeled "Commerce," "United States Constitution," "State Rights," "Habeas Corpus," and "Credit." In the aftermath of the assassination, however, the magazine's editor, Mark Lemon, decided that an "avowal that we had been a bit mistaken" would be "manly and just." To express its contrition, *Punch* published a poem by Taylor that was accompanied by a new engraving by Tenniel showing "Britannia" sympathizing with "Columbia" over her loss (see illustration 21 in this volume).

You lay a wreath on murdered LINCOLN's bier,
    You, who with mocking pencil wont to trace,
Broad for the self-complacent British sneer,
    His length of shambling limb, his furrowed face,

His gaunt, gnarled hands, his unkempt, bristling hair,
    His garb uncouth, his bearing ill at ease,
His lack of all we prize as debonair,
    Of power or will to shine, of art to please.

You, whose smart pen backed up the pencil's laugh,
    Judging each step, as though the way were plain:
Reckless, so it could point its paragraph,
    Of chief's perplexity, or people's pain.

Beside this corpse, that bears for winding-sheet
    The Stars and Stripes he lived to rear anew,
Between the mourners at his head and feet,
    Say, scurril-jester, is there room for *you*?

Yes, he had lived to shame me from my sneer,
    To lame my pencil, and confute my pen —

To make me own this hind of princes peer,
    This rail-splitter a true-born king of men.

My shallow judgment I had learnt to rue,
    Noting how to occasion's height he rose,
How his quaint wit made home-truth seem more true,
    How, iron-like, his temper grew by blows.

How humble yet how hopeful he could be:
    How in good fortune and in ill the same:
Nor bitter in success, nor boastful he,
    Thirsty for gold, nor feverish for fame.

He went about his work—such work as few
    Ever had laid on head and heart and hand—
As one who knows, where there's a task to do,
    Man's honest will must Heaven's good grace command;

Who trusts the strength will with the burden grow,
    That God makes instruments to work his will,
If but that will we can arrive to know,
    Nor tamper with the weights of good and ill.

So he went forth to battle, on the side
    That he felt clear was Liberty's and Right's,
As in his peasant boyhood he had plied
    His warfare with rude Nature's thwarting mights—

The uncleared forest, the unbroken soil,
    The iron-bark, that turns the lumberer's axe,
The rapid, that o'erbears the boatman's toil,
    The prairie, hiding the mazed wanderer's tracks,

The ambushed Indian, and the prowling bear—
    Such were the needs that helped his youth to train:
Rough culture—but such trees large fruit may bear,
    If but their stocks be of right girth and grain.

So he grew up, a destined work to do,
 And lived to do it: four long-suffering years'
Ill-fate, ill-feeling, ill-report, lived through,
 And then he heard the hisses change to cheers,

The taunts to tribute, the abuse to praise,
 And took both with the same unwavering mood:
Till, as he came on light, from darkling days,
 And seemed to touch the goal from where he stood,

A felon hand, between the goal and him,
 Reached from behind his back, a trigger prest,—
And those perplexed and patient eyes were dim,
 Those gaunt, long-labouring limbs were laid to rest!

The words of mercy were upon his lips,
 Forgiveness in his heart and on his pen,
When this vile murderer brought swift eclipse
 To thoughts of peace on earth, good-will to men.

The Old World and the New, from sea to sea,
 Utter one voice of sympathy and shame!
Sore heart, so stopped when it at last beat high,
 Sad life, cut short just as its triumph came.

A deed accurst! Strokes have been struck before
 By the assassin's hand, whereof men doubt
If more of horror or disgrace they bore;
 But thy foul crime, like CAIN'S, stands darkly out,

Vile hand, that brandest murder on a strife,
 Whate'er its grounds, stoutly and nobly striven;
And with the martyr's crown crownest a life
 With much to praise, little to be forgiven!

May 6, 1865

John Nichol

Reunion

Unlike *Punch*, the Scottish literary scholar John Nichol (1833–1894) had no need after Lincoln's death to make amends for earlier mockery. Appointed in 1862 as the first Regius Professor of English Language and Literature at the University of Glasgow, Nichol spent the Civil War advocating for the Union cause "in the press and on the platform alike" with "an energy and ardour which ran strongly counter to the prevailing sentiment of his Glasgow townsmen." He published his tribute to Lincoln on May 13, 1865, in the weekly *Spectator*.

An end at last! The echoes of the war—
    The weary war beyond the western waves—
Die in the distance. Freedom's rising star
    Beacons above a hundred thousand graves:

The graves of heroes who have won the fight,
    Who in the storming of the stubborn town
Have rung the marriage peal of might and right,
    And scaled the cliffs and cast the dragon down.

Pæans of armies thrill across the sea,
    Till Europe answers—"Let the struggle cease,
The bloody page is turned; the next may be
    For ways of pleasantness and paths of peace!"—

A golden morn—a dawn of better things—
    The olive-branch—clasping of hands again—
A noble lesson read to conquering kings—
    A sky that tempests had not scoured in vain.

This from America we hoped and him
    Who ruled her "in the spirit of his creed."
Does the hope last when all our eyes are dim,
    As History records her darkest deed?

The pilot of his people through the strife,
  With his strong purpose turning scorn to praise,
E'en at the close of battle reft of life,
  And fair inheritance of quiet days.

Defeat and triumph found him calm and just,
  He showed how clemency should temper power,
And dying left to future times in trust
  The memory of his brief victorious hour.

O'ermastered by the irony of fate,
  The last and greatest martyr of his cause;
Slain like Achilles at the Scæan gate,
  He saw the end, and fixed "the purer laws."

May these endure and, as his work, attest
  The glory of his honest heart and hand, —
The simplest, and the bravest, and the best, —
  The Moses and the Cromwell of his land.

Too late the pioneers of modern spite,
  Awestricken by the universal gloom,
See his name lustrous in Death's sable night,
  And offer tardy tribute at his tomb.

But we who have been with him all the while,
  Who knew his worth, and loved him long ago,
Rejoice that in the circuit of our isle
  There is no room at last for Lincoln's foe.

Ford's Theatre playbill for April 14, 1865, the night of the assassination.

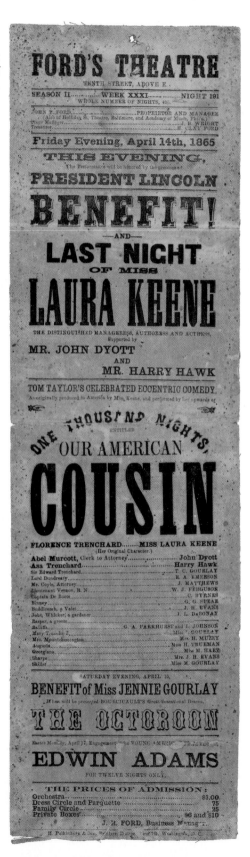

The last photograph of Lincoln, taken on the White House balcony, March 6, 1865, by Henry F. Warren.

Mary Lincoln in mourning attire.

The
presidential
box at Ford's
Theatre in
April 1865.

Ford's Theatre c. 1860–65.

Lincoln Borne by Loving Hands by Carl Bersch, c. 1895, painting after sketches made on April 14, 1865. Bersch witnessed Lincoln being removed from Ford's Theatre across the street to William Petersen's boarding house. On the right, a celebration of Lee's surrender is interrupted by the men carrying the wounded President.

Drawing of Lincoln's deathbed scene by Hermann Faber, a medical artist on the Surgeon General's staff. It was purportedly sketched within a few hours of Lincoln's death on the morning of April 15.

Secretary of the Navy Gideon Welles is seated, far left, with Chief Justice Salmon P. Chase standing behind him. Seated in front of Lincoln are his personal physician, Dr. Robert King Stone, and Dr. Joseph K. Barnes, the Surgeon General. Directly behind Lincoln are Senator Charles Sumner and Dr. Charles H. Crane. Secretary of War Edwin M. Stanton stands, far right, and to his left is Major General Henry W. Halleck, chief of staff of the Union army.

Fanny Seward in 1866. She was in the room during the assassination attempt on her father, Secretary of State William H. Seward.

Broadside reward poster issued by the War Department.

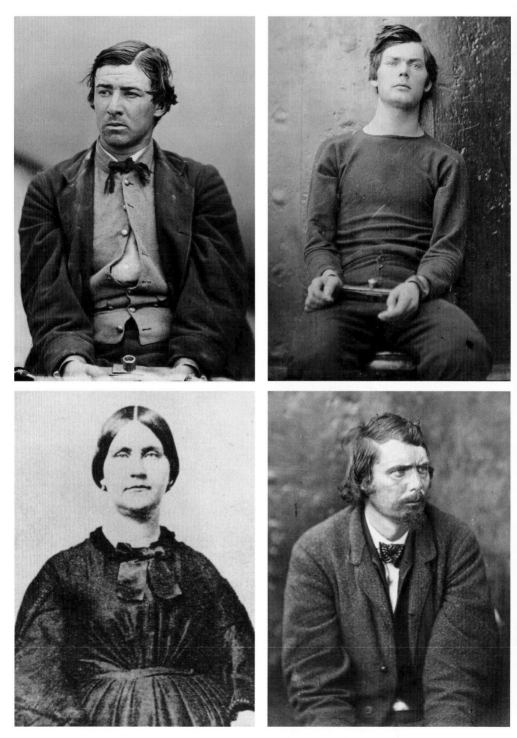

Clockwise from top left: Booth's co-conspirators David Herold, Lewis Powell (alias Payne), George Atzerodt, and Mary Surratt. Photographs of Herold, Powell, and Atzerodt taken in April 1865 by Alexander Gardner while they were imprisoned onboard ironclad monitors in the Washington Navy Yard. This is the last known portrait of Mary Surratt.

Autographed studio portrait of John Wilkes Booth, c. 1860–65.

Sergeant Boston Corbett of the 16th New York Cavalry, the man who shot Booth.

Lincoln's catafalque with coffin during the funeral procession in New York City, photograph by George Stacy.

Mourners in front of the Lincoln home in Springfield, Illinois.

The funeral train that transported Lincoln's body to Illinois,
photographed on a Lake Michigan pier in Chicago.

Lincoln's funeral procession at the corner of Broadway and Union Square in New York City, April 25, 1865, photograph by Robert N. Dennis. The two children visible in the window at the upper left are believed to be six-year-old Theodore Roosevelt and his younger brother Elliott Roosevelt, watching from their grandfather's house.

THE FOUNDER AND THE PRESERVER OF THE UNION.
[*Apotheosis.*]

Entered according to Act of Congress by Thurston, Herline & Co.,
in the year 1865, in the Clerk's Office of the District Court of the
Eastern District of Pennsylvania.

Published by Thurston, Herline & Co., 630 Chestnut St., Phila.

Washington, the father of the country, receives Lincoln as its savior into heaven.
1865 print by Thurston, Herline & Co., Philadelphia.

BRITANNIA SYMPATHISES WITH COLUMBIA.

Illustration by John Tenniel published in *Punch, or the London Charivari*, London, England, May 6, 1865. Columbia sits at the left; a slave with broken chains at the right.

IN MEMORY OF ABRAHAM LINCOLN.

THE REWARD OF THE JUST.

"The Reward of the Just," by D. T. Wiest. Immortality and Father Time carry Lincoln into heaven. In front of the tomb are symbols of the United States: an eagle, with the national shield, and Columbia, bearing a liberty cap. The women to the left represent Faith, Hope, and Charity. Wiest copied his print from an earlier image of Washington by John James Barralet, changing only the president's head and the inscription on the tomb.

The bodies of Mary Surratt, Lewis Powell, David Herold, and George Atzerodt hang from the gallows after their execution at the Washington Arsenal. Photograph by Alexander Gardner, July 7, 1865.

Henrik Ibsen

Abraham Lincoln's Murder

Henrik Ibsen (1828–1906) had not yet written the plays that would help define modern drama when he composed this poem in Rome on April 30, 1865. Published in Norwegian in the Copenhagen newspaper *Fædrelandet* (The Fatherland) on May 15, Ibsen's verses envision the example of American republicanism as a threat to entrenched European despotism, an idea Lincoln himself had espoused in many of his pre-presidential speeches. The third stanza alludes to the Prussian defeat of Denmark in 1864, the Russian suppression of the 1863 uprising in Poland, and the deadly bombardment of Copenhagen by the British navy in 1807.

They fired a shot out there in the West
and the shock throughout Europe rang.
My word! What life all at once expressed
by the whole of the fancy-dress gang!
Old Europe, so ordered, so patently right,
with laws for each rung on the scale,
with honour unblemished, clean and bright,
with proper scorn for all black-not-white,—
you turned quite remarkably pale!

In sealing-wax, eagles and unicorns burn
and all other beasts, no less;
the packet-boat rides on its cable's turn,
despatches, they swarm and they press.
Magnates in cotton, "gloire's" proud son,
the mob from the land of lies,
they reached for the palmfrond of peace as one,
then sounded that shot from a single gun,
and a man falls, one person dies.

And then you were scared. Had Europe's lead
been followed as fit and right?
A Prussian exploit, a Dybbøl-deed,

the world had all witnessed the sight.
No dog eats dog, and no raven raven;—
remember the Poles and that row?
The English action at Copenhaven?
the war-tomb at Flensborg? and "Sønderborg" graven?
So why so indignant now?

That crimson rose there, whose flowers shock
and frighten you here at home,
our Europe it was that supplied the stock,
the West its luxurious loam.
You planted as seedling that stem grown so grand
it reddens America's shore,
you tied on his breast, with your own fair hand,
that patent of martyrdom's blood-red band
that Abraham Lincoln wore.

With broken promises, words betrayed
and with treaties mere paperish toil,
with this season's crimes against oaths last year made
you have fertilised history's soil.
Then at peace with your minds you looked to the day
for noblest of harvests to dawn!
Now it's sprouting, your seed. Look—a blazing display!
You're puzzled, confounded, can't think what to say,—
for stilettos have grown as your corn.

Where law is poised on the dagger's edge
and right on the gallow's sill,
the triumph of dawn has surer pledge
than here, where it's words that can kill.
A passion wakens, a judgement keen
that shatters each lair of lies;—
but first must the worm pick the skull quite clean,
and times must first change from what they have been
to their own self-parodies.

A demon's in charge, one of boundless strength.
Just cross him! do try, if you must!
The Aurea Domus crumbled at length
like Nero's colossus to dust.
But first had the crime that was Rome to spread wide
from the pole of the earth to pole,
the tyrant be worshipped and deified,
the Caesars' gold busts range side by side
as gods on the Capitol.

Then all of it crumbled; circus and camp,
temples and columned roof,
store-rooms, arcades pounded small by the stamp
of the buffalo's armoured hoof.
Then men built anew on those old decays
and clean, for a while, was the air.
Now signs suggest there's a second phase;
the pestilence climbs from its waterlogged maze
and hovers now here, now there.

But if we all sink in corruption's lair
don't count on laments from me
over each of the poisonous flowers that flare
and mass on this age's tree.
Just let the worm burrow. The walls won't decay
till all of the skull's picked clean.
Just let the whole system be wrenched away;
the sooner comes vengeance and Judgment Day
on us for the lies we have been!

May 15, 1865

Oliver Wendell Holmes

For the Services in Memory of Abraham Lincoln

By presidential proclamation June 1, 1865, was "a day of special humiliation and prayer in consequence of the assassination of Abraham Lincoln," observed with secular commemorations as well as by services in churches and synagogues. In Boston Senator Charles Sumner gave an oration on Lincoln and "The Promises of the Declaration of Independence" that was followed by the performance of a hymn written by the poet, essayist, and physician Oliver Wendell Holmes (1809–1894). A critic of abolitionism and advocate of political compromise before the war, Holmes had become an ardent advocate for the Union during the conflict, in which his eldest son and namesake was wounded three times. Holmes would later learn that Lincoln had once praised his poem "The Last Leaf" as "inexpressibly touching."

O thou of soul and sense and breath,
    The ever-present Giver,
Unto Thy mighty angel, death,
    All flesh thou dost deliver;
What most we cherish, we resign,
For life and death alike are Thine,
    Who reignest Lord forever!

Our hearts lie buried in the dust
    With him, so true and tender,
The patriot's stay, the people's trust,
    The shield of the offender;
Yet every murmuring voice is still,
As, bowing to Thy sovereign will,
    Our best loved we surrender.

Dear Lord, with pitying eye behold
    This martyr generation,
Which Thou, through trials manifold,
    Art showing Thy salvation!
O let the blood by murder spilt

Wash out Thy stricken children's guilt,
  And sanctify our nation!

Be Thou Thy orphaned Israel's friend,
  Forsake Thy people never,
In One our broken Many blend,
  That none again may sever!
Hear us, O Father, while we raise
With trembling lips our song of praise,
  And bless Thy name forever!

Frederick Douglass

Address at Cooper Union, New York City

On June 1 a large, mostly African-American audience filled Cooper Union in New York City to hear the nation's leading black abolitionist eulogize the slain President. Frederick Douglass (1818–1895) had written favorably about Lincoln during the 1860 campaign, then harshly criticized him after the election for his attempts to conciliate the South and willingness to enforce the Fugitive Slave Law. From the beginning of the war Douglass had called for immediate emancipation and the arming of black troops, and had judged the President to be inexcusably slow in adopting these measures. Once Lincoln issued the Emancipation Proclamation, and especially after the two men met at the White House to discuss policy in August 1863 and August 1864, Douglass altered his views and began to publicly praise Lincoln. His speech at Cooper Union was summarized in *The New York Times* and *New York Tribune*, but has never been printed in full. The text presented here is taken from the manuscript in the Library of Congress, and preserves Douglass's spelling, capitalization, and punctuation. In two places a bracketed space, i.e., [   ], is used to indicate where an unknown word, or words, was omitted from the manuscript.

I come before you this evening with much diffidence: The rarest gifts, the best eloquence, the highest order of genius to which the nation has given birth, might well be employed here and now, and yet fail of justice to the dignity and solemnity of this occasion.

The character of the illustrious deceased, the position he occupied at the head of our Government, the extraordinary manner of his death, with all the attendant circumstances of the country, are fruitful themes, of the most interesting nature;—themes which must depend upon the historian, rather than upon the orator, for elaborate and appropriate celebration.

Had Abraham Lincoln died from any of the numerous ills to which flesh is heir, and by which men are removed from the scenes of life; Had he reached that good old age, of which his vigorous constitution, and his temperate habits gave promise: Had he seen the end of the great work which it was his good fortune to inaugurate; Had the curtain of death been but gradually drawn around him;—our task this evening, though sad, and painful would be very simple.

But dying as he did die, by the red hand of violence, snatched suddenly away from his work without warning;—killed, murdered, assassinated, not because of personal hate, for no man who knew Abraham Lincoln, could hate him; but solely because he was the President, the faithful, loyal President of the United States—true to his country, and true to the cause of human freedom, taking care that the Constitution and the laws were obeyed; for this reason he was slain, murdered, assassinated, and for this all commanding reason he to day commands our homage and the homage of good men every where as a glorious martyr—one who must be viewed if viewed rightly, in connection with his country and with all that pertains to his country.

Very evidently here is a large field opened, but the most any man can do, with a subject like this, and at a time like this, when every faculty of thought and feeling, is intensely active, when the press, the pulpit and the platform, when poetry and art in all her departments, has been occupied with this one great event for weeks: I say, the most I can do, the most any man can do, is in some humble measure, to give back to the country, the thoughts and feelings which are derived from the country:—The speaker upon occasions like this, is but as the wave to the ocean; he borrows all his weight and volume; from the sea out of which he rises.

To day all over this country—men have been thinking of Abraham Lincoln: Our statesmen scholars and poets—have been celebrating as never before the memory of our martyred President. It is well. He is worthy of it all—and it is becoming in all—to join however humbly in these tokens of respect and veneration.

One thing will be at once conceded by all generous minds; no people or class of people in this country, have a better reason for lamenting the death of Abraham Lincoln, and for desiring to honor and perpetuate his memory, than have the colored people; and yet we are about the only people who have been in any case forbiden to exhibit our sorrow, or to show our respect for the deceased president publicly. The attempt to exclude colored people from his funeral procession in New York—was one of the most disgraceful; and sickening manifestations of moral emptiness, ever exhibited by any nation or people professing to be civilized. But what was A. Lincoln to the colored people or they to him? As compared with the long line of his predecessors, many of whom were merely the facile and servile instruments of the slave power, Abraham Lincoln, while unsurpassed in his devotion, to the welfare of the white race, was also in a sense hitherto without example, emphatically the black mans President: the first to show any respect for their rights as men.

To our white fellow countrymen therefore we say, follow your martyred president to his grave, lay the foundation of his monument broad and strong—let its capstone rise towards the sky—do homage to his character, forever perpetuate his memory, but as you respect genuine sorrow, unfeigned greif, and sincere bereavement, let the colored people of this country—for whom he did so much, have space at least, for one stone in that monument—one which shall tell to after-coming generations the story of their love and gratitude to Abraham Lincoln.

Those love most to whom most is forgiven. One of the most touching scenes connected with the funeral of our lamented President, occurred at the gate of the Presidential mansion. A colored woman standing at the gate weeping, was asked the cause of her tears; Oh! Sir she said we have lost our Moses. But said the gentleman, the Lord will send you another: That may be said the weeping woman, but Ah! we had him. To her mind one as good, or better might come in his stead—but no such possibility to her was equal to—to the reality, actual possession in the person of Abraham Lincoln.

The colored people, from first to last, and through all, whether through good or through evil report, fully believed in Abraham Lincoln. Even though he sometimes smote them, and wounded them severely, yet they firmly trusted in him: This was however, no blind trust unsupported by reason: They early caught a glimpse of the man, and from the evidence of their senses, they believed in him. They viewed him not in the light of separate individual facts—but in the light of his mission—as his manifest relation to events—and in the philosophy of his statesmanship— Viewing him thus they trusted him—as men are seldom trusted. They did not care what forms of expression the President adopted, whether it were justice, expediency, or military necessity so that they saw slavery abolished—and Liberty was established in the country.

Under Abraham Lincolns beneficent rule, they saw themselves being gradually lifted to the broad plain of equal manhood: Under his rule, and by measures approved by him, they saw gradually fading the hand writing of ages which was against them: Under his rule, they saw millions of their bretheren proclaimed free and invested with the right to defend their freedom: Under his rule, they saw the Confederate states—that boldest of all conspiracies against the just rights of human nature, broken to peices, overpowered conquered, shattered to fragments—ground to powder and swept from the face of existence: Under his rule, they saw the Independence of Hayti and Liberia recognized—and the whole colored race steadily rising into the friendly consideration of the American people. In their broad practical common sense, they took no captious exceptions to the unpleasant incidents of their transition from slavery to freedom. All they wanted to know was that those incidents were only transitional not permanent.

But we speak here to night not merely as colored men, but as men among men, and as American citizens—having the same interest in the welfare permanence and prosperity, of the country—that any other class of citizens may be supposed to have. We survey the facts of the hour with reference to this relation to our fellow citizens:—From this outlook we find the prospect bright & glorious.

The greatness and grandeur of the American republic never appeared more conspicuosly than in connection with the death of Abraham Lincoln: Though always great and always powerful, we have seemed to need the presence of some great, and widespread calamity, some over whelming sorrow, to reveal to our selves and the world, in glorified forms, all the elements of our national strength and greatness. While it cannot be affirmed, that our long torn and distracted country, has already reached the desired condition of peace, it may be said, and said in the face of all prophecies of failure—freely indulged in at one time, at home as well as abroad that we have survived the terrible agonies of a feirce and sanguinary rebellion, and have before us a fair prospect of a just and lasting peace, a peace which if *we are wise*, and just, can never be disturbed or broken by the remains of still insolent and designing slave oligarchy.

Already a strong hand is felt upon the helm of state; Already the key note of justice has been sounded; Already the majesty of the Law and the power of the Government are bringing order out of confusion, by making the Law a terror to evil doers, as well as a praise to those who do well: The word has gone forth that traitors and assassins whether of low or of high degree, whether male or female, are to be punished: that loyal and true men are to be rewarded and protected: That slavery the haggard and damning offense of many generations, is to be entirely and for ever abolished: that the emancipated negro, so long outraged and degraded is to be enfranchised and clothed with the dignity of American citizenship: That the poor white man of the south—scornfully denominated by the rich slaveholders, as the poor white trash, so long deceived, misled and plundered by the slaveholding aristocracy—are to be delivered from their political and social debasement: That the loyal and patriot dead, whether dying of wounds on the field or of starvation in Rebel prisons, whether falling in open combat or by the stealthy dagger of the assassin—are to be gratefully remembered and honored forever. That the toil worn, scarred, maimed and battered veterans, of all nationalities and of all colors, now returning home from the scenes of strife, are to be welcomed home, and taught by the respect and gratitude they receive from their country—that they have been fighting for *their* country—and not merely for the empty and delusive hope of a country.

Henceforth we have a new date, a new era for our great Republic: Henceforth a new account is opened, between the government and the people of the United States: Henceforth there is to be no north no south in American politics, but a common country of all for all: Henceforth the nation assumes a new position and a new relation to the nations of the Earth: Henceforth an American citizen may defend his country at the tribunal of the world's judgement, without defending a glaring inconsistency and a scandalous crime: Henceforth there is an end to that compromising statesmanship—which has so deeply demoralized both the Government and the people: Henceforth we shall stand an acknowledged power among the great powers of Europe and exert a beneficent influence in the destiny of nations. Out of the vast and dreadful concatenation of evils which have environed us, brought upon us during these four years of treason rebellion and assassination, we shall yet be the recipients of immeasurable and priceless blessings: It is something that the crash has come and that the worst is known—that the storm cloud has burst, and sent down its bolt and has left the blue sky above, calm and bright as when the morning stars sang to gether for joy!

Spanning the horrible gulf, the fearful chasm—made by the sad, the mournful, and tragic death of our greatly loved; greatly honored greatly trusted and greatly lamented President, we behold from side to side, a perfect bow of promise with all its beautiful beams undimmed, dispelling fear, and kindling hope a new for the future of the Republic.

This occassion therefore, though sad and solemn when we contemplate our martyred president, is not one of gloom, when we consider the future of the country. There is here joy as well as sorrow, gratulation as well as greif, great gain as well as great loss. This last drop in our cup of bitterness was perhaps needed: No nation ever passed an ordeal better fitted to try its strength, or to test the value of its institutions. Know thyself is a wise admonition to nations as well as to individuals, such national self knowledge has been imparted by the war and by this last act of the war. It had long been the settled opinion of European statesmen and philosophers, that our ship of state was too weak for stormy weather. They predicted that though beautiful to the eye, strong to the touch and swift upon the wave, our gallant bark would go down in the first great storm. They had little faith in the wisdom or virtue of the people. And as little in the form and substance of popular government. I have no reproaches for these foreigners of little faith, for it cannot be denied that many thoughtful and patriotic men at home, have doubted and trembled while contemplating the possibility of just such a conflict as that through which we have now so nearly and happily passed.

The cost of the experiment in blood and treasure has been vast, but the results attained and made attainable by it will fully compensate for all loss: Already we are realizing its blessings: At this moment as never before in our history we are enjoying not, I trust, a haughty but a healthy consciousness of our strength: Already there is a feeling of national repose, an assured faith in the ability of the people, and in the stability of Republican Government—such as never before existed.

Happily too: this confidence is not limited to our own country—It is defusing itself through all countries—and over all continents. Writhing under the heel of an imported despotism, the worst of all the despotisms of Europe—Mexico to day, lifts up her dejected and woe smitten head, with revived and reinvigorated hope, and the friends of free institutions throughout the world, will recognize in our great national triumph over rebellion and slavery, a powerful gaurantee, of the ultimate universal establishment of free institutions.

But I will not stop here to argue the value of the results thus far of our conflict. When measured by the hardships endured, and the fearful loss of human life involved, such arguments however just, may savour too much of indifference to human suffering.

A more tranquilizing thought comes to us on this occasion. That thought is the inevitability of the conflict. It was beyond the power of human will or wisdom—to have prevented just what has happened. We should never forget that this dreadful war with all its incidents was a part of—and sprung out of the fundamental elements of our national structure—and was in the nature of things unavoidable. We have but reaped where we had sown. Its hour had come, and there was nothing left but to make room for it, to accept it, and derive from it, whatever advantage it brought. We could no more evade it, than we could unmake our anticedents.

When slavery was first planted in the national soil, treason, rebellion and assassination were planted with it and their bloody fruit was bequeathed to the present generation. And if in the coming reconstruction, we shall encorporate any of the seeds of injustice, any of the remains of slavery, we shall repeat the mistake of our fathers, with the certainty that our children after us will reap a similar harvest of blood to that we have just experienced.

All the great nations of the Earth, no matter how isolated their location, no matter how iron like their ruler no matter how conservative their statesmen, no matter how carefully they exclude the light of new ideas—are fated to pass through what may be termed their historical periods—certain grand epochs, made up by the irrepressible tendencies of their inherent social forces, coming upon them whether they will or not.

Their political astrologers and wisemen, look upward and read as they think the signs of the times they see the crises coming just as they see the storm gathering in the sky. They may utter their warning, but can neither avert nor hinder the event. There is however nothing aimless capricious arbitrary or blind in the oncoming of such periods. They are prepared for—provided for by violation of law, they come when they are ready and they depart when their work is done. Such epochs occurring at different points of time and in different nations, are the great teachers of mankind, they disclose in striking forms and colors, the active elements of the national life good and bad, of each individual nation, making each better acquainted with itself and better known to all other nations.

As a people though less disturbed and more fortunate than most other nations we are no exception to the general rule applying to all. One such period as this happened to us, four score and nine years ago. It was when our delegates sat in solemn assembly in Philadelphia and openly declared our independence of Great Britain—and when the American people, with a courage that never quailed—and a faith that knew no doubt marched through bloody fields during all the length of seven years to make that declaration a solid reality.

Another and mightier than that, is the one compressed within the narrow limits of the last four years. There is not one jot of all this space from the first of June sixty one, to the first of June sixty-five, which is not studded with stupendous events, destined to engage the thoughts, and thrill the hearts of mankind away into the depths of coming ages. I repeat nothing strange has happened unto us. We have been simply playing our appointed parts in the subtle machinery of human advancement and civilization. We had within our midst a gigantic system of injustice, and barbarism, a shocking offense against the enlightened judgement of mankind—a system which the world had out grown, one which we were required by the necessity of our existence and our relations to mankind to put away. Peacibly if we could, forcibly if we must.

In doing this great work for ourselves, we have done other, if not greater service.

To the grand sum of human knowledge as to what men have done, will do, as to what great nations and states have done and will do, when vital interests are involved and powerful human passions are stirred, we have during these four years—added our special and peculiar contribution, such an one as no other nation of modern times could add.

Our experience has been full of instruction and our example brilliant and striking beyond a parrable: The very ends of the earth may look and learn. During this tremendous struggle for national [   ], so feirce, bitter and sanguinary, so long protracted and so desperate, we have illustrated both extremes of human possibilities. As a nation we have exemplified the best and noblest qualities—which distinguish human nature, as well as those which most blot and disgrace it.

The history of this war for the union and for Free Institutions, will possess many thrilling Chapters full of moving incidents, full of battles, sieges, hair breadths escape, of gallant achievements upon flood and field, but it will have none, which will so interest, so *astound* and amaze mankind as that which shall contain a faithful record of the events and scenes which have transpired in our country during the last seven weeks:

We have here the concentrated *virus* the moral poison, accumulated by more than two centuries of human slavery, pouring itself out upon the nation as a vial of wrath in one dreadful and shocking crime the first of its kind in the annals of the country.

The accursed thing, so long defended in the name of the Bible and religion—defended thus while known to live upon blood and tears—the hateful crime, so long defended in the name of law and order, properly celebrates its own death by a crime that sends a shudder around the world.

England, France, Germany all European nations have been literally struck dumb, by this appropriate exhibition of slaveholding hate. It is well that slavery should give this mean and bloody sign of its death, cradled in theft, and living by robbery, it is meet that it should go to its grave under a storm of execration from every quarter of the globe.

Hereafter when men think of slavery, they will think of murder, Hereafter when men think of slaveholders, they will think of assassins: Hereafter when men think of southern chivalry they will think of our starving prisoners at Andersonville, Hereafter when men think of southern honor, they will think of the assassination of Abraham Lincoln.

Deny it who will, Doubt it who may—that hell black deed sprung from the very heart of the aristocratic class of the south.

I know that some of the leaders of the rebellion have affected to deplore it, Some have even ventured to plead their honorable character as proof their innocence of that foul and ghastly crime. But such pleas cannot be received. They are utterly vain and worthless—These slaveholders know, we know, and the world knows where the responsibility for this crime belongs.

The assassin not less than any member of the late Confederate Government, represented a cause, and was the very image and superscription of that cause. Those who have by fraud, treachery robbery broken oaths and piracy, carried on a war during four years to break up this union, with no better or other motive than to make human bondage perpetual, will have to bring better evidence than their own word of honor, to remove from their shoulders this heavy responsibility.

Booth the assassin is of the south. His affiliations such as they were, are of the south. He fired his deadly shot in the interest of the south. His motto of defense after committing the atrocious crime, was copied from the south; From the first of the war he took sides with the south. His first thought upon the commission of the crime, was escape to the south; There is nothing in his morals or manners, or in the crime itself to seperate him from the south—or that should make the south disown him. As types, and representative men of southern civilization—Booth and Brooks stand well together. Brooks, attempted to assassinate Mr Sumner of Massachusetts—a noble representative of New England culture—and statesmanship—and was applauded, publicly applauded all over the south. And I undertake to say, knowing the south as I do—that the same south, or what is left of it, which applauded the assassination of Hon. Charles Sumner—at its inmost heart will applaud the assassination of Abraham Lincoln.

Let us not, mistake public opinion either at the north or the south. This mistake is the danger, the imminent danger of the hour. We have done too much of this in other days.

Public journals, there are all over the north—which have sympathised from the first with the rebels and traitors—just so far as they could do so with safety—are endeavoring to serve their old friends and allies to day by persuading their readers—that the south disowns Booth—and laments as sincerely as we do the death of Abraham Lincoln. To this there is just one word to be said—It comes entirely too late, and is utterly inconsistent with the past. Take the federal soldiers from the so called Confederate states and tomorrow the very elite of the south will drink to the memory of Booth the assassin.

Besides, the crime accords well, with the several attempts to burn up sleeping women and innocent children in hotels. It accords well with the attempt to throw crowded Railway trains from the tracks. It accords well with the torpedo and infernal machine mode of warfare, so universally adopted by the chivalry of the south. It accords well with the horrid profanation of the graves of our brave soldiers, and making ornaments of their bones: It accords well with the massacre at Fort Pillow—It accords well with the system of starvation adopted by the Confederate government in its treatment of our prisoners. And it accords generally with the cowardly ferocity—with which the system of slavery naturally inspires her worshippers:

Men who whip women with their hands tied, and burn their names into their flesh with hot irons—can not be allowed any especial abhorrence of assassination—or for any other crime it may seem for their interest to commit.

Another strong argument in favor of this theory of southern responsibility for the assassination, is found in the fact, that that crime was freely talked of at the south, and the time and the place were specified previously to Mr Lincoln's first inauguration: His journey to Washington was the time and Baltimore was the appointed place for the tragedy. Even men here at the North, by winks and nods, and other intimations, which would not now be tolerated, gave us to understand then, that though elected, Mr Lincoln could never be inaugurated.

That their evil prophecies were not fulfilled, we all know was owing to his travelling by an irregular train and arriving in Baltimore at an unexpected time.

Booth the miserable assassin only did at the last what was meditated threatened, and expected at the very outset of the rebellion.

Great as was his crime, he is at this moment not one whit guiltier, than is General Lee and other Leaders of the rebellion.

The beginning of the rebellion is assassination. The end of the rebellion is assassination—It is consistent throughout. It ends as it began, not a line of analogy is missing. Booth and Beauregard, Payne and President Davis Adzerot and Breckenridge, were servants of a common cause, and will go down in history as clansmen and kinsmen—and brothers beloved in a common conspiracy and a common crime.

It has been sometimes regretted that Booth was not captured alive, that he might have been regularily tried, condemned, sentenced and executed.

I shall waste no unavailing regrets, upon this point. The ends of justice in his case have been satisfied. His punishment has been indeed swift and terrible.

Men at the North where they have dared do so, have been heard to extol the bravery of Booth.

That he had more courage than his captain may be freely admitted. Yet in no honorable or desireable sense was Booth a brave man. His courage was the courage of the thief—the burglar, the highway robber, who murder at midnight and escape in the darkness—by plans and appliances arranged weeks in advance.

His courage was no bar to his suffering: In his ten days wanderings after committing his crime he must have suffered more than a hundred deaths.

I can conceive of no torture more exquisite and extreme than his. Reckless of life as he affected to be, when captured no criminal ever made a more desperate effort to save his life than he did, while there seemed the least chance of saving it.

To imagine the intense anguish he suffered those ten days we need not track him in his perilous flight, with a broken leg at the start, inflamed by liquor and swelling with pain: we need not follow him as he hobbled along—on either side of the Potomac in the darkness seeking safety and finding none. We need not go with him into that dismal swamp wherein he whirled about upon his crutch, startled by every sound like a hunted wolf in an iron trap—hemmed in all sides, all chance of escape cut off, with sleep murdered appetite gone, his broken limb all the while getting worse no friend daring to approach him with succor, the lines of his pursuers steadily drawing more closely around him: as certain for days of final capture, as though the iron hand of the law had already fallen heavily upon him. I say we need not follow him through these scenes to imagine his terrible suffering, nor even to that last scene of all, wherein he piteously begs the by standers to kill him—to put an end to his pains, and remove him from the horrible thing he was—to his own sight.

The simple fact that he had shed innocent blood, and that a whole nation was roused for his capture—and that no assylum awaited him—in any country except the south—and that the south was now utterly impossible to him, will give a distressing idea enough—of the living death through which he dragged himself during those ten terrible days.

No: assassination finds no encouragement in the fate of Booth—as treason finds no countenence in the capture of Davis.

But let us turn away from the hateful assassin, and think of the loved and honored martyr who fell by the hand of the assassin.

The world is old, and its experience vast, but was there ever such an hour caused by the announcement of the death of any monarch, as was caused by the news of the death of Abraham Lincoln? Was ever any people so instantly and so universally overwhelmed with greif? Did ever a great and victorious nation so suddenly pass from triumph to tears—from exaltation and joy to the very dust and ashes of mourning. I know of none and the world knows of none.

The monstrous blow came when, as at no time before during all the war, we were rejoicing in great and decisive victories, the rebel capital had fallen, General Lee had surrendered: Mobile was in our hands; the rebel army was scattered, blown away like the fine dust, before the strong North wind: the press, the loyal press, had put off the wrinckled front of war—and was appealing for clemency in behalf of the defeated rebels. The feeling of resentment and wrath was everywhere giving way to a spirit of forgiveness and oblivion; the whole national horizon seemed fringed with the golden dawn of peace; when all at once, we were startled, amazed, struck down, overwhelmed, by this most foul and dreadful murder. The gentle, the amiable, character of the man— the man, with malice towards none, but charity towards—all—the last man in the world—one would think to tempt the assassins dagger—The thought was full of astonishment as well as horror. The event itself, was so sudden, so tragic, and so out of joint with all seeming probability, so in contradiction to all our feelings that few could at the first believe the dreadful news.

You remember all the circumstances, and yet it seems fit in an address like this that we reiterate their leading features. The story is soon told: While seated with his wife, in a private box at Ford's theatre, set apart by its proprietor, for the President and his family;—while putting off the burdens of state for the moment, observing the play entitled Our American Cousin, which he had been specially invited to witness—all unconscious of danger to himself or to the state: Abraham Lincoln was shot down by an assassin who stood behind him—and died from the wound the ensuing morning: such was the shocking news flashed from Washington on the Fifteenth April—Along with it also came the stunning announcement that Hon: William H. Seward—Secretary of State had been assassinated in his chamber, upon a bed where some thought he had days before laid down to die: and that both himself and his son, the assistant Secretary of State must die from the terrible wounds inflicted by the assassin.

Further on still, there came the intimation hardly needed, that their assassinations were not the self moved, individual outbreaks of the malign passions of miscreants: That they were representative men. They were but as the hands of the clock, in front and in sight, but the cunning machinery that moved them was behind and out of sight. It was seen at the moment that the assassins had only accomplished a part of the bloody work, marked out for their hands. Murder was to have had a more extended circle. All the heads of the State—and the head of the Army, were to have fallen: Men everywhere recognized in it the hand and heart of the rebellion: The life taken was not the life the murderer sought. It was not the President, but the country—they would strike down through him.

But what a day! What a day to the American people was that fourteenth of April. For the moment we seemed suspended over the howling abyss of Anarchy and social chaos: At that moment a breath or an atom might have detached us from the moorings of civil order—and plunged us into national ruin.

One feature of the moment was the feeling of astonishment: In the condition of the country—and the threats so frequently made, the event ought to have been looked for. Men are men, here as elsewhere. History is but repeating itself—said Mr Seward—as soon as able to speak—The remark is strictly philosophical. We ought to have expected it.—Yet it caught us all unprepared.

Had the solid earth opened and swallowed up one of our chief cities, had the tombs, burst beneath our feet, and the sheeted dead walked forth from the dust of ages, the sensation of astonishment and horror could not have been more profound and all pervading.

A hush, a solemn stillness went out over the land, as though each man had heard a voice from heaven, an uninterpreted sound from the sky, and had tremblingly paused to learn its meaning.

Men spoke to each other with bated breath, with voices—broken and scarcely audable. The heads of the people were bowed—like the waves of the sea when first swept by the tempest, only to rise higher later in the storm.

I shall not undertake to describe the grand tumult of emotions that throbbed in all loyal hearts that day. A thought of the assassin caused a shudder, as if one had in the darkness of a lonely way come upon the feirce glaring eyes of a ferocious beast—or trodden upon a poisonous reptile. We were smitten with a feeling of shame for the fiendish possibilities of human nature.

For a moment there stole through men's hearts a strange distrust of each other. They looked at their fellow citizens with a searching glance, which said not so much who are you but what are you and how do you feel at this mournful hour? for none could tell how far the dark spirit of assassination had travelled north nor where the blow would next fall.

Still as I look back to that day, and analize the emotions every where excited, I must say, the one sentiment, the one feeling,—vastly more intense, more prominent and all pervading, than all others; the one that stirred deepest, the hearts of men, and caused their eyes to alternate between tears at one moment, and sparks of fire at another, was a feeling of sorrow—a sense of personal bereavement—in the death of Abraham Lincoln. This one great feeling—overlapped and interlaced all others—and colored every object to the eye and spirits.

What was the real cause of this deep sorrow? Who can explain whence the hold this man had upon the American people? His high official character, no doubt had something to do with it—but very evidently this was not all. Other Presidents have died, though none have been assassinated before President Lincoln—yet none were ever so mourned.

So far as the contingency of the loss of the president was concerned, it was already provided for. It is one of the marvils to the outside world that the confidence of the country—was so easily and promptly transferred from the President dead to the President Living. The death of a monarch is looked to as an event of great political changes if not of revolution—but we have shown that even in times of great troubles and calamities—our country can pass from the hands of one ruler to those of another without noise or detriment of any sort: In this fact we have a renewed garantee of the perpetuity of Republican Institutions.

What then was the cause of our greif? Whence our bereavement: If I affirm that it was not because the country had lost a president, but because the world had lost a man—one whose like we may not see again.

The fact is the people in the very depths of their souls loved Abraham Lincoln. They knew him, *and* knew him as one brother knows another, and they loved him as one brother loves another. He was not only the President of the country, but a member of each loyal family in the country. The very picture of his plain American face, was loved—as the picture of a dear relation.

Abraham Lincoln was no exotic,—no imported growth of king craft or of Priest craft. He was no imitator of foreign customs or copiest of foreign manners, but thoroughly American in all that distinguished his character—There was not a fibre in his whole composition—that did not identify him with his country to the fullest extent. He was a self-made man, the architect of his own fortune. And the American people—indebted to themselves for themselves, saw in him, a full length portrait of themselves. In him they saw their better qualities represented—incarnated, and glorified—and as such they loved him.

Other men have, perhaps, been as much honored, but no American has been so much loved—by the American people.

But we stand even yet, too near the newly made grave of Abraham Lincoln, either for a just analysis of his character—or for a dispassionate review of his official life. The wound caused by his death is yet too deep—too fresh, the sorrow too lasting, and the mind too excited with the scenes of sorrow for just criticism or unbiased Eulogy.

The sad and solemn pageantry of his funeral has not yet faded from our vision: The long and imposing procession winding its way through distant states, towards the setting sun is still in sight. The sable drapery of mourning has scarcely ceased to sadden on dwellings or streets, the booming of distant cannon proclaiming a nation's greif, has hardly ceased to reverberate. Muffled drums are still beating funeral marches to his grave, the national flag still waves sadly at half mast against the hollow sky. While the image of him who has gone, lingers in our hearts, like the last smile of a loving mother—just quitting the shores of time.

It was my privilege to know Abraham Lincoln and to know him well. I saw and conversed with him at different times during his administration, and upon two occasions at least by his special invitation. He was the first American President, who thus rose above the prejudices of his times, and country.

I mention it as a proof of his independence. He knew that he could do nothing—which would call down upon him more feircely the ribaldry of the vulgar—than by showing any respect to a colored man.

I found him as you all know him to have been a plain man. There was neither paint nor varnish about him. His manners were simple, unaffected unstudied. His language was like himself—plain strong, sinewy—and earnest. He stated his views with great clearness and strength. Few men could state a case so strongly and convincingly. His utterances were always to the point and without ornament. Though a western man—he was entirely free from extravagance or exaggeration in thought or speech: He was conscious of the vast responsibilities resting upon him, but bore himself—as one able to bear them successfully. His dignity as the President, never stood in the way of his amibility as a man. He was like his pictures, the same man from whichever side you viewed him. He neither awed by his silence nor silenced by the volubility or authority of his speech. While willing to give, he was equally willing to receive: and so far from feeling ustracised in his presence, he acted upon me as all truly great men act upon their fellow men, as a Liberator,—He set me at perfect Liberty—to state where I differed from him as freely, as where I agreed with him. From the first five minutes I seemed to myself, to have been acquainted with him during all my life. He was one of the most solid men I ever met, and one of the most transparent.

What Mr Lincoln was among white men, How he bore himself towards them, I do not know, but this much I am bound to say, that he was one of the very few white Americans who could converse with a negro without any thing like condecension, and without in anywise reminding him of the unpopularity of his color.

If you will pardon the seeming egotism I will mention a fact or two in further illustration of the character of President Lincoln and of his kindly disposition towards colored people. He seemed to want to know them thoroughly. Born in Kentucky—living in Illinois—accustomed to seeing the colored man in most unfavorable conditions it was natural to expect from him at the first—as those [   ] made to the colored people he called about him during the first years of the war. But Mr Lincoln soon outgrew his colonization ideas and schemes—and came to look upon the Blackman as an American citizen.

On one occasion while conversing with him, his messenger twice announced that Governor Buckinham of Connecticut was in an adjoining room, and was very desirous of seeing him. Tell the Governor to wait— said Mr Lincoln—I want to have a long talk with my friend Douglass. I remained a full hour after this with the President. While Governor Buckinham waited patiently in an adjoining room the Presidents pleasure to see.

This was probably the first time in the history of the country when the Governor of a state, was required to wait for an interview, because the President of the United States, was engaged in conversation with a negro.

Francis B. Carpenter

In Memoriam: Abraham Lincoln

A successful portrait painter, Francis Bicknell Carpenter (1830–1900) worked at the White House from February to July 1864 while painting his heroic canvas *The First Reading of the Emancipation Proclamation,* which depicts Lincoln presenting the proclamation to his cabinet on July 22, 1862. During a visit to Mathew Brady's studio in February 1864, Carpenter had persuaded Lincoln to be photographed looking at a picture album with his son Tad. Released to the public only after the assassination, the photograph became an immediate bestseller. Having played a crucial role in visually defining Lincoln as emancipator and loving family man, Carpenter turned to writing. His article "In Memoriam," printed in *Hours at Home* in June 1865, was followed by "Anecdotes and Reminiscences of President Lincoln," which appeared in the summer of 1865 as an epilogue to Henry J. Raymond's highly popular post-assassination biography, *The Life and Public Services of Abraham Lincoln.* Carpenter would further help shape the memory of Lincoln by publishing a successful memoir, *Six Months at the White House with Abraham Lincoln: The Story of a Picture,* in 1866.

———————

I LEAVE to other and abler pens the proper eulogy of MR. LINCOLN, as a ruler, and a statesman, and the estimate of his work and place in history. Favored during the past year with six months' familiar intercourse with him under the same roof, be it my pleasant task to recall and record for the gratification of those who never came into personal contact with the great and good man, some incidents, of interest now as illustrations of his character and daily life, mostly the result of my own observation.

There is a very natural and proper desire, at this time, to know something of the religious experience of the late President. Statements are in circulation in this connection, which, to those who knew him intimately, seem so *unlike* him, that for one I venture to enter my protest, and to assert that I believe such stories, either to be wholly untrue, or the facts in the case to have been unwarrantably embellished. Of all men in the world, Mr. Lincoln was the most unaffected and truthful. He rarely or never used language loosely or carelessly, or for the sake of compliment. He was the most utterly indifferent to, and unconscious of, the effect he was producing, either upon dignitaries or the common people, of any man ever in public position.

Mr. Lincoln could scarcely be called a *religious* man, in the common acceptation of the term, and yet a sincerer *Christian* I believe never lived. A constitutional tendency to dwell upon sacred things; an emotional nature which finds ready expression in religious conversation and revival-meetings; the culture and development of the religious element till the expression of religious thought and experience becomes almost habitual, were not among his characteristics. Doubtless he felt as deeply upon the great questions of the soul and eternity as any other thoughtful man, but the very tenderness and humility of his nature would not permit the exposure of his inmost convictions, except upon the rarest occasions, and to his most intimate friends. And yet, aside from emotional expression, I believe no man had a more abiding sense of his dependence upon God, or faith in the Divine government, and in the power and ultimate triumph of Truth and Right in the world. In the language of an eminent clergyman of this city, who lately delivered an eloquent discourse upon the life and character of the departed President, "It is not necessary to appeal to apocryphal stories, in circulation in the newspapers— which illustrate as much the assurance of his visitors as the depth of his own sensibility—for proof of Mr. Lincoln's Christian character." If his daily life, and various public addresses and writings, do not show this, surely nothing can demonstrate it.

But while impelled to disbelieve some of the assertions upon this subject, much commented upon in public as well as private, I feel at liberty to relate an incident in this connection, which I have not seen published, and which bears upon its face unmistakable evidence of truthfulness. A lady interested in the work of the Christian Commission, had occasion, in the prosecution of her duties, to have several interviews with the President of a business nature. He was much impressed with the devotion and earnestness of purpose she manifested, and on one occasion, after she had discharged the object of her visit, he leaned back in his chair and said to her: "Mrs.——, I have formed a very high opinion of your Christian character, and now as we are alone, I have a mind to ask you to give me, in brief, your idea of what constitutes a true religious experience." The lady replied at some length, stating that, in her judgment, it consisted of a conviction of one's own sinfulness and weakness, and personal need of the Saviour for strength and support; that views of mere doctrine might and would differ, but when one was really brought to feel his need of

Divine help, and to seek the aid of the Holy Spirit for strength and guidance, it was satisfactory evidence of his having been born again. This was the substance of her reply. When she had concluded, Mr. Lincoln was very thoughtful for a few moments. He at length said very earnestly, "If what you have told me is really a correct view of this great subject, I think I can say with sincerity, that I hope I am a Christian. I had lived," he continued, "until my boy Willie died, without realizing fully these things. That blow overwhelmed me. It showed me my weakness as I had never felt it before, and if I can take what you have stated as a *test*, I think I can safely say that I know something of that *change* of which you speak, and I will further add, that it has been my intention for some time, at a suitable opportunity, to make a public religious profession!"

The desire to know of the *inner* experience of one whose *outward* life had so impressed him, and his own frank and simple utterance thereupon, are so characteristic as to render this account, which was given me by a friend, extremely probable. He was not what I would call a *demonstrative* man. He would listen to the opinions of others on these subjects with great deference, even if he was not able to perceive their force, but would never express what he did not feel in response. I recollect his once saying, in a half soliloquy, when we were alone, just after he had been waited upon by a committee or delegation, with reference to securing his coöperation in having the name of God inserted in the Constitution: "Some people seem a great deal more concerned about the *letter* of a thing, than about its *spirit*," or words to this effect.

Too much has not been said of his uniform meekness and kindness of heart, but there would sometimes be afforded evidence, that one grain of sand too much would break even *this* camel's back. Among the callers at the White House one day, there was an officer who had been cashiered from the service. He had prepared an elaborate defence of himself which he consumed much time in reading to the President. When he had finished, Mr. Lincoln replied that even upon his own statement of the case the facts would not warrant executive interference. Disappointed, and considerably crest-fallen the man withdrew. A few days afterward, he made a second attempt to alter the President's convictions, going over substantially the same ground, and occupying about the same space of time, but without accomplishing his end. The *third* time he succeeded in forcing himself into Mr. Lincoln's presence, who with great forbearance listened to another repetition of the case, to its conclusion, but made no reply. Waiting for a moment, the man gathered from the expression of his countenance that his mind was unconvinced. Turning very abruptly, he said, "Well Mr. President, I see that you are fully determined not to do me justice!" This was too aggravating even for Mr. Lincoln. Manifesting, however, no more feeling than that indicated by a slight compression of the lips, he very quietly arose, laid down a package of papers he held in his hand, and then suddenly seizing the defunct officer by the coat collar, he marched him forcibly to the door, saying as he ejected him into the passage, "Sir, I give you fair warning never to show yourself in this room again. I can bear censure, but not insult!" In a whining tone the man begged for his papers which he had dropped. "Begone, sir," said the President, "Your papers will be sent to you. I never wish to see your face again!"

Late one afternoon a lady with two gentlemen were admitted. She had come to ask that her husband, who was a prisoner of war, might be permitted to take the oath and be released from confinement. To secure a degree of interest on the part of the President, one of the gentlemen claimed to be an acquaintance of Mrs. Lincoln; this however received but little attention, and the President proceeded to ask what position the lady's husband held in the rebel service. "Oh," said she, "he was a captain." "A *captain*," rejoined Mr. Lincoln, "indeed, rather too big a fish to set free simply upon his taking the oath! If he was an officer, it is proof positive that he has been a zealous rebel; I can not release him." Here the lady's friend reiterated the assertion of his acquaintance with Mrs. Lincoln. Instantly the President's hand was upon the bell-rope. The usher in attendance answered the summons. "Cornelius, take this man's name to Mrs. Lincoln, and ask her what she knows of him?" The boy presently returned with the reply that "*the Madam*" (as she was called by the servants) knew nothing of him whatever. "It is just as I suspected," said the President. The party made one more attempt to enlist his sympathy, but without effect. "It is of no use," was the reply. "I can not release him!" and the trio withdrew in high displeasure.

One day the Hon. Thaddeus Stevens called with an elderly lady, in great trouble, whose son had been in the army, but for some offence had been court-martialed, and sentenced either to death or imprisonment at hard labor for a long term, I do not recollect which. There were some

extenuating circumstances, and after a full hearing the President turned
to the representative and said: "Mr. Stevens, do you think this is a case
which will warrant my interference?" "With my knowledge of the facts
and the parties," was the reply, "I should have no hesitation in granting
a pardon." "Then," returned Mr. Lincoln, "I will pardon him," and he
proceeded forthwith to execute the paper. The gratitude of the mother
was too deep for expression, save by her tears, and not a word was said
between her and Mr. Stevens until they were half way down the stairs
on their passage out, when she suddenly broke forth in an excited manner with the words, "I knew it was a copperhead LIE!" "What do you
refer to, madam?" asked Mr. Stevens. "Why, they told me he was an *ugly*
looking man," she replied with vehemence. "He is the *handsomest* man I
ever saw in my life!" And surely for that mother, and for many another,
throughout the land, no carved statue of ancient or modern art, in all
its symmetry, ever can have the charm which will forevermore encircle
that care-worn but gentle face, expressing as was never expressed before,
"MALICE TOWARD NONE—CHARITY FOR ALL."

Never shall I forget the scene early one morning, when, with the
help of some of the workmen and special police at the capitol, the large
painting upon which I was engaged during the six months I was with
Mr. Lincoln, representing the President and cabinet in council on the
Emancipation Proclamation, was first lifted to a place, temporarily, in
the Rotunda. Shortly after it was fixed in its position over the northern
door leading to the Senate, a ray of sunshine came struggling in from the
upper part of the great dome, and fell directly upon the face and head
of the beloved President, leaving all the rest of the picture in shadow.
"Look!" exclaimed one of the policemen, pointing to the canvass, in a
burst of enthusiasm, "that is as it should be, God bless him; may the sun
shine upon his head for ever!"

My attention has been two or three times called to a paragraph now
going the rounds of the newspapers concerning a singular apparition of
himself in a looking glass, which Mr. Lincoln is stated to have seen on
the day he was first nominated at Chicago. The story as told is quite in-
correct, and is made to appear very mysterious, and believing that the
taste for the supernatural is sufficiently ministered unto, without per-
verting the facts, I will tell the story as the President told it to John Hay,
the assistant private secretary, and myself. We were in his room together

about dark the evening of the Baltimore Convention. The gas had just been lighted, and he had been telling us how he had that afternoon received the news of the nomination of Andrew Johnson, for Vice President before he heard of his own.

It seemed that the dispatch announcing his re-nomination had been sent to his office from the War department, while he was at lunch. Directly afterward, without going back to the official chamber, he proceeded to the War department. While there the telegram came, announcing the nomination of Johnson. "What," said he to the operator, "do they nominate a Vice President before they do a President?" "Why," replied the astonished official, "have you not heard of your own nomination? It was sent to the White House two hours ago." "It is all right," replied the President, "I shall probably find it on my return."

Laughing pleasantly over this incident, he said, soon afterward, "a very singular occurrence took place the day I was nominated at Chicago four years ago, which I am reminded of to-night. In the afternoon of the day, returning home from down town, I went up stairs to Mrs. Lincoln's sitting room. Feeling somewhat tired I laid down upon a couch in the room directly opposite a bureau upon which was a looking glass. As I reclined, my eye fell upon the glass and I saw distinctly *two* images of myself, exactly alike, except that one was a little paler than the other. I arose, and laid down again with the same result. It made me quite uncomfortable for a few moments, but some friends coming in, the matter passed out of my mind. The next day while walking in the street, I was suddenly reminded of the circumstance, and the disagreeable sensation produced by it returned. I had never seen any thing of the kind before, and did not know what to make of it. I determined to go home and place myself in the same position, and if the same effect was produced, I would make up my mind that it was the natural result of some principle of refraction or optics, which I did not understand, and dismiss it. I tried the experiment with the same result, and as I had said to myself, accounting for it on some principle unknown to me, it ceased to trouble me." "But," said he, "sometime ago, I tried to produce the same effect *here*, by arranging a glass and couch in the same position, without success." He did not say, as is asserted in the story as printed, that either he or Mrs. Lincoln attached any omen to it whatever. Neither did he say that the double reflection was seen while he was walking about the room. On the contrary it was only visible in a certain position and at a certain angle, and therefore he thought could be accounted for upon scientific principles. I have mentioned this story only to show upon what a slender foundation a marvelous account may be built!

At one of the "levees," a year ago last winter, during a lull in the hand-shaking, he was addressed by two familiar lady friends, one of whom is now the wife of a member of the cabinet. Turning to them with a weary air, he remarked that it was a relief to have now and then those to talk to, who had no favors to ask. The lady referred to is a strong radical—a New Yorker by birth—but for many years a resident with her husband at the West. She replied, playfully, "Mr. President, I *have* one request to make." "Ah!" said he at once, looking grave; "well, what is it?" "That you suppress the infamous ⸺ ⸺" (mentioning a prominent Western journal) was the rejoinder. After a brief pause, Mr. Lincoln asked her if she had ever tried to imagine how she would have felt, in some former administration to which she was opposed, if her favorite newspaper had been seized by the government and suppressed. The lady replied that it was not a parallel case, that in circumstances like those then existing, when the nation was struggling for its very life, such utterances as were daily put forth in that journal, should be suppressed by the strong hand of authority; that the cause of loyalty and good government demanded it. "I fear you do not fully comprehend," returned the President, "the danger of abridging the *liberties* of the people. Nothing but the very sternest necessity can ever justify it. A government had better go to the very extreme of toleration, than to do aught that could be construed into an interference with, or to jeopardize in any degree the common rights of its citizens."

One more example of the exercise of the pardoning power, will conclude this brief sketch. It may excite a smile, as well as a tear; but it may be relied upon as a veritable relation of what actually transpired. A distinguished citizen of Ohio had an appointment with the President one evening at six o'clock. As he entered the vestibule of the White House, his attention was attracted by a poorly-clad young woman who was violently sobbing. He asked her the cause of her distress. She said that she had been ordered away by the servants, after vainly waiting many hours to see the President about her only brother, who had been condemned to death. Her story was this: She and her brother were foreigners, and orphans. They had been in this country several years. Her brother enlisted in the army, but, through bad influences, was induced to desert. He was captured, tried and sentenced to be shot—the old story. The poor girl had obtained the signatures of some persons who had formerly known him, to a petition for a pardon, and, alone, had come to Washington to lay the case before the President. Thronged as the waiting rooms always were, she had passed the long hours of two days trying in vain to get an audience, and had at length been ordered away.

The gentleman's feelings were touched. He said to her that he had come to see the President, but did not know as *he* should succeed. He told her, however, to follow him up stairs and he would see what could be done for her. Just before reaching the door Mr. Lincoln came out, and meeting his friend said good humoredly, "Are you not ahead of time?" The gentleman showed him his watch with the hand upon the hour of six. "Well," returned Mr. Lincoln, "I have been so busy to-day that I have not had time to get a lunch. Go in, and sit down, I will be back directly."

The gentleman made the young woman accompany him into the office, and when they were seated, said to her, "Now my good girl, I want you to muster all the courage you have in the world. When the President comes back, he will sit down in that arm-chair. I shall get up to speak to him, and as I do so, you must force yourself between us, and insist upon his examination of your papers, telling him it is a case of life and death, and admits of no delay." These instructions were carried out to the letter. Mr. Lincoln was at first somewhat surprised at the apparent forwardness of the young woman, but observing her distressed appearance, he ceased conversation with his friend, and commenced an examination of the document she had placed in his hands. Glancing from it to the face of the petitioner, whose tears had broken forth afresh, he studied its expression for a moment and then his eye fell upon her scanty, but neat dress. Instantly his face lighted up. "My poor girl," said he, "you have come here with no governor, or senator or member of congress, to plead your cause. You seem honest and truthful; *and you don't wear hoops*—and I will be whipped, but I will pardon your brother."

Thomas MacKellar

Good Friday, April 14, 1865

A partner in a highly successful Philadelphia type foundry, Thomas MacKellar (1812–1899) was also the editor of the trade journal *Typographic Advertiser* and the author of three volumes of poetry: *Droppings from the Heart* (1844), *Tam's Fortnight Rambles* (1847), and *Lines for the Gentle and Loving* (1853). His eulogy for Lincoln appeared in the April–June 1865 number of the *Typographic Advertiser*.

THIS day has taken its place among days that will never be forgotten while admiration of exalted virtue and detestation of atrocious crime shall thrill the heart of mankind. Good Friday has long been observed in commemoration of that crime of all crimes, the judicial murder of the SON OF THE HIGHEST; and sacred religious sorrow attaches to the day. If any event could invest it with additional pathos and horror, it would be the unprovoked assassination of a ruler like *Abraham Lincoln*, whose character had won the love of the patriotic and the good in all the world. Thought is astounded, and language fails to express the atrociousness of an act so devilish. A pall of darkness, as fearful as if the midnoon sun had been suddenly blotted out, fell on the hearts of all good men when the dreadful announcement was made that our clement, gentle-hearted, and manly-minded President had been vilely slain; and sorrow filled the land. The mechanic and the merchant ceased toiling, and the money-changer was idle. Woman wept, and man cursed the assassin, or knit his brow and was silent. The nation stood still for a time. Religion looked up to God, and said, "The Lord reigns! God is our refuge and strength, a very present help in trouble;" and a spirit of strength and self-control fell upon the people. No anarchy, no convulsion; but a calm, stern determination that law and order should be observed, and justice be fairly meted out. Men of all parties almost universally felt alike; and unity such as the nation had scarcely ever known knit it together almost as one. Political opponents, recanting in effect stump lampoon and electioneering tirade, wrote eulogies eloquent and unequalled; and honours never surpassed were paid to the remains and memory of one who, sprung from

the common people, proved himself the equal of the noblest and purest
that ever sat upon an hereditary throne.

> So deep our grief, it may be silence is
>   The meetest tribute to the father's name:
> A secret shrine in every breast is his,
>   Whom death hath girt with an immortal fame:
> And in this dim recess our thoughts abide,
>   Clad in the garment of unspoken grief,
> As fain the sorrow of the heart to hide
>   That yields no tears to give our wo relief.
> "But death is not to such as he," we sigh,
>   "His heart is still—his pulse may beat no more;
> Yet men so good and loved do never die,
>   But while the tide shall flow upon the shore
> Of time to come, a presence to the eye
>   Of nations shall he be, and evermore
> Shall freemen treasure in historic page
> The martyr-hero of earth's noblest age."

Julia Ward Howe

"Crown his blood-stained pillow"

Julia Ward Howe (1819–1910) co-edited the Boston antislavery newspaper *The Commonwealth* in the early 1850s and published two volumes of poetry and a travel book about Cuba before the Civil War. Her most famous poem, "The Battle-Hymn of the Republic," inspired by a visit to a Union army encampment near Washington, appeared in February 1862. Howe met Lincoln only once, when Senator Charles Sumner and Massachusetts Governor John A. Andrew introduced her to the President at the White House in November 1862. Her poem honoring the slain President was published in the summer of 1865 in *Poetical Tributes to the Memory of Abraham Lincoln*.

Crown his blood-stained pillow
   With a victor's palm;
Life's receding billow
   Leaves eternal calm.

At the feet Almighty
   Lay this gift sincere;
Of a purpose weighty,
   And a record clear.

With deliverance freighted
   Was this passive hand,
And this heart, high-fated,
   Would with love command.

Let him rest serenely
   In a Nation's care,
Where her waters queenly
   Make the West most fair.

In the greenest meadow
   That the prairies show,

Let his marble's shadow
   Give all men to know:

"Our First Hero, living,
   Made his country free;
Heed the Second's giving,
   Death for Liberty."

1865

Phoebe Cary

Our Sun Hath Gone Down

Phoebe Cary (1824–1871) and her older sister Alice (1820–1871) published their first volume of poems together in 1850. The following year Phoebe left Ohio and joined Alice in New York City, where they continued writing and presided over a salon frequented by Horace Greeley, John Greenleaf Whittier, Elizabeth Cady Stanton, and P. T. Barnum. When the London magazine *Punch* expressed contrition for its earlier mockery of Lincoln (see pp. 298–300 in this volume), Alice Cary expressed her disdain in verse ("What need hath he now of a tardy crown, / His name from mocking jest and sneer to save? / When every ploughman turns his furrow down / As soft as though it fell upon his grave"). Phoebe Cary also eulogized the slain president, comparing the nation in its mourning to Rizpah, the bereaved mother in 2 Samuel 21.

Our sun hath gone down at the noonday,
   The heavens are black;
And over the morning the shadows
   Of night-time are back.

Stop the proud boasting mouth of the cannon,
   Hush the mirth and the shout;—
God is God! and the ways of Jehovah
   Are past finding out.

Lo! the beautiful feet on the mountains,
   That yesterday stood;
The white feet that came with glad tidings,
   Are dabbled in blood.

The Nation that firmly was settling
   The crown on her head,
Sits, like Rizpah, in sackcloth and ashes,
   And watches her dead.

Who is dead? who, unmoved by our wailing,
   Is lying so low?

O, my Land, stricken dumb in your anguish,
    Do you feel, do you know,

That the hand which reached out of the darkness
    Hath taken the whole?
Yea, the arm and the head of the people—
    The heart and the soul!

And that heart, o'er whose dread awful silence
    A nation has wept;
Was the truest, and gentlest, and sweetest,
    A man ever kept!

Once this good man, we mourn, overwearied,
    Worn, anxious, oppressed,
Was going out from his audience chamber
    For a season to rest;

Unheeding the thousands who waited
    To honor and greet,
When the cry of a child smote upon him,
    And turned back his feet.

"Three days hath a woman been waiting,"
    Said they, "patient and meek."
And he answered, "Whatever her errand,
    Let me hear; let her speak!"

So she came, and stood trembling before him,
    And pleaded her cause;
Told him all; how her child's erring father
    Had broken the laws.

Humbly spake she: "I mourn for his folly,
    His weakness, his fall;"
Proudly spake she: "he is not a TRAITOR,
    And I love him through all!"

Then the great man, whose heart had been shaken
   By a little babe's cry;
Answered soft, taking counsel of mercy,
   "This man shall not die!"

Why, he heard from the dungeons, the rice-fields,
   The dark holds of ships;
Every faint, feeble cry which oppression
   Smothered down on men's lips.

In her furnace, the centuries had welded
   Their fetter and chain;
And like withes, in the hands of his purpose,
   He snapped them in twain.

Who can be what he was to the people;
   What he was to the State?
Shall the ages bring to us another
   As good, and as great?

Our hearts with their anguish are broken,
   Our wet eyes are dim;
For us is the loss and the sorrow,
   The triumph for him!

For, ere this, face to face with his Father
   Our Martyr hath stood;
Giving into his hand the white record,
   With its great seal of blood!

Mary A. Denison

To Mrs. Lincoln

Mary A. Denison (1826–1911) distinguished herself among those who mourned Lincoln in verse by addressing her poem to the grief-stricken First Lady. A prolific writer of fiction and journalistic sketches under her own name and the pennames Clara Vance and N. I. Edson, Denison published *Edna Etheril, the Boston Seamstress*, the first of her sixty novels, in 1847. Largely forgotten for most of the twentieth century, she has recently received favorable attention for her antislavery novel *Old Hepsy* (1858), a tragic story of miscegenation, incest, and murder stemming from an illicit affair between a white woman and a mixed-race man.

———————————

If it be any joy to know
That a whole nation mourns thy woe;
That clasped hands and bowed down head
Bear witness for the mighty dead;
That he was loved as ne'er before
A chief in peace or chief in war;
Take this one drop of balm—and less
By that thy draught of bitterness!

If it be any joy to feel
That thine is now the nation's weal;
That every home would gladly be
A shelter, and a shrine for thee;
That every heart throbs high to make
Some sacrifice for his dear sake:
Take this one thought of comfort,—less
May be thy draught of bitterness.

If it be any joy to see
One glimpse of thy high destiny,
As she who wore a martyr's love—
And wears an angel's now, above—
As she who felt the throbs that swelled
That heart, by hearts of millions knelled:

Take this sweet sympathy—and less
By that thy draught of bitterness!

Oh! wife of our dear patriot—see—
Our land sheds tear for tear with thee;
Yet, widow of the nation! God
Speaks to thee, through the broken sod;
"I am thy God— thou yet shall see
It was not death, but victory!
And even now my love shall bless
And drain thy cup of bitterness."

James Russell Lowell

FROM *Ode Recited at the Harvard Commemoration*

A poet, literary critic, magazine editor, and professor of Romance languages at Harvard, James Russell Lowell (1819–1891) admired and often praised Lincoln while occasionally dealing out sharp criticism as well. When Harvard held a Commemoration Day to honor its Union veterans and war dead, Lowell, who had lost three nephews in the conflict, was asked to compose and recite an ode for the occasion. Shortly after the July 21 ceremony, he added a canto about the fallen president; it first appeared when the Commemoration Ode was published in the September 1865 *Atlantic Monthly* to wide acclaim.

VI

Such was he, our Martyr-Chief,
  Whom late the Nation he had led,
  With ashes on her head,
Wept with the passion of an angry grief:
Forgive me, if from present things I turn
To speak what in my heart will beat and burn,
And hang my wreath on his world-honored urn.
    Nature, they say, doth dote,
    And cannot make a man
    Save on some worn-out plan,
    Repeating us by rote:
For him her Old World moulds aside she threw,
    And, choosing sweet clay from the breast
    Of the unexhausted West,
With stuff untainted shaped a hero new,
Wise, steadfast in the strength of God, and true.
    How beautiful to see
Once more a shepherd of mankind indeed,
Who loved his charge, but never loved to lead;
One whose meek flock the people joyed to be,
    Not lured by any cheat of birth,
    But by his clear-grained human worth,
And brave old wisdom of sincerity!

They knew that outward grace is dust;
They could not choose but trust
In that sure-footed mind's unfaltering skill,
    And supple-tempered will
That bent like perfect steel to spring again and thrust.
  His was no lonely mountain-peak of mind,
  Thrusting to thin air o'er our cloudy bars,
  A sea-mark now, now lost in vapors blind;
  Broad prairie rather, genial, level-lined,
  Fruitful and friendly for all human kind,
Yet also nigh to Heaven and loved of loftiest stars.
    Nothing of Europe here,
Or, then, of Europe fronting mornward still,
    Ere any names of Serf and Peer
  Could Nature's equal scheme deface;
  Here was a type of the true elder race,
And one of Plutarch's men talked with us face to face.
  I praise him not; it were too late;
And some innative weakness there must be
In him who condescends to victory
Such as the Present gives, and cannot wait,
  Safe in himself as in a fate.
    So always firmly he:
    He knew to bide his time,
    And can his fame abide,
Still patient in his simple faith sublime,
    Till the wise years decide.
  Great captains, with their guns and drums,
    Disturb our judgment for the hour,
    But at last silence comes;
  These all are gone, and, standing like a tower,
  Our children shall behold his fame,
    The kindly-earnest, brave, foreseeing man,
Sagacious, patient, dreading praise, not blame,
  New birth of our new soil, the first American.

1865

Walt Whitman

Hush'd Be the Camps To-Day
When Lilacs Last in the Dooryard Bloom'd
O Captain! My Captain!

The poet Walt Whitman (1819–1892) spent much of the Civil War in Washington, visiting wounded soldiers in hospitals while working as a government clerk. Although he never met Lincoln, Whitman saw him in the streets on numerous occasions and studied him closely, writing in August 1863 about his "dark brown face, with the deep cut lines, the eyes, &c., always to me with a deep latent sadness in the expression." On April 15 news of the assassination reached Whitman while he was visiting his family in Brooklyn. "Lincoln's death—black, black, black," he wrote in a notebook, and then observed the expressions of people he saw on the streets, a "strange mixture of horror, fury, tenderness, & a stirring wonder brewing." Within days he wrote "Hush'd Be the Camps To-Day" and added it to the proofs of *Drum-Taps*, his first collection of new poems since 1860. Believing that his poetic treatment of the war was incomplete without further engagement with Lincoln's death, Whitman had only one hundred copies of *Drum-Taps* issued in May, holding back an additional four hundred copies while he composed a lengthy elegy for the slain President. "When Lilacs Last in the Dooryard Bloom'd" and the more conventional—and hugely popular—"O Captain! My Captain!" appeared in *Sequel to Drum-Taps*, a collection of eighteen poems that was bound together with the second issue of *Drum-Taps* and published on October 28, 1865. (The texts of the poems presented here are taken from the 1881 edition of *Leaves of Grass* and incorporate Whitman's final revisions.)

Hush'd be the Camps To-Day
(MAY, 1865.)

Hush'd be the camps to-day,
And soldiers let us drape our war-worn weapons,
And each with musing soul retire to celebrate,
Our dear commander's death.

No more for him life's stormy conflicts,
Nor victory, nor defeat—no more time's dark events,
Charging like ceaseless clouds across the sky.

But sing poet in our name,
Sing of the love we bore him—because you, dweller in camps,
    know it truly.

As they invault the coffin there,
Sing—as they close the doors of earth upon him—one verse,
For the heavy hearts of soldiers.

When Lilacs Last in The Dooryard Bloom'd

1

When lilacs last in the dooryard bloom'd,
And the great star early droop'd in the western sky in the night,
I mourn'd, and yet shall mourn with ever-returning spring.

Ever-returning spring, trinity sure to me you bring,
Lilac blooming perennial and drooping star in the west,
And thought of him I love.

2

O powerful western fallen star!
O shades of night—O moody, tearful night!
O great star disappear'd—O the black murk that hides the star!
O cruel hands that hold me powerless—O helpless soul of me!
O harsh surrounding cloud that will not free my soul.

3

In the dooryard fronting an old farm-house near the
    white-wash'd palings,
Stands the lilac-bush tall-growing with heart-shaped leaves of
    rich green,
With many a pointed blossom rising delicate, with the
    perfume strong I love,
With every leaf a miracle—and from this bush in the
    dooryard,

With delicate-color'd blossoms and heart-shaped leaves of
    rich green,
A sprig with its flower I break.

4

In the swamp in secluded recesses,
A shy and hidden bird is warbling a song.

Solitary the thrush,
The hermit withdrawn to himself, avoiding the settlements,
Sings by himself a song.
Song of the bleeding throat,
Death's outlet song of life, (for well dear brother I know,
If thou wast not granted to sing thou would'st surely die.)

5

Over the breast of the spring, the land, amid cities,
Amid lanes and through old woods, where lately the violets
    peep'd from the ground, spotting the gray debris,
Amid the grass in the fields each side of the lanes, passing the
    endless grass,
Passing the yellow-spear'd wheat, every grain from its shroud
    in the dark-brown fields uprisen,
Passing the apple-tree blows of white and pink in the
    orchards,
Carrying a corpse to where it shall rest in the grave,
Night and day journeys a coffin.

6

Coffin that passes through lanes and streets,
Through day and night with the great cloud darkening the
    land,
With the pomp of the inloop'd flags with the cities draped in
    black,
With the show of the States themselves as of crape-veil'd
    women standing,

With processions long and winding and the flambeaus of the
    night,
With the countless torches lit, with the silent sea of faces and
    the unbared heads,
With the waiting depot, the arriving coffin, and the sombre
    faces,
With dirges through the night, with the thousand voices
    rising strong and solemn,
With all the mournful voices of the dirges pour'd around the
    coffin,
The dim-lit churches and the shuddering organs—where
    amid these you journey,
With the tolling tolling bells' perpetual clang,
Here, coffin that slowly passes,
I give you my sprig of lilac.

                              7
(Nor for you, for one alone,
Blossoms and branches green to coffins all I bring,
For fresh as the morning, thus would I chant a song for you
    O sane and sacred death.

All over bouquets of roses,
O death, I cover you over with roses and early lilies,
But mostly and now the lilac that blooms the first,
Copious I break, I break the sprigs from the bushes,
With loaded arms I come, pouring for you,
For you and the coffins all of you O death.)

                              8
O western orb sailing the heaven,
Now I know what you must have meant as a month since I
    walk'd,
As I walk'd in silence the transparent shadowy night,
As I saw you had something to tell as you bent to me night
    after night,

As you droop'd from the sky low down as if to my side,
  (while the other stars all look'd on,)
As we wander'd together the solemn night, (for something I
  know not what kept me from sleep,)
As the night advanced, and I saw on the rim of the west how
  full you were of woe,
As I stood on the rising ground in the breeze in the cool
  transparent night,
As I watch'd where you pass'd and was lost in the netherward
  black of the night,
As my soul in its trouble dissatisfied sank, as where you sad
  orb,
Concluded, dropt in the night, and was gone.

9

Sing on there in the swamp,
O singer bashful and tender, I hear your notes, I hear your call,
I hear, I come presently, I understand you,
But a moment I linger, for the lustrous star has detain'd me,
The star my departing comrade holds and detains me.

10

O how shall I warble myself for the dead one there I loved?
And how shall I deck my song for the large sweet soul that
  has gone?
And what shall my perfume be for the grave of him I love?

Sea-winds blown from east and west,
Blown from the Eastern sea and blown from the Western sea,
  till there on the prairies meeting,
These and with these and the breath of my chant,
I'll perfume the grave of him I love.

11

O what shall I hang on the chamber walls?
And what shall the pictures be that I hang on the walls,
To adorn the burial-house of him I love?

Pictures of growing spring and farms and homes,
With the Fourth-month eve at sundown, and the gray smoke
lucid and bright,
With floods of the yellow gold of the gorgeous, indolent,
sinking sun, burning, expanding the air,
With the fresh sweet herbage under foot, and the pale green
leaves of the trees prolific,
In the distance the flowing glaze, the breast of the river, with
a wind-dapple here and there,
With ranging hills on the banks, with many a line against the
sky, and shadows,
And the city at hand with dwellings so dense, and stacks of
chimneys,
And all the scenes of life and the workshops, and the
workmen homeward returning.

12

Lo, body and soul—this land,
My own Manhattan with spires, and the sparkling and
hurrying tides, and the ships,
The varied and ample land, the South and the North in the
light, Ohio's shores and flashing Missouri,
And ever the far-spreading prairies cover'd with grass and
corn.

Lo, the most excellent sun so calm and haughty,
The violet and purple morn with just-felt breezes,
The gentle soft-born measureless light,
The miracle spreading bathing all, the fulfill'd noon,
The coming eve delicious, the welcome night and the stars,
Over my cities shining all, enveloping man and land.

13

Sing on, sing on you gray-brown bird,
Sing from the swamps, the recesses, pour your chant from the
bushes,
Limitless out of the dusk, out of the cedars and pines.

Sing on dearest brother, warble your reedy song,
Loud human song, with voice of uttermost woe.

O liquid and free and tender!
O wild and loose to my soul—O wondrous singer!
You only I hear—yet the star holds me, (but will soon depart,)
Yet the lilac with mastering odor holds me.

14

Now while I sat in the day and look'd forth,
In the close of the day with its light and the fields of spring,
    and the farmers preparing their crops,
In the large unconscious scenery of my land with its lakes and
    forests,
In the heavenly aerial beauty, (after the perturb'd winds and
    the storms,)
Under the arching heavens of the afternoon swift passing,
    and the voices of children and women,
The many-moving sea-tides, and I saw the ships how they sail'd,
And the summer approaching with richness, and the fields all
    busy with labor,
And the infinite separate houses, how they all went on, each
    with its meals and minutia of daily usages,
And the streets how their throbbings throbb'd, and the cities
    pent—lo, then and there,
Falling upon them all and among them all, enveloping me
    with the rest,
Appear'd the cloud, appear'd the long black trail,
And I knew death, its thought, and the sacred knowledge of
    death.

Then with the knowledge of death as walking one side of me,
And the thought of death close-walking the other side of me,
And I in the middle as with companions, and as holding the
    hands of companions,
I fled forth to the hiding receiving night that talks not,

Down to the shores of the water, the path by the swamp in
     the dimness,
To the solemn shadowy cedars and ghostly pines so still.

And the singer so shy to the rest receiv'd me,
The gray-brown bird I know receiv'd us comrades three,
And he sang the carol of death, and a verse for him I love.

From deep secluded recesses,
From the fragrant cedars and the ghostly pines so still,
Came the carol of the bird.

And the charm of the carol rapt me,
As I held as if by their hands my comrades in the night,
And the voice of my spirit tallied the song of the bird.

Come lovely and soothing death,
Undulate round the world, serenely arriving, arriving,
In the day, in the night, to all, to each,
Sooner or later delicate death.

Prais'd be the fathomless universe,
For life and joy, and for objects and knowledge curious,
And for love, sweet love—but praise! praise! praise!
For the sure-enwinding arms of cool-enfolding death.

Dark mother always gliding near with soft feet,
Have none chanted for thee a chant of fullest welcome?
Then I chant it for thee, I glorify thee above all,
I bring thee a song that when thou must indeed come, come
     unfalteringly.

Approach strong deliveress,
When it is so, when thou hast taken them I joyously sing the dead,
Lost in the loving floating ocean of thee,
Laved in the flood of thy bliss O death.

From me to thee glad serenades,
Dances for thee I propose saluting thee, adornments and feastings
for thee,
And the sights of the open landscape and the high-spread sky are
fitting,
And life and the fields, and the huge and thoughtful night.

The night in silence under many a star,
The ocean shore and the husky whispering wave whose voice I know,
And the soul turning to thee O vast and well-veil'd death,
And the body gratefully nestling close to thee.

Over the tree-tops I float thee a song,
Over the rising and sinking waves, over the myriad fields and the
prairies wide,
Over the dense-pack'd cities all and the teeming wharves and ways,
I float this carol with joy, with joy to thee O death.

15

To the tally of my soul,
Loud and strong kept up the gray-brown bird,
With pure deliberate notes spreading filling the night.

Loud in the pines and cedars dim,
Clear in the freshness moist and the swamp-perfume,
And I with my comrades there in the night.

While my sight that was bound in my eyes unclosed,
As to long panoramas of visions.

And I saw askant the armies,
I saw as in noiseless dreams hundreds of battle-flags,
Borne through the smoke of the battles and pierc'd with
missiles I saw them,
And carried hither and yon through the smoke, and torn and
bloody,

And at last but a few shreds left on the staffs, (and all in
    silence,)
And the staffs all splinter'd and broken.

I saw battle-corpses, myriads of them,
And the white skeletons of young men, I saw them,
I saw the debris and debris of all the slain soldiers of the war,
But I saw they were not as was thought,
They themselves were fully at rest, they suffer'd not,
The living remain'd and suffer'd, the mother suffer'd,
And the wife and the child and the musing comrade suffer'd,
And the armies that remain'd suffer'd.

16

Passing the visions, passing the night,
Passing, unloosing the hold of my comrades' hands,
Passing the song of the hermit bird and the tallying song of
    my soul,
Victorious song, death's outlet song, yet varying ever-altering
    song,
As low and wailing, yet clear the notes, rising and falling,
    flooding the night,
Sadly sinking and fainting, as warning and warning, and yet
    again bursting with joy,
Covering the earth and filling the spread of the heaven,
As that powerful psalm in the night I heard from recesses,
Passing, I leave thee lilac with heart-shaped leaves,
I leave thee there in the door-yard, blooming, returning with
    spring.

I cease from my song for thee,
From my gaze on thee in the west, fronting the west,
    communing with thee,
O comrade lustrous with silver face in the night.

Yet each to keep and all, retrievements out of the night,

The song, the wondrous chant of the gray-brown bird,
And the tallying chant, the echo arous'd in my soul,
With the lustrous and drooping star with the countenance
    full of woe,
With the holders holding my hand nearing the call of the bird,
Comrades mine and I in the midst, and their memory ever to
    keep, for the dead I loved so well,
For the sweetest, wisest soul of all my days and lands—and
    this for his dear sake,
Lilac and star and bird twined with the chant of my soul,
There in the fragrant pines and the cedars dusk and dim.

O Captain! My Captain!

O Captain! my Captain! our fearful trip is done,
The ship has weather'd every rack, the prize we sought is won,
The port is near, the bells I hear, the people all exulting,
While follow eyes the steady keel, the vessel grim and daring;
    But O heart! heart! heart!
        O the bleeding drops of red,
            Where on the deck my Captain lies,
                Fallen cold and dead.

O Captain! my Captain! rise up and hear the bells;
Rise up—for you the flag is flung—for you the bugle trills,
For you bouquets and ribbon'd wreaths—for you the shores
    a-crowding,
For you they call, the swaying mass, their eager faces turning;
    Here Captain! dear father!
        This arm beneath your head!
            It is some dream that on the deck,
                You've fallen cold and dead.

My Captain does not answer, his lips are pale and still,
My father does not feel my arm, he has no pulse nor will,

The ship is anchor'd safe and sound, its voyage closed and
   done,
From fearful trip the victor ship comes in with object won;
     Exult O shores, and ring O bells!
      But I with mournful tread,
        Walk the deck my Captain lies,
          Fallen cold and dead.

Mary Lincoln

Letter to Francis B. Carpenter

Despite her grief-stricken seclusion in the White House in the weeks following the assassination, Mary Lincoln (1818–1882) had been able to successfully exert her will in a dispute over her husband's burial. As the funeral train neared Illinois, a committee of prominent Springfield citizens pressed to have Lincoln interred in a specially built tomb in the middle of the city. She refused, insisting that he be buried in Oak Ridge Cemetery and threatening to have his body moved to Chicago if her wishes were ignored. Mary Lincoln finally left the White House on May 22. Unable to bear the prospect of returning to her home in Springfield, she moved into a series of Chicago hotels with her sons Robert and Tad. In November 1865, she wrote to the artist Francis B. Carpenter, who had been commissioned by a New York publisher to paint a portrait of the Lincoln family in 1861, before the death of Willie Lincoln. She sent Carpenter a picture along with a surprisingly intimate recollection of her last carriage ride with her husband. Although Mary Lincoln would later praise Carpenter's family portrait, in 1867 she became angry when his memoir *Six Months at the White House* was retitled *The Inner Life of Abraham Lincoln* and dismissed him as "this *stranger*," a "silly adventurer" who had "scarcely" known the President at all.

Chicago Nov 15th

My Dear Sir:

Your last letter, has been received—It would be utterly impossible for me, in my present nervous state, to sit for a photograph—although, I should like to oblige you, very much. There is an excellent painted likeness of me, at Brady's in N.Y. taken in *1861*—have you, ever seen it? I am sure you will like it & I believe, it was taken, in a black velvet. I enclose you one of my precious, sainted Willie. You have doubtless heard, how *very* handsome a boy, he was considered—with a pure, gentle nature, always unearthly & in intellect *far, far* beyond his years—When I reflect, as I am always doing, upon the overwhelming loss, of that, *most* idolized boy, and the crushing blow, that deprived me, of my *all in all*, in this life, I wonder that I retain my reason & live. There are hours of each day, that my mind, cannot be brought to realize, that *He*, who is considered, so great and good, a God, has *thus* seen fit to afflict us! How difficult it is to be reconciled to such a bereavement, how much sooner, each one, of our

356

stricken family, if the choice had been left to us, would have preferred "passing away," ourselves.

It strikes me strangely, how such a rumor, should be circulated— that Robert is in Europe. The thought of leaving home, I am sure, has never *once*, entered his mind. He is diligently applying himself, to his law studies—a most devoted Son & brother. Every thing is *so fabulously* high *here*, that his third of the estate, an income of $1800 apiece—with taxes deducted—It requires the most rigid economy, with Robert & the rest of us to clothe ourselves, plainly & weekly settle our board-bills. Is not this, a sad change for us! As a matter of course living, every where, *now* in the U.S. is high—Yet I cannot express to you, how painful to me, it is, to have *no* quiet home, where I can freely indulge my sorrows—*this*, *is* yet another of the crosses, appointed unto me. With my beloved husband, I should have had, a heart, for any fate, if "need be." Dear little Taddie! was named, for my husband's father, Thomas Lincoln—no *T*—for a middle name—was *nicknamed, Taddie*, by his loving Father. Taddie—is learning to be as diligent in his studies, as he used to be *at play* in the W. H. he appears to be rapidly making up, for the great amount of time, he lost in W— As you are aware, *he* was always a *marked character*. Two or three weeks since, a lady in an adjoining room, gave him, a copy of Mr Raymond's life of the President, for me to read & return to her. After reading it, I remarked to Robert, in Taddie's presence, that it was *the most* correct history, of his Father, that has been written—Taddie immediately spoke up & said, "Mother, I am going to save, all the little money, you give me and get one of them." R. told him, he need not, as he would buy, a copy. I press the poor little fellow closer, *if possible*, to my heart, in memory of the sainted Father, who loved *him*, *so very dearly*, as well as the rest of us—How I wish you could have seen my dear husband, the last three weeks of his life! Having a realizing sense, that the unnatural rebellion, was near its close, & being most of the time, *away* from W, where he had endured such conflicts of mind, within the last four years, feeling *so encouraged*, he freely gave vent to his cheerfulness. Down the Potomac, he was almost boyish, in his mirth & reminded me, of his original nature, what I had always remembered of him, in our own home—free from care, surrounded by those he loved so well & *by whom*, he was so idolized. *The Friday*, I never saw him so supremely cheerful—his manner was even playful. At three o'clock, in the afternoon, he drove out with

me in the open carriage, in starting, I asked him, if any one, should accompany us, he immediately replied—"No—I prefer to ride by ourselves
to day." During the drive he was so gay, that I said to him, laughingly,
"Dear Husband, you almost startle me by your great cheerfulness," he
replied, "and well I may feel so, Mary, I consider *this day*, the war, has
come to a close—and then added, "We must *both*, be more cheerful in the
future—between the war & the loss of our darling Willie—we have both,
been very miserable." Every word, then uttered, is deeply engraven, on
my poor broken heart. In the evening, his mind, was fixed upon having
some relaxation & bent on the theater. Yet I firmly believe, that if he
had remained, at the W. H. on that night of darkness, when the fiends
prevailed, he would have been horribly *cut to pieces*—Those fiends, had
too long contemplated, this inhuman murder, to have allowed, *him*, to
escape. Robert informs me, that the best likeness of himself, is at Gol-
din's, in Washington, taken last spring. We have none, unframed. The
attitude in the one, you sent me, of myself, is very good, my hands are
always *made* in *them*, very large and I look too stern. The drapery of the
dress, was *not* sufficiently flowing—and my hair, should not be so low
down, on the forehead & so much dressed. I am sending you a long &
most hastily written letter, which I pray you excuse. My sons desire to be
remembered to you. Whilst I remain

Very Sincerely
Mary Lincoln

Herman Melville

The Martyr

When Herman Melville (1819–1891) published "The Martyr" in his first volume of poetry, *Battle-Pieces and Aspects of the War*, in August 1866, he included an endnote (printed below) expressing relief that his worst fears regarding the popular passions aroused at the time of Lincoln's murder had not come to pass. In March 1861 the author of *Moby-Dick* had traveled to the capital in the hope of obtaining a consular appointment in Florence from the new Lincoln administration. Melville did not get the position, but he did meet the President at a White House reception. "Old Abe is much better looking than I expected & younger looking," he wrote to his wife. "He shook hands like a good fellow—working hard at it like a man sawing wood at so much per cord."

———————————

INDICATIVE OF THE PASSION OF THE PEOPLE
ON THE 15TH OF APRIL, 1865.

Good Friday was the day
   Of the prodigy and crime,
When they killed him in his pity,
   When they killed him in his prime
Of clemency and calm—
     When with yearning he was filled
     To redeem the evil-willed,
And, though conqueror, be kind;
   But they killed him in his kindness,
   In their madness and their blindness,
And they killed him from behind.

     There is sobbing of the strong,
     And a pall upon the land;
     But the People in their weeping
       Bare the iron hand:
     Beware the People weeping
     When they bare the iron hand.

He lieth in his blood—
   The father in his face;
They have killed him, the Forgiver—
   The Avenger takes his place,*
The Avenger wisely stern,
     Who in righteousness shall do
     What the heavens call him to,
And the parricides remand;
   For they killed him in his kindness,
   In their madness and their blindness,
And his blood is on their hand.

       There is sobbing of the strong,
       And a pall upon the land;
       But the People in their weeping
           Bare the iron hand:
       Beware the People weeping
       When they bare the iron hand.

1866

---

*At this period of excitement the thought was by some passionately welcomed that the Presidential successor had been raised up by heaven to wreak vengeance on the South. The idea originated in the remembrance that Andrew Johnson by birth belonged to that class of Southern whites who never cherished love for the dominant one; that he was a citizen of Tennessee, where the contest at times and in places had been close and bitter as a Middle-Age feud; that himself and family had been hardly treated by the Secessionists.

But the expectations built hereon (if, indeed, ever soberly entertained), happily for the country, have not been verified.

Likewise the feeling which would have held the entire South chargeable with the crime of one exceptional assassin, this too has died away with the natural excitement of the hour.

Walt Whitman

This Dust Was Once the Man

Whitman first published this poem in *Passage to India* (1871), where it appeared
with "When Lilacs Last in the Dooryard Bloom'd," "O Captain! My Captain!,"
and "Hush'd Be the Camps To-day" in a section titled "President Lincoln's Burial
Hymn." The four poems were later printed together in the 1881 edition of *Leaves of
Grass* under the title "Memories of President Lincoln."

This dust was once the man,
Gentle, plain, just and resolute, under whose cautious hand,
Against the foulest crime in history known in any land or age,
Was saved the Union of these States.

1881

Frederick Douglass

Oration in Memory of Abraham Lincoln, Washington, D.C.

Eleven years after the assassination, Frederick Douglass delivered the oration at the dedication in Washington of the Freedmen's Monument to Abraham Lincoln. Funded entirely by contributions from African Americans, Thomas Ball's statue group depicted a freed slave kneeling before Lincoln—or perhaps rising symbolically from his bondage—a design Douglass disapproved of, believing "a more manly attitude would have been indicative of freedom." In front of an audience that included much of official Washington, Douglass delivered an assessment of Lincoln strikingly different from the one he had offered at Cooper Union in 1865. Instead of being "emphatically the black mans President: the first to show any respect for their rights as men," Douglass now declared that Lincoln had been "preeminently the white man's President, entirely devoted to the welfare of white men," and that blacks were "at best only his step-children." Whatever contributed to his changing views—the passage of time, disillusionment with the weakening Republican commitment to reconstruction—the result was an exceptionally provocative and insightful speech.

Friends and Fellow-Citizens:

I warmly congratulate you upon the highly interesting object which has caused you to assemble in such numbers and spirit as you have to-day. This occasion is in some respects remarkable. Wise and thoughtful men of our race, who shall come after us, and study the lesson of our history in the United States; who shall survey the long and dreary spaces over which we have travelled; who shall count the links in the great chain of events by which we have reached our present position, will make a note of this occasion; they will think of it and speak of it with a sense of manly pride and complacency.

I congratulate you, also, upon the very favorable circumstances in which we meet to-day. They are high, inspiring, and uncommon. They lend grace, glory, and significance to the object for which we have met. Nowhere else in this great country, with its uncounted towns and cities, unlimited wealth, and immeasurable territory extending from sea to sea, could conditions be found more favorable to the success of this occasion than here.

We stand to-day at the national centre to perform something like a national act—an act which is to go into history; and we are here where every pulsation of the national heart can be heard, felt, and reciprocated. A thousand wires, fed with thought and winged with lightning, put us in instantaneous communication with the loyal and true men all over this country.

Few facts could better illustrate the vast and wonderful change which has taken place in our condition as a people than the fact of our assembling here for the purpose we have to-day. Harmless, beautiful, proper, and praiseworthy as this demonstration is, I cannot forget that no such demonstration would have been tolerated here twenty years ago. The spirit of slavery and barbarism, which still lingers to blight and destroy in some dark and distant parts of our country, would have made our assembling here the signal and excuse for opening upon us all the flood-gates of wrath and violence. That we are here in peace to-day is a compliment and a credit to American civilization, and a prophecy of still greater national enlightenment and progress in the future. I refer to the past not in malice, for this is no day for malice; but simply to place more distinctly in front the gratifying and glorious change which has come both to our white fellow-citizens and ourselves, and to congratulate all upon the contrast between now and then: the new dispensation of freedom with its thousand blessings to both races, and the old dispensation of slavery with its ten thousand evils to both races—white and black. In view, then, of the past, the present, and the future, with the long and dark history of our bondage behind us, and with liberty, progress, and enlightenment before us, I again congratulate you upon this auspicious day and hour.

Friends and fellow-citizens, the story of our presence here is soon and easily told. We are here in the District of Columbia, here in the city of Washington, the most luminous point of American territory; a city recently transformed and made beautiful in its body and in its spirit; we are here in the place where the ablest and best men of the country are sent to devise the policy, enact the laws, and shape the destiny of the Republic; we are here, with the stately pillars and majestic dome of the Capitol of the nation looking down upon us; we are here, with the broad earth freshly adorned with the foliage and flowers of spring for our church, and all races, colors, and conditions of men for our congregation—in a word, we are here to express, as best we may, by appropriate forms and ceremonies, our grateful sense of the vast, high, and pre-eminent services rendered to ourselves, to our race, to our country, and to the whole world by Abraham Lincoln.

The sentiment that brings us here to-day is one of the noblest that can stir and thrill the human heart. It has crowned and made glorious the high places of all civilized nations with the grandest and most enduring works of art, designed to illustrate the characters and perpetuate the memories of great public men. It is the sentiment which from year to year adorns with fragrant and beautiful flowers the graves of our loyal, brave, and patriotic soldiers who fell in defence of the Union and liberty. It is the sentiment of gratitude and appreciation, which often, in presence of many who hear me, has filled yonder heights of Arlington with the eloquence of eulogy and the sublime enthusiasm of poetry and song; a sentiment which can never die while the Republic lives.

For the first time in the history of our people, and in the history of the whole American people, we join in this high worship, and march conspicuously in the line of this time-honored custom. First things are always interesting, and this is one of our first things. It is the first time that, in this form and manner, we have sought to do honor to an American great man, however deserving and illustrious. I commend the fact to notice; let it be told in every part of the Republic; let men of all parties and opinions hear it; let those who despise us, not less than those who respect us, know that now and here, in the spirit of liberty, loyalty, and gratitude, let it be known everywhere, and by everybody who takes an interest in human progress and in the amelioration of the condition of mankind, that, in the presence and with the approval of the members of the American House of Representatives, reflecting the general sentiment of the country; that in the presence of that august body, the American Senate, representing the highest intelligence and the calmest judgment of the country; in presence of the Supreme Court and Chief-Justice of the United States, to whose decisions we all patriotically bow; in the presence and under the steady eye of the honored and trusted President of the United States, with the members of his wise and patriotic Cabinet, we, the colored people, newly emancipated and rejoicing in our blood-bought freedom, near the close of the first century in the life of this Republic, have now and here unveiled, set apart, and dedicated a monument of enduring granite and bronze, in every line, feature, and figure of which the men of this generation may read, and those of after-coming generations may read, something of the exalted character and great works of Abraham Lincoln, the first martyr President of the United States.

Fellow-citizens, in what we have said and done to-day, and in what we may say and do hereafter, we disclaim everything like arrogance and assumption. We claim for ourselves no superior devotion to the character, history, and memory of the illustrious name whose monument we have here dedicated to-day. We fully comprehend the relation of Abraham Lincoln both to ourselves and to the white people of the United States. Truth is proper and beautiful at all times and in all places, and it is never more proper and beautiful in any case than when speaking of a great public man whose example is likely to be commended for honor and imitation long after his departure to the solemn shades, the silent continents of eternity. It must be admitted, truth compels me to admit, even here in the presence of the monument we have erected to his memory, Abraham Lincoln was not, in the fullest sense of the word, either our man or our model. In his interests, in his associations, in his habits of thought, and in his prejudices, he was a white man.

He was pre-eminently the white man's President, entirely devoted to the welfare of white men. He was ready and willing at any time during the first years of his administration to deny, postpone, and sacrifice the rights of humanity in the colored people to promote the welfare of the white people of this country. In all his education and feeling he was an American of the Americans. He came into the Presidential chair upon one principle alone, namely, opposition to the extension of slavery. His arguments in furtherance of this policy had their motive and mainspring in his patriotic devotion to the interests of his own race. To protect, defend, and perpetuate slavery in the States where it existed Abraham Lincoln was not less ready than any other President to draw the sword of the nation. He was ready to execute all the supposed constitutional guarantees of the United States Constitution in favor of the slave system anywhere inside the slave States. He was willing to pursue, recapture, and send back the fugitive slave to his master, and to suppress a slave rising for liberty, though his guilty master were already in arms against the Government. The race to which we belong were not the special objects of his consideration. Knowing this, I concede to you, my white fellow-citizens, a pre-eminence in this worship at once full and supreme. First, midst, and last, you and yours were the objects of his deepest affection and his most earnest solicitude. You are the children of Abraham Lincoln. We are at best only his step-children; children by adoption, children by force of circumstances and necessity. To you it especially belongs to sound his praises, to preserve and perpetuate his memory, to multiply his statues, to hang his pictures high upon your walls, and commend his example, for to you he was a great and glorious friend and benefactor. Instead of supplanting you at this altar, we would exhort you to build high his monuments: let them be of the most costly material, of the most cunning workmanship; let their forms be symmetrical, beautiful, and perfect; let their bases be upon solid rocks, and their summits lean against the unchanging blue, overhanging sky, and let them endure forever! But while in the abundance of your wealth, and in the fulness of your just and patriotic devotion, you do all this, we entreat you to despise not the humble offering we this day unveil to view; for while Abraham Lincoln saved for you a country, he delivered us from a bondage, according to Jefferson, one hour of which was worse than ages of the oppression your fathers rose in rebellion to oppose.

Fellow-citizens, ours is no new-born zeal and devotion—merely a thing of this moment. The name of Abraham Lincoln was near and dear to our hearts in the darkest and most perilous hours of the Republic. We were no more ashamed of him when shrouded in clouds of darkness, of doubt, and defeat than when we saw him crowned with victory, honor, and glory. Our faith in him was often taxed and strained to the uttermost, but it never failed. When he tarried long in the mountain; when he strangely told us that we were the cause of the war; when he still more strangely told us to leave the land in which we were born; when he refused to employ our arms in defence of the Union; when, after accepting our services as colored soldiers, he refused to retaliate our murder and torture as colored prisoners; when he told us he would save the Union if he could with slavery; when he revoked the Proclamation of Emancipation of General Frémont; when he refused to remove the popular commander of the Army of the Potomac, in the days of its inaction and defeat, who was more zealous in his efforts to protect slavery than to suppress rebellion; when we saw all this, and more, we were at times grieved, stunned, and greatly bewildered; but our hearts believed while they ached and bled. Nor was this, even at that time, a blind and unreasoning superstition. Despite the mist and haze that surrounded him; despite the tumult, the hurry, and confusion of the hour, we were able to take a comprehensive view of Abraham Lincoln, and to make reasonable allowance for the circumstances of his position. We saw him, measured him, and estimated him; not by stray utterances to injudicious and tedious delegations, who often tried his patience; not by isolated facts torn from their connection; not by any partial and imperfect glimpses, caught at inopportune moments; but by a broad survey, in the light of the stern logic of great events, and in view of that divinity which shapes our ends, rough hew them how we will, we came to the conclusion that the hour and the man of our redemption had somehow met in the person of Abraham Lincoln. It mattered little to us what language he might employ on special occasions; it mattered little to us, when we fully knew him, whether he was swift or slow in his movements; it was enough for us that Abraham Lincoln was at the head of a great movement, and was in living and earnest sympathy with that movement, which, in the nature of things, must go on until slavery should be utterly and forever abolished in the United States.

When, therefore, it shall be asked what we have to do with the memory of Abraham Lincoln, or what Abraham Lincoln had to do with us, the answer is ready, full, and complete. Though he loved Cæsar less than Rome, though the Union was more to him than our freedom or our future, under his wise and beneficent rule we saw ourselves gradually lifted from the depths of slavery to the heights of liberty and manhood; under his wise and beneficent rule, and by measures approved and vigorously pressed by him, we saw that the handwriting of ages, in the form of prejudice and proscription, was rapidly fading away from the face of our whole country; under his rule, and in due time, about as soon after all as the country could tolerate the strange spectacle, we saw our brave sons and brothers laying off the rags of bondage, and being clothed all over in the blue uniforms of the soldiers of the United States; under his rule we saw two hundred thousand of our dark and dusky people responding to the call of Abraham Lincoln, and with muskets on their shoulders, and eagles on their buttons, timing their high footsteps to liberty and union under the national flag; under his rule we saw the independence of the black republic of Hayti, the special object of slaveholding aversion and horror, fully recognized, and her minister, a colored gentleman, duly received here in the city of Washington; under his rule we saw the internal slave-trade, which so long disgraced the nation, abolished, and slavery abolished in the District of Columbia; under his rule we saw for the first time the law enforced against the foreign slave-trade, and the first slave-trader hanged like any other pirate or murderer; under his rule, assisted by the greatest captain of our age, and his inspiration, we saw the Confederate States, based upon the idea that our race must be slaves, and slaves forever, battered to pieces and scattered to the four winds; under his rule, and in the fullness of time, we saw Abraham Lincoln, after giving the slaveholders three months' grace in which to save their hateful slave system, penning the immortal paper, which, though special in its language, was general in its principles and effect, making slavery forever impossible in the United States. Though we waited long, we saw all this and more.

Can any colored man, or any white man friendly to the freedom of all men, ever forget the night which followed the first day of January, 1863, when the world was to see if Abraham Lincoln would prove to be as good as his word? I shall never forget that memorable night, when in a distant city I waited and watched at a public meeting, with three thousand others not less anxious than myself, for the word of deliverance which we have heard read to-day. Nor shall I ever forget the outburst of joy and thanksgiving that rent the air when the lightning brought to us the emancipation proclamation. In that happy hour we forgot all delay, and forgot all tardiness, forgot that the President had bribed the rebels to lay down their arms by a promise to withhold the bolt which would smite the slave-system with destruction; and we were thenceforward willing to allow the President all the latitude of time, phraseology, and every honorable device that statesmanship might require for the achievement of a great and beneficent measure of liberty and progress.

Fellow-citizens, there is little necessity on this occasion to speak at length and critically of this great and good man, and of his high mission in the world. That ground has been fully occupied and completely covered both here and elsewhere. The whole field of fact and fancy has been gleaned and garnered. Any man can say things that are true of Abraham Lincoln, but no man can say anything that is new of Abraham Lincoln. His personal traits and public acts are better known to the American people than are those of any other man of his age. He was a mystery to no man who saw him and heard him. Though high in position, the humblest could approach him and feel at home in his presence. Though deep, he was transparent; though strong, he was gentle; though decided and pronounced in his convictions, he was tolerant towards those who differed from him, and patient under reproaches. Even those who only knew him through his public utterances obtained a tolerably clear idea of his character and his personality. The image of the man went out with his words, and those who read them, knew him.

I have said that President Lincoln was a white man, and shared the prejudices common to his countrymen towards the colored race. Looking back to his times and to the condition of his country, we are compelled to admit that this unfriendly feeling on his part may be safely set down as one element of his wonderful success in organizing the loyal American people for the tremendous conflict before them, and bringing them safely through that conflict. His great mission was to accomplish two things: first, to save his country from dismemberment and ruin; and second, to free his country from the great crime of slavery. To do one or the other, or both, he must have the earnest sympathy and the powerful co-operation of his loyal fellow-countrymen. Without this primary and essential condition to success his efforts must have been vain and utterly fruitless. Had he put the abolition of slavery before the salvation of the Union, he would have inevitably driven from him a powerful class of the American people and rendered resistance to rebellion impossible. Viewed from the genuine abolition ground, Mr. Lincoln seemed tardy, cold, dull, and indifferent; but measuring him by the sentiment of his country, a sentiment he was bound as a statesman to consult, he was swift, zealous, radical, and determined.

Though Mr. Lincoln shared the prejudices of his white fellow-countrymen against the negro, it is hardly necessary to say that in his heart of hearts he loathed and hated slavery.* The man who could say, "Fondly do we hope, fervently do we pray, that this mighty scourge of war shall soon pass away, yet if God wills it continue till all the wealth piled by two hundred years of bondage shall have been wasted, and each

---

* "I am naturally anti-slavery. If slavery is not wrong, nothing is wrong. I cannot remember when I did not so think and feel"—*Letter of Mr. Lincoln to Mr. Hodges, of Kentucky, April* 4, 1864.

drop of blood drawn by the lash shall have been paid for by one drawn by the sword, the judgments of the Lord are true and righteous altogether," gives all needed proof of his feeling on the subject of slavery. He was willing, while the South was loyal, that it should have its pound of flesh, because he thought that it was so nominated in the bond; but farther than this no earthly power could make him go.

Fellow-citizens, whatever else in this world may be partial, unjust, and uncertain, time, time! is impartial, just, and certain in its action. In the realm of mind, as well as in the realm of matter, it is a great worker, and often works wonders. The honest and comprehensive statesman, clearly discerning the needs of his country, and earnestly endeavoring to do his whole duty, though covered and blistered with reproaches, may safely leave his course to the silent judgment of time. Few great public men have ever been the victims of fiercer denunciation than Abraham Lincoln was during his administration. He was often wounded in the house of his friends. Reproaches came thick and fast upon him from within and from without, and from opposite quarters. He was assailed by Abolitionists; he was assailed by slaveholders; he was assailed by the men who were for peace at any price; he was assailed by those who were for a more vigorous prosecution of the war; he was assailed for not making the war an abolition war; and he was most bitterly assailed for making the war an abolition war.

But now behold the change: the judgment of the present hour is, that taking him for all in all, measuring the tremendous magnitude of the work before him, considering the necessary means to ends, and surveying the end from the beginning, infinite wisdom has seldom sent any man into the world better fitted for his mission than Abraham Lincoln. His birth, his training, and his natural endowments, both mental and physical, were strongly in his favor. Born and reared among the lowly, a stranger to wealth and luxury, compelled to grapple single-handed with the flintiest hardships of life, from tender youth to sturdy manhood, he grew strong in the manly and heroic qualities demanded by the great mission to which he was called by the votes of his countrymen. The hard condition of his early life, which would have depressed and broken down weaker men, only gave greater life, vigor, and buoyancy to the heroic spirit of Abraham Lincoln. He was ready for any kind and any quality of work. What other young men dreaded in the shape of toil, he took hold of with the utmost cheerfulness.

A spade, a rake, a hoe,
A pick-axe, or a bill;
A hook to reap, a scythe to mow,
A flail, or what you will.

All day long he could split heavy rails in the woods, and half the night long he could study his English Grammar by the uncertain flare and glare of the light made by a pine-knot. He was at home on the land with his axe, with his maul, with gluts, and his wedges; and he was equally at home on water, with his oars, with his poles, with his planks, and with his boat-hooks. And whether in his flat-boat on the Mississippi river, or at the fireside of his frontier cabin, he was a man of work. A son of toil himself, he was linked in brotherly sympathy with the sons of toil in every loyal part of the Republic. This very fact gave him tremendous power with the American people, and materially contributed not only to selecting him to the Presidency, but in sustaining his administration of the Government.

Upon his inauguration as President of the United States, an office, even where assumed under the most favorable conditions, fitted to tax and strain the largest abilities, Abraham Lincoln was met by a tremendous crisis. He was called upon not merely to administer the Government, but to decide, in the face of terrible odds, the fate of the Republic.

A formidable rebellion rose in his path before him; the Union was already practically dissolved; his country was torn and rent asunder at the centre. Hostile armies were already organized against the Republic, armed with the munitions of war which the Republic had provided for its own defence. The tremendous question for him to decide was whether his country should survive the crisis and flourish, or be dismembered and perish. His predecessor in office had already decided the question in favor of national dismemberment, by denying to it the right of self-defence and self-preservation—a right which belongs to the meanest insect.

Happily for the country, happily for you and for me, the judgment of James Buchanan, the patrician, was not the judgment of Abraham

Lincoln, the plebeian. He brought his strong common sense, sharpened in the school of adversity, to bear upon the question. He did not hesitate, he did not doubt, he did not falter; but at once resolved that at whatever peril, at whatever cost, the union of the States should be preserved. A patriot himself, his faith was strong and unwavering in the patriotism of his countrymen. Timid men said before Mr. Lincoln's inauguration, that we had seen the last President of the United States. A voice in influential quarters said "Let the Union slide." Some said that a Union maintained by the sword was worthless. Others said a rebellion of 8,000,000 cannot be suppressed; but in the midst of all this tumult and timidity, and against all this, Abraham Lincoln was clear in his duty, and had an oath in heaven. He calmly and bravely heard the voice of doubt and fear all around him; but he had an oath in heaven, and there was not power enough on the earth to make this honest boatman, back-woodsman, and broad-handed splitter of rails evade or violate that sacred oath. He had not been schooled in the ethics of slavery; his plain life had favored his love of truth. He had not been taught that treason and perjury were the proof of honor and honesty. His moral training was against his saying one thing when he meant another. The trust which Abraham Lincoln had in himself and in the people was surprising and grand, but it was also enlightened and well founded. He knew the American people better than they knew themselves, and his truth was based upon this knowledge.

Fellow-citizens, the fourteenth day of April, 1865, of which this is the eleventh anniversary, is now and will ever remain a memorable day in the annals of this Republic. It was on the evening of this day, while a fierce and sanguinary rebellion was in the last stages of its desolating power; while its armies were broken and scattered before the invincible armies of Grant and Sherman; while a great nation, torn and rent by war, was already beginning to raise to the skies loud anthems of joy at the dawn of peace, it was startled, amazed, and overwhelmed by the crowning crime of slavery—the assassination of Abraham Lincoln. It was a new crime, a pure act of malice. No purpose of the rebellion was to be served by it. It was the simple gratification of a hell-black spirit of revenge. But it has done good after all. It has filled the country with a deeper abhorrence of slavery and a deeper love for the great liberator.

Had Abraham Lincoln died from any of the numerous ills to which flesh is heir; had he reached that good old age of which his vigorous constitution and his temperate habits gave promise; had he been permitted to see the end of his great work; had the solemn curtain of death come down but gradually—we should still have been smitten with a heavy grief, and treasured his name lovingly. But dying as he did die, by the red hand of violence, killed, assassinated, taken off without warning, not because of personal hate—for no man who knew Abraham Lincoln could hate him—but because of his fidelity to union and liberty, he is doubly dear to us, and his memory will be precious forever.

Fellow-citizens, I end, as I began, with congratulations. We have done a good work for our race to-day. In doing honor to the memory of our friend and liberator, we have been doing highest honors to ourselves and those who come after us; we have been fastening ourselves to a name and fame imperishable and immortal; we have also been defending ourselves from a blighting scandal. When now it shall be said that the colored man is soulless, that he has no appreciation of benefits or benefactors; when the foul reproach of ingratitude is hurled at us, and it is attempted to scourge us beyond the range of human brotherhood, we may calmly point to the monument we have this day erected to the memory of Abraham Lincoln.

Alexander H. Stephens

Remarks at the U.S. Capitol

Few people would have anticipated in April 1865 that Alexander H. Stephens (1812–1883), the Confederate vice president, would one day speak at a ceremony honoring Lincoln, much less one held in the U.S. Capitol. A former Whig who had served with Lincoln in the Thirtieth Congress, Stephens had opposed immediate secession in the Georgia convention of January 1861, but then accepted election to the Confederate vice presidency. In March 1861 he gave a widely reported speech in which he declared that the "corner-stone" of the new Confederacy "rests upon the great truth, that the negro is not equal to the white man; that slavery—subordination to the superior race—is his natural and normal condition." Stephens opposed conscription, the suspension of habeas corpus, and other war measures adopted by Jefferson Davis, and spent much of the conflict at his home in Georgia. Arrested by Union troops in May 1865, he was imprisoned for five months before being released on parole. In 1872 Congress passed an amnesty act that allowed most former Confederate officials to hold political office again, and the following year Stephens was elected to Congress. When the philanthropist Elizabeth Thompson purchased Francis B. Carpenter's painting *The First Reading of the Emancipation Proclamation* for $25,000 in 1877 and presented it to the nation, Congress decided to formally receive the gift in a joint session. The ceremony was held on February 12, 1878, the sixty-ninth anniversary of Lincoln's birth. As a symbol of the sectional reconciliation that so many white Americans now sought, the two speakers chosen for the occasion were Ohio Republican congressman James A. Garfield, a former Union brigadier general (and future president), and Stephens.

Mr. STEPHENS, of Georgia. Mr. President, there is but little left to say in the performance of the part assigned me in the programme arranged for this august occasion. As to the merits of the picture and the skill of the artist, my friend from Ohio [Mr. GARFIELD] has dwelt at large. I can but indorse all he has so well said on that subject. Of the munificent gift of the donor, he has also left me nothing to add. The present of a twenty-five-thousand-dollar painting to the Government well deserves commendation. Few instances of this sort have occurred in the history of our country; I know of none. The example of this generous lady in the encouragement of art may well be followed by others.

Mr. President, with regard to the subject of the painting I propose, if strength permits, to submit a few remarks: first, as to the central figure, the man; after that, as to the event commemorated. I knew Mr. Lincoln well. We met in this House in December, 1847. We were together during the Thirtieth Congress. I was as intimate with him as with any other man of that Congress, except perhaps one. That exception was my colleague, Mr. Toombs. Of Mr. Lincoln's general character I need not speak. He was warm hearted; he was generous; he was magnanimous; he was most truly, as he afterward said on a memorable occasion, "with malice towards none, with charity for all."

In bodily form he was above the average; and so in intellect; the two were in symmetry. Not highly cultivated, he had a native genius far above the average of his fellows. Every fountain of his heart was ever overflowing with the "milk of human kindness." So much for him personally. From my attachment to him, so much the deeper was the pang in my own breast as well as of millions at the horrible manner of his "taking off." That was the climax of our troubles and the spring from which came afterward "unnumbered woes." But of those events no more now. Widely as we differed on public questions and policies, yet as a friend I may say:

> No farther seek his merits to disclose,
>   Or draw his frailties from their dread abode;
> (There they alike in trembling hope repose,)
>   The bosom of his Father and his God.

So much I have felt it my duty on this occasion to say in behalf of one with whom I held relations so intimate and one who personally stood so high in my estimation.

Now as to the great historic event which this picture represents and which it is designed to commemorate.

This is perhaps a subject which, as my friend from Ohio has said, the people of this day and generation are not exactly in a condition to weigh rightfully and judge correctly. One thing was remarked by him which should be duly noted. That was this: Emancipation was not the chief object of Mr. Lincoln in issuing the proclamation. His chief object, the ideal to which his whole soul was devoted, was the preservation of the Union. Let not history confuse events. That proclamation, pregnant as it was with coming events, initiative as it was of ultimate emancipation, still originated in point of fact more from what was deemed the necessities of war than from any bare humanitarian view of the matter. Life is all a mist; and in the dark our fortunes meet us.

This was evidently the case with Mr. Lincoln. He in my opinion was like all the rest of us, an instrument in the hands of that Providence above us, that "Divinity which shapes our ends, rough-hew them how we will." I doubt much, as was indicated by my friend from Ohio, whether Mr. Lincoln at the time realized the great result. Mark you, the proclamation itself did not declare free all the colored people of the Southern States: it applied only to those parts of the country then in resistance to the Federal authorities. If the emancipation of the colored race, which is one of the greatest epochs in our day and will be so marked in the future history of this country, be a boon or a curse to them, (a question which, under Providence, is yet to be solved, and which depends much upon themselves,) then, representing the Southern States here, I must claim in their behalf that the freedom of that race was never finally consummated, and could not be until the Southern States sanctioned the thirteenth amendment, which they did, every one of them, by their own former constituencies. Before the upturning of southern society by the reconstruction acts the white people there came to the conclusion that their domestic institution known as slavery better be abolished. They accepted the proposition for emancipation by a voluntary, uncontrolled sanction of the proposed thirteenth amendment to the Constitution of the United States. This sanction was given by the original constituency of those States, the former governing white race, and without that sanction the thirteenth amendment never could have been incorporated in the fundamental law. That is the charter of the colored man's freedom. Mr. Lincoln's idea, as embodied in his first proclamation of September 22, 1862, as well as that of January 1, 1863, was consummated by the adoption of the thirteenth amendment of the Constitution of the United States, and without that the proclamation had nothing but the continued existence of the war to sustain it. Had the States in resistance laid down their arms by the 1st of January, 1863, the Union would have been saved but the condition of the slave so called would have been unchanged. Upon the subject of emancipation itself it may here be stated, the pecuniary view, the politico-economic question involved, the amount of property invested under the system, though that was vast, not less than $2,000,000,000, weighed in my estimation no more than a drop in the bucket compared with the great ethnological problem now in the process of solution.

Mr. President, as to this institution called slavery in the Southern States, many errors existed and many exceedingly unjust prejudices. Prejudice! What wrongs, what injuries, what mischiefs, what lamentable consequences have resulted at all times from this perversity of the intellect! Of all the obstacles to the advancement of truth and human progress in every department of knowledge, in science, in art, in government, and in religion, in all ages and climes, not one on the list is more formidable, more difficult to overcome and subdue than this horrible distortion of the moral as well as intellectual faculties.

I could enjoin no greater duty upon my countrymen now, North and South, as I said upon a former occasion, than the exercise of that degree of forbearance which would enable them to conquer their prejudices. One of the highest exhibitions of the moral sublime the world ever witnessed was that of Daniel Webster, the greatest orator I ever heard, combining thought with elocution, when in an open barouche in the streets of Boston he proclaimed in substance to a vast assembly of his constituents—unwilling hearers—that they had conquered an uncongenial clime; they had conquered a sterile soil; they had conquered the winds and currents of the ocean; they had conquered most of the elements of nature; but they must yet learn to conquer their prejudices.

I would say this is to the people of the North as well as to the people of the South.

Indulge me a moment upon this subject of the institution of slavery, so called, in the Southern States. Well, Mr. President and Mr. Speaker, it was not an unmitigated evil. It was not, thus much I can say, without its compensations. It is my purpose now, however, to bury, not to praise, to laud, "nor aught extenuate."

It had its faults, and most grievously has the country, North and South, for both were equally responsible for it, answered them. It also, let it be remembered, gave rise to some of the noblest virtues that adorn civilization. But let its faults and virtues be buried alike forever.

I will say this: if it were not the best relation for the happiness and welfare of both races, morally, physically, intellectually, and politically, it was wrong; and ought to have been abolished. This I said of it years before secession, and I repeat it still. But as I have said, this is no time now to discuss those questions.

I have seen something of the world and traveled somewhat, and I have never yet found on earth a paradise. The Southern States are no exception. Wherever I have been, I have been ready to exclaim with Burns —

> But oh! what crowds in every land
> Are wretched and forlorn!
> * * *
> Man's inhumanity to man
> Makes countless thousands mourn.

It was so at the South. It was so at the North. It is so yet. It is so in every part of the world that I have seen. The question of the proper relation of the races is one of the most difficult problems which statesmen or philanthropists, legislators or jurists, ever had to solve. The former polity of the Southern States upon this subject is ended, and I do not think it inappropriate on this occasion to indulge in some remarks with regard to the future. Since the emancipation, since the former ruling race have been relieved of their direct heavy responsibility for the protection and welfare of their dependents, it has been common to speak of the colored race as "the wards of the nation."

May I not say with appropriateness in this connection and due reverence, in the language of Georgia's greatest intellect, (Toombs,) "They are rather the wards of the Almighty," committed now under a new state of things to the rulers, the law-makers, the law-expounders, and the law-executors throughout this broad land, within their respective constitutional spheres, to take care of and provide for in that complicated system of government under which we live. I am inclined, sir, so to regard and so to speak of them—not in exceptional cases, but as a mass. In the providence of God why their ancestors were permitted to be brought over here it is not for us to say, but they have a location and habitation here, especially in the South; and since the changed condition of their status, though it was the leading cause of the late terrible conflict of arms between the States, yet I think I may venture to affirm there is not one within the circle of my acquaintance, or in the whole southern country, who would now wish to see the old relation restored.

If there is one in all the South who would desire such a change back I am not aware of it. Well, then, this changed status creates new duties. The wardship has changed hands. Men of the North and of the South, of the East and of the West—I care not of what party—I would to-day, on this commemorative occasion, urge upon every one within the sphere of duty and humanity, whether in public or private life, to see to it that there be no violation of the divine trust.

Mr. President and Mr. Speaker, one or two other reflections may not be out of place on this occasion. In submitting them I shall but repeat, in substance, what I said in my own State nearly twelve years ago. What is to be the future?

During the conflict of arms I frequently almost despaired of the liberties of our country both South and North. War seldom advances while it always menaces the cause of liberty, and most frequently results in its destruction. The union of these States at first I always thought was founded upon the assumption that it was the best interest of all to remain united, faithfully performing each for itself its own constitutional obligations under the compact. When secession was resorted to as a remedy it was only to avoid a greater evil that I went with my State, holding it to be my duty so to do, but believing all the time that if successful, for which end I strove most earnestly, after the passions of the hour and of the day were over the great law which produced the Union at first, "mutual interest and reciprocal advantage," that grand truth which Great Britain learned after seven years of the revolutionary war, and put in the preamble to the preliminary articles of peace in 1781, would reassert itself, and that at no distant day a new Union soon would again be formed.

My earnest desire, however, throughout was that whatever might be done, might be peaceably done; might be the result of calm, dispassionate, and enlightened reason, looking to the permanent interests and welfare of all. And now, after the severe chastisement of war, if the general sense of the whole country shall come back to the acknowledgment of the original assumption, that it is for the best interests of all the States to be so united, as I trust it will—the States still being "separate as the billows but one as the sea"—this thorn in the body politic now being removed, I can perceive no reason why under such restoration, the flag no longer waving over provinces but States, we as a whole, with "peace, commerce, and honest friendship with all nations and entangling alliances with none," may not enter upon a new career, exciting increased wonder in the Old World by grander achievements hereafter to be made than any heretofore attained by the peaceful and harmonious workings of our matchless system of American federal institutions of self-government. All this is possible if the hearts of the people be right. It is my earnest wish to see it. Fondly would I indulge my fancy in gazing on such a picture of the future. With what rapture may we not suppose the spirits of our fathers would hail its opening scenes from their mansions above. But if, instead of all this, sectional passions shall continue to bear sway; if prejudice shall rule the hour; if a conflict of classes or of labor and capital or of races shall arise; if the embers of the late war shall be kept aglowing until with new fuel they shall flame up again, then our late great troubles and disasters were but the shadow, the *penumbra* of that deeper and darker eclipse which is to totally obscure this hemisphere and blight forever the anxious anticipations and expectations of mankind! Then, hereafter, by some bard it may be sung—

> The star of hope shone brightest in the West.
> The hope of liberty, the last, the best;
> It, too, has set upon her darkened shore,
> And hope and freedom light up earth no more.

[Loud applause.]

Walt Whitman

The Death of Lincoln

Whitman delivered his lecture on Lincoln's death three times from 1879 to 1881 and published it in *Specimen Days & Collect* in 1882. He would give it on another seven occasions from 1886 to 1890, including a special anniversary performance in New York on April 14, 1887, that was attended by Mark Twain, William Dean Howells, James Russell Lowell, John Hay, Edmund Clarence Stedman, and General William T. Sherman. Although some of the incidents presented by Whitman are clearly fanciful, such as the "some two hundred" angry Union soldiers who supposedly stormed through Ford's Theatre with fixed bayonets after the shooting, it is likely that his account drew on the recollections of his intimate friend Peter Doyle, who was in the audience at Ford's Theatre on April 14.

----

*Lecture deliver'd in New York, April 14, 1879 —
in Philadelphia, '80 — in Boston, '81.*

How often since that dark and dripping Saturday — that chilly April day, now fifteen years bygone — my heart has entertain'd the dream, the wish, to give of Abraham Lincoln's death, its own special thought and memorial. Yet now the sought-for opportunity offers, I find my notes incompetent, (why, for truly profound themes, is statement so idle? why does the right phrase never offer?) and the fit tribute I dream'd of, waits unprepared as ever. My talk here indeed is less because of itself or anything in it, and nearly altogether because I feel a desire, apart from any talk, to specify the day, the martyrdom. It is for this, my friends, I have call'd you together. Oft as the rolling years bring back this hour, let it again, however briefly, be dwelt upon. For my own part, I hope and desire, till my own dying day, whenever the 14th or 15th of April comes, to annually gather a few friends, and hold its tragic reminiscence. No narrow or sectional reminiscence. It belongs to these States in their entirety — not the North only, but the South — perhaps belongs most tenderly and devoutly to the South, of all; for there, really, this man's birth-stock. There and thence his antecedent stamp. Why should I not say that thence his manliest traits — his universality — his canny, easy ways and words upon the surface — his inflexible determination and courage at heart? Have you never realized it, my friends, that Lincoln, though grafted on the West, is essentially, in personnel and character, a Southern contribution?

And though by no means proposing to resume the Secession war to-night, I would briefly remind you of the public conditions preceding that contest. For twenty years, and especially during the four or five before the war actually began, the aspect of affairs in the United States, though without the flash of military excitement, presents more than the survey of a battle, or any extended campaign, or series, even of Nature's convulsions. The hot passions of the South—the strange mixture at the North of inertia, incredulity, and conscious power—the incendiarism of the abolitionists—the rascality and *grip* of the politicians, unparallel'd in any land, any age. To these I must not omit adding the honesty of the essential bulk of the people everywhere—yet with all the seething fury and contradiction of their natures more arous'd than the Atlantic's waves in wildest equinox. In politics, what can be more ominous, (though generally unappreciated then)—what more significant than the Presidentiads of Fillmore and Buchanan? proving conclusively that the weakness and wickedness of elected rulers are just as likely to afflict us here, as in the countries of the Old World, under their monarchies, emperors, and aristocracies. In that Old World were everywhere heard underground rumblings, that died out, only to again surely return. While in America the volcano, though civic yet, continued to grow more and more convulsive—more and more stormy and threatening.

In the height of all this excitement and chaos, hovering on the edge at first, and then merged in its very midst, and destined to play a leading part, appears a strange and awkward figure. I shall not easily forget the first time I ever saw Abraham Lincoln. It must have been about the 18th or 19th of February, 1861. It was rather a pleasant afternoon, in New York city, as he arrived there from the West, to remain a few hours, and then pass on to Washington, to prepare for his inauguration. I saw him in Broadway, near the site of the present Post-office. He came down, I think from Canal street, to stop at the Astor House. The broad spaces, sidewalks, and street in the neighborhood, and for some distance, were crowded with solid masses of people, many thousands. The omnibuses and other vehicles had all been turn'd off, leaving an unusual hush in that busy part of the city. Presently two or three shabby hack barouches made their way with some difficulty through the crowd, and drew up at the Astor House entrance. A tall figure step'd out of the centre of these barouches, paus'd leisurely on the sidewalk, look'd up at the granite walls and looming architecture of the grand old hotel—then, after a relieving stretch of arms and legs, turn'd round for over a minute to slowly and good-humoredly scan the appearance of the vast and silent crowds. There were no speeches—no compliments—no welcome—as far as I could hear, not a word said. Still much anxiety was conceal'd in that quiet. Cautious persons had fear'd some mark'd insult or indignity to the President-elect—for he possess'd no personal popularity at all in New York city, and very little political. But it was evidently tacitly agreed that if the few political supporters of Mr. Lincoln present would entirely abstain from any demonstration on their side, the immense majority, who were any thing but supporters, would abstain on their side also. The result was a sulky, unbroken silence, such as certainly never before characterized so great a New York crowd.

Almost in the same neighborhood I distinctly remember'd seeing Lafayette on his visit to America in 1825. I had also personally seen and heard, various years afterward, how Andrew Jackson, Clay, Webster, Hungarian Kossuth, Filibuster Walker, the Prince of Wales on his visit, and other celebres, native and foreign, had been welcom'd there—all that indescribable human roar and magnetism, unlike any other sound in the universe—the glad exulting thunder-shouts of countless unloos'd throats of men! But on this occasion, not a voice—not a sound. From the top of an omnibus, (driven up one side, close by, and block'd by the curbstone and the crowds,) I had, I say, a capital view of it all, and especially of Mr. Lincoln, his look and gait—his perfect composure and coolness—his unusual and uncouth height, his dress of complete black, stovepipe hat push'd back on the head, dark-brown complexion, seam'd and wrinkled yet canny-looking face, black, bushy head of hair, disproportionately long neck, and his hands held behind as he stood observing the people. He look'd with curiosity upon that immense sea of faces, and the sea of faces return'd the look with similar curiosity. In both there was a dash of comedy, almost farce, such as Shakspere puts in his blackest tragedies. The crowd that hemm'd around consisted I should think of thirty to forty thousand men, not a single one his personal friend—while I have no doubt, (so frenzied were the ferments of the time,) many an assassin's knife and pistol lurk'd in hip or breast-pocket there, ready, soon as break and riot came.

But no break or riot came. The tall figure gave another relieving stretch or two of arms and legs; then with moderate pace, and accompanied by a few unknown looking persons, ascended the portico-steps of the Astor House, disappear'd through its broad entrance—and the dumb-show ended.

I saw Abraham Lincoln often the four years following that date. He changed rapidly and much during his Presidency—but this scene, and him in it, are indelibly stamped upon my recollection. As I sat on the top of my omnibus, and had a good view of him, the thought, dim and inchoate then, has since come out clear enough, that four sorts of genius, four mighty and primal hands, will be needed to the complete limning of this man's future portrait—the eyes and brains and finger-touch of Plutarch and Eschylus and Michel Angelo, assisted by Rabelais.

And now—(Mr. Lincoln passing on from this scene to Washington, where he was inaugurated, amid armed cavalry, and sharpshooters at every point—the first instance of the kind in our history—and I hope it will be the last)—now the rapid succession of well-known events, (too well known—I believe, these days, we almost hate to hear them mention'd) —the national flag fired on at Sumter—the uprising of the North, in paroxysms of astonishment and rage—the chaos of divided councils—the call for troops—the first Bull Run—the stunning cast-down, shock, and dismay of the North—and so in full flood the Secession war. Four years of lurid, bleeding, murky, murderous war. Who paint those years, with all their scenes?—the hard-fought engagements—the defeats, plans, failures—the gloomy hours, days, when our Nationality seem'd hung in pall of doubt, perhaps death—the Mephistophelean sneers of foreign lands and attachés—the dreaded Scylla of European interference, and the Charybdis of the tremendously dangerous latent strata of secession sympathizers throughout the free States, (far more numerous than is supposed)—the long marches in summer—the hot sweat, and many a sunstroke, as on the rush to Gettysburg in '63—the night battles in the woods, as under Hooker at Chancellorsville—the camps in winter—the military prisons—the hospitals—(alas! alas! the hospitals.)

The Secession war? Nay, let me call it the Union war. Though whatever call'd, it is even yet too near us—too vast and too closely overshadowing—its branches unform'd yet, (but certain,) shooting too far into the future—and the most indicative and mightiest of them yet ungrown. A great literature will yet arise out of the era of those four years, those scenes—era compressing centuries of native passion, first-class pictures, tempests of life and death—an inexhaustible mine for the histories, drama, romance, and even philosophy, of peoples to come—indeed the verteber of poetry and art, (of personal character too,) for all future America—far more grand, in my opinion, to the hands capable of it, than Homer's siege of Troy, or the French wars to Shakspere.

But I must leave these speculations, and come to the theme I have assign'd and limited myself to. Of the actual murder of President Lincoln, though so much has been written, probably the facts are yet very indefinite in most persons' minds. I read from my memoranda, written at the time, and revised frequently and finally since.

The day, April 14, 1865, seems to have been a pleasant one throughout the whole land—the moral atmosphere pleasant too—the long storm, so dark, so fratricidal, full of blood and doubt and gloom, over and ended at last by the sun-rise of such an absolute National victory, and utter break-down of Secessionism—we almost doubted our own senses! Lee had capitulated beneath the apple-tree of Appomattox. The other armies, the flanges of the revolt, swiftly follow'd. And could it really be, then? Out of all the affairs of this world of woe and failure and disorder, was there really come the confirm'd, unerring sign of plan, like a shaft of pure light—of rightful rule—of God? So the day, as I say, was propitious. Early herbage, early flowers, were out. (I remember where I was stopping at the time, the season being advanced, there were many lilacs in full bloom. By one of those caprices that enter and give tinge to events without being at all a part of them, I find myself always reminded of the great tragedy of that day by the sight and odor of these blossoms. It never fails.)

But I must not dwell on accessories. The deed hastens. The popular afternoon paper of Washington, the little "Evening Star," had spatter'd all over its third page, divided among the advertisements in a sensational manner, in a hundred different places, *The President and his Lady will be at the Theatre this evening. . . .* (Lincoln was fond of the theatre. I have myself seen him there several times. I remember thinking how funny it was that he, in some respects the leading actor in the stormiest drama known to real history's stage through centuries, should sit there and be so completely interested and absorb'd in those human jack-straws, moving about with their silly little gestures, foreign spirit, and flatulent text.)

On this occasion the theatre was crowded, many ladies in rich and gay costumes, officers in their uniforms, many well-known citizens, young folks, the usual clusters of gas-lights, the usual magnetism of so many people, cheerful, with perfumes, music of violins and flutes—(and over all, and saturating all, that vast, vague wonder, *Victory*, the nation's victory, the triumph of the Union, filling the air, the thought, the sense, with exhilaration more than all music and perfumes.)

The President came betimes, and, with his wife, witness'd the play from the large stage-boxes of the second tier, two thrown into one, and profusely draped with the national flag. The acts and scenes of the piece—one of those singularly written compositions which have at least the merit of giving entire relief to an audience engaged in mental action or business excitements and cares during the day, as it makes not the slightest call on either the moral, emotional, esthetic, or spiritual nature—a piece, ("Our American Cousin,") in which, among other characters, so call'd, a Yankee, certainly such a one as was never seen, or the least like it ever seen, in North America, is introduced in England, with a varied fol-de-rol of talk, plot, scenery, and such phantasmagoria as goes to make up a modern popular drama—had progress'd through perhaps a couple of its acts, when in the midst of this comedy, or non-such, or whatever it is to be call'd, and to offset it, or finish it out, as if in Nature's and the great Muse's mockery of those poor mimes, came interpolated that scene, not really or exactly to be described at all, (for on the many hundreds who were there it seems to this hour to have left a passing blur, a dream, a blotch)—and yet partially to be described as I now proceed to give it. There is a scene in the play representing a modern parlor, in which two unprecedented English ladies are inform'd by the impossible Yankee that he is not a man of fortune, and therefore undesirable for marriage-catching purposes; after which, the comments being finish'd, the dramatic trio make exit, leaving the stage clear for a moment. At this period came the murder of Abraham Lincoln. Great as all its manifold train, circling round it, and stretching into the future for many a century, in the politics, history, art, &c., of the New World, in point of fact the main thing, the actual murder, transpired with the quiet and simplicity of any commonest occurrence—the bursting of a bud or pod in the growth of vegetation, for instance. Through the general hum following the stage pause, with the change of positions, came the muffled sound of a pistol-shot, which not one-hundredth part of the audience heard at the time—and yet a moment's hush—somehow, surely, a vague startled thrill—and then, through the ornamented, draperied, starr'd and striped spaceway of the President's box, a sudden figure, a man, raises himself with hands and feet, stands a moment on the railing, leaps below to the stage, (a distance of perhaps fourteen or fifteen feet,) falls out of position, catching his boot-heel in the copious drapery, (the American flag,) falls on one knee, quickly recovers himself, rises as if nothing had happen'd, (he really sprains his ankle, but unfelt then)—and so the figure, Booth, the murderer, dress'd in plain black broadcloth, bare-headed, with full, glossy, raven hair, and his eyes like some mad animal's flashing with light and resolution, yet with a certain strange calmness, holds aloft in one hand a large knife—walks along not much back from the footlights— turns fully toward the audience his face of statuesque beauty, lit by those basilisk eyes, flashing with desperation, perhaps insanity—launches out in a firm and steady voice the words *Sic semper tyrannis*—and then walks with neither slow nor very rapid pace diagonally across to the back of the stage, and disappears. (Had not all this terrible scene—making the mimic ones preposterous—had it not all been rehears'd, in blank, by Booth, beforehand?)

A moment's hush—a scream—the cry of *murder*—Mrs. Lincoln leaning out of the box, with ashy cheeks and lips, with involuntary cry, pointing to the retreating figure, *He has kill'd the President.* And still a moment's strange, incredulous suspense—and then the deluge!—then that mixture of horror, noises, uncertainty—(the sound, somewhere back, of a horse's hoofs clattering with speed)—the people burst through chairs and railings, and break them up—there is inextricable confusion and terror— women faint—quite feeble persons fall, and are trampled on—many cries of agony are heard—the broad stage suddenly fills to suffocation with a dense and motley crowd, like some horrible carnival—the audience rush generally upon it, at least the strong men do—the actors and actresses are all there in their play-costumes and painted faces, with mortal fright showing through the rouge—the screams and calls, confused talk—redoubled, trebled—two or three manage to pass up water from the stage to the President's box—others try to clamber up—&c., &c.

In the midst of all this, the soldiers of the President's guard, with others, suddenly drawn to the scene, burst in—(some two hundred altogether)—they storm the house, through all the tiers, especially the upper ones, inflamed with fury, literally charging the audience with fix'd bayonets, muskets and pistols, shouting *Clear out! clear out! you sons of*——
. . . . . Such the wild scene, or a suggestion of it rather, inside the play-house that night.

Outside, too, in the atmosphere of shock and craze, crowds of people, fill'd with frenzy, ready to seize any outlet for it, come near committing murder several times on innocent individuals. One such case was especially exciting. The infuriated crowd, through some chance, got started against one man, either for words he utter'd, or perhaps without any cause at all, and were proceeding at once to actually hang him on a neighboring lamp-post, when he was rescued by a few heroic policemen, who placed him in their midst, and fought their way slowly and amid great peril toward the station house. It was a fitting episode of the whole affair. The crowd rushing and eddying to and fro—the night, the yells, the pale faces, many frighten'd people trying in vain to extricate themselves—the attack'd man, not yet freed from the jaws of death, looking like a corpse—the silent, resolute, half-dozen policemen, with no weapons but their little clubs, yet stern and steady through all those eddying swarms—made a fitting side-scene to the grand tragedy of the murder. They gain'd the station house with the protected man, whom they placed in security for the night, and discharged him in the morning.

And in the midst of that pandemonium, infuriated soldiers, the audience and the crowd, the stage, and all its actors and actresses, its paint-pots, spangles, and gas-lights—the life blood from those veins, the best and sweetest of the land, drips slowly down, and death's ooze already begins its little bubbles on the lips.

Thus the visible incidents and surroundings of Abraham Lincoln's murder, as they really occur'd. Thus ended the attempted secession of these States; thus the four years' war. But the main things come subtly and invisibly afterward, perhaps long afterward—neither military, political, nor (great as those are,) historical. I say, certain secondary and indirect results, out of the tragedy of this death, are, in my opinion, greatest. Not the event of the murder itself. Not that Mr. Lincoln strings the principal points and personages of the period, like beads, upon the single string of his career. Not that his idiosyncrasy, in its sudden appearance and disappearance, stamps this Republic with a stamp more mark'd and enduring than any yet given by any one man—(more even than Washington's;)—but, join'd with these, the immeasurable value and meaning of that whole tragedy lies, to me, in senses finally dearest to a nation, (and here all our own)—the imaginative and artistic senses— the literary and dramatic ones. Not in any common or low meaning of those terms, but a meaning precious to the race, and to every age. A long and varied series of contradictory events arrives at last at its highest poetic, single, central, pictorial denouement. The whole involved, baffling, multiform whirl of the secession period comes to a head, and is gather'd in one brief flash of lightning-illumination—one simple, fierce deed. Its sharp culmination, and as it were solution, of so many bloody and angry problems, illustrates those climax-moments on the stage of universal Time, where the historic Muse at one entrance, and the tragic Muse at the other, suddenly ringing down the curtain, close an immense act in the long drama of creative thought, and give it radiation, tableau, stranger than fiction. Fit radiation—fit close! How the imagination—how the student loves these things! America, too, is to have them. For not in all great deaths, nor far or near—not Cæsar in the Roman senate-house, or Napoleon passing away in the wild night-storm at St. Helena—not Paleologus, falling, desperately fighting, piled over dozens deep with Grecian corpses—not calm old Socrates, drinking the hemlock—outvies that terminus of the secession war, in one man's life, here in our midst, in our own time—that seal of the emancipation of three million slaves—that parturition and delivery of our at last really free Republic, born again, henceforth to commence its career of genuine homogeneous Union, compact, consistent with itself.

Nor will ever future American Patriots and Unionists, indifferently over the whole land, or North or South, find a better moral to their lesson. The final use of the greatest men of a Nation is, after all, not with reference to their deeds in themselves, or their direct bearing on their times or lands. The final use of a heroic-eminent life—especially of a heroic-eminent death—is its indirect filtering into the nation and the race, and to give, often at many removes, but unerringly, age after age, color and fibre to the personalism of the youth and maturity of that age, and of mankind. Then there is a cement to the whole people, subtler, more underlying, than any thing in written constitution, or courts or armies—namely, the cement of a death identified thoroughly with that people, at its head, and for its sake. Strange, (is it not?) that battles, martyrs, agonies, blood, even assassination, should so condense—perhaps only really, lastingly condense—a Nationality.

I repeat it—the grand deaths of the race—the dramatic deaths of every nationality—are its most important inheritance-value—in some respects beyond its literature and art—(as the hero is beyond his finest portrait, and the battle itself beyond its choicest song or epic.) Is not here indeed the point underlying all tragedy? the famous pieces of the Grecian masters—and all masters? Why, if the old Greeks had had this man, what trilogies of plays—what epics—would have been made out of him! How the rhapsodes would have recited him! How quickly that quaint tall form would have enter'd into the region where men vitalize gods, and gods divinify men! But Lincoln, his times, his death—great as any, any age—belong altogether to our own, and are autochthonic. (Sometimes indeed I think our American days, our own stage—the actors we know and have shaken hands, or talk'd with—more fateful than any thing in Eschylus—more heroic than the fighters around Troy—afford kings of men for our Democracy prouder than Agamemnon—models of character cute and hardy as Ulysses—deaths more pitiful than Priam's.)

When, centuries hence, (as it must, in my opinion, be centuries hence before the life of these States, or of Democracy, can be really written and illustrated,) the leading historians and dramatists seek for some personage, some special event, incisive enough to mark with deepest cut, and mnemonize, this turbulent Nineteenth century of ours, (not only these States, but all over the political and social world)—something, perhaps, to close that gorgeous procession of European feudalism, with all its pomp and caste-prejudices, (of whose long train we in America are yet so inextricably the heirs)—something to identify with terrible identification, by far the greatest revolutionary step in the history of the United States, (perhaps the greatest of the world, our century)—the absolute extirpation and erasure of slavery from the States—those historians will seek in vain for any point to serve more thoroughly their purpose, than Abraham Lincoln's death.

Dear to the Muse—thrice dear to Nationality—to the whole human race—precious to this Union—precious to Democracy—unspeakably and forever precious—their first great Martyr Chief.

1882

John Greenleaf Whittier

The Emancipation Group

A replica of the Thomas Ball statue group depicting Lincoln freeing a kneeling slave was unveiled in Park Square, Boston, in December 1879. At the Faneuil Hall ceremony that followed, Andrew Chamberlain, an African-American student at the Boston Latin School, recited a poem composed for the occasion by John Greenleaf Whittier (1807–1892). A dedicated abolitionist who had helped found the American Anti-Slavery Society in 1833, Whittier served as a presidential elector in 1860 and dutifully cast his ballot for Lincoln after the Republicans carried New Hampshire. Although the Ball statue groups in Washington and Boston present a flawed vision of emancipation, they—and the literature they inspired—represent an era in which celebrating the end of slavery was still an essential part of the remembrance of Lincoln.

––––––––––

Boston, 1879

Amidst thy sacred effigies
  Of old renown give place,
O city, Freedom-loved! to his
  Whose hand unchained a race.

Take the worn frame, that rested not
  Save in a martyr's grave—
The care-lined face, that none forgot,
  Bent to the kneeling slave.

Let man be free! The mighty word
  He spake was not his own;
An impulse from the Highest stirred
  These chiselled lips alone.

The cloudy sign, the fiery guide,
  Along his pathway ran,
And Nature, through his voice, denied
  The ownership of man.

We rest in peace where these sad eyes
    Saw peril, strife, and pain;
His was the nation's sacrifice,
    And ours the priceless gain.

O symbol of God's will on earth
    As it is done above!
Bear witness to the cost and worth
    Of justice and of love.

Stand in thy place and testify
    To coming ages long,
That truth is stronger than a lie,
    And righteousness than wrong.

1879

"J. R. P." and The Century Magazine

Lincoln in the South

In January 1887 *The Century Magazine* printed a letter to the editor and an editorial comment under the heading "Lincoln in the South." At the time *The Century* was publishing its highly successful "Battles and Leaders of the Civil War" series, which sought to promote sectional reconciliation by extolling the bravery and sacrifice of soldiers on both sides while avoiding divisive political questions. "J. R. P.," the author of the letter, may have been John Robert Procter (1844–1903), the director of the Kentucky geological survey, who had served as a Confederate artillery officer in Georgia in 1865. The quotation from former Confederate Lieutenant General James Longstreet appeared at the end of his article on the Seven Days in the "Battles and Leaders" series. In his closing paragraph, Longstreet had assessed the performance of Robert E. Lee and Thomas J. (Stonewall) Jackson during the fighting outside Richmond before offering his praise of Lincoln.

In the spring of 1865, during the armistice between Johnston and Sherman, I had gone from camp into Atlanta to learn the news. Senator Wigfall of Texas was in Atlanta, on his way, I think, to the Trans-Mississippi. I was in the rooms of the commandant of the post with some gentlemen, listening to the interesting conversation of Wigfall, when the news of the assassination of Lincoln was brought in. The words of Wigfall and the impression produced by the news upon those present—all Confederate soldiers—so impressed me that I wrote his expressions down in my note-book the same day. An impressive silence of some moments was broken by Wigfall: "Gentlemen, I am—— sorry for this. It is the greatest misfortune that could have befallen the South at this time. I knew Abe Lincoln, and, with all his faults, he had a kind heart; but as for Andy Johnson—" Here he assumed an expression of intense hate and brought his clenched fist with force upon the table—but what he added is too profane to print in these pages.

FRANKFORT, KY., 1886.   *J. R. P.*

In this connection we quote from the article by the Ex-Confederate General Longstreet in THE CENTURY for July, 1885: "Without doubt the greatest man of rebellion times, the one matchless among forty millions for the peculiar difficulties of the period, was Abraham Lincoln."—EDITOR.

John G. Nicolay and John Hay

FROM *Abraham Lincoln: A History*

John G. Nicolay (1832–1901) and John Hay (1838–1905), Lincoln's principal secretaries, were the perfect White House aides—tireless, hardworking, companionable, loyal, and protective. For nearly every day of Lincoln's nearly fifty months as President, the two young men worked and lived at the Executive Mansion, organizing the presidential schedule (when they could), guarding his door, handling his correspondence, delivering his messages, and—in Hay's case—writing anonymous pro-Lincoln articles for several newspapers while intermittently keeping a fascinating diary. After the assassination, Robert Todd Lincoln—by then a close personal friend of Hay—entrusted the two secretaries with securing his father's papers, and in 1874 he gave them exclusive access to the material for their use in writing a biography of President Lincoln. *Abraham Lincoln: A History* was serialized in *Century Magazine* from 1886 to 1890, the same year it was published in ten volumes. Undoubtedly the work of "Lincoln men all the way through," the Nicolay-Hay volumes played a critical role in creating what one historian has called "the Lincoln Memorial Lincoln" by making their subject the central heroic figure of the war for Union and emancipation. The selection presented here is taken from "The Fourteenth of April," a chapter that begins with an account of the flag-raising ceremony held at Fort Sumter on the fourth anniversary of the garrison's surrender before shifting to the cabinet meeting in Washington. (In the narrative, John Hay, who had been commissioned in January 1864, appears as "Major Hay.") Appearing almost twenty-five years after the assassination and drawing upon unimpeachable sources (although Nicolay was absent from Washington when the President fell victim to Booth's bullet), this account can justifiably be called the final word in nineteenth-century recollections of the Lincoln assassination.

In Washington also it was a day, not of exultation, but of deep peace and thankfulness. It was the fifth day after the surrender of Lee; the first effervescence of the intoxicating success had passed away. The President had, with that ever-present sense of responsibility which distinguished him, given his thoughts instantly to the momentous question of the restoration of the Union and of harmony between the lately warring sections. He had, in defiance of precedent and even of his own habit, delivered to the people on the 11th, from the windows of the White House, his well-considered views as to the measures demanded by the times. His whole heart was now enlisted in the work of "binding up the nation's wounds," of doing all which might "achieve and cherish a just and lasting peace."

Grant had arrived that morning in Washington and immediately proceeded to the Executive Mansion, where he met the Cabinet, Friday being their regular day of meeting. He expressed some anxiety as to the news from Sherman, which he was expecting hourly. The President answered him in that singular vein of poetic mysticism which, though constantly held in check by his strong common-sense, formed a remarkable element in his character. He assured Grant that the news would come soon and come favorably, for he had last night had his usual dream which preceded great events. He seemed to be, he said, in a singular and indescribable vessel, but always the same, moving with great rapidity towards a dark and indefinite shore; he had had this dream before Antietam, Murfreesboro', Gettysburg, and Vicksburg. The Cabinet were greatly impressed by this story; but Grant, the most matter-of-fact of created beings, made the characteristic response that "Murfreesboro' was no victory, and had no important results." The President did not argue this point with him, but repeated that Sherman would beat or had beaten Johnston; that his dream must relate to that, as he knew of no other important event which was likely at present to occur.*

The subject of the discussion which took place in the Cabinet on that last day of Lincoln's firm and tolerant rule has been preserved for us in the notes of Mr. Welles. They were written out, it is true, seven years afterwards, at a time when Grant was President, seeking reëlection, and when Mr. Welles had followed Andrew Johnson into full fellowship with the Democratic party. Making whatever allowance is due for the changed environment of the writer, we still find his account of the day's conversation candid and trustworthy. The subject of trade between the States was the first that engaged

"The
Galaxy,"
April, 1872.

---

*This incident is told by the Hon. Gideon Welles in an article printed in "The Galaxy" for April, 1872. It was frequently related by Charles Dickens with characteristic amplifications. See also "George Eliot's Life." Vol. III., p. 82.

the attention of the Cabinet. Mr. Stanton wished it to be carried on under somewhat strict military supervision; Mr. Welles was in favor of a more liberal system; Mr. McCulloch, new to the Treasury, and embarrassed by his grave responsibilities, favored the abolition of the Treasury agencies, and above all desired a definite understanding of the purpose of the Government. The President, seeing that in this divergence of views among men equally able and honest there lay the best chance of a judicious arrangement, appointed the three Secretaries as a commission with plenary power to examine the whole subject, announcing himself as content in advance with their conclusions.

The great subject of the reëstablishment of civil government in the Southern States was then taken up. Mr. Stanton had, a few days before, drawn up a project for an executive ordinance for the preservation of order and the rehabilitation of legal processes in the States lately in rebellion. The President, using this sketch as his text, not adopting it as a whole, but saying that it was substantially the result of frequent discussions in the Cabinet, spoke at some length on the question of reconstruction, than which none more important could ever engage the attention of the Government. It was providential, he thought, that this matter should have arisen at a time when it could be considered, so far as the Executive was concerned, without interference by Congress. If they were wise and discreet, they should reanimate the States and get their governments in successful operation, with order prevailing and the Union reëstablished, before Congress came together in December. The President felt so kindly towards the South, he was so sure of the Cabinet under his guidance, that he was anxious to close the period of strife without overmuch discussion.

He was particularly desirous to avoid the shedding of blood, or any vindictiveness of punishment. He gave plain notice that morning that he would have none of it. "No one need expect he would take any part in hanging or killing these men, even the worst of them. Frighten them out of the country, open the gates, let down the bars, scare them off," said he, throwing up his hands as if scaring sheep. "Enough

Welles, in "The Galaxy."

lives have been sacrificed; we must extinguish our resentments if we expect harmony and union."* He deprecated the disposition he had seen in some quarters to hector and dictate to the people of the South, who were trying to right themselves. He regretted that suffrage, under proper arrangement, had not been given to negroes in Louisiana, but he held that their constitution was in the main a good one. He was averse to the exercise of arbitrary powers by the Executive or by Congress. Congress had the undoubted right to receive or reject members; the Executive had no control in this; but the Executive could do very much to restore order in the States, and their practical relations with the Government, before Congress came together.

Mr. Stanton then read his plan for the temporary military government of the States of Virginia and North Carolina, which for this purpose were combined in one department. This gave rise at once to extended discussion, Mr. Welles and Mr. Dennison opposing the scheme of uniting two States under one government. The President closed the session by saying the same objection had occurred to him, and by directing Mr. Stanton to revise the document and report separate plans for the government of the two States. He did not wish the autonomy nor the individuality of the States destroyed. He commended the whole subject to the most earnest and careful consideration of the Cabinet; it was to be resumed on the following Tuesday; it was, he said, the great question pending—they must now begin to act in the interest of peace.

These were the last words that Lincoln spoke to his Cabinet. They dispersed with these words of clemency and good-will in their ears, never again to meet under his wise and benignant chairmanship. He had told them that morning a strange story, which made some demand upon their faith, but the circumstances under which they were next to come together were beyond the scope of the wildest fancy. The day was one of unusual enjoyment to Mr. Lincoln. His son Robert had returned from the field with General Grant, and the President spent an hour with the

---

*Near the close of the war his old friend, Joseph Gillespie, asked him what was to be done with the rebels. He answered, after referring to the vehement demand prevalent in certain quarters for exemplary punishment, by quoting the words of David to his nephews, who were asking for vengeance on Shimei because "he cursed the Lord's anointed": "What have I to do with you, ye sons of Zeruiah, that ye should this day be adversaries unto me? Shall there any man be put to death this day in Israel?"

young captain in delighted conversation over the campaign. He denied himself generally to the throng of visitors, admitting only a few friends.

Schuyler Colfax, who was contemplating a visit overland to the Pacific, came to ask whether the President would probably call an extra session of Congress during the summer. Mr. Lincoln assured him that he had no such intention, and gave him a verbal message to the mining population of Colorado and the Western slope of the mountains concerning the part they were to take in the great conquests of peace which were coming. In the afternoon he went for a long drive with Mrs. Lincoln. His mood, as it had been all day, was singularly happy and tender. He talked much of the past and the future; after four years of trouble and tumult he looked forward to four years of comparative quiet and normal work; after that he expected to go back to Illinois and practice law again. He was never simpler or gentler than on this day of unprecedented triumph; his heart overflowed with sentiments of gratitude to Heaven, which took the shape usual to generous natures, of love and kindness to all men.

From the very beginning of his Presidency Mr. Lincoln had been constantly subject to the threats of his enemies and the warnings of his friends. The threats came in every form; his mail was infested with brutal and vulgar menace, mostly anonymous, the proper expression of vile and cowardly minds. The warnings were not less numerous; the vaporings of village bullies, the extravagances of excited secessionist politicians, even the drolling of practical jokers, were faithfully reported to him by zealous or nervous friends. Most of these communications received no notice. In cases where there seemed a ground for inquiry it was made, as carefully as possible, by the President's private secretary and by the War Department, but always without substantial result. Warnings that appeared to be most definite, when they came to be examined proved too vague and confused for further attention. The President was too intelligent not to know he was in some danger. Madmen frequently made their way to the very door of the Executive offices and sometimes into Mr. Lincoln's presence.* He

---

*All Presidents receive visits from persons more or less demented. Mr. Hayes, when about to retire one day from his working-room, asked his messenger if there was any one waiting to see him. "Only two, and one of them is crazy." "Send in the sane one," said the President. A grave-looking man was introduced, who announced himself as the emperor of the world. The President rang the bell, and told the messenger if that was his idea of sanity to send in the maniac.

had himself so sane a mind, and a heart so kindly even to his enemies, that it was hard for him to believe in a political hatred so deadly as to lead to murder. He would sometimes laughingly say, "Our friends on the other side would make nothing by exchanging me for Hamlin," the Vice-President having the reputation of more radical views than his chief.

He knew indeed that incitements to murder him were not uncommon in the South. An advertisement had appeared in a paper of Selma, Alabama, in December, 1864, opening a subscription for funds to effect the assassination of Lincoln, Seward, and Johnson before the inauguration. There was more of this murderous spirit abroad than was suspected. A letter was found in the Confederate Archives from one Lieutenant Alston, who wrote to Jefferson Davis immediately after Lincoln's reëlection, offering to "rid his country of some of her deadliest enemies by striking at the very heart's blood of those who seek to enchain her in slavery." This shameless proposal was referred, by Mr. Davis's direction, to the Secretary of War; and by Judge Campbell, Assistant Secretary of War, was sent to the Confederate Adjutant-General indorsed "for attention." We can readily imagine what reception an officer would have met with who should have laid before Mr. Lincoln a scheme to assassinate Jefferson Davis. It was the uprightness and the kindliness of his own heart that made him slow to believe that any such ignoble fury could find a place in the hearts of men in their right minds.

Although he freely discussed with the officials about him the possibilities of danger, he always considered them remote, as is the habit of men constitutionally brave, and positively refused to torment himself with precautions for his own safety. He would sum the matter up by saying that both friends and strangers must have daily access to him in all manner of ways and places; his life was therefore in reach of any one, sane or mad, who was ready to murder and be hanged for it; that he could not possibly guard against all danger unless he were to shut himself up in an iron box, in which condition he could scarcely perform the duties of a President; by the

Pitman, Conspiracy Trial, p. 51. W. Alston to Jefferson Davis. On file in the office of the Judge Advocate-General at Washington. Ibid., p. 52.

hand of a murderer he could die only once; to go continually in fear would be to die over and over. He therefore went in and out before the people, always unarmed, generally unattended. He would receive hundreds of visitors in a day, his breast bare to pistol or knife. He would walk at midnight, with a single secretary or alone, from the Executive Mansion to the War Department and back. He would ride through the lonely roads of an uninhabited suburb from the White House to the Soldiers' Home in the dusk of evening, and return to his work in the morning before the town was astir. He was greatly annoyed when it was decided that there must be a guard stationed at the Executive Mansion, and that a squad of cavalry must accompany him on his daily ride; but he was always reasonable and yielded to the best judgment of others.

Four years of threats and boastings, of alarms that were unfounded, and of plots that came to nothing thus passed away; but precisely at the time when the triumph of the nation over the long insurrection seemed assured, and a feeling of peace and security was diffused over the country, one of the conspiracies, not seemingly more important than the many abortive ones, ripened in the sudden heat of hatred and despair. A little band of malignant secessionists, consisting of John Wilkes Booth, an actor, of a family of famous players, Lewis Powell, alias Payne, a disbanded rebel soldier from Florida, George Atzerodt, formerly a coachmaker, but more recently a spy and blockade runner of the Potomac, David E. Herold, a young druggist's clerk, Samuel Arnold and Michael O'Laughlin, Maryland secessionists and Confederate soldiers, and John H. Surratt, had their ordinary rendezvous at the house of Mrs. Mary E. Surratt, the widowed mother of the last named, formerly a woman of some property in Maryland, but reduced by reverses to keeping a small boarding-house in Washington.

Pitman,
pp. 350, 222.

541 H St.

Booth was the leader of the little coterie. He was a young man of twenty-six, strikingly handsome, with a pale olive face, dark eyes, and that ease and grace of manner which came to him of right from his theatrical ancestors. He had played for several seasons with only indifferent success; his

ABRAHAM LINCOLN.

From a photograph taken March 6, 1865.

value as an actor lay rather in his romantic beauty of person than in any talent or industry he possessed. He was a fanatical secessionist; had assisted at the capture and execution of John Brown, and had imbibed at Richmond and other Southern cities where he had played, a furious spirit of partisanship against Lincoln and the Union party. After the reëlection of Mr. Lincoln, which rang the knell of the insurrection, Booth, like many of the secessionists North and South, was stung to the quick by disappointment. He visited Canada, consorted with the rebel emissaries there, and at last—whether or not at their instigation cannot certainly be said—conceived a scheme to capture the President and take him to Richmond. He spent a great part of the autumn and winter inducing a small number of loose fish of secession sympathies to join him in this fantastic enterprise. He seemed always well supplied with money, and talked largely of his speculations in oil as a source of income; but his agent afterwards testified that he never realized a dollar from that source; that his investments, which were inconsiderable, were a total loss. The

Pitman,
p. 45.

winter passed away and nothing was accomplished. On the 4th of March, Booth was at the Capitol and created a disturbance by trying to force his way through the line of policemen who guarded the passage through which the President walked to the east front of the building. His intentions at this time are not known; he afterwards said he lost an excellent chance of killing the President that day.

He was seized and held back by John W. Westfall, of the Capitol Police.

Pitman, p. 45.

There are indications in the evidence given on the trial of the conspirators that they suffered some great disappointment in their schemes in the latter part of March, and a letter from Arnold to Booth, dated March 27, showed that some of them Ibid., p. 236. had grown timid of the consequences of their contemplated enterprise and were ready to give it up. He advised Booth, before going further, "to go and see how it will be taken in R——d." But timid as they might be by nature, the whole group was so completely under the ascendency of Booth that they did not dare disobey him when in his presence; and after the surrender of Lee, in an access of malice and rage which was akin to madness, he called them together and assigned each his part in the new crime, the purpose of which had arisen suddenly in his mind out of the ruins of the abandoned abduction scheme. This plan was as brief and simple as it was horrible. Powell, alias Payne, the stalwart, brutal, simple-minded boy from Florida, was to murder Seward; Atzerodt, the comic villain of the drama, was assigned to remove Andrew Johnson; Booth reserved for himself the most difficult and most conspicuous rôle of the tragedy; it was Herold's duty to attend him as a page and aid in his escape. Minor parts were assigned to stage carpenters and other hangers-on, who probably did not understand what it all meant. Herold, Atzerodt, and Surratt had previously deposited at a tavern at Surrattsville, Maryland, owned by Mrs. Surratt, but kept by a man named Lloyd, a quantity of ropes, carbines, ammunition, and whisky, which were to be used in the abduction scheme. On the 11th of April Mrs. Surratt, being at the tavern, told Lloyd to have the shooting irons in readiness, and on Friday, the 14th, again visited the place and told him they would probably be called for that night.

The preparations for the final blow were made with feverish haste; it was only about noon of the 14th that Booth learned the President was to go to Ford's Theater that night. It has always been a matter of surprise in Europe that he should have been at a place of amusement on Good Friday; but the day was not kept sacred in America, except by the members of certain churches. It was not, throughout the country, a day of religious observance. The President was fond of the theater; it was one of his few means of recreation. It was natural enough that, on this day of profound national thanksgiving, he should take advantage of a few hours' relaxation to see a comedy. Besides, the town was thronged with soldiers and officers, all eager to see him; it was represented to him that appearing occasionally in public would gratify many people whom he could not otherwise meet. Mrs. Lincoln had asked General and Mrs. Grant to accompany her; they had accepted, and the announcement that they would be present was made as an advertisement in the evening papers; but they changed their minds and went North by an afternoon train. Mrs. Lincoln then invited in their stead Miss Harris and Major Henry R. Rathbone, the daughter and the stepson of Senator Ira Harris. The President's carriage called for these young people, and the four went together to the theater. The President had been detained by visitors, and the play had made some progress when he arrived. When he appeared in his box the band struck up "Hail to the Chief," the actors ceased playing, and the audience rose, cheering tumultuously; the President bowed in acknowledgment of this greeting and the play went on.

From the moment Booth ascertained the President's intention to attend the theater in the evening his every action was alert and energetic. He and his confederates, Herold, Surratt, and Atzerodt, were seen on horseback in every part of the city. He had a hurried conference with Mrs. Surratt before she started for Lloyd's tavern. He intrusted to an actor named Matthews a carefully prepared statement of his reasons for committing the murder, which he charged him to give to the publisher of the "National Intelligencer," but which Matthews,

John F.
Coyle, MS.
Statement.

in the terror and dismay of the night, burned without showing to any one. Booth was perfectly at home in Ford's Theater, where he was greatly liked by all the employees, without other reason than the sufficient one of his youth and good looks. Either by himself or with the aid of his friends he arranged his whole plan of attack and escape during the afternoon. He counted upon address and audacity to gain access to the small passage behind the President's box; once there, he guarded against interference by an arrangement of a wooden bar to be fastened by a simple mortice in the angle of the wall and the door by which he entered, so that the door could not be opened from without. He even provided for the contingency of not gaining entrance to the box by boring a hole in its door, through which he might either observe the occupants or take aim and shoot. He hired at a livery stable a small, fleet horse, which he showed with pride during the day to barkeepers and loafers among his friends.

The moon rose that night at ten o'clock. A few minutes before that hour he called one of the underlings of the theater to the back door and left him there holding his horse. He then went to a saloon near by, took a drink of brandy, and, entering the theater, passed rapidly through the crowd in rear of the dress circle and made his way to the passage leading to the President's box. He showed a card to a servant in attendance and was allowed to pass in. He entered noiselessly, and, turning, fastened the door with the bar he had previously made ready, without disturbing any of the occupants of the box, between whom and himself there yet remained the slight partition and the door through which he had bored the hole. Their eyes were fixed upon the stage; the play was "Our American Cousin," the original version by Tom Taylor, before Sothern had made a new work of it by his elaboration of the part of *Dundreary*.

No one, not even the comedian on the stage, could ever remember the last words of the piece that were uttered that night—the last Abraham Lincoln heard upon earth. The whole performance remains in the memory of those who heard it a vague phantasmagoria, the actors the thinnest of specters. The awful tragedy in the box makes everything else seem pale and unreal. Here were five human beings in a narrow space—the greatest man of his time, in the glory of the most stupendous success in our history, the idolized chief of a nation already mighty, with illimitable vistas of grandeur to come; his beloved wife, proud and happy; a pair of betrothed lovers, with all the promise of felicity that

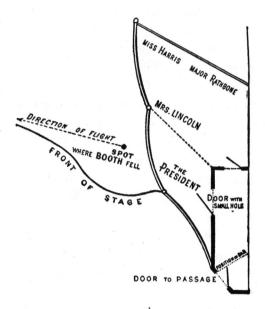

DIAGRAM OF THE BOX IN FORD'S THEATER.
(COPIED FROM THE DRAWING IN THE WAR DEPARTMENT.)

youth, social position, and wealth could give them; and this young actor, handsome as Endymion upon Latmos, the pet of his little world. The glitter of fame, happiness, and ease was upon the entire group, but in an instant everything was to be changed with the blinding swiftness of enchantment. Quick death was to come on the central figure of that company—the central figure, we believe, of the great and good men of the century. Over all the rest the blackest fates hovered menacingly —fates from which a mother might pray that kindly death would save her children in their infancy. One was to wander with the stain of murder on his soul, with the curses of a world upon his name, with a price set upon his head, in frightful physical pain, till he died a dog's death in a burning barn; the stricken wife was to pass the rest of her days in melancholy and madness; of those two young lovers, one was to slay the other, and then end his life a raving maniac.

The murderer seemed to himself to be taking part in a play. Partisan hate and the fumes of brandy had for weeks kept his brain in a morbid state. He felt as if he were playing Brutus off the boards; he posed, expecting applause. Holding a pistol in one hand and a knife in the other, he opened the box door, put the pistol to the President's head, and fired; dropping the weapon, he took the knife in his right hand, and when Major Rathbone sprang to seize him he struck savagely at him. Major Rathbone received the blow on his left arm, suffering a wide and deep wound. Booth, rushing forward, then placed his left hand on the railing of the box and vaulted lightly over to the stage. It was a high leap, but nothing to such a trained athlete. He was in the habit of introducing what actors call sensational leaps in his plays. In "Macbeth," where he met the weird sisters, he leaped from a rock twelve feet high. He would have got safely away but for his spur catching in the folds of the Union flag with which the front of the box was draped. He fell on the stage, the torn flag trailing on his spur, but instantly rose as if he had received no hurt, though in fact the fall had broken his leg; he turned to the audience, brandishing his dripping knife, and shouting the State motto of Virginia, "Sic Semper Tyrannis,"* and fled rapidly across the stage and out of sight. Major Rathbone had shouted, "Stop him!" The cry went out, "He has shot the President." From the audience, at first stupid with surprise, and afterwards wild with excitement and horror, two or three men jumped upon the stage in pursuit of the flying assassin; but he ran through the familiar passages, leaped upon his horse, which was in waiting in the alley behind, rewarded with a kick and a curse the call-boy who had held him, and rode rapidly away in the light of the just risen moon.

The President scarcely moved; his head drooped forward slightly, his eyes closed. Colonel Rathbone, at first not regarding his own grievous hurt, rushed to the door of the box to summon aid. He found it barred, and on the outside some one was beating and clamoring for entrance. He opened the door; a young officer named Crawford entered; one or two army surgeons soon followed, who hastily examined the wound. It was at once seen to be mortal. It was afterwards ascertained that a large

---

*Mr. Leopold de Gaillard, writing on the 29th of April, 1865, refers to these words of Booth, which he calls a "stupid phrase," and not American in character. "I remember," he adds, "but one assassination adorned with a Latin quotation, but it took place in Florence, and in the sixteenth century. Lorenzino treacherously killed his cousin, Alexander de Medici, who was in reality a tyrant, and left in writing near the body the line of Virgil on Brutus: *Vincet amor patriæ laudumque immensa cupido*. It was the thirst of fame which was the real incentive to these savage deeds."—"Gazette de France," April 30, 1865.

STAGE AND PROSCENIUM BOXES OF FORD'S THEATER AS THEY

This drawing was made from two photographs by Brady, lent by W. R. Speare of Washington. One of the photographs (of the President's box, on the opposite page), supposed to be the earlier of the two, differs from the other photograph (showing the stage and all the boxes) as regards the three silk flags, apparently regimental flags, fixed at the sides and middle column of the box. Joseph S. Sessford, at the time assistant treasurer of the theater,

APPEARED ON THE NIGHT OF PRESIDENT LINCOLN'S ASSASSINATION.

is authority for the statement that the second photograph (presented to Mr. Speare by L. Moxley, who had it from Mr. Sessford) was taken three or four days after the assassination, when none of the decorations, except the regimental flags, had been removed. The portrait between the flags is an engraving of Washington.

derringer bullet had entered the back of the head on the left side, and, passing through the brain, had lodged just behind the left eye. By direction of Rathbone and Crawford, the President was carried to a house across the street and laid upon a bed in a small room at the rear of the hall, on the ground floor. Mrs. Lincoln followed, half distracted, tenderly cared for by Miss Harris. Rathbone, exhausted by loss of blood, fainted, and was carried home. Messengers were sent for the members of the Cabinet, for the Surgeon-General, for Dr. Robert K. Stone, the President's family physician; a crowd of people rushed instinctively to the White House and, bursting through the doors, shouted the dreadful news to Robert Lincoln and Major Hay, who sat gossiping in an upper room, Mr. Nicolay being absent at Charleston, at the flag-raising over Sumter. They ran downstairs. Finding a carriage at the door, they entered it to go to Tenth street. As they were driving away, a friend came up and told them that Mr. Seward and most of the Cabinet had been murdered. The news was all so improbable that they could not help hoping it was all untrue. But when they got to Tenth street and found every thoroughfare blocked by the swiftly gathering thousands, agitated by tumultuous excitement, they were prepared for the worst. In a few minutes those who had been sent for, and many others, were gathered in the little chamber where the chief of the state lay in his agony. His son was met at the door by Dr. Stone, who with grave tenderness informed him that there was no hope. After a natural outburst of grief young Lincoln devoted himself the rest of the night to soothing and comforting his mother.

The President had been shot a few minutes past ten. The wound would have brought instant death to most men, but his vital tenacity was extraordinary. He was, of course, unconscious from the first moment; but he breathed with slow and regular respiration throughout the night. As the dawn came, and the lamplight grew pale in the fresher beams, his pulse began to fail; but his face even then was scarcely more haggard than those of the sorrowing group of statesmen and generals around him. His automatic moaning, which had continued through the night, ceased; a look of unspeakable peace came upon his worn features. At twenty-two minutes after seven he died. Stanton broke the silence by saying, "Now he belongs to the ages." Dr. Gurley kneeled by the bedside and prayed fervently. The widow came in from the adjoining room supported by her son and cast herself with loud outcry on the dead body.

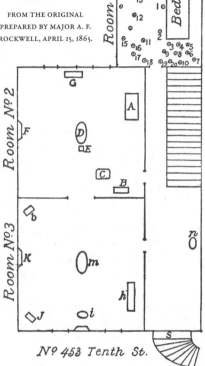

DIAGRAM OF THE HOUSE
IN WHICH PRESIDENT
LINCOLN DIED.

FROM THE ORIGINAL
PREPARED BY MAJOR A. F.
ROCKWELL, APRIL 15, 1865.

No. 453 Tenth St.

ROOM No. 1.—The following indicates the position of persons present, when the Surgeon-General announced the death of the President at 7:22 A.M., April 15, 1865:

1. Surgeon-General Barnes (sitting on the side of the bed, holding the hand of the President).
2. Rev. Dr. Gurley.
3. Surgeon Crane (holding the President's head).
4. Robert Lincoln.
5. Senator Sumner.
6. Assistant Secretary M. B. Field.
7. Major John Hay, Private Secretary of the President.
8. Secretary Welles.
9. General Halleck.
10. Attorney-General Speed.
11. General Meigs (Quartermaster-General).
12. Secretary Usher.
13. Secretary Stanton.
14. Governor Dennison.
15. Major Thomas T. Eckert (Chief of Telegraph Corps at War Dep't).
16. Mrs. Kinney.
17. Miss Kinney.
18. Col. Thomas M. Vincent (War Dep't).
19. Col. L. H. Pelonze (War Dep't).
20. Major A. F. Rockwell (War Dep't).
21. Secretary Hugh McCulloch (occupied this position during the night, but was not present at the closing scene).

The few others noted were persons unknown to Colonel Rockwell. [Generals Augur, Farnsworth, and Todd, Drs. Stone, Leale, Taft, and Abbott, and Alexander Williamson (tutor at the White House) were among them.

ROOM No. 2.—This room was used for the preliminary examination of witnesses. A stenographer was seated at the center table (D) from 12 to 8 in the morning. The Secretary (Stanton) wrote his dispatches to General Dix (with lead pencil) at the same table (C).

A, Bed. B, Washstand. C, Table. D, Table. E, Chair. F, Fireplace. G, Dressing Case.

ROOM No. 3.—This room was occupied by Mrs. Lincoln, Robert Lincoln, and two or three friends.

Mrs. Lincoln occupied the sofa (H) through the night.

H, Sofa. I, Table. J and L, Etagères. K, Fireplace.

HALL.—Carpet covered with oilcloth, stained with drops of blood.

N, Hat Rack. S, Large blood spot on doorstep.

Tenth Street   S))⟩⟩——————→N

Fords Theatre

CODA

Among the many unprecedented roles Abraham Lincoln played during his presidency—emancipator, radical interpreter of the Constitution, commander-in-chief of the world's largest army—one of the most important was as the nation's mourner-in-chief. As the rebellion intensified and the death toll mounted, Lincoln endeavored to console individuals he knew personally, those whose losses had been brought to his attention, and ultimately the entire country, grieving together under the crushing burden of some 750,000 wartime deaths.

Lincoln's first celebrated letter of condolence was sent on May 25, 1861, to the parents of Colonel Elmer E. Ellsworth, a dashing young New York Zouave officer who had been killed by the proprietor of an Alexandria, Virginia, hotel after he tore down a Confederate flag flying from its roof. Ellsworth, the first Union officer killed in the conflict, had read law in Lincoln's office before the war, and the President accorded the young hero a White House funeral even as he wrote this sublime note to his mother and father.

The next year, Lincoln wrote with equal earnestness to Fanny Mc-Cullough, the twenty-two-year-old daughter of an officer killed in a nighttime battle near Coffeeville, Mississippi, on December 5, 1862. Lieutenant Colonel William McCullough of the 4th Illinois Cavalry had served before the war as clerk of the McLean County circuit court in Bloomington, where Lincoln had made his acquaintance. Lincoln's most famous personal condolence letter went on November 21, 1864, to Mrs. Lydia Bixby, five of whose sons had reportedly "died gloriously on the field of battle." Although no original copy has ever been found in Lincoln's hand, and some have attributed its composition to presidential secretary John Hay, the letter was published in the *Boston Transcript* as an authentic presidential communication on November 25. As it turned out, Mrs. Bixby's losses had been exaggerated. Only two of her sons had died in battle; one was honorably discharged and returned home to Boston, one had deserted from the Union army three years earlier, and one was captured and either deserted or died in a Confederate prison.

Lincoln's two most famous presidential speeches focused intently on the meaning of death. In the Gettysburg Address, he not only eulogized the Union soldiers who died in the war's largest battle so that the nation might live, but calculated their deaths as central to the nation's rebirth. Yet in his Second Inaugural Address only twenty months later, the war-weary President insisted that all of the conflict's sacrifices had been ordained by a God determined to punish both North and South for so long tolerating the sin of slavery. This Lincoln may have preached "malice toward none" and "charity for all," but believed that centuries of suffering under the lash had to be repaid by the ongoing suffering by the sword. In the final reckoning, at least to America's mourner-in-chief, there could be no consolation without atonement.

To Ephraim D. and Phoebe Ellsworth

To the Father and Mother of Col.   Washington D.C.
Elmer E. Ellsworth: May 25. 1861

My dear Sir and Madam,   In the untimely loss of your noble son, our affliction here, is scarcely less than your own. So much of promised usefulness to one's country, and of bright hopes for one's self and friends, have rarely been so suddenly dashed, as in his fall. In size, in years, and in youthful appearance, a boy only, his power to command men, was surpassingly great. This power, combined with a fine intellect, an indomitable energy, and a taste altogether military, constituted in him, as seemed to me, the best natural talent, in that department, I ever knew. And yet he was singularly modest and deferential in social intercourse. My acquaintance with him began less than two years ago; yet through the latter half of the intervening period, it was as intimate as the disparity of our ages, and my engrossing engagements, would permit. To me, he appeared to have no indulgences or pastimes; and I never heard him utter a profane, or an intemperate word. What was conclusive of his good heart, he never forgot his parents. The honors he labored for so laudably, and, in the sad end, so gallantly gave his life, he meant for them, no less than for himself.

In the hope that it may be no intrusion upon the sacredness of your sorrow, I have ventured to address you this tribute to the memory of my young friend, and your brave and early fallen child.

May God give you that consolation which is beyond all earthly power. Sincerely your friend in a common affliction—

A. LINCOLN

To Fanny McCullough

Dear Fanny
Executive Mansion,
Washington, December 23, 1862.

It is with deep grief that I learn of the death of your kind and brave Father; and, especially, that it is affecting your young heart beyond what is common in such cases. In this sad world of ours, sorrow comes to all; and, to the young, it comes with bitterest agony, because it takes them unawares. The older have learned to ever expect it. I am anxious to afford some alleviation of your present distress. Perfect relief is not possible, except with time. You can not now realize that you will ever feel better. Is not this so? And yet it is a mistake. You are sure to be happy again. To know this, which is certainly true, will make you some less miserable now. I have had experience enough to know what I say; and you need only to believe it, to feel better at once. The memory of your dear Father, instead of an agony, will yet be a sad sweet feeling in your heart, of a purer, and holier sort than you have known before.

Please present my kind regards to your afflicted mother.

Your sincere friend   A. LINCOLN.

Miss. Fanny McCullough.

To Lydia Bixby

Executive Mansion,
Washington, Nov. 21, 1864.

Dear Madam, — I have been shown in the files of the War Department a statement of the Adjutant General of Massachusetts, that you are the mother of five sons who have died gloriously on the field of battle.

I feel how weak and fruitless must be any words of mine which should attempt to beguile you from the grief of a loss so overwhelming. But I cannot refrain from tendering to you the consolation that may be found in the thanks of the Republic they died to save.

I pray that our Heavenly Father may assuage the anguish of your bereavement, and leave you only the cherished memory of the loved and lost, and the solemn pride that must be yours, to have laid so costly a sacrifice upon the altar of Freedom. Yours, very sincerely and respectfully,

A. LINCOLN.

Mrs. Bixby.

The Gettysburg Address

Four score and seven years ago our fathers brought forth on this continent, a new nation, conceived in Liberty, and dedicated to the proposition that all men are created equal.

Now we are engaged in a great civil war, testing whether that nation, or any nation so conceived and so dedicated, can long endure. We are met on a great battle-field of that war. We have come to dedicate a portion of that field, as a final resting place for those who here gave their lives that that nation might live. It is altogether fitting and proper that we should do this.

But, in a larger sense, we can not dedicate—we can not consecrate—we can not hallow—this ground. The brave men, living and dead, who struggled here, have consecrated it, far above our poor power to add or detract. The world will little note, nor long remember what we say here, but it can never forget what they did here. It is for us the living, rather, to be dedicated here to the unfinished work which they who fought here have thus far so nobly advanced. It is rather for us to be here dedicated to the great task remaining before us—that from these honored dead we take increased devotion to that cause for which they gave the last full measure of devotion—that we here highly resolve that these dead shall not have died in vain—that this nation, under God, shall have a new birth of freedom—and that government of the people, by the people, for the people, shall not perish from the earth.

Second Inaugural Address

Fellow Countrymen: March 4, 1865

At this second appearing to take the oath of the presidential office, there is less occasion for an extended address than there was at the first. Then a statement, somewhat in detail, of a course to be pursued, seemed fitting and proper. Now, at the expiration of four years, during which public declarations have been constantly called forth on every point and phase of the great contest which still absorbs the attention, and engrosses the energies of the nation, little that is new could be presented. The progress of our arms, upon which all else chiefly depends, is as well known to the public as to myself; and it is, I trust, reasonably satisfactory and encouraging to all. With high hope for the future, no prediction in regard to it is ventured.

On the occasion corresponding to this four years ago, all thoughts were anxiously directed to an impending civil-war. All dreaded it—all sought to avert it. While the inaugeral address was being delivered from this place, devoted altogether to *saving* the Union without war, insurgent agents were in the city seeking to *destroy* it without war—seeking to dissolve the Union, and divide effects, by negotiation. Both parties deprecated war; but one of them would *make* war rather than let the nation survive; and the other would *accept* war rather than let it perish. And the war came.

One eighth of the whole population were colored slaves, not distributed generally over the Union, but localized in the Southern part of it. These slaves constituted a peculiar and powerful interest. All knew that this interest was, somehow, the cause of the war. To strengthen, perpetuate, and extend this interest was the object for which the insurgents would rend the Union, even by war; while the government claimed no right to do more than to restrict the territorial enlargement of it. Neither party expected for the war, the magnitude, or the duration, which it has already attained. Neither anticipated that the *cause* of the conflict might cease with, or even before, the conflict itself should cease. Each looked for an easier triumph, and a result less fundamental and astounding. Both read the same Bible, and pray to the same God; and each invokes His aid against the other. It may seem strange that any men should dare to ask a just God's assistance in wringing their bread from the sweat of other men's faces; but let us judge not that we be not judged. The prayers of both could not be answered; that of neither has been answered fully. The Almighty has His own purposes. "Woe unto the world because of offences! for it must needs be that offences come; but woe to that man by whom the offence cometh!" If we shall suppose that American Slavery is one of those offences which, in the providence of God, must needs come, but which, having continued through His appointed time, He now wills to remove, and that He gives to both North and South, this terrible war, as the woe due to those by whom the offence came, shall we discern therein any departure from those divine attributes which the believers in a Living God always ascribe to Him? Fondly do we hope—fervently do we pray—that this mighty scourge of war may speedily pass away. Yet, if God wills that it continue, until all the wealth piled by the bond-man's two hundred and fifty years of unrequited toil shall be sunk, and until every drop of blood drawn with the lash, shall be paid by another drawn with the sword, as was said three thousand years ago, so still it must be said "the judgments of the Lord, are true and righteous altogether."

With malice toward none; with charity for all; with firmness in the right, as God gives us to see the right, let us strive on to finish the work we are in; to bind up the nation's wounds; to care for him who shall have borne the battle, and for his widow, and his orphan—to do all which may achieve and cherish a just, and a lasting peace, among ourselves, and with all nations.

CHRONOLOGY

SOURCES AND ACKNOWLEDGMENTS

INDEX

Chronology, May 1864–March 1869

1864   John Wilkes Booth (b. 1838) ends successful stage career on May 28, giving his last paid performance as an actor in Boston production of *The Corsican Brothers*. Visits western Pennsylvania to oversee his investments in oil drilling ventures. Meets in Baltimore in early August with school friend Samuel Arnold and former neighbor Michael O'Laughlen, both former Confederate soldiers. Booth enlists them in plot to abduct President Abraham Lincoln while he is traveling between the White House and the Soldiers' Home outside Washington, take him to Richmond, and use him as a hostage in order to force the resumption of prisoner exchanges. (In July 1862 the Union and Confederate armies negotiated an agreement on prisoner exchanges that began to break down in the summer of 1863 because of the Confederate refusal to treat black soldiers and their officers as prisoners of war. In April 1864 Lieutenant General Ulysses S. Grant suspended general prisoner exchanges until the Confederates agreed to treat black and white prisoners equally and to recognize the validity of the surrender terms given to the Confederate garrisons at Vicksburg and Port Hudson in July 1863.) Booth ends involvement in the oil industry in September and begins transferring his assets to family members. Transfer may have been precaution against possible future confiscation by the federal government. Maryland voters narrowly approve new state constitution abolishing slavery, October 12–13. During visit to Montreal, October 18–27, Booth meets with Confederate agents Patrick Martin and George Sanders and possibly informs them of his abduction plot. Martin gives Booth letter of introduction to Dr. William Queen, a Confederate sympathizer in Charles County, Maryland, and may also provide Booth with funds. Lincoln is reelected on November 8, defeating Democrat George B. McClellan with 55 percent of the popular vote and 212 of 233 electoral votes. Booth visits Queen at his home near Bryantown, Maryland, November 12–13. Begins planning escape route from Washington through pro-Confederate southern Maryland and across the Potomac River into Virginia. Visits his sister Asia Booth Clarke in Philadelphia and gives her packet of papers for safekeeping, including letter, addressed "To whom it may concern," justifying his plot to capture Lincoln. Appears with brothers Edwin and Junius Brutus in special benefit performance of *Julius Caesar* in New York City, November 25, playing Mark Antony. Returns to Charles County, December 18–19, and is introduced to Dr. Samuel Mudd, a Confederate sympathizer and former slave-owner. Recruits Thomas Harbin, a Confederate agent from Charles County, into abduction plot. Encounters Mudd in Washington in late December and is introduced by him to John Surratt, a clandestine Confederate courier who joins Booth's conspiracy.

1865   Booth purchases two Spencer repeating carbines, six Colt revolvers, three bowie knives, and two pairs of handcuffs during visit to New

York City in early January. Harbin and Surratt recruit George Atzerodt, a resident of Port Tobacco, Maryland, with experience running
the Union blockade on the lower Potomac. (Conspiracy now also
includes David Herold, a Washington druggist's clerk familiar with
the Charles County countryside.) With Lincoln no longer traveling
to his summer residence at the Soldiers' Home, Booth proposes to
Arnold and O'Laughlen that they abduct the President during a performance at Ford's Theatre. While visiting Baltimore in late January
Surratt meets and recruits Lewis Powell, alias Payne, a former Confederate soldier from Florida.

General prisoner exchanges resume in February after the Confederates offer to exchange all Union prisoners.

Lincoln is inaugurated for second term on March 4 with Booth in
the audience. Booth outlines plan to abduct Lincoln from Ford's
Theatre at meeting with several co-conspirators on March 15. Arnold
objects to theater scheme, points out that prisoner exchanges have
been resumed, and challenges Booth to take action by the end of the
week. On afternoon of March 17 Booth meets with Arnold, O'Laughlen, Powell, Herold, Atzerodt, and Surratt outside Washington
boardinghouse owned by Mary Surratt, John Surratt's widowed
mother, and tells them that Lincoln is visiting Campbell Hospital
near the Soldiers' Home. Conspirators prepare to seize the President
as he returns by carriage to the White House, but ambush is abandoned when Booth learns that Lincoln has changed his plans and is
not at the hospital. The next day, Herold, Atzerodt, and John Surratt
hide two Spencer carbines at the tavern owned by Mary Surratt in
Surrattsville (now Clinton), a crossroads in Prince George's County,
Maryland. That evening, Booth gives his last stage performance, appearing as Duke Pescara in a benefit performance of Richard Sheil's
tragedy *The Apostate* at Ford's Theatre. Lincoln leaves Washington on
March 23 for extended stay at Grant's headquarters at City Point,
Virginia. At meeting with Arnold and O'Laughlen on March 31,
Booth claims to have abandoned his plot against Lincoln.

Union assault breaks Confederate lines outside Petersburg on April
2, forcing General Robert E. Lee to evacuate his troops from Petersburg and Richmond as the Confederate government flees its capital.
John Surratt leaves Washington on April 3 and travels to Montreal
carrying messages for Confederate agents in Canada. Lincoln tours
Richmond on April 4. Secretary of State William H. Seward breaks
his jaw and right arm in carriage accident in Washington, April 5.
Lincoln returns to Washington on April 9, Palm Sunday, the same day
that Lee surrenders to Grant at Appomattox Court House. On April
11 Mary Surratt tells John Lloyd, who is renting her tavern in Surrattsville, to make ready the carbines hidden there in March. That
evening, Lincoln gives speech at the White House on reconstruction
in which he endorses limited black suffrage. Booth is in the audience
and reportedly vows to kill the President. Powell is seen outside the
Seward home on Lafayette Square in Washington, April 13. On the
morning of April 14 Atzerodt rents room in Kirkwood House, hotel

where Vice President Andrew Johnson is living. Booth learns that the President and Mary Lincoln will be attending evening performance of comedy *Our American Cousin* at Ford's Theatre with General Grant and Julia Grant as their guests. Writes letter to *National Intelligencer* newspaper justifying his actions and gives to actor John Mathews. Learns that Grant is leaving the city and will not be attending the theater. Mary Surratt visits tavern in late afternoon, gives Lloyd a field glass belonging to Booth, and tells him the carbines will be retrieved that night. Booth meets with Atzerodt, Powell, and Herold to review his plan: Booth will assassinate Lincoln at the theater, Atzerodt will kill Johnson at the Kirkwood House, and Powell will murder Seward in his home, with the three attacks to take place shortly after 10 P.M. Herold will accompany Powell to Lafayette Square, then join Booth in his escape through Maryland. The President and Mary Lincoln arrive at Ford's around 8:30 P.M., accompanied by their guests, Clara Harris and Major Henry Rathbone. Armed with a single-shot .44-caliber derringer and a large knife, Booth enters the presidential box at about 10:30 P.M. Booth shoots Lincoln in the back of the head, wounds Rathbone during brief struggle, then leaps onto the stage and escapes from the theater before fleeing the scene on horseback. At about the same time, Powell gains entry to the Seward house, where he wounds the secretary of state, two of his sons, a male nurse, and a messenger before escaping on horseback. Atzerodt loses his nerve, gets drunk, and flees without ever approaching Johnson. After two surgeons examine Lincoln and agree that his wound is mortal, the unconscious President is carried across the street to the Petersen house. Booth and Herold separately cross the Anacostia River by way of the Navy Street bridge before rendezvousing in Maryland. Powell hides in northeast Washington. Mathews reads Booth's letter to the *National Intelligencer* and then burns it. Secretary of War Edwin M. Stanton arrives at Petersen house and takes charge of investigation as witnesses from Ford's Theatre identify Booth as the assassin. Booth and Herold reach tavern in Surrattsville after midnight and take the field glasses and a carbine from Lloyd before leaving. At about 4 A.M. on April 15 they reach the farm of Dr. Samuel Mudd near Bryantown. Mudd treats Booth, who had fractured his left tibia either in his leap onto the stage or in a subsequent horse fall. Lincoln dies without regaining consciousness at the Petersen house at 7:22 A.M. Andrew Johnson is sworn in as president by Chief Justice Salmon P. Chase at 11 A.M. Investigators in Washington connect Booth to John Surratt, Atzerodt, and Herold, and Baltimore provost marshal links him to Arnold and O'Laughlen. Atzerodt leaves Washington and makes way toward Germantown, Maryland, where his uncle lives. John Surratt learns of assassination in Elmira, New York, and flees to Canada (will later make his way to England and then Italy). Booth and Herold leave the Mudd farm on the afternoon of April 15 and reach estate of Samuel Cox early on April 16. Cox has his overseer take them to hiding place in the pine woods of Zekiah Swamp. On the morning of April 17 two detectives sent by the Baltimore provost marshal arrest Arnold at

Fortress Monroe, Virginia. O'Laughlen surrenders to authorities in
Baltimore. Edman (Ned) Spangler, a stagehand suspected of helping
Booth escape from Ford's Theatre, is arrested in Washington. After
receiving tip that suspicious persons were seen at Mary Surratt's
boardinghouse, military search the house on the night of April 17.
Powell walks in during search disguised as laborer looking for work
and is taken into custody along with Mary Surratt. Servant from Seward
house recognizes Powell as the assailant from April 14. War Department
continues investigation into the assassination, resulting in the arrest of
hundreds of potential suspects and witnesses; investigators also pursue
numerous false sightings of Booth throughout the country, although
manhunt remains focused on Maryland. Major General William T.
Sherman and General Joseph E. Johnston meet near Durham Station,
North Carolina, on April 18 and sign agreement providing military
and political terms for the surrender of the remaining Confederate
armies. Funeral services are held for Lincoln in the White House on
April 19 before his body is taken to lie in state at the Capitol. Atzerodt
is arrested by Union soldiers at his uncle's home in Germantown in
the early hours of April 20 after talking carelessly about the assassination. Booth and Herold attempt to cross the Potomac on the night of
April 20 in a skiff provided by Thomas Jones, a local Confederate
agent. They turn back after encountering a Union gunboat and land
at Nanjemoy Creek, where a Confederate sympathizer lets them
hide in a shack. Funeral train carrying Lincoln's body and the exhumed remains of his son Willie leaves Washington for Springfield,
Illinois, on the morning of April 21, reversing the route taken by
Lincoln as president-elect in February 1861. Train stops in Baltimore
before reaching Harrisburg on night of April 21. The same day,
President Johnson and the cabinet reject the Sherman-Johnson
surrender agreement for being too lenient. Funeral train arrives in
Philadelphia on April 22. That night, Booth and Herold cross the
Potomac and land at Machodoc Creek in King George County,
Virginia. With help from Thomas Harbin, they make their way to
home of Dr. Richard Stuart, who tells them to spend the night in
the cabin of a nearby black family. Funeral train leaves Philadelphia
on April 24 and arrives in Jersey City, where Lincoln's body is taken
across the Hudson to lower Manhattan. The same day, Dr. Samuel
Mudd is arrested after having been questioned several times by federal authorities. Booth and Herold meet William Jett, a former
Confederate soldier, in Port Conway and cross the Rappahannock
River by ferry with him. Jett accompanies them to the Garrett farm
two miles southwest of Port Royal, then proceeds to nearby village of
Bowling Green. In Washington, Colonel Lafayette Baker, a senior
investigator for the War Department, sees telegram reporting that
two suspicious men had crossed the Potomac on April 16. Baker decides to expand search into region of Virginia between the Potomac
and Rappahannock. He sends detectives Everton Conger and Luther
Byron Baker (his cousin) and a twenty-six-man detachment from the
16th New York Cavalry by boat to Belle Plain, Virginia. After lying in

state at City Hall, Lincoln's body is conveyed through the streets of New York on April 25 and then sent by train to Albany. The same day, Conger and the cavalry arrive in Port Conway, where witnesses identify photographs of Booth and Herold and tell Conger to look for Jett in Bowling Green. Conger and his men apprehend Jett, who tells them Booth is at the Garrett farm. In the early hours of April 26 the cavalry detachment surrounds the tobacco barn where Booth and Herold are sleeping. When Booth refuses to surrender, Conger sets fire to the barn. Herold surrenders, but when Booth moves toward the barn door carrying Spencer carbine, Sergeant Boston Corbett shoots him with a .44-caliber revolver, partially severing Booth's cervical spinal cord. Booth is carried from the barn and dies two hours later at dawn on April 26. The same day, the funeral train leaves Albany and arrives in Buffalo. Johnston surrenders Confederate forces in the Carolinas, Georgia, and Florida on terms similar to those given to Lee at Appomattox. Booth's body is autopsied in Washington on April 27 and then secretly buried under the floor of a storeroom in the Washington Arsenal (now Fort McNair). The same day, the funeral train leaves Buffalo, arriving in Cleveland, April 28, Columbus, April 29, and Indianapolis, April 30.

After receiving legal opinion from Attorney General James Speed, President Johnson orders on May 1 that Booth's co-conspirators be tried by a nine-member military commission. (Order is drafted by Stanton, who strongly favors a military trial.) The same day, after stopping in Michigan City, Indiana, the funeral train arrives in Chicago. On May 2 Johnson issues a proclamation accusing Jefferson Davis and five Confederate agents who had operated in Canada of having "incited, concerted, and procured" Lincoln's assassination. Funeral train arrives in Springfield on May 3 after trip covering more than 1,600 miles. Lincoln is buried in Oak Ridge Cemetery, May 4. The same day, the Confederate forces in Alabama, Mississippi, and eastern Louisiana surrender. Military commission meets at Washington Arsenal on May 10 as Arnold, Atzerodt, Herold, Mudd, O'Laughlen, Powell (under his alias Payne), Spangler, and Mary Surratt are formally charged with conspiring to assassinate Lincoln, Johnson, Seward, and Grant. Jefferson Davis and seven Confederate agents are named as unindicted co-conspirators. The same day, Davis is captured by Union cavalry near Irwinville, Georgia. Judge Advocate General Joseph Holt and his assistants Henry Burnett and John Bingham begin presenting prosecution witnesses on May 12. Government argues that assassination conspiracy is part of wider Confederate policy of illegal warfare involving the deliberate starvation of Union prisoners, plans to destroy Northern cities and steamboats by arson, and attempts to spread yellow fever.

Confederate forces in the Trans-Mississippi surrender on June 2. Defense attorneys present closing arguments in assassination conspiracy trial, June 19–23. John Bingham delivers summation for the prosecution, June 27–28, defending legitimacy of military trial. Commission decides verdicts, June 29–30. Atzerodt, Herold, Powell, and Mary

Surratt are sentenced to death, while Arnold, Mudd, and O'Laughlen
are given life sentences and Spangler receives six years. Five members
of the commission sign clemency petition for Surratt and give it to
Holt.

President Johnson approves verdicts on July 5. (Johnson later
claims that Holt never showed him the clemency petition, a charge
Holt will deny.) Condemned prisoners are informed of their sentences
on July 6. Atzerodt, Herold, Powell, and Surratt are hanged at the
Washington Arsenal on July 7. Arnold, Mudd, O'Laughlen, and
Spangler are sent on July 17 to Fort Jefferson, military prison on Dry
Tortugas, island in the Gulf of Mexico seventy miles west of the
Florida Keys. Cabinet advises Johnson on July 21 that Jefferson Davis
should be tried for treason in federal court in Virginia, as press reports
cast increasing doubt on evidence linking him to the assassination.
(Testimony before military commission linking Davis and Confeder-
ate agents in Canada to the Booth conspiracy is eventually discredited.
Davis is later indicted for treason, but is released on bail in May 1867
and never brought to trial.)

1866   John Surratt is discovered serving in the Papal Guard in Italy under
         an assumed name. Arrested by Papal authorities on November 7, he
         escapes and flees to Alexandria, Egypt, where he is apprehended on
         November 27. U.S. Supreme Court releases opinions in *Ex parte
         Milligan* on December 17. In case arising from an 1864 prosecution
         of antiwar Democrats in Indiana, the majority of the Court rules that
         civilians cannot be tried by military commissions in jurisdictions
         where the civilian courts remain open.

1867   Charged with aiding and abetting in Lincoln's murder, John Surratt
         goes on trial in civilian court in Washington, D.C., on June 10. Pros-
         ecution and defense witnesses present conflicting testimony regarding
         Surratt's whereabouts on April 14, 1865. Trial ends on August 10 after
         jury deadlocks 8–4 in favor of acquittal. Michael O'Laughlen dies of
         yellow fever in Dry Tortugas on September 23.

1868   Surratt is indicted for treason on June 18. U.S. district court in south-
         ern Florida dismisses habeas corpus petition filed by Mudd, ruling on
         September 9 that the *Milligan* decision does not apply to his case
         because Lincoln's assassination was a military crime subject to military
         trial. Treason indictment against John Surratt is dismissed on Septem-
         ber 24 for having been filed after the statute of limitation had expired,
         and Surratt is released from custody.

1869   President Johnson pardons Mudd, February 8, and Spangler and Ar-
         nold, March 2.

Sources and Acknowledgments

Great care has been taken to locate and acknowledge all owners of copyrighted material included in this book. If any owner has inadvertently been omitted, acknowledgment will gladly be made in future printings.

The most common sources are indicated by these abbreviations:

CWAL   *The Collected Works of Abraham Lincoln*, ed. Roy P. Basler (8 vols., New Brunswick, N.J.: Rutgers University Press, 1953). Copyright © 1953 by the Abraham Lincoln Association. Used by permission of the Abraham Lincoln Association.

OR   *The War of the Rebellion: A Compilation of the Official Records of the Union and Confederate Armies* (128 vols., Washington, D.C.: Government Printing Office, 1880–1901).

Pitman   *The Assassination of President Lincoln and the Trial of the Conspirators*, compiled and arranged by Benn Pitman (New York: Moore, Wilstach & Baldwin, 1865).

Poore   *The Conspiracy Trial for the Murder of the President*, edited by Ben Perley Poore, 3 vols. (Boston: J. E. Tilton and Company, 1866).

Frederick A. Aiken. Argument for Mary Surratt: *Pitman*, 298–99.

Anglo-African. Caste Hate at the Great Funeral: *The Anglo-African*, April 29, 1865.

George Bancroft. Oration in Union Square, New York City: *Obsequies of Abraham Lincoln in Union Square, New York, April 25, 1865* (New York: D. Van Nostrand, 1865), 9–20.

James Madison Bell. Poem in Commemoration of Lincoln: *The Poetical Works of James Madison Bell* (Lansing, Mich.: Wynkoop Hallenbeck Crawford, 1901), 154–55.

John A. Bingham. Argument for the Prosecution: *Pitman*, 379–80, 397.

John Wilkes Booth. Diary, April 17, April 22, 1865: *"Right or Wrong, God Judge Me": The Writings of John Wilkes Booth*, ed. John Rhodehamel and Louise Taper (Urbana and Chicago: University of Illinois Press, 1997), 154–55. © 1997 by the Board of Trustees of the University of Illinois. "To whom it may concern": *The New York Times*, April 21, 1865.

William Cullen Bryant. Ode: *Obsequies of Abraham Lincoln in Union Square, New York, April 25, 1865* (New York: D. Van Nostrand, 1865).

Francis B. Carpenter. "In Memoriam:" *Hours at Home*, June 1865.

Phoebe Cary. "Our Sun Hath Gone Down:" *Poetical Tributes to the Memory of Abraham Lincoln* (Philadelphia: J. B. Lippincott & Co., 1865), 37–40.

Mary Chesnut. Diary, April 22–23, 1865: *Mary Chesnut's Civil War*, ed. C. Vann Woodward (New Haven: Yale University Press, 1981), 791–92, 795. Copyright © 1981 by C. Vann Woodward, Sally Bland Meets, Barbara C. Carpenter, Sally

Bland Johnson, and Katherine W. Herbert. Used by permission of Yale University Press.

Charles Carlton Coffin. Scenes in Richmond: *Boston Journal*, April 10, 1865.

William T. Coggleshall. From *The Journeys of Abraham Lincoln*: *The Journeys of Abraham Lincoln: from Springfield to Washington, 1861, as President Elect; and from Washington to Springfield, 1865, as President Martyred* (Columbus, Ohio: Ohio State Journal, 1865), 293–99, 302–3.

Everton J. Conger. Testimony Before the Military Commission: *Poore*, 1: 312–18.

Boston Corbett. Testimony Before the Military Commission: *Poore*, 1: 322–26.

L. M. Dawn. Farewell Father, Friend and Guardian: *Memorial Record of the Nation's Tribute to Abraham Lincoln*, compiled by B. F. Morris (Washington, D.C.: W. H. & O. H. Morrison, 1865), 227.

Mary A. Dennison. To Mrs. Lincoln: *Poetical Tributes to the Memory of Abraham Lincoln* (Philadelphia: J. B. Lippincott & Co., 1865), 222–23.

Benjamin Disraeli. Remarks in the House of Commons: *Appendix to Diplomatic Correspondence of 1865; The Assassination of Abraham Lincoln, Late President of the United States of America* (Washington, D.C.: Government Printing Office, 1866), 154–55.

William E. Doster. Argument for Lewis Powell: *Pitman*, 311. Argument for George Atzerodt: *Pitman*, 304–5.

Frederick Douglass. Address at Cooper Union, New York City: Manuscript, Frederick Douglass Papers, Library of Congress. Oration in Memory of Abraham Lincoln, Washington, D.C.: *Oration by Frederick Douglass Delivered on the Occasion of the Unveiling of the Freedmen's Monument in Memory of Abraham Lincoln in Lincoln Park, Washington, D.C., April 14th, 1876* (Washington, D.C.: Gibson Brothers, 1876), 1–15.

Helen Du Barry. Letter to Ann Amelia Bratt: "Eyewitness Account of Lincoln's Assassination," *Journal of the Illinois State Historical Society*, vol. 39, no. 3 (September 1946), 366–69. Used by permission of the Illinois State Historical Society.

Thomas T. Eckert. Testimony Before the House Judiciary Committee: *Testimony taken before the Judiciary Committee of the House of Representatives in the Investigation of the Charges against Andrew Johnson. Second Session Thirty-Ninth Congress, and First Session Fortieth Congress, 1867* (Washington, D.C.: Government Printing Office, 1867), 674.

Ralph Waldo Emerson. Remarks at the Services Held in Concord, Massachusetts: *Miscellanies* (Boston and New York: Houghton, Mifflin and Company, 1883), 305–15.

Wilbur Fisk. Letter to *The Green Mountain Freeman*: *Hard Marching Every Day: The Civil War Letters of Private Wilbur Fisk, 1861–1865*, ed. Emil and Ruth Rosenblatt (Lawrence: University Press of Kansas, 1992), 323–26. Copyright © 1983, 1992 by Emil Rosenblatt. Used by permission of the University Press of Kansas.

Lawrence A. Gobright. Associated Press Dispatch: L. A. Gobright, *Recollections of Men and Things at Washington, during the third of a century* (Philadelphia: Claxton, Remsen & Haffelfinger, 1869), 351–54.

Horace Greeley. The Nation's Loss: *New York Tribune*, April 17, 1865.

Clara Harris. Letter to Mary: Manuscript, New-York Historical Society. Used by permission. Letter to M——: *The Independent*, June 20, 1889.

Harry Hawk. Letter to William Hawk: *Washington Evening Star*, April 24, 1865.

Oliver Wendell Holmes. For the Services in Memory of Abraham Lincoln: *Poetical Tributes to the Memory of Abraham Lincoln* (Philadelphia: J. B. Lippincott & Co., 1865), 73–74.

Julia Ward Howe. "Crown his blood-stained pillow": *Poetical Tributes to the Memory of Abraham Lincoln* (Philadelphia: J. B. Lippincott & Co., 1865), 15–16.

Henrik Ibsen. Abraham Lincoln's Murder: *Ibsen's Poems: in versions by John Northam* (Oslo: Norwegian University Press, 1986), 92–94.

"J.R.P." and *The Century Magazine*. Lincoln in the South: *The Century Magazine*, January 1887.

George Julian. Diary, April 15–19, 1865: "George Julian's Journal—The Assassination of Lincoln," *Indiana Magazine of History*, Vol. XI, No. 4 (December 1915).

Elizabeth Keckly. From *Behind the Scenes: Behind the Scenes, or, Thirty Years a Slave, and Four Years in the White House* (New York: G. W. Carleton & Co., 1868), 174–93.

Charles A. Leale. Report on the Death of President Lincoln: Helena Iles Papaioannou and Daniel W. Stowell, "Dr. Charles A. Leale's Report on the Assassination of Abraham Lincoln," *Journal of the Abraham Lincoln Association*, Vol. 34, No. 1 (2013). © 2013 by the Board of Trustees of the University of Illinois. Used by permission of the Abraham Lincoln Association.

Emma LeConte. Diary, April 21, 1865: Electronic edition, The University of North Carolina at Chapel Hill: http://docsouth.unc.edu/fpn/leconteemma/leconte .html. Accessed February 18, 2014.

Abraham Lincoln. Letter to Ephraim D. and Phoebe Ellsworth: *CWAL*, 4:385–86. Letter to Fanny McCullough: *CWAL*, 6:16–17. Letter to Lydia Bixby: *CWAL*, 8:116–17. The Gettysburg Address: *CWAL*, 7:22–23. Second Inaugural Address: *CWAL*, 8:332–33.

Mary Lincoln. Letter to Francis B. Carpenter: Justin G. Turner and Linda Levitt Turner, *Mary Todd Lincoln: Her Life and Letters* (New York: Alfred A. Knopf, 1972), 283–85.

John M. Lloyd. Testimony Before the Military Commission: *Poore*, 1:115–20.

Louisville Journal. President Lincoln's Death—The Spirit and Comments of the Press. *Louisville Journal*, April 19, 1865.

James Russell Lowell. From Ode Recited at the Harvard Commemoration: *Atlantic Monthly*, September 1865.

James Lusby. Testimony Before the Military Commission: *Poore*, 3:67–68.

Thomas MacKellar. Good Friday, April 14, 1865: *Typographic Advertiser*, April–July 1865.

Manton Marble. From *The New York World*: The Assassination of President Lincoln and Secretary Seward, *New York World*, April 15, 1865. The Late President Lincoln, *New York World*, April 17, 1865.

James M. Mason. Letter to *The Index*: *The New York Times*, May 11, 1865.

Herman Melville. The Martyr: *Battle-Pieces and Aspects of the War* (New York: Harper & Brothers, 1866), 141–42, 252.

Richard C. Morgan. Testimony Before the Military Commission: *Poore*, 2:9–11.

Sarah Morgan. Diary, April 19, 1865: *The Civil War Diary of Sarah Morgan*, ed. Charles East (Athens: The University of Georgia Press, 1991), 605–8. Copyright © 1991 by The University of Georgia Press. Used by permission of The University of Georgia Press.

Morning Star. Editorial, April 27, 1865: *Appendix to Diplomatic Correspondence of 1865; The Assassination of Abraham Lincoln, Late President of the United States of America* (Washington, D.C.: Government Printing Office, 1866), 385–87.

National Anti-Slavery Standard. Obsequies of the Martyred President: *National Anti-Slavery Standard*, April 29, 1865.

New York Times. The Obsequies: *New York Times*, April 20, 1865. End of the Assassins: *New York Times*, July 8, 1865.

New York Tribune. Editorial on the New York Funeral Procession: *New York Tribune*, April 24, 1865.

John Nichol. Reunion: *The Spectator*, May 13, 1865.

John G. Nicolay and John Hay. From *Abraham Lincoln: A History*: *Abraham Lincoln: A History*, vol. X, 280–302.

Taylor Peirce. Letter to Catharine Peirce: *Dear Catharine, Dear Taylor: The Civil War Letters of a Union Soldier and His Wife*, ed. Richard L. Kiper, letters transcribed by Donna B. Vaughn (Lawrence: University Press of Kansas, 2002), 384–86. Copyright © 2002 by University Press of Kansas. Used by permission.

James W. C. Pennington. The Funeral of President Lincoln and the Colored People: *The Anglo-African*, May 13, 1865.

Wendell Phillips. The Lesson of President Lincoln's Death: *Universal Suffrage, and Complete Equality in Citizenship, the Safeguards of Democratic Institutions: shown in discourses by Henry Ward Beecher, Andrew Johnson, and Wendell Phillips* (Boston: Geo. C. Rand & Avery, 1865), 14–16.

Franklin Pierce. Speech at Concord, New Hampshire: *The Lincoln Memorial: A Record of the Life, Assassination, and Obsequies of the Martyred President* (New York: Bunce & Huntington, 1865), 86–87.

Henry R. Rathbone. Affidavit: *The Lincoln Memorial: A Record of the Life, Assassination, and Obsequies of the Martyred President* (New York: Bunce & Huntington, 1865), 61–63.

Henry J. Raymond. From *The New York Times*: The Murder of President Lincoln, *New York Times*, April 16, 1865; The Nation's Bereavement, *New York Times*, April 17, 1865.

Whitelaw Reid. Dispatch from Washington: *Cincinnati Gazette*, April 26, 1865.

Frances (Fanny) Seward. Diary, April 14, 1865: Transcription online at http://www.lib.rochester.edu/index.cfm?page=1420&Print=436. Accessed February 18, 2014. Used by permission of American Heritage Publishing.

Matthew Simpson. Funeral Address at the Burial of President Lincoln: *Funeral Address at the Burial of President Lincoln, at Springfield, Illinois, May 4, 1865* (New York: Carlton & Porter, 1865), 3–21.

Edwin M. Stanton. Telegrams to John A. Dix: *OR*, series 1, vol. 46, pt. 3, 780–81. Letter to Charles Francis Adams: *OR*, series 1, vol. 46, pt. 3, 784–85. Reward Announcement: *OR*, series 1, vol. 46, pt. 3, 847–48.

Edmund Clarence Stedman. Abraham Lincoln Assassinated Good Friday, 1865: *New York Tribune*, April 17, 1865.

Alexander H. Stephens. Remarks at the U.S. Capitol: *Congressional Record*, 45th Congress, 2nd Session, 970–71.

William O. Stoddard. Recollection of the Lincoln Assassination: *Lincoln's White House Secretary: The Adventurous Life of William O. Stoddard*, ed. Harold Holzer (Carbondale: Southern Illinois University Press, 2007), 343–46. Copyright © 2007 by the Board of Trustees, Southern Illinois University. Used by permission.

Frederick Stone. Argument for David Herold: *Pitman*, 274.

George Templeton Strong. Diary, April 15–17, 1865: *Diary of the Civil War, 1860–1865*, ed. Allan Nevins (New York: The Macmillan Company, 1962), 582–88. Reprinted with permission of Scribner, a Division of Simon & Schuster, Inc., from *The Diary of George Templeton Strong*, edited by Allan Nevins and Milton Halsey Thomas. Copyright © 1952 by The Macmillan Publishing Company; copyright renewed © 1980 by Milton Halsey Thomas. All rights reserved.

Charles Sabin Taft. Abraham Lincoln's Last Hours: *The Century Magazine*, February 1893.

James Tanner. Letter to Henry F. Walch: Howard H. Peckham, "James Tanner's Account of Lincoln's Death," *The Abraham Lincoln Quarterly*, vol. 2, no. 4, December 1942, 176–83. Transcription from Pitman shorthand by Gertrude Maginn. Used by permission of the Abraham Lincoln Association.

Tom Taylor. Abraham Lincoln, Foully Assassinated April 14, 1865: *Punch*, May 6, 1865.

Queen Victoria. Letter to Mary Lincoln: Manuscript, Abraham Lincoln Papers, Library of Congress.

Louis J. Weichmann. Testimony Before the Military Commission: *Poore*, 1:75–78, 1:89–91.

Gideon Welles. Diary, April 14–21, 1865: *Diary of Gideon Welles*, volume II, ed. Howard K. Beale (New York: W. W. Norton & Company, Inc., 1960), 283–94. Copyright © 1960 by W. W. Norton & Company, Inc. Manuscript, Gideon Welles Papers, Library of Congress.

Walt Whitman. Hush'd Be the Camps To-Day. When Lilacs Last in the Dooryard Bloom'd. O Captain! My Captain! This Dust was Once the Man: *Complete Poetry and Collected Prose*, ed. Justin Kaplan (New York: Library of America, 1982), 459–68. Originally published in 1881. The Death of Lincoln: *Complete*

Poetry and Collected Prose, ed. Justin Kaplan (New York: Library of America, 1982), 1036–47. Originally published in 1882.

John Greenleaf Whittier. The Emancipation Group: *The Poetical Works of John Greenleaf Whittier* (Boston: Houghton, Mifflin and Company, 1882), 513–14.

Isaac Mayer Wise. Sermon at Cincinnati: *The Israelite*, April 28, 1865.

ILLUSTRATIONS

1. Ford's Theatre playbill for April 14, 1865, courtesy of the University of Delaware Library.
2. Photograph of Abraham Lincoln, March 6, 1865, by Henry F. Warren. Courtesy of the Library of Congress, Prints & Photographs Division.
3. Mary Lincoln in mourning attire, from the Lincoln Financial Foundation Collection, courtesy of the Allen County Public Library and Indiana State Museum.
4. The presidential box at Ford's Theatre, courtesy of the Library of Congress, Prints & Photographs Division.
5. Ford's Theatre c. 1860–65, courtesy of the Library of Congress, Prints & Photographs Division.
6. *Lincoln Borne by Loving Hands* by Carl Bersch, c. 1895, courtesy of Art Resource, NY.
7. Drawing of Lincoln's deathbed scene by Hermann Faber, courtesy of the Library of Congress, Prints & Photographs Division.
8. Fanny Seward in 1866, courtesy of the Seward House Museum, Auburn, New York.
9. Broadside reward poster issued by the War Department, courtesy of the Library of Congress, Rare Book & Special Collections Division.
10–13. Photographs of David Herold, Lewis Powell (alias Payne), and George Atzerodt, by Alexander Gardner, courtesy of the Library of Congress, Prints & Photographs Division. Mary Surratt, last known portrait, courtesy of Surratt House Museum in Clinton, Maryland / The Maryland National Capital Park and Planning Commission.
14. Half-length studio portrait of John Wilkes Booth, c. 1860–65. Courtesy of the Library of Congress, Prints & Photographs Division.
15. Sergeant Boston Corbett, courtesy of the Library of Congress, Prints & Photographs Division.
16. Lincoln's catafalque in New York City, photograph by George Stacy. Courtesy of the Library of Congress, Prints & Photographs Division.
17. Lincoln's funeral train photographed on a Lake Michigan pier in Chicago, courtesy of Getty Images.
18. Mourners in front of the Lincoln home in Springfield, Illinois, courtesy of the Abraham Lincoln Presidential Library and Museum.
19. Lincoln's funeral procession in New York City, photograph by Robert N. Dennis. Courtesy of the Theodore Roosevelt Birthplace National Historic Site.
20. "The Founder and the Preserver of the Union. (*Apotheosis*)" by Thurston, Herline & Co. Courtesy of the Lincoln Museum Collection.
21. "Britannia Sympathises With Columbia" by John Tenniel. Courtesy of the Lincoln Museum Collection.
22. "The Reward of the Just" by D. T. Wiest, courtesy of the Chicago History Museum.
23. Hanging of the conspirators, July 7, 1865, photograph by Alexander Gardner. Courtesy of the Library of Congress, Prints & Photographs Division.

Index